Frances Fox Piven and
Richard A. Cloward

REGULATING THE POOR

Frances Fox Piven is Distinguished Professor of Political Science, Graduate School and University Center, City University of New York. Richard A. Cloward, a social worker and sociologist, is on the faculty of the Columbia University School of Social Work. Their co-authored books include *The Politics of Turmoil* (1974), *Poor People's Movements* (1987), *The New Class War* (1982), *Why Americans Don't Vote* (1988), and, with Fred Block and Barbara Ehrenreich, *The Mean Season* (1987). They have won various international and national awards, including both the C. Wright Mills and Lee/Founders Awards of the Society for the Study of Social Problems.

REGULATING THE POOR

The Functions of Public Welfare

Updated Edition

Frances Fox Piven and Richard A. Cloward

Vintage Books
A Division of Random House, Inc.
New York

SECOND VINTAGE EDITION, OCTOBER 1993

Copyright © 1971, 1993 by Frances Fox Piven and Richard A. Cloward

Library of Congress Cataloging-in-Publication Data
Piven, Frances Fox.
Regulating the poor: the functions of public welfare / Frances Fox Piven, Richard A. Cloward.—Updated ed.
p.   cm.
Includes bibliographical references and index.
ISBN 0-679-74516-5
1. Public welfare—United States.   I. Cloward, Richard A.
II. Title.
HV95.P57   1993
361.973—dc20   93-17460
CIP

Manufactured in the United States of America

B

DEDICATED

TO

the welfare protest movement that arose in the 1960's;

and to its leader,

George A. Wiley

ACKNOWLEDGMENTS

In preparing the original edition, we were greatly aided by the comments of Winifred Bell, Herbert Gans, Alvin Schorr, and David Fanshell. Harriet Hoptner of the Columbia University Library gave us invaluable bibliographical assistance, and Sara Blackburn and Martha Gilmor helped edit the manuscript.

Fred Block, Timothy Casey, Henry Freedman, Herbert Gans, Michael Goldfield, and Charles Noble generously took time to review and comment on the updated edition. Margaret Groarke performed helpful library assistance.

We are again indebted to our friend and literary agent, Frances Goldin.

CONTENTS

Contents

THREE

PART II
Relief and the Years of Stability: 1940–1960

FOUR

FIVE

PART III
Relief and the Urban Crisis

SIX

SEVEN

TWELVE

INTRODUCTION
to the Updated Edition

The original version of *Regulating the Poor* was published in 1971, just as the rise in the welfare rolls associated with the turmoil of the 1960s was peaking. We thought that the expansion of relief was an accomplishment, flaws in the American relief system notwithstanding. The readier availability of cash and in-kind assistance eased some of the worst poverty, especially among women and children.

But we did not think liberal relief-giving would last. We expected that the expansion of relief would set in motion forces pressing for "reform," including restrictions on aid and measures to force women on welfare to work. During the more than two decades since the first edition was published, our predictions were confirmed. Grant levels were driven down, the rolls were slashed, and workfare programs of one sort or another have proliferated.

Because we believe that the analysis set out in this book is substantially correct, we left the original ten chapters intact in this revised edition, and added two chapters. Chapter 11 provides a description and explanation of the restrictive turn in relief policy and practices from the 1970s into the 1990s. In Chapter 12, we locate our theoretical perspective in relation to the growing literature on welfare state development in the rich countries of the West produced since the original publication of *Regulating the Poor.* Most of this work is about a broad range of social welfare policies. *Regulating the Poor,* by contrast, is about poor relief, which continues to play a large and distinctive role in the United States. In this final chapter, we draw on a range of theories of welfare state development to explain why the United States continues to be a "poor relief" state.

Finally, in an appendix to Chapter 12, we review a series of published empirical studies, conducted by others, which test the propositions contained in *Regulating the Poor*.

Frances Fox Piven
Richard A. Cloward
March 1993

INTRODUCTION

This book is about relief-giving and its uses in regulating the political and economic behavior of the poor. Our object is not so much to describe the public welfare system (as relief-giving is known in the United States), for that has been done often enough. Rather, we seek to explain why relief arrangements exist, and why—from time to time—the relief rolls precipitously expand or contract.

The key to an understanding of relief-giving is in the functions it serves for the larger economic and political order, for relief is a secondary and supportive institution. Historical evidence suggests that relief arrangements are initiated or expanded during the occasional outbreaks of civil disorder produced by mass unemployment, and are then abolished or contracted when political stability is restored. We shall argue that expansive relief policies are designed to mute civil disorder, and restrictive ones to reinforce work norms. In other words, relief policies are cyclical—liberal or restrictive depending on the problems of regulation in the larger society with which government must contend. Since this view clearly belies the popular supposition that government social policies, including relief policies, are becoming progressively more responsible, humane, and generous, a few words about this popular supposition and its applicability to relief are in order.

There is surely no gainsaying that the role of government has expanded in those domestic matters called "social welfare." One has only to look at the steadily increasing expenditures by local, state, and national governments for programs in housing, health care, education, and the like. These expenditures have been prompted by the repercussions that result when such matters as housing or health care are left entirely to the untrammeled forces of the marketplace. Decisions that are reasonable to the profit-maker are obviously not necessarily reasonable to the various groups that are affected, and they may demand that government intervene to protect them. Moreover, once governmental action is inaugurated, the groups who benefit become a supporting constituency and press for further gains. But most such social welfare activity has not greatly aided the poor, precisely because the poor ordinarily have little influence on government. Indeed, "social welfare" programs designed for other groups frequently ride roughshod over the poor, as when New Deal agricultural subsidies resulted in the displacement of great numbers of tenant farmers and sharecroppers, or when urban renewal schemes deprived blacks of their urban neighborhoods.

However, some social welfare programs *do* benefit those at the bottom of the economic order. The most important examples are old-age pensions and unemployment insurance. As the industrial market system became dominant in Western countries, it was less necessary that everyone work; some people, such as the aged, gradually became economically obsolete and were permitted to drop out of the labor force. Moreover, the vagaries of the market system made it desirable that governments institute a buffer against temporary unemployment, such as unemployment insurance.

Although old-age pension and unemployment insurance schemes in the West have improved over time, and to that extent confirm the popular view that the policies of "welfare capitalism" are becoming more responsive and responsible, access to these benefits has not been unconditional. Generally speaking, eligibility for pensions or unemployment insurance is established through the occupational role, and can actually be obtained only if the individual is certified as unneeded in the labor force, whether because of old age or retrenchment. Moreover, some occupations which draw on unskilled and low-wage workers (e.g., many agricultural workers and domestic servants in the United States) have been denied the benefits of these insurance schemes. These workers are left to get what they can from the relief system. In any case, even those certified as unneeded in the labor force have generally been maintained at such low levels of income as to suggest that social insurance programs are not fully free of the taint of being a form of relief.

As for relief programs themselves, the historical pattern is clearly not one of progressive liberalization; it is rather a record of periodically expanding and contracting relief rolls as the system performs its two main functions: maintaining civil order and enforcing work. This general interpretation is elaborated in Chapter 1, with illustrations drawn from other countries and earlier historical periods.

The bulk of the book deals with the contemporary American public welfare system. There have been two major relief explosions in the United States—the first during the Great Depression of the 1930's and the second during the affluent years of the 1960's. Chapters 2 and 3 focus on the rise of mass disorder and the launching of the first national relief programs during the Great Depression, as well as on the consequences that giving relief had for the control of disorder. In Chapters 4 and 5, we show how, during the relatively stable years of the 1940's and 1950's, relief arrangements were designed to reinforce work norms. Finally, in Chapters 6 through 10, we take up the economic sources of the civil disorder that broke out and spread during the 1960's and that resulted in a great upsurge in the relief rolls, especially after 1964.

The argument that relief programs are initiated to deal with dislocations in the work system that lead to mass disorder, and are then retained (in an altered form) to enforce work, is not a familiar one. Considering that a not inconsiderable literature has been written on the subject of relief, the unfamiliarity of this idea merits explanation.

Those who write about relief are usually enmeshed in the relief system, either as its ideologues or as its administrators. Understandably enough, they are strained to justify the system, although they may identify flaws in it. (Indeed, administrative critiques—from those of George Nichols, head of the Royal Poor Law Commission in 1834, to those of Daniel Moynihan, Presidential Adviser on welfare matters—constitute the bulk of the relief literature.) Most writers view the system as shaped by morality—by their good intentions, or by the mistaken intentions of others. Consequently, the economic and political functions of relief-giving have not been clearly seen. Indeed, much of the literature on relief—whether the arid moralisms and pieties of nineteenth-century writers or the ostensibly "value-neutral" analyses of twentieth-century professionals and technicians—merely serves to obscure the central role of relief agencies in the regulation of marginal labor and in the maintenance of civil order.

Some insights about the larger functions of the relief system are available from historians who have studied relief systems in the course of explaining a larger train of historical developments. We refer the reader particularly to Polanyi, Trevelyan, the Hammonds, and the Webbs. The advantages of the historian's perspective are obvious. For one, the very scope of events that fall within the range of historical inquiry tends to suggest connections between relief practices and larger social institutions that have generally escaped notice by students of relief. For another, the historian ordinarily has some distance from the institutions of which he or she writes, and is not strained to justify them. Even so, while some historians have pointed to a particular use or abuse of relief at a particular time and place, none has undertaken to generalize the functions of relief as an institution. It is that task which we set for ourselves.

One disclaimer ought to be entered at the outset. We

have already suggested that relief-giving is partly designed to enforce work. Our argument, however, is not against work. We take it for granted that all societies require productive contributions from most of their members, and that all societies develop mechanisms to ensure that those contributions will be made. In the market economy, the giving of relief is one such mechanism. But much more should be understood of this mechanism than merely that it reinforces work norms. It also goes far toward defining and enforcing the terms on which different classes of people are made to do different kinds of work; relief arrangements, in other words, have a great deal to do with maintaining social and economic inequities. The indignities and cruelties of the dole are no deterrent to indolence among the rich; but for the poor person, the specter of ending up on "the welfare" or in "the poorhouse" makes any job at any wage a preferable alternative. And so the issue is not the relative merit of work itself; it is rather how some people are made to do the harshest work for the least reward.

November 1, 1970

Frances Fox Piven
Richard A. Cloward

REGULATING THE POOR

CHAPTER ONE

Relief, Labor, and Civil Disorder: An Overview

Since the early sixteenth century, many Western governments have come to make provision for the care of the destitute, often known as poor relief. (In the United States, such provisions are now called public assistance or public welfare.) The purpose of this chapter is to suggest why relief arrangements are established, and why they persist.

Relief arrangements are ancillary to economic arrangements. Their chief function is to regulate labor, and they do that in two general ways. First, when mass unemployment leads to outbreaks of turmoil, relief programs are ordinarily initiated or expanded to absorb and control enough of the unemployed to restore order; then, as turbulence subsides, the relief system contracts, expelling those who are needed to populate the labor market. Relief also performs a labor-regulating function in this shrunken state, however. Some of the aged, the disabled, the insane, and others who are of no use as workers are left on the relief rolls, and their treatment is so degrading and punitive as to instill in the laboring masses a fear of the fate that awaits them should they relax into beggary and pauperism. To demean and punish those who do not work is to exalt by contrast even the meanest labor at the meanest wages. These regulative functions of relief, and their periodic expansion and contraction, are made necessary by several strains toward instability inherent in capitalist economies.

Problems of Controlling Labor by Market Incentives

All human societies compel most of their members to work, to produce the goods and services that sustain the community. All societies also define the work their members must do and the conditions under which they must do it. Sometimes the authority to compel and define is fixed in tradition, sometimes in the bureaucratic agencies of a central government. Capitalism, however, relies primarily upon the mechanisms of a market—the promise of financial rewards or penalties—to motivate men and women to work and to hold them to their occupational tasks.

Basic to capitalist economic arrangements is change. The economy is kept in constant flux by entrepreneurs searching out new and bigger markets and cheaper methods of production and distribution. These changes in the organization of production and distribution create continuous shifts in labor needs: workers must acquire new skills; they must move to new locales; a stream of uninitiated people must be made to fill new and different occupations in a changing productive system. Because of this fluidity, work roles under capitalism cannot be assigned by tradition. Nor can responsibility for the allocation of labor conveniently be lodged in the bureaucracies of a central government, for in a market system a great variety of dispersed entrepreneurs control production and define labor requirements. In the place of tradition or governmental authority, capitalist societies control people and work tasks precisely as they control goods and capital—through a market system.

Under capitalism, the distribution of workers is mainly the result of monetary incentives or disincentives: profits or wages, or the threat of no profits or no wages. As these incentives ebb and flow in response to economic changes, most people are more or less continuously induced to change and adapt. Continual change in labor requirements also means that, at any given moment, some people are left unemployed. In subsistence economies everyone works; the labor force is virtually synonymous with the population. But capitalism makes labor conditional on market demand, with the result that some amount of unemployment becomes a permanent feature of the economy.[1] In other words, change and fluctuation and unemployment are chronic features of capitalism.

But periodically change takes on catastrophic proportions. Sometimes this is the result of the natural disasters that afflict all societies, such as crop failures or rapid population growth, which disturb the ongoing pattern of work and its rewards. To such travails capitalism adds abrupt, erratic, and extreme fluctuations in production and distribution, leading to massive and precipitous modifications in the requirements for labor. The two main sources of the catastrophic changes that distinguish capitalism are depression and rapid modernization.

During the economic downturns or depressions that have marked the advance of capitalism, the structure of

---

[1] Many critics of capitalism have argued that the maintenance of a surplus of unemployed workers is not simply a by-product of market fluidity but a deliberately contrived condition, designed to ease the flow of labor and to lessen the bargaining power of workers in market transactions. The periodic intervention of government to increase the pool of unemployed by slowing the rate of economic growth and the use of government power to force men to work for any bidder lend credence to these views, as we will ourselves argue later in this chapter when we discuss the way relief practices are designed to maintain a labor pool.

market incentives simply collapses; with no demand for labor, there are no monetary rewards to guide and enforce work. During periods of rapid modernization—whether the replacement of handicraft by machines, the relocation of factories in relation to new sources of power or new outlets for distribution, or the demise of family subsistence farming as large-scale commercial agriculture spreads—portions of the laboring population may be rendered obsolete or at least temporarily maladjusted. Market incentives do not collapse; they are simply not sufficient to compel people to abandon one way of working and living in favor of another.

In principle, of course, these dislocated people become part of a labor supply to be drawn upon by a changing and expanding labor market. As the history of Western market systems shows, however, people do not adapt so readily to drastically altered methods of work and to the new and alien patterns of social life dictated by that work. They may resist leaving their traditional communities and the only life they know. Bred to labor under the discipline of sun and season, however severe that discipline may be, they may resist the discipline of factory and machine, which, though it may be no more severe, may seem so because it is alien. The process of human adjustment to these economic changes has ordinarily entailed generations of mass unemployment, distress, and disorganization.

Now, if human beings were invariably given to enduring these travails with equanimity, there would be no governmental relief systems at all. But often they do not, and for reasons that are not difficult to see. The regulation of civil behavior in all societies is intimately dependent on stable occupational arrangements. So long as people are fixed in their work roles, their activities and outlooks are also fixed; they do what they must and think what they must. Each behavior and attitude is shaped by the reward of a good harvest or the penalty of a bad one, by the factory paycheck or the danger of losing it. But mass unemployment breaks that bond, loosening people from the main institution by which they are regulated and controlled.[2]

Moreover, mass unemployment that persists for any length of time diminishes the capacity of other institutions to bind and constrain people. Occupational behaviors and outlooks underpin a way of life and determine familial, communal, and cultural patterns. When large numbers of people are suddenly barred from their traditional occupations, the entire structure of social control is weakened and may even collapse. There is no harvest or paycheck to enforce work and the sentiments that uphold work; without work, people cannot conform to familial and communal roles; and if the dislocation is widespread, the legitimacy of the social order itself may come to be questioned. The result is usually civil disorder—crime, mass protests, riots— a disorder that may even threaten to overturn existing social and economic arrangements. It is then that relief programs are initiated or expanded.

However, simply providing aid to quiet the unemployed will not stop disorder; it may even permit it to worsen, for although the remedy may prevent workers' starvation, the trigger that sets off disorder is not economic distress itself but the deterioration of social control. To restore order, the society must create the means to reassert its authority. Because the market is unable to control men's behavior, at least for a time, a surrogate system of social control must be evolved, at least for a time. Moreover, if the surrogate sys-

---

[2] Marie Jahoda describes the total disorientation of the workers in the Austrian village of Marienthal when its only factory stopped production during the depression of the 1930's: "The unemployed men lost their sense of time. When asked at the end of a day what they had done during it, they were unable to describe their activities. 'Real' time . . . was vague and nebulous. Activities such as fetching wood from the shed, which could not have consumed more than ten minutes, were recorded as if they had filled a morning. . . . The men's waking day was shortened to twelve or thirteen hours. . . . Rational budget planning was abandoned in favor of expenditure on trinkets, while essentials could not be paid for" (56–57, 69–72). Complete citations will be found in the bibliography at the end of each chapter.

tem is to be consistent with normally dominant patterns, it must restore people to work roles. Thus, even while obsolete or unneeded laborers are temporarily given relief, they are generally succored only on condition that they labor, whether in public workhouses and labor yards or by being contracted and indentured to private entrepreneurs. To illustrate these views we turn to some examples of the emergence and expansion of relief-giving in early European capitalist societies. Our purpose is not to give a legislative or administrative history—that has been done by other writers—but to provide a background for our subsequent discussion of the sources of contemporary relief crises in the United States.

Civil Disorder and the Initiation or Expansion of Relief-Giving

Western relief systems originated in the mass disturbances that erupted during the long transition from feudalism to capitalism beginning in the sixteenth century. As a result of the declining death rates in the previous century, the population of Europe grew rapidly; as the population grew, so did transiency and beggary. To deal with these threats to civil order, many localities legislated severe penalties against vagrancy. Even before the sixteenth century, the magistrates of Basel had defined twenty-five different categories of beggars, together with appropriate punishments for each. But penalties alone did not deter begging, especially when economic distress was severe and the numbers affected were large. Consequently, some localities began to augment punishment with provisions for the relief of the vagrant poor.

As early as 1516, the Scottish theologian John Major, who taught at the University of Paris, declared: "If the Prince or Community should decree that there should be no beggar in the country, and *should provide for the im-*

potent, the action would be praiseworthy and lawful." [3]
In 1520, Martin Luther urged the German nobility not
only to abolish beggary but to provide for their own poor.
In 1523 Luther published a detailed relief scheme for Leis-
nig, in Saxony, which prohibited begging and provided for
a common chest to aid the old, the weak, and those poor
householders who had "honourably labored at their craft or
in agriculture" but who could no longer find the means to
support themselves. Ordinances modeled on Luther's in-
junctions were rapidly instituted in the German municipalities,[4] and in 1530 the German emperor Charles the
Fifth issued an edict outlawing beggary and directing each
municipality to maintain its poor.[5]

A French town that initiated such an arrangement early
in the sixteenth century was Lyons,[6] which was troubled
both by a rapidly growing population and by the economic
instability associated with the transition to capitalism. By
1500 Lyons' population had already begun to increase.
During the decades that followed, the town became a prosperous commercial and manufacturing center—the home
of the European money market and of expanding new
trades in textiles, printing, and metalworking. As it thrived
it attracted people, not only from the surrounding countryside, but even from Italy, Flanders, and Germany. All told,
the population of Lyons probably doubled between 1500
and 1540.

All this was very well as long as the newcomers could be

---

[3] Quoted in Ashley, Vol. II, 341. Emphasis added.

[4] Webb and Webb, Part I, 31–32.

[5] In 1531 the emperor elaborated his earlier edict in a scheme that
prohibited vagrancy and begging under pain of prison and the lash, and
commanded every city in the Netherlands to provide for its poor by putting the able-bodied to work while caring for indigent women and orphans
(*ibid.,* 32; de Schweinitz, 33).

[6] Ypres, in Flanders, initiated a scheme very similar to Lyons' in 1525.
Bruges, Paris, and Rome also inaugurated relief systems at about the same
time. We use Lyons only as an illustration of developments that were going
forward in many places. For a detailed description of the circumstances
leading to Lyons' welfare program, see Davis.

absorbed by industry. But not all were, with the result that the town came to be plagued by beggars and vagrants. Moreover, prosperity was not continuous: some trades were seasonal and others were periodically troubled by foreign competition. With each economic downturn, large numbers of workers were thrown out of work. They—and especially their children, who were preferred as beggars for the sympathy they elicited—recurrently took to the streets to plead for charity, cluttering the very doorsteps of the better-off classes. Lyons was most vulnerable during periods of bad harvest, when famine not only drove up the cost of bread for urban artisans and journeymen but brought hordes of peasants into the city, where they sometimes paraded through the streets in great numbers to exhibit their misfortune.

Thus the economic distress resulting from population changes and agricultural and other natural disasters which had characterized life throughout the Middle Ages was exacerbated by the vagaries of an evolving market economy. Consequently, turbulence among the poor reached a new pitch. In 1529 food riots erupted, with thousands of Lyonnais looting granaries and the homes of the wealthy; in 1530, artisans and journeymen armed themselves and marched through the streets; in 1531, mobs of starving peasants literally overran the town.

Such charity as had previously been given in Lyons was primarily the responsibility of the church or of those of the more prosperous who sought to purchase their salvation through almsgiving. If almsgiving were to serve a religious end for the prosperous, the destitute could hardly be prohibited from begging. But this method of caring for the needy obviously stimulated rather than discouraged begging and created a public nuisance to the better-off citizens (one account of the times describes famished peasants so gorging themselves as to die on the very doorsteps where they were fed). Moreover, to leave charity to church or citizen meant that few got aid, and those not necessarily according to their need. The result was that mass disorders periodically erupted.

The increase in disorder led the rulers of Lyons to conclude that the giving of charity should no longer be governed by private whim. Consequently, in 1534, churchmen, notables, and merchants joined together to establish a centralized administration for disbursing aid. All charitable donations were consolidated under a central body, the "Aumône-Générale," whose responsibility was to "nourish the poor forever." A list of the needy was established by a house-to-house survey, and tickets for relief were issued to those who qualified. Standards were fixed in allotting bread and money, the sick were sent to a hospital for free medical care, and not least, begging was strictly prohibited.

Indeed, most of the features of modern welfare—from criteria to discriminate the worthy poor from the unworthy to strict procedures for surveillance of recipients and measures for their rehabilitation—were present in Lyons' new relief administration.[7] By the 1550's, about 10 per cent of the town's population was receiving relief, while the number of patients in the Lyons hospital for the poor had tripled.[8] The notables and merchants who promoted this scheme did not so much take pride in their charity as in their aspiration to make of Lyons "a vision of peace."

Within two years of the establishment of relief in Lyons, King Francis I ordered each parish in France to register its poor and to provide for the "impotent" out of a fund of contributions. Elsewhere other townships began to devise

---

[7] Foreigners were more kindly dealt with than in many other places (this was, after all, a center of foreign commerce); generally they were given a night's lodging before they were sent on their way.

[8] The hospital was in fact used to incarcerate some paupers as well as to care for the sick. Juan Luis Vivès, a humanitarian of the time, wrote in his plan for relief in Bruges, dated January 6, 1526: "I call 'hospitals' those places where the sick are fed and cared for, where a certain number of paupers is supported, where boys and girls are reared, where abandoned infants are nourished, where the insane are confined, and where the blind dwell. . . ." (11). Four centuries later, the almshouse or workhouse was performing roughly the same function in England and America.

similar systems to deal with the vagrants and mobs cast up by famine, rapid population growth, and the transition from feudalism to capitalism. A "new statecraft relative to destitution" was emerging:

> What we see ever-increasingly realised, alike in Germany, the Netherlands, Switzerland, England, and, to some extent, France and Scotland, is that no policy of mere represson availed to stop either mendicancy on the one hand, or vagrancy on the other; that (as distinguished from a fortuitous distribution of voluntary gifts to necessarily selected individuals) a systematic and ubiquitous provision had to be made locally by some organ of government for all those who were actually in need of the means of existence, whatever the cause of their destitution. . . .[9]

England also felt these disturbances, and just as it pioneered in developing an intensively capitalist economy, so it was at the forefront in developing nation-wide, public relief arrangements to replace purely local and private charity.[10] During the closing years of the fifteenth century, the emergence of the wool industry in England began to transform the economic and social arrangements governing agriculture. As sheep raising became more profitable, much land was converted from tillage to pasturage, and large numbers of peasants were displaced by an emerging entrepreneurial gentry which either bought their land or cheated them out of it.[11] The impact on the dispossessed farmers

---

[9] Webb and Webb, Part I, 29.

[10] William Ashley commented on the similarity of these schemes: "We need not suppose that the English legislation was a mere imitation of what was being done elsewhere; the same causes were everywhere at work, leading to the same general results" (Part II, 350).

[11] "We may to-day recognise the opening of the sixteenth century as a period of special economic stress, whether we emphasise the agrarian revolution that was dislocating the manorial organisation, or the growth of manufactures in the towns, involving the production of an urban proletariat; or the rapid increase of commerce, with its unsettlement of one national industry after another" (Webb and Webb, Part I, 43).

was one that was to become familiar in successive periods of agricultural modernization. Sir Thomas More described their plight in 1516:

> The husbandmen be thrust out of their own, or else either by covin or fraud, or by violent oppression they be put besides it, or by wrongs and injuries they be so wearied, that they be compelled to sell all: by one means therefore or by other, either by hook or crook they must needs depart away, poor, silly, wretched souls, men, women, husbands, wives, fatherless children, widows, woeful mothers, with their young babes, and their whole household small in substance and much in number, as husbandry requireth many hands. Away they trudge, I say, out of their known and accustomed houses, finding no place to rest in. All their household stuff, which is very little worth, though it might well abide the sale, yet being suddenly thrust out, they be constrained to sell it for a thing of naught. And when they have wandered abroad till that be spent, what can they then else do but steal, and then justly pardy be hanged, or else go about a begging. And yet then also they be cast in prison as vagabonds, because they go about and work not: whom no man will set at work, though they never so willing profer themselves thereto.[12]

A statute of 1488–1489 comments with alarm on the resulting disorders:

> [F]or where in some towns two hundred persons were occupied and lived by their lawful labors, now be there occupied two or three herdsmen, and the residue fall in idleness, the husbandry which is one of the greatest commodities of this realm is greatly decayed, churches destroyed, the service of God withdrawn, the bodies there buried not prayed for, the patron and curates wronged, the defense of this land against our enemies outward

---

[12] More, 33, as quoted in de Schweinitz, 10.

feebled and impaired; to the great displeasure of God, to the subversion of the policy and good rule of this land, and remedy be not hastily therefore purveyed.[13]

Early in the sixteenth century, the national government moved to try to forestall such disorders. In 1528 the Privy Council, anticipating a fall in foreign sales as a result of the war in Flanders, tried to induce the cloth manufacturers of Suffolk to retain their employees.[14] In 1534, a law passed under Henry VIII attempted to limit the number of sheep in any one holding in order to inhibit the displacement of farmers and agricultural laborers and thus forestall potential disorders. Beginning in the 1550's, the Privy Council attempted to regulate the price of grain in poor harvests.[15] But the entrepreneurs of the new market economy were not so readily curbed, so that during this period another method of dealing with labor disorders, especially vagrancy, was evolved.

Until this time, communities in England, as in other

---

[13] Quoted in de Schweinitz, 9. Nor were the disorders merely idleness and decay. "When the sense of oppression became overwhelming, the popular feeling manifested itself in widespread organised tumults, disturbances and insurrections, from Wat Tyler's rebellion of 1381, and Jack Cade's march on London of 1460, to the Pilgrimage of Grace of 1536, and Kett's Norfolk rising of 1549—all of them successfully put down, but sometimes not without great struggle, by the forces which the Government could command. But vagrancy was not actually prevented; nor, as we shall presently describe, was the habit of making a living by wandering on the roads brought to an end" (Webb and Webb, Part I, 27–28).

[14] de Schweinitz, 80.

[15] "The activities of the Privy Council had been steadily growing during the latter decades of the sixteenth century. In the earlier part of the century these orders seem to have been concerned mainly with the prevention of vagrancy and tumult—in short, with the security of the realm and the maintenance of law and order. Gradually we see them, with increasing frequency, endeavouring to prevent an actual shortage of food, and the high prices occasioned thereby, by compelling farmers to bring to market their hoarded stocks, putting pressure on corn-dealers, causing maximum prices to be fixed in local markets, and promoting both the purchase of corn in bulk from abroad and its distribution to the poor at less than cost price. In the special stress of 1586–1587 this action of the Privy Council was elaborated into a nationwide policy . . ." (Webb and Webb, Part I, 66).

European countries, sanctioned almsgiving as a means of personal salvation, and one third of parish church funds was set aside for this purpose. Early in the sixteenth century, however, the national government moved to replace parish arrangements for charity with a nationwide system of relief. In 1531, an act of Parliament decreed that local officials search out and register those of the destitute deemed to be impotent, and give them a document authorizing begging. Almsgiving to others was outlawed. As for those who sought alms without authorization, the penalty was public whipping till the blood ran.

Thereafter, other arrangements for relief were rapidly instituted. An act passed in 1536, during the reign of Henry VIII, required local parishes to take care of their destitute and to establish a procedure for the collection and administration of donations for that purpose by local officials.[16] (In the same year Henry VIII began to expropriate monasteries, helping to assure secular control of charity.[17]) With these developments, the penalties for beggary were made more severe, including an elaborate schedule of branding, enslavement, and execution for repeated offenders. Even so, by 1572 beggary was said to have reached alarming proportions, and in that year local responsibility for relief was more fully spelled out by the famous Elizabethan Poor Laws, which established a local

---

[16] In 1563, these contributions for relief were made compulsory (de Schweinitz, 25).

[17] The Webbs suggest the motive for thus restricting the church: "Throughout the whole period . . . [up to 1597], the King, his Council and his Parliament, were enacting and carrying out laws relating to the poor of a character exactly opposite to that of the almsgiving of the mediaeval Church or to that of the benevolent institutions established by pious founders, Craft Guilds and municipal corporations. All these activities were derived from the obligation of the Christian to relieve the suffering of 'God's poor.' The King and his nobles were intent upon an altogether different object, namely, maintaining order—that is (as governments always understand it) the maintenance of the then-existing order, based on a social hierarchy of rulers and ruled, of landowners and those who belonged to the land" (Part I, 23).

tax, known as the poor rate, as the means for financing the care of paupers and required that justices of the peace serve as the overseers of the poor.

In the closing years of the sixteenth century, the price of grain rose almost continuously, causing considerable hardship among the laborers. After 1594, bad harvests sharpened their miseries, especially in 1596–1597, when "Unemployment was frequent, poverty was everywhere . . . there was . . . constant danger of revolt." [18] When Parliament convened in October 1597, it acted to clarify and systematize the provisions for relief, especially the system of taxation, and the practice of making relatives responsible for paupers. "The coincidence between the coming of the free wage-labourer and an organised public provision for the destitute cannot, in the nature of things, be exactly proved," write the Webbs,[19] but the indications are convincing, and were to become more convincing still as the system of free labor expanded and changed.

After this period of activity, the parish relief machinery lapsed into disuse. But then a depression in cloth manufacture in 1620, followed by bad harvests and high prices in 1621–22, produced new outbreaks of disorder. The Privy Council established a special commission charged with enforcing the Poor Laws,[20] and by the 1630's the relief rolls had expanded enormously.[21] Relief was curtailed again with the onset of the Civil War, when high pay enticed much of the surplus agricultural population into the army. A long period of contraction then ensued, apparently accounted for by rising wages under Cromwell

---

[18] Edward P. Cheyney, *History of England*, 1926, Vol. II, 36, as quoted in Webb and Webb, Part I, 62.

[19] Webb and Webb, Part I, 44, n. 2.

[20] *Ibid.*, 75–100. Trevelyan writes of the Privy Council during this period that it "had a real regard for the interests of the poor, with which the interests of public order were so closely involved" (170–171).

[21] According to E. M. Leonard, there was more poor relief in England from 1631 to 1640 than ever before or since (266).

and by the paralysis of the central machinery of government after the war.

Relief arrangements were reactivated and expanded again, however, during the massive agricultural dislocations of the late eighteenth century. Most of the English agricultural population had by then lost its landholdings; in place of the subsistence farming found elsewhere in Europe, a three-tier system of landowners, tenant farmers, and agricultural workers had evolved in England.[22] The vast majority of the people were a landless proletariat, hiring out by the year to tenant farmers. The margin of their subsistence, however, was provided by common and waste lands, on which they gathered kindling, grazed animals, and hunted game to supplement their meager wages. Moreover, the use of the commons was part of the English villager's birthright, his sense of place and pride. It was the disruption of these arrangements and the ensuing disorder that led to the new expansion of relief.

By the middle of the eighteenth century, an increasing population, advancing urbanization, and the growth of manufacturing had greatly expanded markets for agricultural products, mainly for cereals to feed the urban population and for wool to supply the cloth manufacturers. These new markets, together with the introduction of new agricultural methods (such as cross-harrowing), led to large-scale changes in agriculture. To take advantage of rising prices and new techniques, big landowners moved to expand their holdings still further by buying up

---

[22] "In 1851, when the first nationally reliable figures were collected, there were about 225,000 farms in Britain, about half of them between 100 and 300 acres in size, and all of them averaging just over 110 acres. In other words, what passed for a small farm in England would certainly have counted as a giant farm beside the small holdings of typical peasant economies. Just over 300,000 people described themselves as 'farmers and graziers.' These cultivated their farms essentially by employing the 1.5 million men and women who described themselves as agricultural labourers, shepherds, farm-servants . . ." (Hobsbawm and Rudé, 24).

small farms and, armed with parliamentary "Bills of Enclosure," by usurping the common and waste lands which
had enabled many small cottagers to survive.[23] Although
this process began much earlier, it accelerated rapidly
after 1750; by 1850, well over 6 million acres of common
land—or about one quarter of the total arable acreage—
had been consolidated into private holdings and turned
primarily to grain production.[24] Half of this acreage was
enclosed between 1760 and 1800, a period during which
the rate of parliamentary acts of enclosure ran ten times
higher than in the previous forty years. For great numbers
of agricultural workers, enclosure meant no land on which
to grow subsistence crops to feed their families, no grazing
land to produce wool for home spinning and weaving, no
fuel to heat their cottages, and new restrictions against
hunting. It meant, in short, deprivation of a major
source of subsistence for the poor.[25]

New markets also stimulated a more businesslike approach to farming. Landowners demanded the maximum
rent from tenant farmers, and tenant farmers in turn began to deal with their laborers in terms of cash calculations. Specifically, this meant a shift from a master-servant
relationship to an employer-employee relationship, but on
the harshest terms. Where laborers had previously worked
by the year and frequently lived with the farmer, they
were now hired for only as long as they were needed and
were then left to fend for themselves.[26] Pressures toward

---

[23] Enclosure was also encouraged by the high rentals paid by factories
located in outlying areas, and especially by the prospects of coal-mining,
from which the landed gentry drew great fortunes in royalties.

[24] Hobsbawm and Rudé, 27. There were about four thousand parliamentary acts for enclosure during this hundred-year span, most of them
in the 1760's and 1770's and during the war period of 1793–1816.

[25] A comprehensive account of the life of the villagers after enclosure
is provided in Hammond and Hammond, 1948, Vols. I and II.

[26] The loss of "gleaning rights" illustrates how the commercialization
of farming affected the precarious margin of the laborers' existence. More
efficient farming methods deprived them of the right to pick the fields
clean after the harvest. The Hammonds estimate that such gleaning rights
represented the equivalent of six or seven weeks' wages (1948, Vol. I, 103).

short-term hiring also resulted from the large scale cultivation of grain crops for market, which called for a seasonal labor force, as opposed to mixed subsistence farming, which required year-round laborers. The use of cash rather than produce as the medium of payment for work, a rapidly spreading practice, encouraged partly by the long-term inflation of grain prices, added to the laborer's hardships.[27] Finally, the rapid increase in rural population [28] at a time when the growth of woolen manufacturing continued to provide an incentive to convert land from tillage to pasturage produced a larger labor surplus, leaving agricultural laborers with no leverage in bargaining for wages with their tenant-farmer employers.[29] The result was widespread unemployment and terrible hardship among agricultural workers.

None of these changes took place without resistance from small farmers and laborers who, while they had known hardship before, were now being forced out of a way of life and even out of their villages. Some rioted when "Bills of Enclosure" were posted; some petitioned the Parliament for their repeal.[30] During the last decade of the eighteenth century, when hardship was made more acute by a succession of poor harvests, there were widespread food riots.[31] But their protests could not curb the

---

[27] Hobsbawm and Rudé, 38–42.

[28] Between 1701 and 1831, the population of the agricultural counties almost doubled, from 1,563,000 to 2,876,000. Moreover, after 1751, emigration fell off sharply, draining off only about 40 per cent of the natural increase (*ibid.*, 43).

[29] The laborers' vulnerability was assured by laws prohibiting workers from combining for the purpose of exerting influence to reduce hours or raise wages. There were forty such laws on the books by 1800. New statutes in 1799 and 1800 effectively prohibited all joint action by the workers (Hammond and Hammond, 1917, 112–142).

[30] The Hammonds give an account of the futile protests, over a period of some thirty years, by villagers in the vicinity of Oxford (1948, Vol. I, 83–92).

[31] Hobsbawm and Rudé suggest increases in poaching as another index of disorder. Poaching was motivated both by the need for food and as a protest against enclosure. They offer the following estimates (77):

market processes that were at work. As for the distress of the displaced laborers, the laissez-faire commentators of the time pontificated that this was the necessary concomitant of economic productivity and progress.

A solution to disorder was needed, however, and that solution turned out to be relief.[32] During the late eighteenth and early nineteenth centuries, the English countryside was periodically besieged by turbulent masses of the displaced rural poor and the towns were racked by Luddism, radicalism, trade-unionism, and Chartism,[33] even while the ruling classes worried about what the French Revolution might augur for England.

If compassion was not a strong enough force to make the ruling classes attend to the danger that the poor might starve, fear would certainly have made them think

---

Commitments to the County Jails in Norfolk 1800–30, and Norwich, Wymondham, Aylsham, Walsingham from 1807.

1800–04	250	1819	639	1826	784
1805–09	277	1820	811	1827	839
1810–14	309	1821	722	1828	745
1815	415	1822	943	1829	899
1816	489	1823	728	1830	916
1817	579	1824	700		
1818	669	1825	812		

The landowning gentry of Britain responded to the incursions of poachers on their newly enclosed lands by legislating a series of brutal penalties (Hammond and Hammond, 1948, Vol. I, 183–204).

[32] The relief system was by no means the only solution. This was an era of brutal repression; indeed, in no other domestic matters was Parliament so active as in the elaboration of the criminal codes. At the same time, troops were spread across the country and quartered in barracks (rather than in the homes of citizens) to avoid the possibility that they would identify with the rebellious population (Hammond and Hammond, 1917, 37–94).

[33] "At no other period in modern British history," writes Hobsbawm of this period, especially the decades between Waterloo and the 1840's, "have the common people been so persistently, profoundly, and often desperately dissatisfied. At no other period since the seventeenth century can we speak of large masses of them as revolutionary . . ." (Vol. II, 55). It should be said that agitation arose from both the middle and working classes. After Parliament extended the franchise to the middle classes in 1832, however, the workers' movement was effectively isolated and weakened.

of the danger that the poor might rebel. . . . Thus fear and pity united to sharpen the wits of the rich, and to turn their minds to the distresses of the poor.[34]

It was at this time that the poor relief system—first created in the sixteenth century to control the earlier disturbances caused by population growth and the commercialization of agriculture—became a major institution.[35] Between 1760 and 1784, taxes for relief—the "poor rate"— rose by 60 per cent; they doubled by 1801, and rose by 60 per cent more in the next decade.[36] By 1818, the poor rate was over six times as high as it had been in 1760. Hobsbawm estimates that up to the 1850's, upwards of 10 per cent of the English population were paupers.[37] The relief system, in short, was expanded in order to absorb and regulate the masses of discontented people uprooted from agriculture but not yet incorporated into industry.[38] Its importance in maintaining civil order in England was suggested by John Stuart Mill in 1863:

[T]he hatred of the poor for the rich is an evil that is almost inevitable where the law does not guarantee the poor against the extremity of want. The poor man, in

---

[34] Hammond and Hammond, 1948, Vol. I, 118.

[35] Hobsbawm and Rudé (76) compute the paupers relieved as a percentage of the total population in 1815 as follows:

Berks.	17	Suffolk	12.25
Wilts.	15	Cambs.	11.5
Sussex, Essex	14	Kent	11.25
Dorset, Oxford	13	Herts., Norfolk, Northants.	11
Bucks.	12.75	Hereford, Leicester	10.5
Hunts.	12.5	Beds., Salop., Hants.	10

[36] Mantoux, 437; de Schweinitz, 114; Nicholls, Vol. II, 133, 438. During this period, expenditures under the poor law nearly equaled the entire peacetime cost of the English national government, excluding the army and navy (Webb and Webb, Part II, Vol. I, 2).

[37] Hobsbawm, 70. The Webbs estimate a "pauper host of a million or so actually in receipt of relief" in the early 1830's (Part II, Vol. I, 105).

[38] Karl Polanyi observes of this period that "by and large, the nearly sixteen thousand Poor Law authorities of the country managed to keep the social fabric of village life unbroken and undamaged" (88).

France, notwithstanding the charitable relief that he may
get, has always before his eyes the possibility of death by
starvation; whereas in England he knows that, in the last
resort, he has a claim against private property up to the
point of bare subsistence; that not even the lowest proletarian is absolutely disinherited from his place in the
sun. It is to this that I attribute the fact that, in spite of
the aristocratic constitution of wealth and social life in
England, the proletarian class is seldom hostile, either
to the institution of private property or to the classes who
enjoy it.[39]

Restoring Order by Restoring Work

Relief arrangements deal with disorder, not simply by
giving aid to the displaced poor, but by granting it on condition that they behave in certain ways and, most important, on condition that they work. Any institution that
distributes the resources men and women depend upon for
survival can exert control over them: the occasion of giving vitally needed assistance can easily become the occasion of inculcating the work ethic, for example, and of
enforcing work itself, for those who resist risk the withdrawal of that assistance. Once the destitute of sixteenth-
century Lyons were identified and registered, those declared eligible for help were watched over by the rectors,
who prohibited them from spending money at taverns or at
cards and made surprise visits to their homes in search of
evidence of immorality. More important, an effort was

---

[39] Mill, Vol. I, 307. Trevelyan makes a similar judgment of poor relief
in England which he says "is one reason why there was never anything
like the French Revolution in our country, and why through all our political, religious and social feuds from the Seventeenth to the Nineteenth
Centuries the quiet and orderly habits of the people, even in times of
distress, continued upon the whole as a national characteristic." Furthermore, "That we dispensed so long with a proper police force is a testimony of the average honesty of our ancestors and to the value of the old
Poor Law. in spite of all its defects" (230).

made to redirect the employable poor of Lyons into the work force: schools were set up to teach pauper children to read and write, and boys were apprenticed to the new industries. The town even subsidized new manufacturers on condition that training would be provided for pauper children. Any employables who turned to begging, on the other hand, were chained and set to work digging sewers and ditches.

The arrangements, both historical and contemporary, through which relief recipients have been made to work vary: some communities are relatively benevolent, others harsh; some communities develop a monolithic system, others have diverse arrangements; some are efficient, others lax. But, broadly speaking, the enforcement of work is accomplished in two main ways: work is provided under public auspices, whether in the recipient's home, in a labor yard, or in a workhouse; or work is provided in the private market, whether by contracting or indenturing the poor to private employers, or through subsidies designed to induce employers to hire paupers. And although a relief system may at any time use both of these methods of enforcing work, one or the other usually becomes predominant, depending on the economic conditions that first gave rise to disorder.

Publicly subsidized work tends to be used during business depressions, when the demand for labor in the private market collapses. Conversely, arrangements to channel paupers into the labor market are more likely to be used when rapid changes in markets or technology render a segment of the labor supply temporarily maladapted. In the first case, the relief system augments a shrunken labor market; in the other, its policies and procedures are shaped to overcome the poor fit between labor-market requirements and the characteristics of the labor force.

Public work is as old as public relief. The municipal relief systems initiated on the Continent in the first quarter of the sixteenth century often included some form of public works.[40] In England, the same statute of 1572 that established taxation as the method for financing poor relief charged the overseers of the poor with putting vagrants to work. Shortly afterwards, in 1576, local officials were directed to acquire a supply of raw goods—wool, hemp, iron—which was to be delivered to the needy for processing in their homes, their wages to be fixed according to "the desert of the work." The purpose was explicit:

> . . . to the intent youth may be accustomed and brought up in labor and work, and then not like to grow to be idle rogues, and to the intent also that such as be already grown up in idleness and so rogues at this present, may not have any just excuse in saying that they cannot get any service or work, and then without any favor or toleration worthy to be executed, and that other poor and needy persons being willing to work may be set on work.[41]

The favored method of ensuring that "youth may be accustomed and brought up in labor and work" throughout most of the history of relief was the workhouse. In 1723, an act of Parliament permitted the local parishes to establish workhouses and to refuse aid to those poor who would not enter; [42] within ten years, there were said to be about fifty workhouses in the environs of London. Workhouses were also established elsewhere in Europe, where the rations, health conditions, and morale were usually better than in institutions under the thriving English capitalism. In 1790, when Bavaria was plagued by beggars, the city of Munich established an institution for the manufacture of army clothing where the poor were presumably to be inducted into the virtues of industry by a steady regimen of work.

The destitute have also sometimes been paid to work in the general community or in their own homes. In the late

---

[40] See Webb and Webb, Part I, 29–41.

[41] Quoted in de Schweinitz, 26.

[42] In fact the parishes, responding to local exigencies, continued to provide various forms of "outdoor" relief (Webb and Webb, Part I, 121–125).

1790's, the town of Hamburg initiated a public works program designed (in the words of Baron Kaspar von Voght, the chief author of the scheme) "to prevent *any man from securing a shilling which he was able to earn himself . . . for if the manner in which relief is given is not a spur to industry, it becomes undoubtedly a premium to sloth and profligacy*." To deter profligacy while dealing with vagrancy, the respectable citizens of Hamburg decided that, "six-sevenths of our poor being women and children," they should be set to work spinning flax in their homes. Men and boys were to make rope, clean streets, or mend roads. Relief payments were deliberately kept below market wages: "It was our determined principle," the Baron wrote, "to reduce this support lower than what any industrious man or woman could earn. . . ." Finally the Baron could report: "For the last seven years . . . hardly a beggar has been seen in Hamburg. . . . We not only did much toward the relief of the poor, but . . . we gained some steps toward the more desirable, yet but slowly attainable, end, the *preventing some of the causes of poverty*." [43]

A somewhat similar method of enforcing work evolved in England during the bitter depression of 1840–1841. As unemployment mounted, the poor in some of the larger cities protested against having to leave their families and communities to enter workhouses in order to obtain relief, and in any case, in some places the workhouses were already full. As a result, various public spaces were designated as "labor yards" to which the unemployed could come by the day to pick oakum, cut wood, and break stone, for which they were paid in food and clothing. [44] The

---

[43] Quoted in de Schweinitz, 91–94.

[44] During the same period, Ireland also made great use of work relief in coping with the widespread political unrest created by the "Great Potato Famine." In 1845, the first year of the famine, approximately 750,000 persons were employed on public works projects, out of a total population of slightly more than 8 million persons. In the second year of the famine, however, the situation became so desperate that public works were abandoned and free soup was distributed to more than 3 million

method was used periodically throughout the second half of the nineteenth century; at times of severe distress, very large numbers of the able-bodied poor were supported in this way.[45] A similar massive use of public work under relief auspices occurred in the United States during the 1930's, when millions of the unemployed were subsidized through the Works Progress Administration.

Quite different methods of enforcing work are used when the demand for labor is steady but maladaptions in the labor supply, caused by changes in methods of production, result in unemployment. In such circumstances, relief agencies ordinarily channel paupers directly into the private market. For example, the rapid expansion of English manufacturing during the late eighteenth and early nineteenth centuries[46] produced a commensurately expanded need for factory operatives. But it was no easy matter to get them. People who had been agricultural laborers, independent artisans, or workers in domestic industries (i.e., piecework manufacturing in the home) did not adjust easily to the new and alien discipline of the factory. The Hammonds write of this period:

> The men and women of Lancashire and Yorkshire felt of this new power that it was inhuman, that it disregarded all their instincts and sensibilities, that it brought into their lives an inexorable force, destroying and scattering their customs, their traditions, their freedom, their ties of family and home. . . . [T]o all the evils from which the domestic worker had suffered, the Industrial Revolution added discipline. . . . The workman was summoned by the factory bell; his daily life was arranged by factory

persons. Even so, more than a million died of starvation or fever. For a general discussion of Irish work relief programs since the eighteenth century, see Mac-Donagh, 27–30.

[45]Webb and Webb, Part II, Vol. I, 365–367.

[46]"The number of power-looms in England rose from 2,400 in 1813 to 55,000 in 1829, 85,000 in 1833 and 224,000 in 1850 . . ." (Hobsbawn, 47). Overall, the rate of growth in industrial production averaged about 40 per cent per decade from 1810 to 1850 (*ibid.*, 51).

hours; he worked under an overseer . . .; if he broke one
of a long series of minute regulations he was fined, and
behind all this scheme of supervision and control there
loomed the great impersonal system.[47]

And they resisted the new discipline. Between 1778 and
1830, there were repeated revolts by laborers in which local
tradesmen and farmers often participated.[48] The revolts
failed, of course; the new industry moved forward in-
exorably, taking the more dependent and tractable under
its command. Despite the higher wages of the factory, the
operatives were mainly women and children at the beginning, and mainly pauper children.

The burgeoning English textile industry solved its labor
problems during the latter part of the eighteenth century
by using parish children, some only four or five years old, as
factory operatives.[49] Manufacturers negotiated regular bar-
gains with the parish authorities, ordering lots of fifty or
more children from the poorhouses. (In at least one known
instance, a Lancashire manufacturer agreed to the stipula-
tion of a London parish that he take one idiot for every
twenty sound children delivered.) [50] To secure their acquiescence, the youngsters were told that once at the cotton

---

[47] Hammond and Hammond, 1917, 18–19.

[48] Hobsbawm, 50. Some independent workers, such as the hand weavers,
were virtually starved into submission before they would enter the factories. Subsequent adjustments as factory methods advanced were not much
easier: "Industrialization multiplied the number of handloom weavers
and framework-knitters. . . . Thereafter it destroyed them by slow strangu-
lation: militant and thoughtful communities like the Dunfermline linen
workers broke up in demoralization, pauperization and emigration in the
1830s. Skilled craftsmen were degraded into sweated outworkers, as in the
London furniture trades . . ." (*ibid.*, 71).

[49] Somewhat earlier, various schemes had been sponsored by philanthropists to incarcerate paupers, especially pauper children, in institutions
that would train them to work under the new discipline. The philanthropists had high hopes that these enterprises would become models for
profit-making poor relief. In this regard, they failed. As for training, the
new manufacturers were soon showing themselves to be the better task-
masters in dealing with young paupers—a beneficent service in which
they took a not inconsiderable pride.

[50] Hammond and Hammond, 1917, 145.

mills or ironmongers they would live like ladies and gentlemen on roast beef and plum pudding.[51]

Parish children were an ideal labor source for new manufacturers. The young paupers could be shipped to remote
factories,[52] located to take advantage of the streams from
which power was drawn. (With the shift from water power
to steam in the nineteenth century, factories began to locate in towns where they could employ local children; with
that the system of child labor became a system of "free"
child labor.[53]) The children were also preferred for their
docility[54] and for their light touch at the looms. Moreover, pauper children could be had for a bit of food and a
bed, and they provided a very stable labor supply, for they
were held fast at their labors by indentures, usually until
they were twenty-one. Sir Robert Owen, noted as an industrial reformer, restricted the labor of the children in
his workshops to thirteen hours a day and ordered that
they be allowed a daily romp in the yard for their health.
This was exceptionally humane; many children did not
survive the terms of their indentures.

The parish children were thus in demand by manufacturers, who found it no great problem to force their helpless young serfs to work. But when the demand for labor is
too slack to absorb a potential work force, or when market
terms are insufficiently compelling to keep them working,
the relief system may subsidize the employment of paupers—as when the magistrates of Lyons provided subsidies

---

[51] Mantoux, 411.

[52] In 1816, when parish children were no longer essential in any case,
Parliament limited the distance children might be shipped to forty miles
(Hammond and Hammond, 1917, 156).

[53] In the early days of the factory system, workers refused to let their
own children enter the mills, but their reluctance was overcome in time
by the sheer force of destitution (ibid., 156).

[54] When Sir Robert Peel (apparently either regretting his own methods
of becoming rich or satisfied that he was rich enough) attempted to get a
factory act passed that would prohibit night work for children, the mill
owners protested that free laborers would not work at night except on
terms disadvantageous to the manufacturers (ibid., 152).

to manufacturers who employed pauper children. In rural England during the late eighteenth century, as more and more of the population was being displaced by the commercialization of agriculture, this method was used on a very large scale. To be sure, a demand for labor was developing in the new manufacturing establishments that would in time absorb many of the uprooted rural poor. But this did not happen all at once: rural displacement and industrial expansion did not proceed at the same pace or in the same areas, and in any case the drastic shift from rural village to factory system took time. During the long interval before people forced off the land were absorbed into manufacturing, many remained in the countryside as virtual vagrants; others migrated to the towns, where they crowded into hovels and cellars, subject to the vicissitudes of rapidly rising and falling markets, their ranks continually enlarged by new rural refugees. And as the masses of unemployed swelled, disorder spread.

These conditions were not the result of a collapse in the market. Indeed, grain prices rose during the second half of the eighteenth century, and they rose spectacularly during the Revolutionary and Napoleonic wars. Rather, it was the expanding market for agricultural produce which, by stimulating enclosure and business-minded farming methods, led to unemployment and destitution. Meanwhile, population growth, which meant a surplus of laborers, left the workers little opportunity to resist the destruction of their traditional way of life—except by crime, riots, and incendiarism. To cope with these disturbances, relief expanded, but in such a way as to absorb and discipline the laborers by supporting the faltering labor market with subsidies.

The subsidy system is widely credited to the sheriff and magistrates of Berkshire,[55] who, in a meeting at Speenham-

---

[55] There were ample precedents for the method recommended at Speenhamland. In the late seventeenth century, some parishes began to give

land in 1795, decided on a scheme by which the Poor Law authorities would supplement the wages of agricultural workers if these wages fell below a published scale.[56] It was a time when exceptional scarcity of food led to riots all over England,[57] sometimes suppressed only by calling out the troops. With this "double panic of famine and revolution," [58] the subsidy scheme spread, especially in counties where large amounts of acreage had been enclosed.[59]

The local parishes implemented the subsidy system in different ways. Under the "roundsman" arrangement, the parish overseers sent anyone who applied for aid from house to house to get work. If he or she found work, the employer was obliged to feed and pay him or her a small sum (6d) per day, with the parish adding another small sum (4d). Elsewhere, the parish authorities contracted directly with farmers to have paupers work for a given price, with the parish paying the combined wage and relief supplement directly to the pauper. In still other places, parish authorities parceled out the unemployed to farmers, who were obliged to pay a set rate or make up the difference in higher taxes.[60] Everywhere, however, the main principle was the same: an unemployed and turbulent populace was being pacified with public allowances, but these allowances were used to restore order by enforcing work, at very low wage levels. Relief, in short, served as a support for a disturbed labor market and as a discipline for a disturbed rural so-

---

supplements to workers who could not feed their families on their wages; and Gilbert's Act of 1782 provided for subsidized work outside the workhouse for the able-bodied poor in the parishes incorporated under the Act (Webb and Webb, Part I, 170–171).

[56] The notables of Berkshire first turned down, by a considerable majority, a proposal to fix a minimum wage for laborers to correspond to the high price of corn.

[57] For a description of these outbreaks, see Hammond and Hammond, 1948, Vol. I, 116–118.

[58] The phrase belongs to H. R. Pretyman, *Dispauperization*, 1878, 27, as quoted in Webb and Webb, Part I, 172.

[59] In 1796, Parliament again followed the rulers of Berkshire by voting down minimum wage legislation in favor of wage subsidies through the relief system (de Schweinitz, 72–73).

[60] *Ibid.*, 73–74.

ciety. "The meshes of the Poor Law were spread over the entire labour system." [61]

But the Poor Law was not at variance with the labor system or with the interests of the groups that dominated that system. Quite the contrary. The farmers got cheap labor, and the poor rates did not encroach on the rent profits of the landed gentry. Indeed, relief allowances were closely articulated with market conditions, although in principle they were supposed to be scaled to "bread and children." In 1795 the Berkshire magistrates had recommended an allowance sufficient to provide a man with three gallon loaves per week, but the allowances were progressively cut, especially after the grain market began to fall at the close of the Napoleonic wars.[62] Between 1816 and 1821, several counties cut the allowance to two gallon loaves or a little more; by 1826 there were some counties in which a man was deemed to need only one and a half gallon loaves.[63] These relief cuts reflected the sharp fall in wages as farmers tried to maintain profits in the face of declining grain prices—a market maneuver made possible by the over-supply of labor, but implemented by the relief system.[64]

---

[61] Hammond and Hammond, 1948, Vol. I, 162.

[62] After 1815 the landed interests succeeded in breaking the fall in prices by securing the enactment of Corn Laws, a measure which kept food prices high even while allowances were being reduced, and thus further worsened the laborers' condition.

[63] Hobsbawm and Rudé, 51.

[64] The Speenhamland plan is generally held accountable for the steadily worsening condition of the English agricultural laborers during the first third of the nineteenth century, the view being that, by assuring a minimum allowance, it sapped the laborers' incentive to work productively, deterred farmers from raising wages, and eventually created a condition of such sodden dependence as to permit allowances to be cut to the starvation level. Karl Polanyi adds that Speenhamland held back the free labor market, by which he means the urban industrial labor market. As for the first point, it seems to us that the Speenhamland scheme is being blamed for far more basic conditions: namely, a surplus labor force, rising grain prices, and the dislocations caused by the commercialization of farming. As for the latter, if Speenhamland retarded the onset of an industrial labor market, it did so because it was necessary to moderate the social disturbances entailed—which we believe has always been, and still is, a major function of relief, and not peculiar to Speenhamland.

The English Speenhamland plan, while it enjoys a certain notoriety, is by no means unique. The most recent example of a scheme for subsidizing paupers in private employ is the reorganization of American public welfare proposed in the summer of 1969 by President Nixon; while the mechanisms by which relief recipients would be channeled into the labor market were not precisely elaborated in his initial proposal, the general parallel with the events surrounding Speenhamland is striking. The United States relief rolls expanded in the 1960's to absorb a laboring population made superfluous by agricultural modernization in the South, a population that became turbulent in the wake of forced migration to the cities. As the relief rolls grew to deal with these disturbances, pressure for "reforms" also mounted. Key features of the reform proposals include a national minimum allowance of $1,600 per year for a family of four, coupled with an elaborate system of penalties and incentives to force families to work. In effect, the proposal was intended to support and strengthen a disturbed low-wage labor market by providing what was called in nineteenth-century England a "rate in aid of wages."

Enforcing Low-Wage Work
During Periods of Stability

Even in the absence of cataclysmic change, market incentives may be insufficient to compel all people at all times to do the particular work required of them. Incentives may be too meager and erratic, or people may not be sufficiently socialized to respond to them properly. To be sure, the productivity of a fully developed capitalist economy would allow wages and profits sufficient to entice the population to work; and in a fully developed capitalist society, most people would also be reared to want what the market holds out to them. They would expect, even sanctify, the rewards of the marketplace and acquiesce in its vagaries.

But no fully developed capitalist society actually exists. (Even today in the United States, the most advanced capitalist country, certain regions and population groups—such as Southern tenant farmers—remain on the periphery of the wage market and are only partially socialized to the ethos of the market.) Capitalism evolved slowly and spread slowly. During most of this evolution, the market provided meager rewards for most workers, and none at all for some. For many, this is still so. And during most of this evolution, large sectors of the laboring classes were not fully socialized to the market ethos. The relief system, we contend, has made an important contribution toward overcoming these persisting weaknesses in the capacity of the market to direct and control people.

Once an economic convulsion subsides and civil order is restored, relief systems are not ordinarily abandoned. The rolls are reduced, to be sure, but the shell of the system usually remains, ostensibly to provide aid to the aged, the insane, the disabled, and such other unfortunates as may be without economic utility. However, the manner in which these "impotents" have always been treated, in the United States and elsewhere, suggests a purpose quite different from remediation of their destitution. For these residual persons have been universally degraded for lacking economic value and ordinarily relegated to the foul quarters of the workhouse, with its strict penal regimen and its starvation diet. Such institutions were repeatedly proclaimed the sole source of aid during times of stability, and for a reason bearing directly on the maintenance of work norms in a market system.

Conditions in the workhouse were intended to ensure that no one with any conceivable alternatives would seek public aid. Nor can there be any doubt of that intent. This statement by the Poor Law Commissioners in 1834, for example, admits of no other interpretation:

> Into such a house none will enter voluntarily; work, confinement, and discipline, will deter the indolent and

vicious; and nothing but extreme necessity will induce any to accept the comfort which must be obtained by the surrender of their free agency, and the sacrifice of their accustomed habits and gratifications. *Thus the parish officer, being furnished an unerring test of the necessity of applicants, is relieved from his painful and difficult responsibility; while all have the gratification of knowing that while the necessitous are abundantly relieved, the funds of charity are not wasted by idleness and fraud.*[65]

The method worked. Periods of relief expansion were generally followed by "reform" campaigns to abolish all "outdoor" aid and restrict relief to those who entered the workhouse—as in England in 1722, 1834, and 1871 and in the United States in the 1880's and 1890's—and these campaigns almost invariably resulted in a sharp reduction in the number of applicants seeking aid.

The harsh treatment of those who had no alternative except to fall back upon the parish and accept "the offer of the House" terrorized the impoverished masses.[66] That, too, was a matter of deliberate intent. The workhouse was designed to spur people to contrive ways of supporting themselves by their own industry, *to offer themselves to any employer on any terms*. It did this by making pariahs of those who could not support themselves; they served as an object lesson, a means of celebrating the virtues of work by the terrible example of their agony.[67] Three years after the Poor

---

[65] *The Report from His Majesty's Commissioners for Inquiring into the Administration and Practical Operation of the Poor Laws*, 1834, 271, as quoted in de Schweinitz, 123.

[66] And terrorized is the right word, for workhouse conditions were terrifying even in an age when life for the laboring classes was always brutal. Conditions were such that a House of Commons investigation conducted in 1767 found that only 7 of 100 infants born or received into workhouses had survived for two years (de Schweinitz, 66).

[67] Hobsbawm comments on the intent of the Poor Law: "The residuum of paupers could not, admittedly, be left actually to starve, but they ought not to be given more than the absolute minimum—provided it was less than the lowest wage offered in the market—and in the most discouraging conditions. The Poor Law was not so much intended to help the unfortunate as to stigmatize the self-confessed failures of society" (69).

Law Commissioners of 1834 decreed the abolition of outdoor relief and the expansion of the system of workhouses.
Disraeli accurately said of this reform that "it announces
to the world that in England poverty is a crime." [68]

The deterrent doctrine of relief [69] enunciated in 1834
provided a formula for relief-giving in the urban industrial
labor market, which is known as the principle of "less
eligibility":

> The first and most essential of all conditions, a principle
> which we find universally admitted, even by those whose
> practice is at variance with it, is, that his [the relief
> recipient's] situation on the whole shall not be made
> really or apparently so eligible [i.e., desirable] as the
> situation of the independent laborer of the lowest class.[70]

Deterrent relief practices have their contemporary equiv-
alents, as we will demonstrate in later chapters. For while
the conditions of relief in the United States today are less
harsh, the main tendency is still far from progressive liberalization. Rather, the pattern is cyclical: long periods of
restrictiveness are interrupted periodically by short periods
of liberalization. Thus the relief system created by the Social Security Act of 1935 in the United States was adminis-

---

[68] Monypenny, Vol. I, 374. As a practical matter, however, the reform
was at best only partially implemented. Tumultuous behavior among the
poor persisted, becoming especially severe during the depressions in the
1840's, so that, much to the disgust of the "reformers," outdoor relief continued to be given on a large scale. "Out of the 595 unions into which
England is divided, they [the Poor Law Commissioners] have issued a pro-
hibitory order [calling for the abolition of outdoor relief] to 478. But the
order is subject to so many exceptions, that out of 1,470,970 relieved [in
1845] only 215,325 were inmates of the workhouse" (Senior, 326).

[69] "Psychological torture," Polanyi says of the 1834 reform, "was coolly
advocated and smoothly put into practice by mild philanthropists as a
means of oiling the wheels of the labor mill" (82). This reform was the
first major accomplishment of the British middle classes after their en-
franchisement in 1832, and no doubt owes some of its brutal vigor to the
manufacturing interests represented in the middle classes.

[70] *The Report from His Majesty's Commissioners for Inquiring into
the Administration and Practical Operation of the Poor Laws*, 1834, 228,
as quoted in de Schweinitz, 123.

tered for more than two decades to ensure that as few of the poor as possible obtained as little as possible from it. The principle of "less eligibility" was reflected in statute, policy, and day-to-day practice: not only were grants kept at levels "more severe than that of the lowest class of laborers who obtain their livelihood by honest industry," which meant in some states that the recipients received too little to sustain life, but the punishment and degradation that the Poor Law authorities were confident would make relief recipients "less eligible" had their modern parallel in such practices as mass searches and raids of recipients' homes. During the 1960's, however, for reasons to be discussed in the latter half of this book, many of these restrictions collapsed and the rolls rose precipitously. But even as this occurred, pressures to reorganize the system also mounted.

We should not leave this discussion of how the relief system reinforces market incentives without noting that other governmental mechanisms to achieve the same end predate the emergence of relief systems and have persisted alongside them. As early as 1349, when the British populace was depleted by the Black Plague, the feudal lords promulgated a Statute of Laborers to deal with the fact that the resulting labor shortage enabled workers to try to obtain higher wages:

> Because that many valiant beggars, as long as they may live of begging, do refuse to labor, giving themselves to idleness and vice, and sometime to theft and other abominations; none upon the said pain of imprisonment, shall under the color of pity or alms, give anything to such, which may labor, or presume to favor them towards their desires, so that thereby they may be compelled to labor for their necessary living.[71]

A companion statute enacted by Parliament in 1350 forbade laborers from traveling from their regular places of

---

[71] Quoted in de Schweinitz, 1.

residence so long as any employer there wanted to hire them at whatever wage levels had previously been paid. Efforts to regulate the supply of labor by law persisted: in 1548, any organized efforts by laborers to fix wages and hours were prohibited; in 1563, the principles of earlier statutes were reaffirmed in a law requiring the unemployed to work for any who wanted them, and empowering the justices of the peace to fix *maximum* wages and to penalize any employer who paid in excess of the standard; in 1601, the Law of Settlement empowered local authorities to remove from their respective jurisdictions those newcomers whose assets were so few that they occupied a property renting for less than ten pounds a year.[72] Through such coercive measures as these, government enforced work during the transition from feudal labor relations to free-market labor relations, and enforced it on terms dictated by employers. Laborers could not organize, they could not refuse work, they could not exploit labor shortages to demand higher wages, and they could not move to new localities to find better working conditions.[73]

The function of these labor statutes was closely related

---

[72] The Laws of Settlement were repealed with the growing need for factory laborers in 1795, but even before that they were used not so much to prohibit the movement of labor as to direct it: "A careful study of the evidence seems to lead to the conclusion that the Laws of Settlement . . . did not stop the flow of labour, but that they regulated it in the interest of the employing class. . . . [W]hen it suited an employer to let fresh workers in, he would, *qua* overseer, encourage them to come with or without certificates; but when they were once in and 'settled' he would refuse them certificates to enable them to go and try their fortunes elsewhere, in parishes where a certificate was demanded with each poor new-comer" (Hammond and Hammond, 1948, Vol. I, 111–112).

[73] Writing in 1776 in *An Inquiry Into the Nature and Causes of the Wealth of Nations*, Adam Smith testified as to the extent and effectiveness of these constraints: "There is scarce a poor man in England of forty years of age, I will venture to say, who has not in some part of his life felt himself cruelly oppressed by this ill contrived law of settlement" (quoted by de Schweinitz, 43). Adam Smith wrote, of course, from the perspective of a philosopher of the free market, at a time when market processes were far better developed and far more effective in allocating and disciplining labor.

to that of the deterrent relief practices [74] that evolved in England during periods of economic stability. The penalties of pauperism reinforced the coercive structure of labor law and to some extent came to replace it. Both arrangements had the same general purpose—to augment the regulation of labor by compensating for the vagaries and weaknesses of a pattern of control based largely on market incentives.

Relief and the Political Process

The landed gentry who ruled Britain until 1832, and the manufacturing classes who joined them as rulers afterwards, responded to popular unrest partly because they feared revolution, partly because they recoiled from the trouble and property losses caused by disorderly mobs, and perhaps even, on some occasions, because they shared with the populace a sense of what was right and just. But government and politics in contemporary capitalist societies are different, or so it would seem. Two features are of particular relevance to the modern relief system: the enlarged role of national government, and the role of electoral institutions.

The modernization of any society generally entails expansion of the power and authority of its national government. However, when disruptions in the economy lead to occupational dislocation, causing widespread distress and discontent, it is usually local government that first experiences the tremors and moderates them by extending relief. The necessary incremental adjustments are made by local

---

[74] "Labor organization, according to the Statute of Artificers, rested on three pillars: enforcement of labor, seven years' apprenticeship, and yearly wage assessments by public officials. . . . The Statute of Artificers and the Poor Law together provided what might be called a Code of Labor" (Polanyi, 86–87).

legislative bodies or by local officials who possess discretion over relief arrangements.

But institutions do not ordinarily adjust easily, not only because of internal bureaucratic rigidities but also because change requires that the fiscal and political supports for the institution must be revised: for example, if local relief rolls rise, the parish poor rate or the state sales tax must be increased, and that may anger local taxpayers. Accordingly, the ability of local government to respond to such crises is inhibited even while the limited expansion of relief that is taking place strains and overloads the fiscal, administrative, and political underpinnings of the relief system. When local relief practices and capacities begin to break down, the national government is likely to intervene.

Correlatively, if expanding local relief begins to intrude on the operations of the labor market, the national government will intervene to force the contraction of relief, especially if disorder is not widespread. The national government of England intervened to assure the provision of local relief in the 1530's and again in the 1630's, but it enforced the contraction of relief in 1722 and 1834; the Federal Government in the United States intervened to assure a massive expansion of relief during the Great Depression (and again in the 1960's), but moved to contract relief arrangements in the late 1930's.

The electoral system is another modern, and especially a capitalist, phenomenon. In a feudal or oligarchical polity, the poor could demonstrate their discontent only by begging, stealing, marching, burning, or rioting. These mass disturbances were a form of political action, a means by which the poor occasionally forced some degree of accommodation from their rulers. But civil disorder is far more costly and threatening in a highly organized and complex society, especially as urbanization and industrialization increase. To minimize disturbances, an elaborate mechanism has evolved in capitalist societies—slowly in England, more rapidly in the United States, unfettered by residual political traditions: namely, the universal franchise and the periodic election of political office holders. The votes of an enfranchised populace serve as a barometer of unrest, and the periodic contests for electoral office are intended to exert pressure on political leaders to deal with widespread discontent in the larger society.

To win and hold office, political leaders must weld together a majority made up of diverse groups. Here, as in England, majorities have been precarious. This means that the tenure of officeholders is intimately dependent on the stability of institutions in the larger society, especially economic institutions, for any breakdown in their functioning stirs unrest and conflict and causes disaffection and division among voters. Price inflation, housing shortages, rising local taxes, widespread unemployment, or demands for racial integration may lead to the threatened or actual disaffection of segments of the population from existing political leadership. Where in the past such disaffection was signaled primarily by disorder in the streets, the electoral system is designed to channel it into the voting booth. The electoral system is, moreover, sensitive to the outbreaks of disorder that do occur, for disorder generally leads large masses of voters to shift their votes to new leaders and parties.

Whether expressed in the streets or at the polls, the disaffection of any large segment of voters can wreak havoc with electoral majorities. Political incumbents try to use the power and resources of government to intervene in the institutional arrangements that breed dissension or to develop public programs intended to recapture the allegiance of disaffected blocs. If they fail, they may lose their office to contenders who promise to deal with the sources of unrest more effectively. During periods of electoral upset, in other words, political leaders proffer concessions to win the allegiance of disaffected voting blocs. It is this objective—the political "reintegration" of disaffected groups—that impels electoral leaders to expand relief programs at times of political crisis engendered by economic distress. Indeed, it was this objective that accounted for the initiation of a national public welfare system in the United States during the Great Depression, the subject to which we now turn.

REFERENCES

Ashley, W. J., *An Introduction to English Economic History and Theory*, Part II, *The End of the Middle Ages*. New York, G. P. Putnam's Sons, 1893.

Davis, Natalie Zemon, "Poor Relief, Humanism and Heresy." Paper given at the Newberry Library Renaissance Conference in Chicago, April 16, 1966 (mimeographed).

de Schweinitz, Karl, *England's Road to Social Security: From the Statute of Laborers in 1349 to the Beveridge Report of 1942*. Philadelphia, University of Pennsylvania Press, 1943.

Hammond, J. L. and Barbara, *The Town Labourer, 1760–1832: The New Civilisation*. London, Longmans, Green & Company, 1917.

Hammond, J. L. and Barbara, *The Village Labourer*. London, Longmans, Green & Company, 1948. 2 vols. (Guild Books Nos. 239 and 240.)

Hobsbawm, E. J., *Industry and Empire: The Making of Modern English Society*, Vol. II, *1750 to the Present Day*. New York, Pantheon Books, 1968.

Hobsbawm, E. J., and Rudé, George, *Captain Swing*. New York, Pantheon Books, 1968.

Jahoda, Marie, Lazarsfeld, Paul F., and Zeisel, Hans, *Die Arbeitslosen von Marienthal. Ein soziographischer Versuch mit einem Anhang zur Geschichte der Soziographie*, 2nd ed. Allensbach, Verlag für Demoskopie, 1960.

Leonard, E. M., *The Early History of English Poor Relief*. Cambridge, University Press, 1900.

MacDonagh, Oliver, *Ireland*. Englewood Cliffs, N. J., Prentice-Hall, 1968.

Mantoux, Paul, *The Industrial Revolution in the Eighteenth Century: An Outline of the Beginnings of the Modern Factory System in England*. New York, Harper & Row, 1962.

Mill, John Stuart, *The Letters of John Stuart Mill*, ed. Hugh

S. R. Elliot, Vol. I. London, Longmans, Green & Company, 1910.

Monypenny, William Flavelle, *The Life of Benjamin Disraeli, Earl of Baconsfield*, Vol. I, *1804–1837*. New York, The Macmillan Company, 1911.

More, Sir Thomas, *Utopia*. Cambridge, University Press, 1935.

Nicholls, Sir George, *A History of the English Poor Law, in Connection with the State of the Country and the Condition of the People*, Vol. II, *A.D. 1714 to 1853*. New York, G. P. Putnam's Sons, 1898.

Polanyi, Karl, *The Great Transformation*. Boston, Beacon Press, 1957.

Senior, Nassau W., *Industrial Efficiency and Social Economy*, Vol. II. New York, Henry Holt & Company, 1928.

Trevelyan, G. M., *English Social History: A Survey of Six Centuries, Chaucer to Queen Victoria*. London, Longmans, Green & Company, 1942.

Vivès, Juan-Luis, *Concerning the Relief of the Poor or Concerning Human Need: A Letter Addressed to the Senate of Bruges, January 6, 1526*, trans. Margaret M. Sherwood. New York, New York School of Philanthropy (now Columbia University School of Social Work), 1917. (Studies in Social Work, No. 11.)

Webb, Sidney and Beatrice, *English Poor Law History*, Part I, *The Old Poor Law*. Hamden, Conn., Archon Books, 1963.

Webb, Sidney and Beatrice, *English Poor Law History*, Part II, *The Last Hundred Years*. London, Longmans, Green & Company, 1929. Vols. I and II (*English Local Government*, Vol. 8.)

PART I

Relief and the Great Depression

CHAPTER TWO

Economic Collapse, Mass Unemployment, and the Rise of Disorder

The first major relief crisis in the United States occurred during the Great Depression. By 1935, upwards of 20 million people were on the dole. But it would be wrong to assume that this unprecedented volume of relief-giving was a response to widespread economic distress, for millions had been unemployed for several years before obtaining aid. What led government to proffer aid, we shall argue, was the rising surge of political unrest that accompanied this economic catastrophe. Moreover, once relief-giving had expanded, unrest rapidly subsided, and then aid was cut back—which meant, among other things, that large numbers of people were put off the rolls and thrust into a labor market still glutted with unemployed. But with stability restored, the continued suffering of these millions had little political force.

Relief developed slowly in the United States. For one thing, except in the South, agriculture was conducted mainly by independent farmers on their own land; there was no large rural proletariat as in England. For another, when industrialization did set in, it grew rapidly, more or less absorbing the growing population. Nor did economic distress, which periodically deepened, ordinarily lead to such serious outbreaks of disorder as to provoke relief concessions, partly because the open land of the frontier served, until the late nineteenth century, to drain off some of the deprived and discontented, and partly because such outbreaks as did occur were not especially disruptive in so sparsely settled a country.

These factors also helped to nurture the strident American belief in economic individualism—the unshakable conviction held by poor and affluent alike that rags could indeed be converted into riches. The doctrine of self-help through work which distinguished nineteenth-century capitalism flourished in its purest and fiercest form in the United States. By contrast with other countries, where some residue remained of earlier Christian teachings that poverty was a blessing that should inspire charity in the rich and meekness in the poor, poverty in the United States came to be regarded as "the obvious consequence of sloth and sinfulness. . . . The promise of America was not affluence, but independence; not ease, but a chance to work for oneself, to be self-supporting, and to win esteem through hard and honest labor." [1] The very notion of a relief system seemed blasphemous.

As a result, what arrangements there were for relief tended to be scattered and fragmentary. Each township or county cared for its hungry in whatever manner it saw fit, if at all. Local arrangements for the care of paupers were varied: the giving of food, incarceration in almshouses, or indentured service.

With urbanization and industrialization, pauperism began to become a problem, especially in the cities, and diverse local arrangements for relief began to multiply.[2]

---

[1] Bremner, 16–17.

[2] Before such local arrangements were finally reorganized in the 1930's, New Hampshire had 700 different officials administering public relief in

Gradually the practice of auctioning off and indenturing paupers was replaced by the institution of the almshouse or workhouse. The first almshouse opened in Boston in 1740. By 1884, there were about six hundred in New England. Eventually most states passed laws designating almshouses as the primary method of caring for the poor, although it remained for the local communities to finance and operate them.

Despite the hardships of immigration, migration, and cyclical depressions that began to plague the industrializing cities of the late nineteenth century, the principle remained firmly established that poor relief, if it was to be given at all, was a local rather than state or federal responsibility. Federal aid was periodically sought and given in cases of disasters such as flood and drought, but not for the disaster of unemployment.[3] Some moves in the Congress to obtain federal aid for the unemployed during the depressions of 1893–1894, 1914, and 1921 failed. The doctrine that was to hold sway for almost a century was articulated by President Pierce in 1854:

> [Should Congress] make provision for such objects, the fountains of charity will be dried up at home, and the several States, instead of bestowing their own means on the social wants of their own people, may themselves, through the strong temptation, which appeals to States as to individuals, become humble suppliants for the bounty of the Federal Government, reversing their true relation to this Union.[4]

---

245 separate county, city, and town units; Pennsylvania had 967 administrators in 425 districts; Ohio had 1,535 different poor relief districts (Brown, 14–15).

[3] Congressional disaster appropriations (for victims of fire, flood, earthquakes, tornadoes, and grasshopper ravages) date from 1827, according to a statement inserted into the record of the United States Senate in 1933. These appropriations were pushed through in response to pressure by farmers who were ready to qualify their staunch belief in self-help in the face of "acts of God."

[4] Taken from a message vetoing a bill to give lands to the states to build institutions for the insane, who were generally confined with paupers. In fact, about one quarter of the population of New England almshouses

Early in the twentieth century, the states began to establish pensions for the blind, the aged, and widows ("Mothers' Aid" pensions). For the most part, however, these programs were not mandatory; implementation remained a
local (usually county) prerogative, and only a few states
shared costs with localities.[5]

When the Great Depression struck in the 1930's, there
were only these local relief arrangements, virtually unchanged since colonial times, to deal with the disaster. All
the old methods—from almshouse to indentured service—
were still in use. In many places, private charities were the
sole recourse for the destitute.[6]

Mass Unemployment and the Persistence of Relief Restrictions

Unemployment was already rising in 1928. At first the
trouble was defined as a temporary business downturn, and
it was widely said that the resulting distress could be
handled by local efforts. The nation was stubbornly unwilling to recognize that an economic catastrophe impended.
News of the Depression as such rarely appeared on the
front pages of newspapers until after 1932. Instead there
were stories of personal tragedy resulting from the disaster:
a speculator's suicide or an unemployed worker who
murdered his starving family. Newspapers urged better-
off citizens to look about for odd jobs for the unemployed;

---

was made up of the insane (*Congressional Globe*, 1854, 1061–1063, as
quoted in Breckinridge, 226–227).

[5] Even by 1934, after five years of depression, 24 states had enacted
pension programs for the blind, but only 11 had appropriated any money;
of the 28 states with old-age pension schemes, only 16 had funded them;
and of the 45 states with Mothers' Aid programs, only 14 had provided
any funds at all (Douglas, 7; Brown, 26–28).

[6] During the severe depression of 1914–1915, for example, it was left
to the New York Association for Improving the Condition of the Poor to
initiate work projects for the unemployed in New York City (Colcord, 13).

city leaders initiated "make-a-job" campaigns and "household helper" schemes; [7] some communities set aside plots for vegetable gardens to ease the plight of the jobless.[8] Thus the Lynds quote a Middletown editorial in 1930: "It is an open secret that there has been considerable suffering . . . which is likely to continue for several weeks. . . . Now is a good time for people who can afford it to have all their odd jobs done to help the unemployed. . . . That is much better than outright charity, however necessary the latter may be in emergencies." [9] The problem was regarded as temporary and thus capable of being handled by the traditional methods of individual self-help and local charity.

But rising unemployment did not portend a temporary business downturn. By the spring of 1929, when a seasonal decrease in unemployment was expected, the number of men out of work approached 3 million; by January 1930, the figure topped 4 million; it rose to 5 million in September and reached 8 million by the spring of 1931. Unemployment continued to rise until, in the spring of 1933, about 15 million men—or about one third of the work force—had become jobless.[10] Expressed in index numbers adjusted for seasonal variations, the employment index fell from 108 in August 1929 to 61 in July 1932, or by more

---

[7] In these "make-a-job" or "man-a-block" campaigns, unemployed men were assigned to residential blocks to do snow removal and the like while the householders were canvassed for small donations. During 1929–1930, such schemes were started in Buffalo, Cincinnati, Kansas City, Milwaukee, and Louisville, among other places. In Philadelphia, the mayor appointed a committee to organize street selling of fruit (*ibid.*, 166).

[8] A plan said to be in use in Chickasha, Oklahoma, and later recommended by Secretary of War Patrick Hurley for application in other local communities, involved scraping the food left on restaurant plates into large containers and giving the scraps to the unemployed—on condition that they chop wood donated by farmers (see Hopkins, 26–28).

[9] Lynd and Lynd, 105.

[10] These estimates are from Nathan. However, unemployment estimates by respectable authorities varied widely. At the peak, reached in March 1933, unemployment was estimated at 17,920,000 by the National Research League, while the National Industrial Conference Board estimated 13,300,000.

than 40 per cent. Meanwhile, those who were still working had to take reductions in pay and hours, so that wages fell by one third, to an average of $17 per week.[11]

An economic crisis of unprecedented magnitude had struck. But the federal government remained aloof. What action Hoover took was directed at supporting and stimulating bankers, railroads, farmers—the entrepreneurial groups that, according to official American gospel, had made the economy run before and would make it run again. But even these steps were crippled by doctrinal reservations about government interference with the economy. When the stock market did not recover immediately, as Hoover had predicted it would after the crash of October 1929, he exhorted businessmen to hold prices and wages firm, as if to seal off the Wall Street disaster. As price devaluation nevertheless worsened and became widespread, Hoover took the position that the economy was experiencing a healthful deflation of unnatural speculative values preliminary to the resumption of business on a sound basis. His chief interim prescription was to call for the expansion of private and public construction; however, given his preoccupation with a balanced budget, so little public money was invested that the construction industry actually declined substantially in the early years of the Depression. To explain rapidly falling wages, the President argued that wage cuts were justified by the need to create a profit margin for businessmen in the face of falling price levels—this in order to assure the rejuvenation of business, and through business to bring the return of prosperity to all Americans, in the American way. Throughout these years, officials continually proclaimed that recovery was always "just around the corner." [12]

---

[11] U.S. Bureau of the Census, 1941, 340, 346.

[12] Dr. John A. Ryan, of the Catholic University, reported that when he went to Hoover in June 1930 as a member of a committee to ask the President to press for a 3-billion-dollar public works program, the President replied: "Gentlemen, you have come sixty days too late. The depression is over" (Hopkins, 88).

As for the growing masses of the unemployed, Hoover limited himself mainly to offering rhetorical encouragement to local charity efforts. In October 1930, he appointed Colonel Arthur Woods to head a President's Emergency Committee for Employment. Colonel Woods telephoned governors around the country to inquire into the unemployment situation, attempted to estimate the numbers out of work, and, apparently impressed that the situation was serious, recommended to the President that he seek substantial appropriations from Congress for public works. Instead, the President told Congress in December 1930 that "the fundamental strength of the Nation's economic life is. unimpaired," and that federal expenditures for public works were "already at the maximum limit warranted by financial prudence as a continuing policy."[13] Accordingly, several resolutions introduced in Congress to aid victims of drought were defeated, as was a measure to appropriate 25 million dollars for Red Cross drought and unemployment relief.[14] Instead, the federal government called on private employers to maintain payrolls.

With over 8 million unemployed in August 1931, the Emergency Committee for Employment was replaced by the President's Organization on Unemployment Relief. Like its predecessor, it had neither funds nor powers,[15] and so it worked to publicize the need for charity, to reaffirm the virtues of local responsibility, and to call for better "coordination" of local efforts—as if mass destitution were mainly a result of administrative confusion among the vari-

---

[13] *Ibid.*, 18–25.

[14] *Ibid.*, 33–36.

[15] Will Rogers described the man appointed to head the new Emergency Committee as ". . . the biggest hello man in the world, a very fine high caliber man, but what a job he has got! Mr. Hoover just told him 'Gifford, I have a remarkable job for you; you are to feed the several million unemployed.' 'With what?' says Gifford. 'That's what makes the job remarkable. If you had something to do it with, it wouldn't be remarkable'" (*ibid.*, 62–63).

ous local charity agencies. The federal stance is suggested by an advertisement which the President's Committee co-sponsored with the Association of Community Chests and Councils during a fund-raising campaign in the fall of 1931:

> Between October 19 and November 25 America will feel the thrill of a great spiritual experience. In those few weeks millions of dollars will be raised in cities and towns throughout the land, and the fear of cold and hunger will be banished from the hearts of thousands. . . .

The ad prompted the following interchange between Senator Edward Costigan and Walter S. Gifford, head of the President's Organization on Unemployment Relief (and president of the American Telephone and Telegraph Company) during hearings on relief bills which were then pending in the Senate:

Senator Costigan: First, let me ask you whether you feel that the fear of cold and hunger has been banished from the hearts of thousands?

Mr. Gifford: Undoubtedly; not of everyone but of thousands. That is a very modest statement, I think.

Senator Costigan: Does it still remain in the hearts of thousands?

Mr. Gifford: I think so. There is no doubt about that.

Senator Costigan: Is it your feeling that we, as a people, ought to follow the practice of advertising ourselves into the thrill of great spiritual experiences? [16]

The National Association of Manufacturers [17] and the U.S. Chamber of Commerce echoed the sentiment against

---

[16] See U.S. Senate, 1932, 327. See also Gifford, 466.

[17] "The Platform of American Industry," drawn up under the auspices of the National Association of Manufacturers in 1932 stated: "We oppose the enactment of compulsory laws which give to the individual a right to payments while unemployed from a fund created by legislative order and subject to continuing political pressure for increases without relation to

federal aid, proclaiming it a menace that would weaken the moral fiber of every individual, community, and state. "The spontaneous generosity of our people," the Chamber assured the nation, "has never failed." [18] Repeatedly, as the crisis worsened, President Hoover asserted that the federal government could not permit local communities to abandon their "precious possession of local initiative and responsibility." In a message to Congress in December 1931, he insisted that the trouble was in fact being taken care of by "local initiative":

> Through the President's Organization for Unemployment Relief, public and private agencies were successfully mobilized last winter to provide employment and other measures against distress. . . . Committees of leading citizens are now active at practically every point of unemployment. In the large majority they have been assured the funds necessary which, together with local government aids, will meet the situation. . . .
>
> I am opposed to any direct or indirect government dole. The breakdown and increased unemployment in Europe is due in part to such practices. Our people are providing against distress from unemployment in true American fashion. . . .[19]

Indeed, the President went so far as to find positive good in the calamity:

---

periods of employment and contribution. Experience demonstrates that such public doles tend to continue and exaggerate the evil by subsidizing uneconomic factors in industry" (Hopkins, 74).

[18] Silas Strawn, president of the U.S. Chamber of Commerce, wrote as follows to a congressional committee in February 1932 after the Chamber had taken a straw vote on the issue: "On the ground that needed relief should be provided through private contributions and by state and local governments, 2,534 votes were cast against federal appropriations, and 197 votes in favor" (*ibid.*, 74–75).

[19] Brown, 98–99. During the great Irish potato famine of the 1840's, when more than one million peasants died, similar restrictions upon relief-giving were justified by similar concern about the moral fiber of the Irish people: "Committed to laissez faire dogmatism, British politicians . . . argued that Famine relief should not interfere with normal commercial activity, compete with private business, discourage personal initiative, make the Irish people psychologically dependent on Government handouts, or interfere with private property or private responsibility" (McCaffery, 65).

The evidence of the Public Health Service shows an actual decrease of sickness and infant and general mortality below normal years. No greater proof could be adduced that our people have been protected from hunger and cold and that the sense of social responsibility in the Nation has responded to the need of the unfortunate.[20]

Nor, at this stage, was Congress ready to take action on direct relief payments, despite a Democratic victory in the congressional election of 1930 which had reduced the Republicans to a minority in the House and had split the Senate.[21] Senator Robert F. Wagner introduced legislation in 1931 which called for 2 billion dollars for federal public works, federal employment services, and federal unemployment insurance. The Congress passed the first two measures, which Hoover promptly vetoed, but unemployment insurance (a form of direct relief) was voted down. In February 1932, Senators Robert M. La Follette, Jr. and Edward P. Costigan introduced a bill calling for a federal grant of 375 million dollars to the states for unemployment relief, and that too was voted down.[22] Senator Gore of Oklahoma expressed the views of many in the Congress when he said that you could no more relieve a depression by legislation "than you can pass a resolution to prevent disease." [23]

But distress deepened. More families used up their savings and exhausted their credit. Some people had been without work for as long as three years, and still unemployment

---

[20] U.S. Senate, 1932, 116.

[21] There were forty-eight Democratic Senators, forty-eight Republicans, and one independent. In the House, the Democrats had a fifty-seat majority. However, the Democratic Party was in the hands of Eastern conservatives who generally cooperated with the Hoover administration. In fact, the leaders of the National Democratic Committee assured the President, after their mid-term congressional victory, that they would not be partisan (see Rauch, 16).

[22] Schlesinger, 1957, 225-226. Senators La Follete and Costigan persisted in introducing unemployment relief legislation in every session of the Seventy-second Congress, all of which either died in committee or failed to pass (Hopkins, 73).

[23] Schlesinger, 1957, 226.

grew. In 1932, applications for relief were estimated to have increased by 40 per cent, but many were rejected; local public and private relief agencies had been pushed beyond their capacity. In Philadelphia and Chicago, the relief offices closed. Across the country, meager relief grants were cut still further.

Farm income also fell disastrously, down from 7 billion dollars in 1929 to 2 billion dollars in 1932 [24] (although until 1931 the Hoover Administration had made some modest efforts to buy up farm surpluses and encourage voluntary crop reduction). Indeed, the fall in farm prices was eventually deeper, although less sudden, than other price declines. Severe drought in 1931 left the farmers of the Plains country especially hard hit. True to the business doctrine, Hoover proposed government loans for the farmers, to be used, however, only to restore property values by buying implements and feeding livestock, and to be secured by their property. Some Western senators objected that farmers could not feed their livestock while their families were going hungry; the Administration countered that direct relief was no business of the federal government but should be provided by local private and public agencies.

In the meantime, some of the urban states began to try to deal with local distress. A number of states that had legislation on the books permitting local jurisdiction to establish pensions for the orphaned, the aged, or the blind moved to require localities to implement these programs, and some states even appropriated matching funds. In 1931, on Governor Roosevelt's initiative, New York established an emergency program which supplemented local

---

[24] Farm prices had been in a slump even before the Depression. Earlier in the century farm production had expanded immensely, partly as a result of the demand created by immigration, and then by World War I, when the United States fed both its armies and its allies. With the war ended and immigration declining, farm prices fell to extremely low levels in the 1920's and then collapsed altogether after 1929 (see U.S. Bureau of the Census, 1941, 310–346, 496, 804).

relief funds with an initial 20 million dollars. New Jersey, Pennsylvania, Ohio, and Wisconsin quickly followed with similar emergency outlays, and other states began to underwrite municipal relief bonds. By the end of 1932, twenty-four states were providing some form of financial aid to localities for relief.

The federal government finally took a small step toward providing relief in 1932. Overriding an initial presidential veto, Democratic leaders pushed through the Emergency Relief Act of 1932, which provided the Reconstruction Finance Corporation [25] with 300 million dollars to supplement local relief funds by making loans to the states (repayable with interest in July 1935). By this time, there were about 12 million people out of work (less than a quarter of whom were getting relief, according to a survey by the American Association of Social Workers, and what they got barely kept them alive). These loans were designed to make it easier for states and localities to spend their own money for relief by allowing them to borrow from their share of federal highway appropriations (one of several types of interference with local responsibility that the federal government had not been reluctant to undertake). Since it was left to the states to request the money, and since the states were liable for repayment, and since a Hoover-oriented RFC administration did not encourage them, the states had borrowed only 30 million dollars by the close of 1932.[26]

---

[25] The RFC was created earlier in 1932 primarily to make loans to banks, consistent with the Hoover doctrine of supporting business as a means to recovery. As it turned out, half of the money was loaned to only three banks (see Schlesinger, 1957, 238).

[26] See Brown, 126, and Schlesinger, 1957, 241. In principle, localities as well as states could borrow these relief funds, but only as definite local obligations to be secured by the usual methods. Many localities had already exceeded their constitutional borrowing powers. As for the states, some were simply reluctant to assume responsibility for relief, and others were bogged down by the necessity of securing legislative authority and setting up an administrative apparatus to distribute the funds. In any case, even if the total appropriation had been distributed, it would not

Six months later, the federal administration forsook its traditional posture and launched a massive emergency relief program. The forces that finally led to this turnabout are worth examining.

Local Efforts to Cope with the Unemployed

If national political figures could at first turn a deaf ear to the cries of the unemployed, local officials could not. As unemployment spread, more and more people descended on relief agencies with pleas for aid. Nor could they simply be turned away, as relief agencies were wont to do. For one thing, the obvious distress on all sides belied the customary American view that the fault lay with those in need. So long as most people could find work, the very poor could be dismissed as lazy and improvident. Now there simply was no work. For another, the unemployed were also voters, and the possibility of their political defection was not lost on local politicians, particularly in industrial towns, where the workers were in the majority as well as unemployed. (By contrast, two decades later, in the 1950's, when millions of black poor were driven from the rural South to the cities by agricultural modernization, there was virtually no response from local relief agencies to the needs of these impoverished people. One reason was that the black newcomers were generally not integrated into the urban political apparatus. Since they had little political force, little had to be conceded to them, at least at first.)

The burden on public and private relief agencies was enormous, and they staggered under it. The Community Chests, which represented private social agencies, had al-

have come near to meeting the need. Governor Pinchot of Pennsylvania estimated that if 60 million dollars were spent in his state alone, each of the unemployed would get thirteen cents' worth of food each day for a year (Hopkins, 92).

ways presented themselves in their annual appeals as shouldering the responsibility for relief, and so they felt compelled to try to carry a large share of the load. Indeed, throughout the early years of the Depression, the Chests continued to insist in their public reports and statements that they, rather than public agencies, were the appropriate vehicle to handle relief problems. (It came as something of a shock to private agencies when the Bureau of Registration for Social Statistics of the University of Chicago reported to the National Conference of Social Work in 1929 that 71 per cent of relief expenditures in the country were in fact public.) Fund-raising appeals aside, private agencies had in truth been financing a variety of more respectable services, such as child guidance, recreation, health care, and the like. Caught between their own proclamations and spreading unemployment, the Chests were reluctantly compelled to put a larger portion of their budgets into cash relief. Prior to the Depression, only about 10 per cent of Chest funds had been expended for cash aid; by 1932, relief costs absorbed as much as 35 per cent of Chest funds in many communities. But even with a greater flow of contributions [27] and the diversion of resources from other services to relief, charity budgets hardly met the rising demand for aid.

Most of the relief load had to be carried by local tax revenues. Reports from several major cities showed that relief expenditures by local agencies in these cities had increased from $22,338,114 in the first three months of 1929 to $73,757,300 during the corresponding period in 1931. The number of families receiving relief averaged 33,861 per month in the first quarter of 1929; by early 1931 the monthly average had increased to 1,287,778 families.[28]

---

[27] In part the increase was attributable to the proliferation of Community Chests. If the same 171 Chests are examined, they raised $60,678,000 in 1929, and $78,542,000 in 1932 (Brown, 412).

[28] While these figures include private relief, the overwhelming portion was carried by public agencies (Brown, 73–74). The Mayor's Unemployment

Municipalities, townships, and counties had to strain to meet these escalating relief budgets. The local citizenry were exhorted to greater charity; ad hoc schemes were invented to raise funds, such as taxing municipal employees the equivalent of a day's salary each month (a device sometimes joined in by private corporations, which contributed to philanthropy by taxing their employees). In New York City, where "outdoor relief" (as distinct from workhouses) had been forbidden by the charter of 1898, local philanthropists convened in July 1930 to raise 8.5 million dollars to put 25,000 of the unemployed to work at municipal jobs. Meanwhile, the police precincts distributed direct relief to the most destitute from funds contributed by city employees.[29]

In Illinois, where severe unemployment spread from Chicago to the downstate coal-mining areas, the public schools were assigned to make a survey of relief needs, and 3 million dollars was raised from "gifts" by the employees of large corporations and by state employees who found their paychecks reduced each month.[30] Some towns tried to economize by establishing commissaries where relief vouchers could be exchanged for food, but the savings thus achieved were dubious, and the device outraged local storekeepers who were managing to stay afloat mainly because of the business they did in relief vouchers. Such schemes did not go far toward meeting the mounting costs of relief, and in any case the methods of financing fell heavily on small proprietors and civil servants and on those of the working classes who were still employed.[31]

Committee of Detroit sent a petition to President Hoover in July 1931 pointing out that the total budget of the Detroit Community Fund was less than the City of Detroit had spent on relief in February and March alone (Hopkins, 48).

[29] Brophy and Hallowitz, 43.

[30] Brown, 72.

[31] "Local relief," Governor Gifford Pinchot of Pennsylvania bitterly remarked in the *Survey*, "means making the poor man pay. . . . Local

With relief costs rapidly mounting, local officials soon found themselves pressed on all sides. The business community called for economy in municipal services and tax relief for themselves. Large property owners in Chicago went so far as to organize a tax boycott; there, as in other cities, the wealthy simply misrepresented their holdings even while appealing to workers to give of their scant earnings to charity campaigns for the unemployed.[32] In some areas, the farmers—ardent believers in self-sufficiency, especially for city folk—were also outraged at the increased county expenditures.

The "business downturn" continued and worsened, and the masses of unemployed grew. National income fell from 82 billion dollars in 1929 to 40 billion dollars in 1932; reported corporate income fell from 11 billion dollars to 2 billion dollars; the value of industrial and railroad stock fell by 80 per cent; and production fell by 50 per cent.[33] Shanty towns sprang up on the outskirts of the cities; in New York the unemployed took over an empty packing plant; others built shacks in the bed of an abandoned reservoir in Central Park, calling it "Hoover Valley." And still more people crowded the relief offices, many of them drawn from the respectable middle class, people stunned by the collapse of the racy prosperity of the 1920's which left them hat-in-hand, begging for a dole. Most got nothing. By 1932, only one quarter of the unemployed were receiving relief. In New York City, such lucky families obtained an average grant of $2.39 per week; in most places, people got only a little food.[34] Even so, relief costs soared:

---

relief means release for the rich, not relief for the poor." So, obviously, did the "spread the work" scheme (cutting the work week so as to employ more men), which was advocated by the Hoover administration in 1931–1932.

[32] Schlesinger, 1957, 253.

[33] U.S. Bureau of the Census, 1941.

[34] In Baltimore, for example, the average relief allotment was eighty cents per week, in commodities (Greenstein).

TABLE I

*Expenditures for Relief from Public and Private Funds
in 120 Urban Areas, 1929–1932* [35]

	Amounts in Thousands
1929	43,745
1930	71,425
1931	172,749
1932	308,185

To make the problem worse, tax revenues fell off sharply. Municipalities tried to float bonds to pay for relief, but by the winter of 1931–1932 many found their credit exhausted; even at exorbitant interest rates, banks would not buy the bonds.[36]

The Rise of Mass Disorder

Without work, a way of life began to collapse. People could not support their families, they lost their farms and their homes, the young did not marry, and many took to the road. Most people suffered quietly, confused and shamed by their plight. But not all were so acquiescent. With signs of disaster on all sides and with millions in desperate straits, attitudes toward destitution were momentarily reversed. Many began to define their hardships, not as an individual fate, but as a collective disaster, not as a mark of individual failure, but as a fault of "the system." As the legitimacy of economic arrangements weakened, anger and protest escalated. The Depression thus gave rise to the largest movement of the unemployed in the history of this country.

Groups of men out of work congregated at local relief

---

[35] Winslow, 26.

[36] Measured in dollars per $1,000 of personal income, the interest expenditure of state and local government rose from $7.34 in 1927 to $14.79 in 1932 (Maxwell, 182).

agencies, cornered and harassed administrators, and took over offices until their demands were met—which usually meant that money or goods were distributed to them.[37] Relief officials, who were accustomed to discretionary giving to a meek clientele and were not much governed by any fixed set of regulations, usually acquiesced in the face of aggressive protests. Unwilling or unable to withstand "direct action" tactics, officials in local and private charities gradually forfeited the discretion to give or withhold aid and relinquished cherished procedures of investigation and surveillance over recipients. Each victory over relief officials added morale and momentum to the movement of the unemployed and further weakened the doctrine that being "on the county" represented a public confession of failure.[38] And because disturbances in local centers succeeded in getting people money or goods, the movement spread throughout the country.

In Chicago, for example, where many of the homeless unemployed had taken refuge in the municipal lodging houses, the Unemployed Council organized five thousand men to march on the headquarters of the lodging houses, demanding three meals a day, free medical attention, tobacco twice a week, the right to hold Council meetings in

---

[37] Similar conditions produced similar protests during earlier depressions in the United States, although never on such a large scale. For example, during the 1850's rallies of the unemployed were organized to demand jobs on city works, and in the depression of 1873–1879 demonstrations in New York City drew ten to fifteen thousand people who had to be dispersed by the police. During the same period, Chicago anarchists organized a march on the Chicago Relief and Aid Society, swamping the intake office and leading to "unprecedentedly wide relief-giving" (Seymour, August 1937, 8).

[38] At such times of disturbance, and only at such times, are relief procedures and relief agents typically condemned by recipients. In the issue of *Call to Action* dated July 20, 1933 (the organ of the Port Angeles, Washington, Unemployed Council and Affiliated Action Committee), the following statement can be found: " 'Home Visitors' or 'snoopers' are only relief workers on a cash basis. They are picked for their ability as snoopers and stool pigeons only. They ask you so damn many questions that there is nothing personal left to you anyway."

the lodging houses, and the assurance of no discrimination against Council members. When relief funds were cut by 50 per cent, the unemployed marched again and the cut was rescinded. Chicago was also the scene of frequent "rent riots," especially in the black neighborhoods, where unemployment reached catastrophic proportions and evictions were frequent.[39] Groups of as many as a hundred men, often led by Communist Party members,[40] would assemble to put an evicted family's furniture back into the apartment or house (even when the family was not present).[41] These tactics frequently culminated in beatings, arrests, and even killings, but they also forced relief officials to give out money for rent payments.[42] After a rent riot in August 1931, in which three policemen were injured, evictions were suspended, at least temporarily,[43] and some of the rioters got work relief. As one official tells the story, the riot

> . . . flared up the whole community. I spent the next forty-eight hours in the streets down there, trying to quiet things down.
>
> I went to see Ryerson and the Committee of leading businessmen . . . I said the only way to stop this business is to put these evicted men to work at once. This was on a Saturday. They said, "We don't have the money." I said, "You better get some." By Monday morning, they had the money, and we put three hundred of those men to work in the parks that day.[44]

---

[39] Gosnell reports that unemployment in some sections of Chicago's South Side ghetto in 1931 ran over 85 per cent. In the period from August 11 to October 31, 1931, there were 2,185 cases before Renter's Court, 38 per cent of which involved blacks (1937, 321–329).

[40] The Communists were especially alert and vigorous agitators on the bread lines, in the flophouses, among the loiterers at factory gates, and in the intake sections of relief offices (Seymour, August 1937, 11).

[41] Abbott, Chap. 14.

[42] Seymour, December 1937, 14. Seymour reports that approximately sixty-five arrests were made for rent riot activities in Chicago during a six-month period in 1932.

[43] Gosnell, 1937, 330–331.

[44] Dr. Martin Bickham, as quoted in Terkel, 396.

In New York, group action by the unemployed began with resistance to evictions on the Lower East Side. In 1930 and 1931, the number of evictions increased daily, and small bands of men began to use strong-arm tactics to prevent marshals from putting furniture on the street. Sometimes they were successful, but even if they were not, physical resistance had become the only resort for people forced out of their homes. A Union Square protest meeting was broken up by the police with considerable brutality. As a result of wide publicity in the press, a second meeting several weeks later attracted an estimated 100,000 people; this time there was no police brutality, and the Mayor agreed to form a committee to collect funds to be distributed to the unemployed.[45]

A survey conducted somewhat later in the Depression revealed that almost all of the district relief administrators in New York City reported that they had frequent dealings with unemployed groups; that these groups were disruptive; and that the groups frequently won their demands.[46] Five of the relief offices were observed continuously over a thirty-day period, during which 196 demands by unemployed groups were recorded, of which 107 were granted.

The disruption was by no means confined to relief offices nor to relief officials. By the spring of 1930, marches and demonstrations in local communities and state capitals, involving thousands of people, had become commonplace; [47] in December 1931, participants in the first of two Communist-led national hunger marches on Washington were met on the ramps leading to the Capitol by police

---

[45] Brophy and Hallowitz, 5–6.

[46] Thus, of the forty-two administrators interviewed, thirty-nine reported "contacts" with groups at least twice a week, and thirty-three reported that the groups shouted, picketed, and refused to leave the relief offices (*ibid.*, 63–65).

[47] On March 6th, declared "World Unemployment Day," one million people were said to have joined in demonstrations across the country (Seymour, August 1937, 12).

armed with rifles and riot guns (backed up by machine-gun nests concealed in the stonework above).[48]

Goaded by cuts in relief, demonstrations often culminated in violence, with consequent arrests and jailings. In March 1932, a procession of thousands of jobless marched from downtown Detroit to the Ford River Rouge plant in Dearborn, where they were met by the Dearborn police. When ordered to halt, the marchers kept moving, and the police opened fire, killing four and wounding several others before the crowd broke ranks. The bodies were laid in state under a red banner bearing Lenin's portrait, and afterwards thousands of Detroit workers walked behind the coffins to the sound of the Russian funeral march of 1905.[49]

In May, a group of World War I veterans set off from Portland to Washington to plead with Congress for earlier payment of a bonus for wartime services due to them by law only in 1945. They were the well-remembered Bonus Expeditionary Force. Their trek across the country attracted national attention, especially after a skirmish with the National Guard in East St. Louis, and veterans from other areas hit the road. By June there were twenty thousand veterans camped on the marshy banks of the Anacostia River in Washington, waiting for President Hoover to grant them an audience. On June 17, the bonus bill was defeated in the Senate. But still the men stayed and waited, many now joined by their wives and children. On the evening of July 28 a skittish Administration ordered the Army to clear the camp with cavalry, infantry, and tanks. Men, women, and children fled as their shacks were burned behind them. The veterans did not resist, and no shots

---

[48] In December 1932 the second march, numbering about three thousand and led by Herbert Benjamin, head of the Communist-organized Unemployed Councils, was held at bay by troops and police on the outskirts of Washington for three days, after which the marchers were permitted to walk through the Capitol accompanied by police and tanks.

[49] Schlesinger, 1957, 255–256.

were fired. They were not rebelling; they were pleading. But still, discontent had reached dangerous proportions and was beginning to express itself in dangerous ways.

Disorder
and Electoral Realignment

By 1932, then, the crisis in the nation could no longer be concealed by doctrinal optimism, and RFC loans were by no means coping with the situation. The crisis had three main elements. The first was widespread destitution, with the accompanying disintegration of normal life patterns. Only 4 million people were getting relief of any kind—a fraction of the millions in the families of the unemployed. In most localities, relief consisted only of food, and not much of that. The Philadelphia Community Council described the situation as one of "slow starvation and progressive disintegration of family life." Countless people were losing their homes and their farms. There were signs of alarming increases in tuberculosis and pellagra.[50]

Compounding the calamity of mass destitution was the fiscal plight of localities; many had been brought to the verge of bankruptcy by relief costs. Some cities stopped paying their municipal employees;[51] many halted other public services; others simply defaulted on their bonds.[52]

---

[50] President Hoover produced statements from the Surgeon General to the effect that the state of public health had improved with the Depression, to which the United Hospital Fund of New York City responded with statistics showing an abnormal and progressive increase in illness, and the Pennsylvania Secretary of Public Health reported alarming increases in malnutrition and tuberculosis (Schlesinger, 1957, 241–250; Brown, 138).

[51] The City of Chicago, for example, owed its schoolteachers 20 million dollars in back pay (Hopkins, 92–93).

[52] During the five years prior to 1932, the number of defaults had averaged about 45 a year. On November 1, 1932, 678 localities were listed; two years later the number had risen to 2,654 (Maxwell, 181–182).

Early in February 1932, as part of a campaign for a bill to provide federal loans for unemployment relief, Senator La Follette sent out a questionnaire to mayors all over the country asking about current numbers of people on relief, anticipated increases, the amounts of relief aid being given, whether the city was in a position to float bond issues to meet relief needs, and whether the mayor favored federal appropriations to "aid in providing more adequate relief for the needy or in lessening the burden on local taxpayers." In their replies,[53] the mayors described widespread distress and clamored for federal aid. Not only were they administering relief on a starvation basis, but virtually every municipality claimed to be on the verge of bankruptcy and faced the prospect of having to cut off relief altogether.

Finally, while most of the populace seemed sullen, confused, and in despair, discontent was mounting, and discontent could turn to turmoil. Economic distress had produced unprecedented disorder and the specter of cataclysmic disorder. Communist-led rallies and marches in New York City drew thousands of people who participated because they were hungry and wanted jobs. Farmers in Iowa overturned milk trucks in a desperate demand that the price they received at market cover at least their costs of production.[54] In Chicago, where half the working force was unemployed and Socialists and Communists were organizing mass demonstrations, the Mayor pleaded for the federal government to send 150 million dollars for relief immediately rather than federal troops later. By the spring of 1932, riots had broken out in the coal-mining areas of

---

[53] Senator La Follette had the replies read into the *Congressional Record*, 3099–3260.

[54] By the summer of 1932, protests by farmers were escalating rapidly. To stem the fall in farm prices, some farmers organized strike actions to keep their products off the market. Trucks bound for market were blocked by spiked logs and threshing cables laid across roads; in many places, for example, dairy farmers declared an embargo on milk, overturned trucks, and emptied milk cans.

Kentucky, and the Administration was being warned of the imminent spread of violence—and Communism—in the Kentucky mountains. Congressman Hamilton Fish, Jr., announced to House of Representatives that "if we don't give [security] under the existing system, the people will change the system. Make no mistake about that." Even the American Legion declared that the crisis could not be "promptly and efficiently met by existing political methods."

Taken together, these events signaled political disaffection on a scale unparalleled in the American experience. The people were turning against their leaders and against the regime—against Hoover, against business, even against "the American way." What direction that disaffection would take was to depend on the responsiveness of political leaders and the adaptability of the regime. More specifically, it was to depend on the ability of the electoral system to register discontent, to shake up political leadership and to force the governmental action needed to restore order.

The Republican Party had been formed in 1854 as a coalition of Northern business and labor interests, joined for a time by Midwestern farm groups, all welded together by a common struggle against the Southern and agrarian interests which dominated the Democratic Party at the time. In the intervening years, the party fell under the domination of Eastern businessmen, despite a short-lived effort by Theodore Roosevelt to restore labor and farmers to the coalition. With Eastern business interests at the helm, the party came to power with the toppling of the Wilson Administration in 1920. Thereafter it reigned securely; the Republicans received substantial majorities throughout the 1920's, particularly in the Northern industrial states. Hoover took office in 1928 with a margin of seventeen Republicans in the Senate and one hundred in the House.

Nor could it be said, in terms of class or sectional interests, that the Democratic Party was the party of opposition. In 1924, the agrarian populist wing of the party had been soundly defeated by Eastern conservatives, represented by business leaders like John J. Raskob and machine politicians like Alfred E. Smith, and these men remained in control in 1932. But with economic conditions worsening and discontent mounting as the presidential contest of 1932 approached, the stage was set for the most dramatic electoral realignment in American political history.

The chief catalyst in the realignment was, of course, Franklin Delano Roosevelt, who, in his efforts to capture the Democratic nomination and the 1932 election, forged the rhetoric of the New Deal and the coalition to back it. Moving from a base as Governor of New York, Roosevelt began to cultivate national political support in 1931. Over the next year, he developed the popular themes, if not yet the programs, with which he would successfully appeal first to the party and then to the country: the nation faced a grave emergency that called for bold public programs, on behalf not of the rich but of the poor, programs that would "build from the bottom up and not from the top down, that put their faith once more in the forgotten man at the bottom of the economic pyramid." [55]

Roosevelt won the Democratic nomination on the fourth ballot, having been opposed by most of the older party leaders, from Al Smith of the urban East to William Gibbs McAdoo of the rural West. James Reed, one of his opponents, rose to speak after Roosevelt's nomination: "It is the highest duty of the Democratic Party," he said, "to get back the old principles and old methods. There has been no improvement on the . . . economic philosophy of John Stuart Mill, and there never will be an improvement." [56] Roosevelt took up the challenge: he began his

---

[55] Roosevelt, Vol. I, 159–206, 625.
[56] Schlesinger, 1957, 311.

acceptance speech by asserting that the breaking of traditions had already begun, and proclaimed that as President he would reduce agricultural production to raise prices, expose the crookedness of men in places of high finance, put men to work on reforestation projects, and assume greater responsibility for unemployment relief.

These differences within the Democratic Party regarding the proper role of the federal government pervaded and confused the campaign itself. Even Roosevelt's running mate, John N. Garner, announced, "Had it not been for the steady encroachment of the federal government on the rights and duties for [sic] the states, we perhaps would not have the present spectacle of the people rushing to Washington to set right whatever goes wrong." Other Democratic leaders sounded similar themes: Governor Albert C. Ritchie of Maryland assured the country "that the Democratic Party could be relied on to stop federal encroachment on states' rights," and John W. Davis denounced Hoover for "following the road to socialism." [57]

But Roosevelt stuck to his own very different themes. His campaign speeches called for regularization of production, for federal public works and unemployment insurance. And he promised that the federal government would assume responsibility for relief where local aid programs broke down.

Roosevelt won with a plurality of almost 7 million votes. The Democrats carried all but a few Eastern states which were still held by well-organized Republican machines, winning the largest electoral majority since 1864. Three million more people turned out to vote in the election of 1932 than in 1928. Economic catastrophe had resulted in a mass rejection of the party in power: the lower-middle classes joined the foreign-born and the industrial workers of the urban East,[58] the farmers of the West

---

[57] *Ibid.*, 416–417.

[58] Gosnell, in his study of Chicago machine politics, points out that the greatest shifts were noticeable in outlying lower-middle class neighbor-

joined the agrarian South, and all swung into the Democratic camp. Shortly after the election, a major new federal program was launched—a program that, for a brief time, would overturn the traditional principles of American relief-giving.

In the interval between the election and Roosevelt's inauguration, economic conditions worsened. The index of production sank to its lowest point ever; more hunger marches were staged in Washington; farmers formed mobs to resist mortgage foreclosures. By the day the new administration took office in March 1933, every bank in America had closed its doors, signifying to a stunned public and Congress the totality of the collapse. Proclaiming in his inaugural address that "the money-changers have fled from their high seats in the temple of our civilization," Roosevelt moved quickly, in the dead stillness of public panic. On March 9, he signed the Emergency Banking Act, which had been pushed through an acquiescent Congress by unanimous vote in a single day; on March 20, he signed the Economy Act; on March 31, the Civilian Conservation Corps was established; on April 19, the gold standard was abandoned; on May 12, the President signed the Agriculture Adjustment Act and the Federal Emergency Relief Act; on May 18, the Tennessee Valley Authority Act; on May 27, the Truth-in-Securities Act; on June 13, the Home Owners Loan Act; and on June 16, the National Industrial Recovery Act, the Glass-Steagall Banking Act, the Farm Credit Act, and the Railroad Coordination Act.

There was little congressional resistance. For a brief period, the legislative process was becalmed, the actors disoriented by the breakdown of the economy and the political turnabout of 1932. The new administration could

---

hoods. The foreign-born and working classes had gravitated to the Democratic Party long before (1937, 125).

take the initiative. Clearly the election was a mandate to attempt economic relief and recovery, but in doing so Roosevelt could virtually fashion his own political environment.[59] Unencumbered by established ties to constituent interests, Roosevelt launched a variety of measures, each to deal with a different facet of economic breakdown, and each to cultivate and solidify the allegiance of a different constituency: farmers and workers, bankers and businessmen, and the unemployed. Farmers got the Agricultural Adjustment Act, capping their half century of struggle for price supports, cheap credit, and inflated currency.[60] Business and organized labor got the National Industrial Recovery Act, allowing business to limit production and fix prices, and conceding to labor codes governing wages and hours, as well as the right of collective bargaining.[61]

The Expansion of Direct Relief

The destitute and unemployed got relief. In a message to Congress on March 21, three weeks after he had assumed office, the President called for a Civilian Con-

---

[59] "During the whole '33 one-hundred days, Congress, people didn't know what was going on, the public couldn't understand these things that were being passed so fast. They knew something was happening, something good for them" (Raymond Moley, as quoted in Terkel, 250).

[60] The provisions of the Agricultural Adjustment bill which provided for an inflated currency were, uniquely among these early measures, passed over the Administration's resistance. Roosevelt was no radical on fiscal policy. But what added urgency to the arguments of the farm bloc in Congress was the rising wave of disorder in the farm belt. In the winter of 1932-1933, while the bill was being debated, unrest in the corn belt reached a new peak. The Farm Holiday Association led new strikes by farmers who refused to sell their produce, and prevented others from selling; and mobs of farmers forced sheriffs to accept one dollar bills at foreclosure auctions (Rauch, 70-71).

[61] The Administration invited both labor and business to help in the formulation of the bill. When an early version of the act was opposed by business leaders, the Administration simply withdrew its support, substituting a business plan which had been officially adopted by the U.S. Chamber of Commerce two years earlier (ibid., 76).

servation Corps, a public works program, and federal emergency relief. The first two of these programs did little to cope with the suffering in the nation. The Civilian Conservation Corps, established in late March, provided jobs in the national forests at subsistence wages for 250,000 men—out of the 15 million unemployed.[62] The Public Works Administration, established in June under the National Recovery Act, had somewhat greater impact, for it eventually spent very large sums (6 billion dollars by 1939), but it was slow in getting under way and in any case was not designed so much to provide jobs for the unemployed as to fuel the economy. There was no requirement, for example, that only the jobless could be hired on the projects.[63] Meanwhile, Senators Edward P. Costigan, Robert F. Wagner, and Robert N. La Follette, Jr., drew up what was to become the Federal Emergency Relief Act, allocating 500 million dollars at the outset for grants-in-aid to the states for relief of the unemployed, half of which was to be spent on a matching basis (one federal dollar for three state dollars).

It was this measure that reached many of the jobless, and quickly. The Emergency Relief Act was signed on May 12, and Harry Hopkins, a social worker who had ad-

---

[62] In 1933, another Bonus Expeditionary Force descended on Washington. Where Hoover had routed them with cavalry, Roosevelt fed them, had the Navy Band play for them, sent his wife to visit and lead them in song, and then gave them jobs in the Civilian Conservation Corps. Elizabeth Wickenden, who represented the Administration at negotiations with the leaders of the Expeditionary Force, told us that her instructions from the President were simply to "give them anything they want" (except the bonus, of course).

[63] The reader should beware of the profusion of similar-sounding New Deal agencies. The Public Works Administration (PWA) was quite different from the Civil Works Administration (CWA) and the Works Progress Administration (WPA), which will be discussed in the next chapter. These latter agencies were essentially relief-giving instruments. By contrast, under Harold Ickes' vigorous and stubborn direction, PWA projects were chiefly designed and administered to improve and beautify the public domain, and this without a whiff of corruption. Consequently, the projects were slowly and cautiously initiated, and drew heavily on skilled workers who were not unemployed.

ministered the New York State relief program during Roosevelt's governorship, was appointed to head the program. On May 23 the first grants were made to the states; by the beginning of June, forty-five states had received federal grants for relief. When the program was terminated in June 1936, an unprecedented 3 billion dollars of federal money had been allocated for direct relief.[64]

The Federal Emergency Relief Administration (FERA) broke all precedents in American relief-giving. For the first time, the federal government assumed responsibility for relief and appropriated substantial funds to carry out that responsibility. While half of these monies were to be spent through matching state grants, the federal administrator was authorized by Congress to use the remainder for unencumbered grants to states where the need was great and financial resources depleted. Moreover, relief grants were not directed to traditional categories of unemployables—such as widows and orphans—but "to all needy unemployed persons and/or their dependents. Those whose employment or available resources are inadequate to provide the necessities of life for themselves and/or their dependents are included." [65] And while the act stated that the federal administrator should cooperate with state and local agencies, it also allowed for the federalization of state programs that failed to conform with federal standards.

With substantial funds and a relatively free hand in distributing them, FERA pressured the states to increase relief appropriations, although success varied from place to place. Some states continued to spend nothing; others paid as much as 50 per cent of the relief bill. Over-all, the federal government paid for 70 per cent of relief appropriations during the life of FERA.

---

[64] In other words, the federal expenditure averaged about 1 billion dollars a year, at a time when the total national income was only 48 billion dollars. By comparison, although federal welfare expenditures today are about six times as high, the national income has increased twenty-fold.

[65] Quoted in Brown, 231.

TABLE II

Obligations Incurred for Emergency Relief Annually
by Sources of Funds—January 1933 through December 1935
(in thousands) [66]

Calendar Year		Federal		State		Local	
	TOTAL	AMOUNT	PER CENT	AMOUNT	PER CENT	AMOUNT	PER CENT
Total	$4,119	$2,918	70.9	$519	12.6	$681	16.5
1933	794	494	62.2	104	13.0	197	24.8
1934	1,489	1,066	71.6	189	12.7	234	15.7
1935	1,834	1,358	74.0	226	12.3	250	13.7

Note: Includes relief extended to cases under the general relief program, cost of administration, and special programs; beginning in April 1934, these figures also include purchases of materials, supplies and equipment, rentals of equipment, earnings of non-relief persons, and other costs of the Emergency Work Relief Program.

The spirit that animated FERA was recalled by Elizabeth Wickenden (who worked for Harry Hopkins) in these words: "There was one concern—to distribute as much money as possible, as fast as possible. to as many as possible." [67] By the winter of 1934, 20 million people (approximately one sixth of the population) were on the dole, and monthly grant levels had risen from an average of $15.15 per family in May 1933 to an average of $24.53 in May 1934, and to $29.33 in May 1935.[68] Underscoring the change in federal posture, Roosevelt told the Congress on

---

[66] U.S. Federal Works Agency (as reproduced in Brown, 204).

[67] Personal communication.

[68] Consistent with the American relief tradition, however, there were wide variations from state to state. In Kentucky, for example, a family received only $6.78 per month in May of 1934, while a family in New York State received $45.12 (Brown, 249).

June 8, 1934, that "if, as our Constitution tells us, our federal government was established, among other things, 'to promote the general welfare,' it is our plain duty to provide for that security upon which welfare depends."

Of all the new programs, it was FERA that reached those who were most in need. As a matter of fact, in the course of pursuing economic recovery while seeking to conciliate more articulate and better organized interests, many New Deal programs rode roughshod over the most destitute. Federal agricultural policy, for example, was designed to raise farm prices by taking land out of cultivation, an action that also took many tenant farmers and sharecroppers out of the economy. The National Recovery Administration, seeking to placate organized employers and organized labor, permitted racial differentials in wages to be maintained. The Tennessee Valley Authority deferred to local prejudice by not hiring blacks. All this was done not unknowingly, but rather out of a concern for building a broad base of political support for the new programs. It was left to FERA to succor the casualties of the New Deal's pragmatic politics. Since blacks got little from (or were actually harmed by) most programs, 30 per cent of the black population ended up on the direct relief rolls by January 1935.[69]

Still, many of the poor had at least gotten relief. What needs to be understood, however, is that relief was not readily conceded to them. The spread of destitution itself was no great force; for a considerable period of time elites remained aloof from the suffering in their midst. But then the destitute became volatile, and unrest spread throughout the country.[70] It was only when these condi-

---

[69] See Schlesinger, 1960, 433. Because blacks got some relief, FERA aroused fierce resentment in the South. A FERA observer reported from Georgia early in 1934 that for Negroes "to be getting $12 a week—at least twice as much as common labor has ever been paid down there before—is an awfully bitter pill for Savannah people to swallow."

[70] In the same vein, many accounts of Ireland's "Great Potato Famine" in the 1840's attribute the large-scale relief effort undertaken by the British

tions, in turn, produced a massive electoral convulsion that government responded.

REFERENCES

Abbott, Edith, *The Tenements of Chicago, 1908–1935.* Chicago, University of Chicago Press, 1936.

Breckinridge, Sophonisba P., ed., *Public Welfare Administration in the United States: Select Documents.* Chicago, University of Chicago Press, 1927.

Bremner, Robert H., *From the Depths: The Discovery of Poverty in the United States.* New York, New York University Press, 1956.

Brophy, Alice, and Hallowitz, George, "Pressure Groups and the Relief Administration in New York City." Unpublished professional project, New York School of Social Work, 1937. (No. 415-2.)

Brown, Josephine Chapin, *Public Relief 1929–1939.* New York, Henry Holt & Company, 1940.

Colcord, Joanna C., *et al.*, *Emergency Work Relief as Carried Out in Twenty-six American Communities, 1930–1931, with Suggestions for Setting Up a Program.* New York, Russell Sage Foundation, 1932.

Congressional Record, 1932, 75, 3067–3260.

Douglas, Paul H., *Social Security in the United States: An Analysis and Appraisal of the Federal Social Security Act.* New York, McGraw-Hill Book Company, 1936.

Gifford, Walter S., "Cities, Counties, States Can Handle the Situation," *Survey*, February 1, 1932, 67, 466.

Gosnell, Harold F., *Machine Politics: Chicago Model.* Chicago, University of Chicago Press, 1937.

Gosnell, Harold F., *Negro Politicians: The Rise of Negro Politics in Chicago.* Chicago, University of Chicago Press, 1935.

Greenstein, Harry, "The Maryland Emergency Relief Program

---

government to the fear that mounting disorder among the starving peasants might lead to revolution; worse yet, there was the fear that revolt among the Irish might stimulate revolt among the English working classes who, at that time, were none too docile.

—Past and Future." Address delivered before the Maryland Conference of Social Work, February 25, 1935.

Hopkins, Harry L., *Spending to Save: The Complete Story of Relief*. New York, W. W. Norton & Company, 1936.

Lynd, Robert S., and Helen Merrell, *Middletown in Transition: A Study in Cultural Conflicts*. New York, Harcourt, Brace & Company, 1937.

Maxwell, James A., *Financing State and Local Governments*, rev. ed. Washington, Brookings Institution, 1969. (Studies of Government Finance.)

McCaffrey, Lawrence J., *The Irish Question, 1890–1922*. Lexington, University of Kentucky Press, 1968.

Nathan, Robert R., *Estimates of Unemployment in the United States, 1929–35*. Geneva, International Labour Office, 1936.

Pinchot, Gifford, "The Case for Federal Relief," *Survey*, January 1, 1932, 67, 348–349.

Rauch, Basil, *The History of the New Deal 1933–1938*. New York, Creative Age Press, 1944.

Roosevelt, Franklin D., *The Public Papers and Addresses of Franklin D. Roosevelt*, comp. Samuel I. Roseman, Vol. I. New York, Random House, 1938.

Schlesinger, Arthur M., Jr., *The Age of Roosevelt*, Vol. I, *The Crisis of the Old Order, 1919–1933*. Boston, Houghton Mifflin Company, 1957.

Schlesinger, Arthur M., Jr., *The Age of Roosevelt*, Vol. III, *The Politics of Upheaval*. Boston, Houghton Mifflin Company, 1960.

Seymour, Helen. Unpublished report of December 1, 1937 to the Committee on Social Security of the Social Science Research Council.

Seymour, Helen "The Organized Unemployed." Unpublished dissertation submitted to the Division of the Social Sciences, University of Chicago, August 1937.

Social Work Today, August 1934, 19.

Terkel, Studs, *Hard Times: An Oral History of the Great Depression*. New York, Pantheon Books, 1970.

Unemployed Council and Affiliated Action Committee, Port Angeles, Washington, *Call to Action*, July 20, 1933.

U.S. Bureau of the Census, *Relief Expenditures by Governmental and Private Organizations, 1929 and 1931: A Special Report*. Washington, U.S. Government Printing Office, 1931.

U.S. Bureau of the Census, *Statistical Abstract of the United States: 1940*. Washington, U.S. Government Printing Office, 1941.

U.S. Conference of Mayors, *Annual Proceedings, 1933*. Chicago, 1933.

U.S. Senate, *Relief Legislation, 1803–1931*. Statement in hearings before a subcommittee of the Committee on Manufactures on S. 5125, *To Provide Federal Aid for Unemployment Relief*, 73rd Congress, 1st Session, February 3, 1933, Part 2. Washington, U.S. Government Printing Office, 1933.

U.S. Senate, *Unemployment Relief*, Hearings before a subcommittee of the Committee on Manufactures on S. 174 and S. 262, 72nd Congress, 1st Session, December 28–30, 1931, and January 4–9, 1932. Washington, U.S. Government Printing Office, 1932.

Winslow, Emma A., *Trends in Different Types of Public and Private Relief in Urban Areas, 1929–35*. Washington, U.S. Government Printing Office, 1937. (Children's Bureau Pub. No. 237.)

CHAPTER THREE

The New Deal
and Relief

No one liked direct relief—not the President who called for it, the Congress that legislated it, the administrators who operated it, the people who received it. Direct relief was viewed as a temporary expedient, a way of maintaining a person's body, but not his dignity; a way of keeping the populace from shattering in despair, discontent, and disorder, at least for a while, but not of renewing their pride, of bringing back a way of life. For their way of life had been anchored in the discipline of work, and so that discipline had to be restored. The remedy was plain to see: abolish direct relief and put the unemployed to work on subsidized projects. These reforms were soon instituted —and with dramatic results. For a brief time, the federal government became the employer of millions of people (although millions of others remained unemployed).

Partly as a result of massive work relief, the disorder, disarray, and panic that gripped the nation subsided; the New Deal seemed securely at the helm. Then, very rapidly, the work-relief program was cut back. Millions who were unable to find work, together with millions who could not work, were left to get what relief they could from state, local, and private agencies.

From Direct Relief to Work Relief

From the very start of federal relief, there had been efforts to shift from direct relief to work relief. As the months passed, the need seemed even more urgent. In 1933, FERA's field staff reported evidence of Communist activities in such unlikely places as Aberdeen, South Dakota; by 1934, however, when many people were getting direct relief, the staff decided that the more ominous danger was "not one of fighting off a 'red menace' . . . but of fighting off hopelessness; despair; a dangerous feeling of helplessness and dependence." [1] According to a FERA survey, the average unemployed city worker on relief had been out of work for more than two years,[2] and there was evidence, the FERA staff said, that a "gimme" syndrome was spreading. People were beginning to feel "that the government actually owes [relief] to them. And they want more." [3] Many civic leaders expressed concern that relief payments alone did not prevent men, families, and communities from deteriorating; after a time on the dole, they said, family relations eroded and men no longer wanted or expected to work.[4]

EARLY ATTEMPTS

The first move toward work relief was made only a few months after FERA was inaugurated. In November 1933, the President announced the establishment of the Civil

---

[1] Schlesinger, 1958, 272.

[2] In the spring of 1934 FERA conducted a study of workers on the relief rolls in 79 cities (Hopkins, 160–161).

[3] Schlesinger, 1958, 275.

[4] The effects of direct relief were later (1940) described by E. Wight Bakke in what has become a classic study.

Works Administration (CWA), which was to draw on FERA and PWA funds to employ people on "made-work" projects.[5] Harry Hopkins zestfully promised to create four million jobs by mid-December. He missed that target date by only a month; by mid-January well over four million men were at work building roads and schools in cities and towns across the country.

But if direct relief left the mass of Americans and their political leaders dissatisfied because it ran against the grain of American ideology, work relief appeared to threaten the private enterprise system itself. For one thing, it was far more expensive than direct relief: the wages paid exceeded the levels of direct relief grants, and substantial expenditures for administration and materials were required to put people to work. Moreover, work relief raised the specter of government activity in areas hitherto reserved for private enterprise,[6] and CWA minimum-wage scales raised the specter of government interference in the conduct of private enterprise.[7]

---

[5] The President's Executive Order of November 9 allocated 400 million dollars to CWA from the Public Works Administration, as well as an additional 89 million dollars from FERA. "For most practical purposes," Harry Hopkins wrote, "the FERA was temporarily converted into the CWA" (118). In February 1934 Congress allocated an additional 345 million dollars to CWA.

[6] A report to Hopkins in 1934 on the views of businessmen concluded that they opposed work relief because of its cost, and because any project, even ditchdigging, was defined as a government intrusion into competitive business (Schlesinger, 1958, 274).

[7] To reflect market wages, CWA wage scales were varied by region and occupation. But minimum rates were established, and in some places this was unsettling, especially in the South, where the CWA minimum for unskilled labor was substantially more than private employers were accustomed to paying (Hopkins, 118). Governor Talmadge of Georgia in 1934 forwarded an indignant letter from a local farmer to the President: "I wouldn't plow nobody's mule from sunrise to sunset for 50 cents per day when I could get $1.30 [per day] for pretending to work on a DITCH." Roosevelt replied (but over Harry Hopkins' signature) that he took it the Governor approved of paying farm labor 40 to 50 cents a day (Schlesinger, 1958, 274). A Du Pont vice-president echoed the Georgia farmer's complaints in a letter to John J. Raskob: "Five Negroes on my place in South Carolina refused work this spring, after I had taken care of them and given them house rent free and work for three years during bad times,

Goaded by the work relief program, businessmen soon began to oppose federal relief ventures of any kind, despite the fact that, in the period of acute economic paralysis and panic just before the election of 1932, prominent business leaders had themselves finally called for emergency federal relief measures.[8] The revival of business opposition was no doubt also influenced by some signs of economic recovery in 1933 and early 1934. Quick to protest, business leaders raised a familiar banner: relief, they said, should be a local responsibility. That little relief would result in such circumstances was probably not lost upon them either. Asked about the homeless boys riding the rails, Henry Ford replied, "Why it's the best education in the world for those boys, that traveling around." [9] For the moment, the critics had their way, for Roosevelt was eager to conciliate the business community. In the spring of 1934, CWA was closed down (although some work relief projects continued under a program financed by FERA and administered by the states).[10] Nor would the massive work relief program the Administration considered essential become possible until the business community, antagonized by Roosevelt's identification with an increasingly militant

---

saying they had easy jobs with the Government. . . . A cook on my houseboat at Fort Myer quit because the Government was paying him a dollar an hour as a painter" (*ibid.*, 485).

[8] In June 1932, the leading citizens of Chicago sent a wire to Senator Otis F. Glenn of Illinois urging federal relief aid to avert what they described as a catastrophe. The telegram was signed by such notables as Lester Armour, Sewell L. Avery, Colonel Frank Knox, and Silas H. Strawn (President of the U.S. Chamber of Commerce), as well as other executives of the largest Midwestern industries, such as the Pullman Company, the Colgate-Palmolive-Peet Company, Swift and Company, Armour and Company, Carson Pirie Scott, and the Illinois Bell Telephone Company. Most of these men had previously been staunch opponents of federal relief (*ibid.*, 76–77).

[9] *Ibid.*, 274.

[10] Other relief programs designed to provide work also aroused business opposition and were stymied because they appeared to threaten the operations of the private market. Thus, when FERA established the Federal Surplus Relief Corporation enterprises, which were to bring together surplus commodities, idle labor, and idle factories, business reacted angrily, and the program neither expanded nor survived for long (*ibid.*, 278).

labor movement and with other insurgent groups, broke with the President, making his continued efforts at conciliation futile.

THE BREAK WITH BUSINESS

Roosevelt's victory in 1932 did not mean that political stability had been restored in the nation. If anything, massive voting shifts signaled an extraordinary instability, a widespread, spastic rejection of the party in power. Just which groups were included in the Democratic constituency and which were excluded was not yet clear; in any case, allegiances had to be firmed up and a political organization created to hold voting blocs in place.

Roosevelt's early measures were designed to achieve these objectives. Eager to build up political support in all sectors, and especially eager to restore the confidence of the economic sector, Roosevelt tried to placate businessmen in designing his legislative proposals, and at first, shaken by the signs of impending disaster, they were acquiescent or even supportive. Not only had prominent businessmen come out in support of emergency relief measures, for example, but the U.S. Chamber of Commerce endorsed "the philosophy of a planned economy," and in 1933 its delegates gave Roosevelt a standing ovation.[11] As late as October 1934, Roosevelt appealed to the American Bankers Association for "an alliance of all forces intent upon the business of recovery . . . in business and banking, agriculture and industry, and labor and capital. What an all-America team that would be!"[12] When the rupture came, Roosevelt was outraged, for he saw himself and his

---

[11] While most businessmen probably had supported Hoover in 1932, some prominent spokesmen endorsed Roosevelt; others quickly joined them when Roosevelt reopened the banks, cut government spending, and legalized beer within a month of taking office.

[12] Schlesinger, 1958, 499–500.

administration as the saviors of capitalism and the business classes—despite themselves.[13]

The most important measure to conciliate business was
the National Industrial Recovery Act of 1933, which permitted the fixing of prices and production to halt defla-
tionary trends. The President himself remarked in 1934
that "the representatives of trade and industry were permitted to write their ideas into the codes." [14] Businessmen
apparently appreciated these arrangements; when the National Recovery Administration held a series of price hearings in January 1935, two thousand businessmen attended,
almost all of whom (according to *Time*) clamored for price
protection.

But the Administration also tried to cultivate other
groups—farmers, workers, homeowners. Although most of
the measures designed to aid these groups were a matter
of relative indifference to business, some were not. None
generated greater concern than Section 7a of the National
Industrial Recovery Act, which granted organized labor
the right to bargain collectively. In the summer and fall
of 1933, industries across the country tried to disarm Section 7a by establishing company unions. But labor was
restive; stimulated by the promise of 7a, a rash of strikes
spread across the country in 1933 and 1934 focused on the

---

[13] In December 1935, *Fortune* magazine agreed, declaring it "fairly evident to most disinterested critics" that the New Deal "has had the preservation of capitalism at all times in view." Some businessmen also still
agreed, such as W. Averell Harriman and Joseph P. Kennedy, but they
were a small minority in the business community.

[14] Schlesinger, 1958, 162. Gardiner C. Means commented in retrospect,
"The NRA was one of the most successful things the New Deal did . . .
when it was created American business was completely demoralized. Violent price cutting and wage cutting . . . nobody could make any plans for
tomorrow. Everybody was going around in circles. The NRA changed the
attitudes of business and the public. It revived belief that something could
be done. . . . In the two years of the NRA, the index of industrial production went up remarkably. . . . You see, there was little Governmental regulation of the NRA. The Government handed industry over to industry to
run, and offered some minor protection to others in the form of Labor
and Consumer Advisory Boards" (Terkel, 249).

right to organize. Strikers shut down entire cities—Minneapolis, San Francisco, and Toledo—and engaged in pitched battles with police and National Guard, leaving many dead or wounded. A virtual civil war had broken out between business and labor, triggered in part by Section 7a. Nor, having intruded itself into the labor-management arena, could the Administration readily disengage. The war between business and labor, in which federal mediators were repeatedly called upon to arbitrate, had a great deal to do with the rise of business opposition to the New Deal.[15]

While industry struggled with a restive labor movement, Wall Street came under attack from a wider front—American public opinion. Throughout 1933, the sharp practices of the nation's financial titans made daily headlines as a result of investigations by the Senate Banking and Currency Committee, and in February 1934 the President called for stock-exchange regulation, arousing fury among financial leaders. When legislation establishing the Securities Exchange Commission was enacted by an overwhelming congressional vote in the spring of 1934, Wall Street virtually took up arms.

Wall Street's anger was no doubt stimulated by signs of modest economic recovery, especially the recovery of business profits (thanks in part to the protection of prices afforded by NRA controls). By the spring of 1934, the precipitous decline appeared to have halted. The index of production picked up slightly (from 71 in November 1933 to 86 in May 1934); industrial and farm prices were also steadying. National income rose by 9 billion dollars during 1933, reaching 48.6 billion dollars; employment jumped by 2.5 million and unemployment fell by 2 million. Farm

---

[15] After conducting a study of business conditions in fourteen large cities, Edward A. Filene, the Boston department-store owner, reported in March 1934 that the "severest" criticism he encountered among businessmen pertained to government labor policy (Schlesinger, 1958, 471).

income was also up (although one quarter of that increase came from government payments). Moreover, when production, employment, and payrolls again fell in mid-1934, industrial prices nevertheless continued to rise.[16] Feeling its strength returning, business girded itself to fight the twin threats of unionization and regulation.

Just prior to the congressional elections of 1934, prominent industrial leaders—including Alfred P. Sloan and William S. Knudsen of General Motors, Edward F. Hutton and Colby M. Chester of General Foods, J. Howard Pew of Sun Oil, Sewell L. Avery of Montgomery Ward, the Du Ponts, and others—joined with several conservative Democrats who had been dethroned by the New Deal— such as Alfred Smith, John J. Raskob, Jouett Shouse, and John W. Davis [17]—to form the American Liberty League, an organization dedicated to fighting "radicalism" and protecting property rights. The mid-term election would show how little public support they could muster.

Of 35 senatorial seats being contested, the Democrats won 25. In the House, Democratic seats rose from 312 to 322. Of the state capitols, 39 fell into Democratic hands. These gains, in a mid-term contest led Arthur Krock of *The New York Times* to say that the New Deal had won "the most overwhelming victory in the history of American politics." The modest if temporary economic improvement, the easing of distress by direct relief, and the hopeful rhetoric of the New Deal had consolidated large segments of the public behind the new President. The Democrats made gains not only in traditionally Republican areas in the urban North, but in the agricultural states as well. Of course, the South remained steadfast: 24 of the 69 Democratic senators and 108 of the 322 representatives

---

[16] The index of production fell from 86 to 71 between May and November of 1934. Meanwhile, wholesale prices rose from 73.7 to 77.6 (Statistical Abstract of the United States, 1936, 766, 298, 323).

[17] Schlesinger, 1958, 486.

were Southern. The New Deal coalition was taking shape
—labor and ethnic groups in the Northern cities, farmers,
and the South.

COPING WITH INSURGENCY

If the election showed that major class and sectional interests had lined up behind the New Deal, and that business
had lined up against it, subsequent actions by the Roosevelt Administration made the new alignments clearer and
the divisions deeper. Freed from the constraining influence of business, Roosevelt moved boldly after 1934 to
cement his constituency. In so doing he promoted legislation that undercut the various insurgent leaders thrust up
by the unrest of the Depression years. By 1934, these
leaders commanded large followings within different sectors of the emerging New Deal coalition—the militants in
organized labor, the followers of Huey Long, the organizations of the unemployed, the Townsendites, the Cough-
linites. For discontent had not evaporated with the
elections of 1932; rather, it was stilled for a moment by the
promise of a new regime, the confidence a new leader in-
spired. However, as the Depression wore on, with conditions showing little improvement, unrest resurfaced. By
1934, various dissident leaders were drawing upon this
unrest, giving it organizational form and coherence, aspir-
ing to build political movements that would change the
face of America.

Of themselves, these movements were not so formidable;
what gave them leverage was the climate of uncertainty and
the realities of economic instability. The voting returns
were reassuring, but other signs, perhaps more telling for
the future, were not. In the spring of 1934, when the business community was taking courage from the recovery of
production and prices, national income was still only half
what it had been in 1929, and one fourth of the labor force

was still out of work (although many were now at least obtaining direct relief). In the fall of 1934, another economic downturn wiped out the gains made since 1933, surely giving the insurgents added force. For, after five years of hardship and confusion, anything seemed possible, and saints and opportunists, reformers and revolutionists, right wing and left—all thought to grasp the moment to shape the future of America.

To contain these dissident movements and to consolidate them behind the New Deal, Roosevelt promulgated a series of reforms which, though they hardly met the demands of insurgent leaders, were nevertheless sufficient to steal their thunder and capture their followers.[18] Far more important, he moved to deal more decisively with the underlying causes of disorder and insurgency: the breakdown of the economy and the consequent weakening of family, community, and a way of life. To restore stability, it was necessary to restore the occupational role: the long-run solution was economic recovery; the interim solution was work relief.

The Presidential Message to Congress on January 4, 1935, emphasized themes calculated to assuage the discontent spawned by economic catastrophe. The nation still suffered from old inequalities: the overprivileged had not been weeded out or the underprivileged effectively lifted up. Unemployment would not be solved simply by stimulating private enterprise, as the National Recovery Administration had attempted to do; instead, government needed to expand purchasing power among the least privileged groups. In the same vein, Roosevelt called for the enactment of measures championed by the insurgents themselves: protective labor legislation, tax reform, the regula-

---

[18] "I am fighting Communism, Huey Longism, Coughlinism, Townsendism," Roosevelt told an emissary of William Randolph Hearst in May 1935. "I want to save our system, the capitalistic system; to save it is to give some heed to world thought of today. I want to equalize the distribution of wealth" (Schlesinger, 1960, 325).

tion of utilities, programs of social insurance, and a massive system of work relief.[19]

Organized labor's struggle to implement the right to bargain collectively, presumably guaranteed under Section 7a, had generally been a losing one during the first two years of the New Deal. Efforts by Senator Robert F. Wagner in 1934 to secure legislation which would strengthen Section 7a by prohibiting company unions were fiercely opposed by business groups and, under pressure from the President, Senator Wagner backed off. But by 1935, when the Wagner-Connery Labor Relations Bill was introduced, the Administration's attitude toward business had hardened. And while Roosevelt stood aside from the fierce debate between advocates of organized labor and advocates of business,[20] he signed the National Labor Relations Act, going on in 1936 to advocate a strong wages-and-hours bill.[21]

The President had also spoken of tax reform in January 1935. Several months later he sent Congress a special measure on taxation, which some called the "soak-the-rich" scheme. The purpose of the reform, the President said, was to redistribute the tax burden according to the ability to pay. He called for higher taxes on inheritances and gifts, higher individual income taxes, graduated corporate taxes to replace the existing uniform rates, and an intercorporate dividend tax to break up holding companies.

The uproar was deafening. William Randolph Hearst

---

[19] Business, of course, opposed all these measures. The U.S. Chamber of Commerce, for example, declared against social security, the regulation of public utilities, banking legislation, and especially against legislation designed to strengthen the bargaining position of labor (ibid., 272–280).

[20] Judging from the outcry, business virtually panicked. "Industry," said Alfred P. Sloan of General Motors, "if it has any appreciation of its obligations to future generations, will fight this proposal to the very last." "It would out-Stalin Stalin," according to the Associated Industries of Oklahoma. And a group of industry representatives who claimed to employ over half the manufacturing force of the nation denounced the bill as inviting use of "the most dangerous weapons of social coercion" (Schlesinger, 1958, 404–405).

[21] Ultimately passed in 1938 as the Fair Labor Standards Act.

told his editors that the "President's program is essentially communism" and said of Roosevelt that he was "a composite personality which might be labelled Stalin Delano Roosevelt." Businessmen, already angry, now accused Roosevelt of a personal vendetta. Even so good a friend of the New Deal as Governor Herbert H. Lehman of New York questioned the revenue proposals. On the other hand, tax reform was the principal demand of Huey Long's "Share Our Wealth" movement, one of the most formidable of the insurgent groups threatening Roosevelt's emerging political hegemony. Raymond Moley, a prominent member of Roosevelt's "brain trust," commented on Long's role in the struggle for tax reform:

> Huey was a good friend of mine. He was threatening to run for President in 1936. The poll showed that Huey would take ten percent of the vote. I'm sure Farley could confirm this. He would have cut into the Democratic vote all over the country. Roosevelt, in order to counteract that, moved toward the Long program. His tax program . . . was pure Huey: soak the rich. Roosevelt was using the same demagogic tactics. It's possible Huey Long—if he weren't killed—would have busted open the Democratic Party even then.[22]

The reform proposals did not fare well in the Congress; indeed, they were virtually gutted in the Senate.[23] How vigorously the Administration had fought for its reforms is unclear, but little matter. The rhetoric of reform had resounded throughout the land, and if the legislative result was mainly symbolic, the symbolism was not lost on the constituents of the "Share Our Wealth" movement.

The Democratic platform of 1932 had called for both un-

---

[22] Terkel, 253. James Farley, Roosevelt's political manager, had a secret poll made of Long's national support which indicated Long might be able to tip the 1936 election to the Republicans (Burns, 211).

[23] On this point we follow Schlesinger, who concludes that the measure was in the end rendered meaningless, capable of yielding only about 250 million dollars in new revenues annually (1960, 329–334). This conclusion differs sharply from that of Rauch (170–177).

employment and old-age insurance to be implemented "under state laws," and there were subsequent if fumbling moves to get such legislation through the Congress, all of which failed. However, the Message to Congress of January 4, 1935 signaled a new push for social security; indeed, the message flagged "security" as the central objective—surely a popular appeal to the millions who had suffered six years of hardship and fearsome uncertainty. On January 17, the Social Security Bill, which had been under study by a committee appointed by Roosevelt, was introduced with a special message from the President. The measure contained three main proposals. One was for unemployment insurance, to be financed by a federal payroll tax but planned and administered by the states, presumably in accordance with local needs. Another was a proposal for old-age insurance, to be financed by a tax on wages and payrolls that would provide $10 to $85 per month at age 65 to persons in covered employment, such payments to begin in 1942. Finally, the bill offered federal aid to the states if they chose to provide direct relief to various categories of unemployables—the old,[24] the blind, and the orphaned. As noted earlier, many of the states already had such "categorical assistance" programs on the books, and some had begun to fund them as the Depression worsened. In effect, the federal government now proposed to pay a share of costs. In the decades to come, this categorical-assistance program would turn out to be crucial to the security—or insecurity—of many Americans. At the time, however, it did not seem nearly so important as the provisions for insuring the employed against destitution in old age and against the hazards of temporary unemployment.[25]

---

[24] That is, to those who would not be eligible for the proposed old-age insurance program because they were already old, or because they would reach retirement age in an occupation not covered by the insurance scheme (e.g., domestic servants or farm laborers).

[25] Roosevelt said of the act when he signed it that it would give "some measure of protection" against economic peaks of inflation and deflation, lessening the force of possible future depressions (Rauch, 163). The Ad-

All told, the social security proposals were relatively modest considering the demands that many groups had been making: hundreds of thousands of old people, organized in the Townsend movement, wanted an immediate monthly pension of $200 for *every* person over sixty years of age; organized labor opposed financing unemployment insurance by any form of payroll tax. On the other hand, there was powerful opposition to the modest measures the Administration advocated. The National Association of Manufacturers simply did not think that industry should have to pay taxes for the social security of its employees, and Alfred P. Sloan announced that "industry has every reason to be alarmed at the social, economic and financial implications. . . . The dangers are manifest." [26] Nevertheless, the bill passed the House in April 1935 by a vote of 371 to 33 and the Senate several months later by a vote of 76 to 7. [27]

Some of these measures would turn out in the end to have little but symbolic meaning for the mass of Americans. Others would take time to implement, and longer still for their benefits to reach the intended groups. The

---

ministration was also beginning to have forebodings about the prospects of permanent unemployment, forebodings probably based partly on the fact that the numbers of unemployed were not diminishing in proportion to increases in employment: employment was up by 2.5 million in 1934, unemployment was down by only 2 million.

[26] Schlesinger, 1958, 301–315.

[27] Two other pieces of legislation exemplify Roosevelt's effort to conciliate the insurgents after the break with business. The Guffey coal bill, denounced by industry representatives as "the first step in the socialization of all industry," was drafted by the United Mine Workers and passed in August 1935 under pressure of a strike threat by John L. Lewis. It provided for codes governing prices, trade practices, wages and hours, and collective bargaining in the coal industry. The Public Utility Company Act called for the abolition within five years of holding companies that could not demonstrate their usefulness, a measure that evoked outraged opposition by utilities companies (one of which was discovered by a Senate investigating committee to have spent $700,000 mustering opposition to the bill). The Administration fought vigorously for the bill, and a compromise version which limited but did not prohibit holding companies was passed by the Congress and signed on August 28, 1935 (Schlesinger, 1960, 314–315).

aged covered by Social Security, for example, were not to begin receiving benefits until 1942. The measure that did reach many of the poor quickly and on an unprecedented scale was work relief.

THE WORKS PROGRESS ADMINISTRATION

By January 1935 political circumstances were propitious for the abolition of direct relief and the substitution of work relief. In October 1934 Roosevelt publicly declared for the first time that direct relief should be terminated. In a message to Congress on January 4, 1935, he echoed some of the widely held opinions about direct relief: "Continued dependence upon relief induces a spiritual and moral disintegration fundamentally destructive to the national fiber. . . . We must preserve not only the bodies of the unemployed from destitution but also their self-respect, their self-reliance and courage and determination." Accordingly, "The Federal Government must and shall quit this business of [direct] relief." [28] Instead, the aged, disabled, orphaned, and others who could not work—there being some 1.5 million such families or individuals then receiving federal emergency relief—were to be turned back to the states and localities for aid, just as before the New Deal.[29] There would be this difference, however: under the proposed provisions of the Social Security Act, local relief costs for unemployables would be shared by the federal government.

---

[28] *Ibid.*, 267–268.

[29] In fact, federal emergency relief had never been intended for the "unemployables" who were the traditional wards of local relief agencies. But FERA was fielded hastily and in a spirit of relative liberality, so that many unemployables did in fact get aid (nor did local officials object, for they were glad to have the federal government assume the larger part of the cost of relief to unemployables). However, when the emergency relief programs in six states were completely federalized in 1934, local officials were given strict instructions to identify the unemployables and consign them to state relief agencies (Brown, 165, 208–210; Rauch, 158; Schlesinger, 1960, 268).

Having suggested how the unemployables should be disposed of, the President then called for a public works program to provide a job for every able-bodied unemployed person. For this purpose, the annual Budget Message of January 3, 1935, requested 4 billion dollars, to be supplemented by 880 million dollars unspent under previous appropriations.[30] This meant that the government proposed to appropriate for work relief an amount equal to 10 per cent of the total national income of the year just ended.[31]

Although many aspects of the work relief program remained unspecified in the Emergency Relief Appropriation Act of 1935, the act reflected a clear intent to alleviate distress and disorder, but—whether businessmen recognized it or not—without interfering with the "natural" processes of the market. Three and a half million people who were receiving direct relief were to be put to work at a "security wage"—that is, a wage higher than relief payments but lower than prevailing wages—so as not to deter people from seeking private employment. (Accordingly, when the program was enacted, security wages varied as widely as market wages: during the first year, farm laborers hired on work projects in the South were paid $15 per month, while professionals on projects in New York City received $90 a month.)[32] Similarly, the work to be undertaken was to constitute a permanent contribution to the

---

[30] The program was to be financed by adding to the national debt, a method of funding that was itself a major departure from prevailing fiscal doctrine.

[31] Actual annual expenditures did not, however, claim so dramatic a share of national income. During 1936, the first and peak year, 2.2 billion dollars were spent. Except in 1938, a year of severe recession *and* an election, the amount subsequently declined year by year.

[32] Rauch, 164. When the liberal-labor bloc in the Congress pushed through an amendment requiring that WPA workers be paid at the prevailing wage, the President had the amendment killed (Burns, 221). Subsequently, protests by the American Federation of Labor that low security wages tended to depress prevailing wages were appeased by raising hourly security rates to the prevailing level, but reducing the number of hours worked each month so that total wages remained at the security level.

nation while not competing with private enterprise.[33] Aside from these legislative guidelines, implementation of the program was left to the discretion of the Administration, and after considerable debate in the Senate, during which conservatives prophesied the disintegration of the American form of government while progressives tried to double the appropriation, the measure passed and was signed by the President early in April.

Harry Hopkins was appointed Administrator of the new Works Progress Administration (WPA).[34] Since he was already head of FERA, he was to preside over the elimination of that agency by transferring millions of unemployed from the direct relief rolls to the new WPA projects,[35] while turning the "unemployables" over to local relief agencies. Meanwhile, works projects were set up, many of them at first organized by existing administrative agencies of the federal government in their particular fields of operation. New agencies were also created, such as the Agricultural Resettlement Administration,[36] the Rural Electrification Administration, and the National Youth

---

[33] Subsequently Congress wrote additional limitations into the legislation to protect private enterprise: in 1939 the use of WPA funds for construction of buildings costing more than 50,000 dollars was prohibited, and in 1941 the use of WPA funds for the purchase or establishment of any facilities to produce or handle articles in competition with existing industries was explicitly forbidden (Howard, 133).

[34] The agency was renamed The Work Projects Administration in July 1939.

[35] During the first year, over 90 per cent of WPA workers were taken from the relief rolls (Hopkins, 167).

[36] Despite the steady increase in farm income after 1932, the number of farm families on relief rose steadily. In many cases, their farms were already gone, so that they could not benefit from AAA price supports; in other cases, they were tenant farmers who found themselves evicted from their holdings when AAA acreage rental policies, which took land out of cultivation, were introduced. By February 1935, 733,000 farm families were on the rolls, a rise of 75 per cent in sixteen months (Hopkins, 140). In response, the Agricultural Resettlement Administration (ARA) was created to help destitute farm families. The design was admirable: the ARA bought farms and resold them to displaced farmers and farm tenants on easy terms, granted small emergency loans, helped farmers to purchase machinery on a competitive basis, undertook land rehabilitation projects,

Administration. Within five years, WPA's accomplishments included the construction or renovation of 110,000 public buildings, 600 airports, 600,000 miles of roads, and 116,000 bridges and viaducts. And although some of the best-known of these projects involved artists, actors, and teachers, most WPA workers were unskilled laborers.

Work relief is remembered mainly for these accomplishments—for the dams and roads and schools and hospitals and other public facilities built by so many men in so short a time. However, it ought to be remembered for quite another and greater reason. By once more enmeshing people in the work role, the cornerstone of social control in any society, it went far toward moderating civil disorder. Had there been no work relief to quiet the populace, it is difficult to say (even in retrospect) whether the consequent turmoil would not have imperiled the nation's economic and political institutions. But the people were amenable to work relief; indeed, they demanded it, for the "habit" of work, as Harry Hopkins observed, was what they "liked":

> Direct relief might do to tide over a few months or a year, or even longer. But millions had already been out of a job for several years. In addition to want, the unemployed were confronting a still further destructive force, that of worklessness. This feeling became articulate in many quarters, but most particularly among the unemployed themselves. Letters came, delegations arrived, protesting against the indignity of public charity. . . . They were accustomed to making a return for their livelihood. It was a habit [of work] they liked, and from which they chiefly drew their self-respect. The family of a man working on a Works Progress Administration project looks down its nose at neighbors who take their relief straight.[37]

---

and the like. Unfortunately, the program was never operated on a sufficiently large scale. After two years of operation, only 4,441 farm families had been resettled (Rauch, 166–168).

[37] Hopkins, 109. A poll taken by the American Institute of Public Opinion in 1938 showed that respondents favored work relief to the dole by a ratio of nine to one (Howard, 811).

Although work relief was unprecedented in its scale, it was by no means equal to the magnitude of distress. The President had promised 3.5 million jobs; WPA actually provided an average of about 2 million during its first five years of operation. Moreover, job quotas fluctuated wildly from month to month, in no apparent relation to unemployment, so that project workers never knew when they might be laid off. In any case, those who got on at all were lucky. At its peak, WPA accounted for only about one in four of the estimated unemployed.[38]

The remaining millions of unemployed, together with the millions of the destitute who were not employable, were shunted to state and local agencies. Their subsequent hardship elicited little response from the Administration, however, partly because work relief had substantially diminished their numbers. Meanwhile, and more important, many of the erstwhile discontented groups appeared to be mollified by work relief as well as by signs of substantial economic recovery. By 1936 national income had risen to 64.7 billion dollars, up from 39.6 billion dollars in 1933; some 6 million more people were employed; *The New York Times* index of business activity reached 100 in May of 1936 for the first time since 1930.[39] Taken together, these changes generated unprecedented support for the President.

The election of 1936 was, of course, a landslide such as had never before occurred in America. The Republicans acted beaten from the start and conducted a desultory campaign under their candidate, Alfred Landon. The Repub-

---

[38] Based on AF of L estimates of unemployment (see Howard, 854–857). A count made by the Bureau of the Census in 1937 showed that all federal emergency workers (those employed in the Civilian Conservation Corps and the National Youth Administration as well as WPA) accounted for only 18 per cent of the total number unemployed in that year (*ibid.*, 554).

[39] Corporate profits showed an especially remarkable recovery, from minus 2 billion dollars in 1933 to nearly 5 billion dollars in 1936. The Dow-Jones industrial average of stock prices was up 80 per cent over 1933 (Schlesinger, 1960, 571).

lican platform began with the words "America is in peril," but did not propose to repeal New Deal legislation. It even went so far as to pledge to "protect the rights of labor to organize and to bargain collectively through representatives of its own choosing without interference from any source," [40] and supported government regulation of business, including public utilities and securities. [41]

Just before the election, however, the Republicans rallied with an attack against the Social Security Act, whose payroll tax was scheduled to take effect in January 1937. Placards began to go up in factories carrying the message: "You're sentenced to a weekly pay reduction for all your working life. You'll have to serve the sentence unless you help reverse it November 3." Businessmen inserted similar messages in their workers' pay envelopes and Republican spot broadcasts told the working people of America that henceforth they would not have a name, only a New Deal number. [42] Roosevelt's answer came in a speech at Madison Square Garden on October 31: "In 1932," he told the wildly cheering crowd, "the issue was the restoration of American democracy; and the American people were in a mood to win. They did win. In 1936 the issue is the preservation of their victory." Never before had the old enemies, business and financial monopoly, "been so united against one candidate as they stand today. They are unanimous in their hate for me—and I welcome their hatred. I should like to have it said of my first Administration that in it the forces of selfishness and of lust for power met their match." [43]

When the returns were counted, the Democrats had polled 5 million votes more than in 1932, winning the

---

[40] *Current History*, 1936, 44, 53, as quoted in Rauch, 239.

[41] See Rauch, 238–239. Senator Arthur Capper of Kansas observed at an early point in the campaign: "Harmony dripped so steadily from every rafter that I fully expected one of the candidates to withdraw" (Schlesinger, 1960, 610).

[42] Schlesinger, 1960, 635–638.

[43] *Ibid.*, 638–639.

largest presidential vote in history and the largest proportion of electoral votes since 1820. Only Maine and Vermont
went Republican, providing James Farley with the quip,
"As Maine goes, so goes Vermont." [44] In the Congress, three
fourths of the senators and almost four fifths of the representatives were Democrats, the largest Senate majority
since 1869 and the largest House majority since 1855.

The Decline of Insurgency

The years of discontent and disaffection, of protest and possibility, were over; the people had lined up behind the
New Deal. What trouble and turbulence persisted were not
sufficient to rock the New Deal or to alter its course. To see
that this was so we need only review the fate of the insurgent movements which tried both to liberalize relief
policies and to prevent relief cutbacks after 1936: partly
conciliated, partly disarmed, and ultimately debilitated by
the impact of the New Deal, they all failed.

THE OLD PEOPLE'S MOVEMENT

The largest relief movement was initiated by Dr. Francis E.
Townsend. By late 1934, he had rallied hundreds of thousands of old people behind the demands for a monthly pension of $200 for all citizens over sixty years of age, to be
paid on the conditions that they forego gainful employment and that they spend every pension dollar within
thirty days. [45] That the movement attracted such widespread support among the aged was due partly to the fact

---

[44] Roosevelt polled 27,476,673 votes to 16,679,583 for Landon.

[45] The plan would have cost about 24 billion dollars, or half the national income at the time, to be paid for by a "transaction tax" (which was
less obviously regressive than a sales tax). The supporters of the scheme
reasoned that the purchasing power created by giving old people a yearly
income of $2,400 would stimulate business and generate full employment,
thus benefiting everyone.

that old people were very hard hit by unemployment. In 1928, approximately 30 per cent of those sixty-five and over were dependent on others for support; by 1935, the percentage had risen to an estimated 50 per cent—this at a time when the proportion of the aged in the population was rising, having doubled since 1900.

By 1936, there were said to be some 7,000 Townsend clubs throughout the country, each with an average membership of about 300—2 million members in all, if the estimates can be trusted. Most of these people had worked all their lives and considered themselves "solid folk" who had been pauperized by the Depression. Their appeal for aid enjoyed wide popular support; 25 million people signed petitions in favor of the Townsend Plan.[46] It is a measure of the strength of the movement that when a Townsend Plan bill was introduced into the House in 1934, almost two hundred Congressmen absented themselves, while those brave enough to show up voted down the bill without a roll call.[47] What the old folks got instead—and if it did not entirely placate them, it placated their public supporters—was the Social Security legislation, which covered only those aged who worked in selected occupations and industries, with even that to begin only in 1942. This meager legislative concession spelled the demise of the movement, but the Townsendites did not give up without a long fight.

In 1936, the old people's movement joined with Father Charles E. Coughlin and the followers of Huey Long to form the Union Party. How much support this new coalition could muster was at first not clear. Coughlin, the well-known "radio priest," had gained in popularity as the Depression deepened [48]—whether despite, or because of, his

[46] See Holtzman, 88; Swing, 268–270; and Messinger.

[47] Schlesinger, 1960, 33–37.

[48] Just how many actual followers Coughlin had is unclear, but his popularity was undisputed. Schlesinger estimates that he got at least 80,000 letters in a normal week and as many as a million after especially popular

murky and shifting political and economic views. Coughlin
had at first applauded the New Deal as "Christ's Deal," but
he turned against Roosevelt in 1934, accusing him of having "out-Hoovered Hoover." "I will not," he angrily announced, "support a New Deal which protects plutocrats
and comforts Communists." [49] He subsequently attacked
the Administration for nationalizing business and not nationalizing banks. Insofar as Coughlin had a concrete program, it was pro-inflationist, a position with strong appeal
for farmers, small homeowners, and other debtors. Early
in 1936, he campaigned in support of a bill calling for the
issuance of 8 billion dollars in paper money to refinance
farm mortgages. When this measure was voted down, a dis-
gusted Coughlin opened discussions with Townsend about
the formation of a third party.

As for the followers of Huey Long, their strength was
even harder to gauge, for Long was one of the most charis-
matic maverick leaders of the era. As a senator from Louisiana, where he had built a powerful, autocratic political machine, Long had also supported Roosevelt in the beginning,
and that support had been crucial in securing the
President's nomination. But late in 1933, the "Kingfish"
broke with Roosevelt, and began to organize the "Share
Our Wealth" movement, which demanded a federally
guaranteed family income of $5,000 a year.

Long rose to power in Louisiana because of his popularity with the "rednecks," whose support he won by lash-
ing out against the "interests" (at least publicly), by constructing roads, hospitals, and schools, and by a rough and
flamboyant personal style. Nor were his followers confined

---

discourses. Moreover, he collected almost a half million dollars a year in
voluntary contributions. When Station WCAU in Philadelphia polled its
listeners on whether they would prefer Coughlin or the Philharmonic
Orchestra for Sunday afternoon listening, Coughlin outpolled classical
music 187,000 to 12,000 (ibid., 20–21).

[49] Ibid., 25.

to Louisiana; he evoked a response from many of the rural poor generally, and from many of the Southern rural poor in particular.

In March 1934, Long proclaimed that "254 thousand earnest men and women are now dedicated to an unrelenting fight to divide up the wealth of this land of plenty so that children will not starve and their parents beg for crusts." [50] The Share Our Wealth movement burgeoned during 1934 and 1935, and some observers believe that had he not been assassinated by a Louisiana political opponent in 1935, Long's chances for the 1936 Democratic presidential nomination would not have been negligible. But by 1936 Roosevelt had put forward his own tax program (which was later emasculated and enacted as the Wealth Tax Act). Long himself praised Roosevelt's proposals, conceding that the Share Our Wealth clubs would move into the President's camp. As subsequent events would show, it was not the dark accident of Louisiana politics that destroyed both the Share Our Wealth movement and Long's national political fortunes so much as the benign and conciliatory politics of the New Deal.[51]

After Long's assassination, his mantle as leader of the Share Our Wealth movement fell to Gerald L. K. Smith, who joined Townsend and Coughlin to form the Union Party, with Representative William Lemke as its presidential candidate in 1936. In some ways it was an odd alliance; at an earlier point, for instance, Coughlin had opposed the Townsend Plan. But programmatic differences were overshadowed by common political disappointments. And so, having previously denounced "the system" as

---

[50] Quoted in Rauch, 172.

[51] The politics which destroyed Long, Townsend, and Coughlin were not *entirely* benign. After Long broke with FDR, he and his henchmen were harassed by the Internal Revenue Service, and patronage was doled out to his political enemies in Louisiana (Burns, 212). As for Townsend, he was maligned by Senate investigators for the ostensible misuse of club funds. And Coughlin was silenced by his church superiors.

capitalism or communism or both, they now dubbed it the "Franklin Double-crossing Roosevelt" system.[52]

The movement's political prospects were snuffed out in the election of 1936. Compared to the overwhelming millions who voted for Roosevelt, the Union Party polled a mere 882,479 votes. The elements of the party then fragmented and dissipated. Although the Townsend clubs persisted for many years, supporting themselves by selling vitamins and dance tickets, their membership dropped off sharply and their influence quickly dwindled.[53]

THE MOVEMENT OF THE
ABLE-BODIED UNEMPLOYED

The old people, with their dream of ample pensions for all, their hymns, and their beloved leader, were more saints than reformers, and Coughlin, Smith, and Long were more opportunists than revolutionists. But the militant organizations of the unemployed and their radical leaders were quite another political breed, or so it might have seemed. However, they met a fate similar to that of the old people's movement.

In Chapter 2, we described the mass protests by the unemployed at relief offices during the early years of the Depression. During 1934 and 1935, groups of the unemployed continued to agitate, and they were at least partly responsible for the fact that many states and localities participated in federal emergency relief programs. When the federal relief funds for Colorado were discontinued in the winter of 1934 because the state had repeatedly failed to appropriate its share, mobs of the unemployed rioted in relief centers and food stores, and stormed the state legislature. Two weeks later, the General Assembly sent a relief bill to the

---

[52] Schlesinger, 1960, 559.

[53] The Townsendites were estimated to have had about 56,000 members in 1951, or about 2 per cent of their 1936 membership. For an analysis of the transformation of the Townsend movement after 1936, see Messinger.

governor, and federal funding was resumed.[54] An attempt
in Chicago to cut food allowances by 10 per cent in November 1934 led to a large demonstration by the unemployed,
and the city council restored the cut. In the spring of 1935,
the federal government withheld relief when Illinois failed
to provide its share. As relief offices closed down, the unemployed marched, picketed, and demonstrated in Chicago
and Springfield until the state legislature appropriated
funds. When relief was cut in Kansas City, Kansas, later
that year, two thousand of the unemployed assembled in
front of the courthouse, where they prayed and sang hymns
until a new relief appropriation was voted.[55]

The early protests of the unemployed soon attracted
would-be leaders and organizers, many of them from the
Left, who imposed greater structure on the movement. The
first Unemployed Councils, known for their especially
abrasive tactics in attacking relief centers, were organized
by the Communists in 1930.[56] By 1931, several other radical political factions were at work. A. J. Muste formed the
Congress for Progressive Labor Action,[57] which developed
strength in Ohio, West Virginia, Kentucky, North Carolina, and Pennsylvania: its locals were known as Unemployed Leagues or Unemployed Citizens Leagues. The
Leagues also urged the impoverished to engage in self-help
and barter activities—instead of just battering the relief
system—as a way of surviving.[58] In some mining areas, the

---

[54] Cross, 153.

[55] Gilpin, 12.

[56] The Communists had at first tried to bring the unemployed directly
into the party, but without much success. Then, in the winter of 1929–
1930, they turned to organizing unemployed groups, an idea that they
traced to the Petrograd Councils of the Unemployed of 1905 (see Seymour,
August 1937, 9–10).

[57] Muste and other left-wing socialists first started the Congress in the
spring of 1929 as a subgroup of the AF of L, a move which was made in
opposition to "dual unionism," a strategy then being promoted by the
Communist Party (*ibid.*, 17).

[58] See Rogg, 14. An article entitled "Organized Looking into Garbage
Cans" in the March 1, 1933, issue of the *Detroit Hunger Fighter*, a news-
sheet of the Detroit Unemployed Council, impugned such self-help activi-

United Mine Workers provided leadership for the unemployed; the UMW led two hunger marches in Charleston, West Virginia, for example, and joined with the Unemployed Council in Gallup, New Mexico, in leading mass resistance against evictions of miners from homes built on land owned by mining companies. Various brands of socialists also became active, especially in New York, Chicago, and Baltimore; their organizations were later to become the nucleus of the Workers Alliance of America—perhaps the most formidable organization of the able-bodied unemployed in American history.[59]

Other groups appeared in many towns, often under auspices that had nothing to do with radical politics. Local politicians, for example, set up clubs in their wards to handle relief grievances on behalf of individual constituents.[60] In some places trade unions helped and even joined with the unemployed, particularly in the coal regions where unemployment was endemic (although by and large the trade-union movement avoided the unemployed, contenting itself with sending messages of greetings to their meetings).

The membership of the unemployed groups cannot be accurately estimated, and in any case it probably fluctuated widely. People were attracted by the chance of getting relief, and many dropped out once they had received the needed aid.[61] Still, if any gauge is provided by the groups'

---

ties as follows: "The procedure is to go to all kinds of food establishments and trade the labor of unemployed workers for unsalable food, to gather old clothing, etc., as a means of lightening the burden of maintaining the unemployed for the bosses and evading the issue of struggle. . . . 55 per cent of the population cannot live on what the other 45 per cent throw away. . . ."

[59] However, it was not until 1936, after a split which led to the expulsion of the right-wingers, that the national Socialist Party itself became involved with unemployed organizations (Seymour, August 1937, 23).

[60] Gosnell describes such ward activity in Chicago.

[61] Until February 1934 the Unemployed Councils did not have either dues or members; adherents were simply called supporters. At that time the official name was also changed to Unemployment Councils (Seymour, August 1937, 11–13).

own claims, the numbers were astonishing for grass-roots organizations. By 1933, the Ohio Unemployed League estimated its membership at 100,000, distributed among 187 locals throughout the state. The Pennsylvania Unemployed League in 1935 claimed 25,000 members in twelve counties, and the Pennsylvania Security League reported some 70,000 members. In Chicago, New York, and other industrial cities, where more than one third of the population depended on the dole, the groups must have been considerably larger.

The movement of the unemployed originated in local communities; early activities involved agitating and disrupting local relief offices in order to obtain money and goods. But the radical leadership felt that a significant movement depended on unified action growing out of a national structure and program—a massive poor people's union that would compel the Congress to put through radical reforms. The election of a more sympathetic President in 1932 encouraged this way of thinking; the time had come, they felt, to build an organization capable of forcing fundamental economic reforms instead of merely disrupting relief offices for handouts.

The first attempt to form a national organization was made in the fall of 1932, when the Chicago Workers Committee called a meeting of "all Unemployed Leagues that we know of" except "the Communist Party's Unemployed Councils." [62] The result was the formation of the Federation of Unemployed Workers Leagues of America, which called on the incoming President and the Congress to enact legislation for direct relief, public works and slum clearance, unemployment and old-age insurance, a shorter work day, and the prohibition of child labor. Similar meetings were held throughout 1933: a Continental Congress of Workers and Farmers (called through the impetus of national officers of the Socialist Party); a Chicago Conference of the Federation of the Unemployed; and a convention of the Unemployed Leagues of Appalachia.[63]

Efforts to weld a national organization continued in 1934. In March, leaders from socialist-led organizations formed the Eastern Federation of Unemployed and Emergency Workers; in June, the Eastern Federation met with the Illinois Workers Alliance to set up a Provisional National Committee. Finally, at a conference held in Washington in January 1935, a "permanent non-partisan federation of most of the large unemployed organizations in the United States" was formed, called the Workers Alliance of America. Delegates from 500 groups in 16 states, representing some 100,000 members, attended. A National Executive Committee was established and directed by the conference to negotiate unification with the Communists' Unemployed Councils. When a second National Workers Alliance Convention met in April 1936, it drew 900 delegates representing organizations from 36 states, including the Unemployed Councils. By the end of the year, the Alliance claimed 1,600 locals in 43 states, with an estimated dues-paying membership of 300,000.[64] A powerful, radical, nationwide organization of the unemployed seemed to be in sight.

Even as the Workers Alliance came into being, however, so did the legislation of 1935, most importantly the new work relief program. To be sure, work relief hardly came close to satisfying the Alliance's demands, any more than

---

[63] The Conference for Progressive Labor Action which had organized the Unemployed Leagues was disbanded shortly afterwards and absorbed into the American Workers Party (Rogg, 14).

[64] See Seymour, December 1937, 8, and Brophy and Hallowitz, 9. The convention marked the merging of most major groups of the unemployed; the Workers Alliance, the Unemployed Councils, the National Unemployment League, the American Workers Union, and several independent state groups. David Lasser, a Socialist who had been chairman of the first Alliance, was again named chairman, and Herbert Benjamin, a Communist who had been national secretary of the Unemployed Councils, was named organizational secretary. The Communists in the Unemployed Councils, by now well into their "united front" phase, deferred to the Socialists by settling for half as many seats on the new National Executive Board.

the old-age provisions of the Social Security Act had fulfilled the goals of the Townsend Plan. But it was enough to turn the tide, and soon the organized unemployed would be left stranded.

Meanwhile, despite work relief, there was still widespread hardship, for while WPA provided about 2.5 million jobs in 1936, some 7 or 8 million were still unemployed; with FERA abolished, the unemployed, together with the old, the infirm, and the orphaned, were forced to turn to state and local relief agencies, which, as a practical matter, could not handle the burden. Consequently, some localities scaled down their grants, and others simply abolished relief.[65] Distress was especially severe in some industrial states, such as Ohio, Pennsylvania, and Illinois. In New Jersey, licenses to beg were issued instead of relief.[66] For many people, the years after 1935 were as bad as any during the Depression.

The Alliance, committed as it was to obtaining reform through congressional lobbying, reacted by drafting a new relief bill. The bill called for a 6-billion-dollar relief appropriation for the seventeen-month period from February 1, 1936, to June 30, 1937; it also called for relief at decent standards and for "security wages" on work projects at trade-union scales. Of course, the bill failed to pass.

---

[65] Contrary to some accounts, total state and local relief expenditures did not actually drop with the termination of FERA. Under pressure by the federal government to share in the emergency relief program, local expenditures rose sharply, reaching about 450 million dollars annually, and then remained at that level until the end of the Depression (Brown, 340). However, once federal funds for direct relief were withdrawn, that sum was not much, and in any case some states spent much less than others.

[66] Seymour, December 1937, 9. Early in 1936, FERA and WPA initiated several local surveys to ascertain what had happened to former relief recipients not on the WPA rolls. In one area after another they found large numbers of people in dire need, without food or fuel. Some were struggling to live on the pittance granted by local relief agencies; less lucky ones begged, or searched through garbage cans. Similar reports on the situation were issued by the American Association of Social Workers in 1936 and 1937. For a summary of these various findings, see Howard, 77–85.

In April 1937, Alliance leaders met with Harry Hopkins to demand an increase in WPA wages; Hopkins turned them down. In June, the third annual convention of the Workers Alliance, meeting in Milwaukee, called for an appropriation of 3 billion dollars for work relief and 1 billion dollars for direct relief, as well as the establishment of a national planning commission to plan permanent public works programs. The Alliance also sponsored the Schwellenbach-Allen Resolution, which provided that no WPA worker could be discharged who was unable to find suitable private employment. The resolution never reached the floor of the Congress; in fact, Congress adjourned two days before an Alliance-sponsored National Job March reached Washington to lobby for the measure.[67] Instead, Harry Hopkins agreed to establish another joint committee with the Alliance to develop plans for a WPA labor relations board. Undaunted, the Alliance continued to propose legislative programs. In March 1938, a severe recession year, they called a National Conference on Work and Security to "hammer out a real program" of social reconstruction.[68]

The end was soon to come. By the fourth annual Alliance convention, in September 1938, the long succession of legislative defeats had taken its toll. Cleavages among the various factions widened, and, embittered and frustrated, the disparate elements of the movement began to fall out. Thereafter the movement rapidly weakened, and in 1941 the Workers Alliance of America quietly dissolved itself.

While the organizational shells of the various relief movements survived until late in the Depression, they had really been destroyed much earlier by such measures as social security, by labor legislation, by the Wealth Tax Act, by

---

[67] And despite the presence of an advance contingent of some hundreds of marchers (Benjamin, 7).

[68] Rodman, 243.

massive work relief, and by partial economic recovery. Although it was not recognized at the time, the election of 1936 had sounded the death knell for those who believed that anything was possible in America. The signs were there to be read in the election returns: taken together, the extremist parties polled only 2.9 per cent of the vote, down from 3.1 per cent in 1932. Although the insurgent organizations persisted for a time, the underlying popular unrest upon which insurgency draws had been quelled. The little the poor had gotten was enough. Indeed, it was apparently more than enough, for with political stability restored by the great election victory in 1936, the Administration rapidly reduced concessions to the poor, not least by slashing emergency relief measures and by restoring the traditional practices by which relief systems help to maintain the marginal labor pool—all in the name of "reform."

The "Reform" of Relief

Harry Hopkins, writing in 1936, had high hopes for the Works Progress Administration and what it signaled for the American future. The communities of America, he maintained, having experienced the benefits of new WPA parks, roads, schools, and hospitals, and WPA programs for hot school lunches, free theater, and public health services, would never again settle for the shabbiness of public life before WPA. And the American government, having once lifted millions of the poor out of destitution, would not allow them to sink back:

Communities now find themselves in possession of improvements which even in 1929 they would have thought themselves presumptuous to dream of . . . [but] everywhere there had been an overhauling of the word presumptuous. We are beginning to wonder if it is not presumptuous to take for granted that some people should have much, and some should have nothing; that some people are less important than others and should die earlier; that the children of the comfortable should be taller and fatter, as a matter of right, than the children of the poor.[69]

Harry Hopkins was wrong. It was WPA that was presumptuous, for it ran against the grain, it violated the American Way. Once Main Street began to feel that things were better, it wanted to return to that Way.[70] The communities of America had never really accepted WPA,[71] and they settled readily for its withdrawal. The poor settled as well.

By late 1936, WPA rolls were being reduced; early in 1937, it was announced that half of the remaining workers would be discharged. When the President's budget request of January 1937 allocated only 650 million dollars to WPA, there was considerable agitation across the country, but to little avail. During the peak month of March 1936, some 2.9 million workers had been employed; by September 1937 only 1.5 million persons were still on the WPA rolls. With the new recession of 1938, WPA appropriations were

---

[69] Hopkins, 184.

[70] Ed Paulsen, a UNICEF official who spent the early Depression years selling apples, working on the roads, and just drifting, reminisced about why: "Before Roosevelt, the Federal Government hardly touched your life. Outside of the postmaster, there was little local representation. Now people you knew were appointed to government jobs. Joe Blow or some guy from the corner.

"It came right down to Main Street. Half of them loved it, half of them hated it. There was the immediacy of its effect on you. In Aberdeen, Main Street was against it. But they were delighted to have those green relief checks cashed in their cash registers. They'd have been out of business had it not been for them. It was a split thing. They were cursing Roosevelt for the intrusion into their lives. At the same time, they were living off it. Main Street still has this fix" (Terkel, 34).

[71] Terkel tells of an Illinois Writers' Project program which was broadcast over the *Chicago Tribune* station. Colonel McCormick, the publisher, was very proud of the show, which was regularly announced as produced "under the auspices of the Works Progress Administration, Harry Hopkins, Director." But the front page of the *Tribune* nevertheless invariably carried a cartoon of a WPA boondoggler (8–9). Nor were the poor themselves less eager for the "American Way" when they had a chance. For example, the rural poor who were settled in farming cooperatives yearned, with their first profits, to buy back their own farms (see Banfield).

increased to 1.25 billion dollars, and for a brief period the rolls again rose to 3 million. But they were rapidly reduced the following year, when Congress stipulated that those who had been in the program for more than eighteen continuous months should be removed—a measure presumably intended to force project workers to seek private employment. Just how these workers fared is suggested in a report issued by the WPA in January 1940:

> In July and August more than 775,000 WPA project workers were dropped from their jobs in accordance with the 18-months' provision of the 1939 Relief Act. A survey covering more than 138,000 of these workers, in 23 large and representative cities, disclosed that 3 to 4 weeks after their lay-off 7.6 per cent were employed in private jobs. In November, a second interview with the same group showed that 2 to 3 months after dismissal 12.7 per cent, or fewer than 100,000 of the 775,000 workers, were employed in private industry. In industrial centers like Buffalo, Cleveland, Cincinnati, Detroit, and Birmingham, the proportion with jobs was about one in six; in eight of the 23 cities it was about one in ten.[72]

With the onset of World War II, the work relief program was even more sharply reduced and then terminated altogether.[73]

What programs then remained to sustain the poor of America? There were, to be sure, the new insurance plans for aged and unemployed workers passed under the Social

---

[72] Federal Works Agency, January 24, 1940. This study pertained only to those laid off under the 18 months' rule, but the fate of those laid off as a result of over-all quota reductions was not much better. Early in 1939 the WPA surveyed eighty-five such workers in five cities and found that only 29 per cent had found private employment, most at wages below the WPA wage for unskilled labor. About one third were getting some local relief, and one fourth were found to be without any income whatsoever (Roberts, xi).

[73] Unemployment was also declining, to be sure, but not nearly so rapidly as WPA slots. By 1940, WPA was covering only one in five of the jobless—the lowest proportion in its history. When the President announced the termination of the program late in 1942, projected plans for the coming year would have covered only one in six of the unemployed.

Security Act. Both of these insurance provisions, however, covered only certain classes of workers in preferred occupations. Such low wage industries as agriculture and domestic service were exempted. Moreover, as noted earlier, the insurance benefits for the aged became payable only in 1942. As for unemployment insurance, the implementation was left to the states [74] which were free to adopt any level of benefits they wished, to set any waiting periods, and to fix the maximum period of benefit. In any case, both insurance plans applied only to workers who established their eligibility by their sustained participation in the workforce, and then became eligible for aid only by virtue of age or job retrenchments.

The relief program that remained was the provision for the aged, the blind, and the orphaned also contained in the Social Security Act of 1935. Control over relief-giving was substantially returned to the states and localities, with the difference that federal grants-in-aid would be available to supplement their expenditures. And although these measures did not receive much public attention at the time, overshadowed as they were by the provisions of the Act providing unemployment insurance and old-age pensions, they laid the foundations for the contemporary public welfare system.

The new relief legislation did, however, receive considerable attention from some members of Congress, who eliminated various alternative proposals before settling on the final wording. That process suggests some of the concerns that shaped our contemporary public assistance program. For example, an Advisory Committee on Public Employment and Relief (appointed by Frances Perkins, the Secretary of Labor, and composed mainly of social workers) had strongly opposed "categorical" assistance—that is, assistance only to those categories of the poor who were aged,

---

[74] State participation was facilitated by a special federal payroll tax, against which any contributions to a state plan could be offset.

blind, or orphaned—and had called upon the federal government to retain substantial authority over state programs. Similarly, an early draft of the public assistance provisions prepared by the FERA staff had defined "dependent children" broadly, intending the legislation to cover all children who were in severe need, not just those who lacked a parent.[75]

The measures enacted by the Congress were substantially different, however. The simple absence of money was not deemed sufficient to justify coverage, and so the absence of a parent was imposed as a condition for the aid of children, more or less duplicating the old Mothers Aid program; wording to the effect that the aged should receive a grant "compatible with decency and health" was eliminated; the federal administering agency was given little authority over the states, which reflected a growing concern with restoring local options in relief-giving, particularly the option to set grant levels.

Not surprisingly, the main push for narrow coverage and local autonomy in administering these narrow programs came from Southern Congressmen, who were already irritated by what they considered the high-handed practices of the Federal Emergency Relief program. Their concerns were twofold: that the grant levels, if set by the federal government, would undermine the low wage structure in the South;[76] and that a federal supervisory agency, if vested with great authority, would curtail local prerogatives to say who should get relief, thus opening the rolls to blacks and undermining the caste economy of the South. The original wording of the bill reported to the House said that relief could not be denied to a citizen if qualifications regarding age and need were met;[77] the final wording provided only

---

[75] In the same vein, the original Wagner-Lewis bill, introduced with Administration backing, did not fix a maximum per child on the state grant eligible for federal reimbursement (Abbott, II, 240).

[76] *Ibid.*

[77] Douglas, 100–116.

that no citizenship requirement could be used to exclude applicants, thus allowing the state to discriminate against blacks. Finally, there was no provision at all for federal aid to those who had neither blindness nor age nor orphanhood to justify their poverty. The modified and amended provisions were submitted for a vote as part of the Social Security package, which, as noted earlier, passed overwhelmingly and was hailed widely as a major reform.

The state public welfare systems that resulted from this enabling legislation will be taken up in detail in the next two chapters. For now, it is enough to say that between the years 1935 and 1939 most of the states enacted legislation to make use of the categorical grants-in-aid. In the main, the legislation enacted was modeled after the state mothers' aid programs and pension programs for the aged that had existed prior to the passage of the Social Security Act, since most of the traditional "poor relief" restrictions which had been the hallmark of these earlier relief programs were reintroduced. The states exercised their prerogative to establish grant levels by setting them very low. Some states set them much lower than others. In December 1939, for example, Arkansas gave an average of $8.10 a month to families with dependent children and Massachusetts gave such families $61.07. Nationally, levels of aid under categorical assistance averaged about half what employables were earning on federal work relief projects.

Most important, few got any aid at all. Just how few is vividly demonstrated by the future course of the categorical assistance program for dependent children (AFDC).[78] For one thing, many states were slow to implement this program; some had not done so as late as 1940. By December 1940, as a consequence, only 360,000 families had been admitted to the nation's AFDC rolls. Nine states, five of

---

[78] This program was initially called Aid to Dependent Children (ADC), but was subsequently renamed Aid to Families with Dependent Children (AFDC). We shall use the later designation throughout this text.

them in the South, still had fewer than 1,000 families on their rolls; Texas, for example, had a caseload of 85 families, and Mississippi a caseload of 104.

The sluggish growth of the program was reversed by World War II; between December 1940 and December 1945, the rolls dropped by 25 per cent. But with the end of the war, the upward trend resumed; between December 1945 and December 1950, the rolls rose 132 per cent. Even so, only 635,000 families were obtaining AFDC payments in 1950. At this level, caseloads stabilized, rising only 17 per cent between 1950 and 1960 (despite sharply mounting unemployment in both agriculture and in the cities).

The cycle was complete. Turbulence had produced a massive federal direct relief program; direct relief had been converted into work relief; then work relief was cut back and the unemployed were thrown upon state and local agencies, which reduced aid to the able-bodied in most places and eventually eliminated it in many. What remained were the categorical-assistance programs for the impotent poor—the old, the blind, and the orphaned. For the able-bodied poor who would not be able to find employment or secure local relief in the days, months, and years to come, the federal government had made no provision. Nor are there statistics that describe their fate.

REFERENCES

Abbott, Grace, *The Child and the State*, Vol. II. Chicago, University of Chicago Press, 1938.

Bakke, E. Wight, *Citizens Without Work: A Study of the Effects of Unemployment Upon the Workers' Social Relations and Practices*. New Haven, Yale University Press, 1940.

Banfield, Edward C., *Government Project*. Glencoe, Ill., Free Press, 1951.

Benjamin, Herbert, "Why We Marched," *Social Work Today*, October 1937, 5, 7.

Brophy, Alice, and Hallowitz, George, "Pressure Groups and the Relief Administration in New York City." Unpublished professional project, New York School of Social Work, April 8, 1937.

Brown, Josephine Chapin, *Public Relief 1929–1939*. New York, Henry Holt & Company, 1940.

Burns, James MacGregor, *Roosevelt: The Lion and the Fox,* New York, Harcourt, Brace & Company, 1956.

Cross, Frank Clay, "Revolution in Colorado," *Nation*, February 7, 1934, 138, 152–153.

Douglas, Paul H., *Social Security in the United States: An Analysis and Appraisal of the Federal Social Security Act.* New York, Mc-Graw-Hill Book Company, 1939.

Federal Works Agency, *Workers Dropped from WPA in Accordance with the 18-months Provision in the 1939 Relief Act.* Division of Research, Works Projects Administration, January 24, 1940.

Fortune, December 1935.

Gilpin, DeWitt, "Fired for Inefficiency," *Social Work Today*, November 1935, 3, 11–13.

Gosnell, Harold F., *Machine Politics: Chicago Model.* Chicago, University of Chicago Press, 1937.

Holtzman, Abraham, *The Townsend Movement: A Political Study.* New York, Bookman Associates, 1963.

Hopkins, Harry L., *Spending to Save: The Complete Story of Relief.* New York, W. W. Norton & Company, 1936.

Howard, Donald S., *The WPA and Federal Relief Policy.* New York, Russell Sage Foundation, 1943.

Messinger, Sheldon L., "Organizational Transformation: A Case Study of a Declining Social Movement," *American Sociological Review*, 1955, 20, 3–10.

Rauch, Basil, *This History of the New Deal, 1933–1938.* New York, Creative Age Press, 1944.

Roberts, Verl E., *Survey of Workers Separated from WPA Employment in Nine Areas, 1937.* Washington, U.S. Government Printing Office, 1938.

Rodman, Selden, "Lasser and the Workers' Alliance," *Nation*, September 10, 1938, 147, 242–244.

Rogg, Nathan, "The Unemployed Unite," *Social Work Today*, June 1936, 3, 13–15.

Schlesinger, Arthur M., Jr., *The Age of Roosevelt,* Vol. II, *The Coming of the New Deal.* Boston, Houghton Mifflin Company, 1958.

Schlesinger, Arthur M., Jr., *The Age of Roosevelt,* Vol. III,

The Politics of Upheaval. Boston, Houghton Mifflin Company, 1960.

Seymour, Helen, "The Organized Unemployed." A dissertation submitted to the Division of the Social Sciences, University of Chicago, August 1937.

Seymour, Helen, "Report to the Committee on Social Security of the Social Science Research Council." Unpublished, December 1, 1937.

Swing, Raymond Gram, "Dr. Townsend Solves It All," *Nation*, March 6, 1935, 140, 268–270.

Terkel, Studs, *Hard Times: An Oral History of the Great Depression.* New York, Pantheon Books, 1970.

U.S. Bureau of the Census, *Statistical Abstract of the United States: 1936.* Washington, U.S. Government Printing Office, 1937.

U.S. Bureau of the Census, *Statistical Abstract of the United States: 1940.* Washington, U.S. Government Printing Office, 1941.

PART II

*Relief and the
Years of Stability:
1940–1960*

CHAPTER FOUR

Enforcing Low-Wage Work:
Statutory Methods

If public relief arrangements are initiated or expanded to cope with serious threats to civil order posed by large and volatile masses of unemployed, what, then, is the function of the relief system once political crises subside? It is, as we argued in Chapter 1, to enforce work, especially very low-wage work. As political stability is restored, relief practices in each locale are re-shaped day by day to meet labor needs. Although this assertion clearly runs counter to the popular belief that relief agencies shelter and encourage the indolent and slothful, a careful examination of the Aid to Families with Dependent Children program will confute any such belief.

There are two reasons for choosing to examine AFDC. First, the way in which this categorical assistance program was implemented in the 1940's and 1950's reflected the prevailing ambiguity as to whether women and children should be exempted from the requirement to work. Such ambiguity did not so seriously afflict assistance programs for the aged and the blind, who were largely relieved of the moral obligation to work by the pension provisions of the Social Security Act, as well as by the Old Age Assistance and Aid to the Blind programs established under that act. (Even so, however, low payments continued to keep many such persons in the labor force.) The question of whether women and children should be granted aid was further clouded by their relationship to men, for able-bodied males might surreptitiously benefit from grants given to women and children. Consequently, the AFDC program has been closely hedged about with work-maintaining statutes and policies.

The second reason for examining AFDC is that it was in this category that the relief explosion of the 1960's occurred. The nature of that explosion, and why it occurred, are the subject of later chapters in this book. Our task now is to identify the work-maintaining procedures of the AFDC program that prevailed during the 1940's and 1950's—that is, during the years of stability between relief explosions.

Relief practices enforce low-wage labor in a number of ways. One way was discussed with surprising candor when the Illinois State Advisory Committee of the U.S. Commission on Civil Rights convened several years ago to hear complaints about AFDC practices in Southern Illinois.

> *Mr. Whitfield:* Mr. Chairman, I am a resident of Cairo. Soon as the month of May, the public aid would start sending letters to the recipients. Due to seasonable work, your grant is cut and you are supposed to make it up by doing this seasonable work. This seasonable work, as we know, is farm labor. My migrant labor, that's what it is, 50 cents per hour.
>
> I asked my superintendent of public aid, Mr. Lawrence, "Did you have to stand toe-to-toe to me and tell me to take my wife and children and go to the fields and make up this amount of grant that they have cut off of my check," and I

Committee Member: have letters to prove what I am saying, because they are their letters and they are signed by them. . . . Now, I was particularly interested in your reference to a discussion with a public aid worker who suggests that you and your wife and your children obtain field work to make up the difference in your welfare payments. Is it your feeling that he was suggesting this to you because there was available field work or do you feel that public aid recipients are a source of cheap labor for the farmers in this area?

Mr. Whitfield: The public aid recipient is a source of cheap labor for the farmer. We have asked a number of times. I have asked my superintendent of public aid about forcing the people to the fields, why didn't he wait and let us stay back until labor rise [i.e., until labor shortages forced wage levels up], and he said the poor farmers couldn't pay any more, we'd have to go along with this going rate, and this going rate has been the same thing ever since I been in Cairo.

Committee Member: So you think, then, the ability of the farmers in this area to get labor for as little as 50 cents is by reason of the relationship between public aid, the recipient, and the necessity of taking that work?

Mr. Whitfield: That's right.[1]

---

[1] U.S. Commission on Civil Rights, 1966, 99–106 (abridged). Although both this chapter and the next focus on the period between 1940 and 1960, we have sometimes used data which pertain to the 1960's. The reason is that public welfare became a source of great concern in the 1960's, so that more evidence regarding policies and practices was gathered by various groups. Since the 1960's were also a period of liberalization, the use of such data tends to convey the impression of more humane practices than probably prevailed in the 1940's and 1950's.

Although welfare officials may give partial aid only on the condition that the recipient work while on the rolls, or give aid only seasonally, these are not the main ways in which relief practices buttress the low-wage market. The more prevalent practice is simply to refuse aid outright to those of the impoverished who might be potential workers.

Excluding Workers

Since 1935, each state legislature has utilized its broad license under the Social Security Act to design welfare legislation and administrative procedures to accommodate local economic interests. This has produced a remarkable similarity in certain relief practices from one state to another (for example, residence laws which deny payments to persons who have not lived in a locale for a particular period of time), and a rather striking diversity in other respects (for example, widely different payment levels). What explains the diversities, as well as the similarities, is not the vicissitudes of local morals and local politics, as critics sometimes charge, but the objective of regulating the giving of aid so that it meshes with the varying labor requirements of local economic enterprises.

One does not have to delve into the details of relief administration in support of this perspective. The main methods of enforcing work are obvious, and evidence enough. Thus relief systems ordinarily exclude able-bodied men (as well as, at times, able-bodied women and children) no matter how severe their destitution or prolonged their unemployment. Even though on the edge of starvation, potential workers are ordinarily kept in the labor pool. It was not until the Social Security Act was amended in 1961 that the federal government agreed to reimburse states for aid to families with unemployed fathers (AFDC-UP). As of early 1969, however, only twenty-four states had made use of the new option, and the eligibility restrictions were so severe that very few families with unemployed fathers actually got on the rolls—just under 80,000 in the entire country as of February 1969, or 5 per cent of the AFDC rolls. (Significantly, when Congress set out in 1967 to do something about the nation's mounting relief costs, it especially singled out this program for unemployed fathers, adding the requirement that only if the man had a fairly stable record of employment and then became unemployed for at least thirty days could a state place him on the rolls and expect federal reimbursement. Whatever the intent, the effect was that those who worked on a seasonal, irregular, or temporary basis were excluded from the program.)

To deny aid to unemployed men may not, however, prevent them from obtaining it via their women and children. But the states have traditionally denied aid to a mother who is in any way associated with a man, especially if the man lives in her house. These provisions—often called "man-in-the-house" rules—are sometimes condemned on the ground that they drive unemployed fathers away from their families. The official explanation commonly given for these rules is that communities insist upon legislating morality for the hapless relief family. Whatever the motive, however, the consequence is to ensure that no relief funds reach unemployed men circuitously. For if the unemployed or underemployed father "deserts" so that his wife and children can get on relief, he may try to support himself by remaining near his family and sharing in its welfare income. Obviously such an arrangement would reduce a man's vulnerability to marginal employment. But with "man-in-the-house" rules, men run the risk of being tracked down and jailed for non-support by investigators who conduct "midnight" raids or parked-car surveillance of homes. These and similar measures may be justified in the language of moral virtue but their economic effect is to ensure a pool of marginal workers. The men affected must take any work at any age; and if they remain with their families, the chances are that their wives and children will have to work too.

When a large pool of low-paid labor is needed by economic enterprises, men alone may not provide a sufficient supply. Consequently, relief arrangements will be adjusted to keep women in the labor pool; according to a recent study, fully 87 per cent of the welfare mothers in one Northern city had been or were working.[2] Children may also be an important part of the labor supply at certain times and in certain places, leading to similar adjustments by the relief system. Thus, access to the AFDC program has always been blocked by more statutory and administrative restrictions than those programs pertaining to the blind, the aged, or the disabled.[3]

The ways in which women and children have been kept off the rolls are myriad. An especially outlandish way consists of bringing criminal charges of "fornication" against mothers of illegitimate children who apply for assistance. A widely-publicized case of this kind recently occurred in New Jersey. Not only was the mother convicted and given a six-month suspended sentence, but she was forced to name the father who was subsequently convicted and sentenced to a three-month prison term.

Sometimes women and children are allowed on the rolls and then made to work, a practice which has a long history,

---

[2] This figure is taken from a study of women on the AFDC caseload in Philadelphia in 1962, as reported in U.S. Manpower Administration, 98. Keeping mothers in the labor force has a long history in this country, as illustrated by the Mothers' Pension Program. "In Harrisburg, Pennsylvania, three quarters of a group of 116 mothers studied in 1918 were employed. There were 95 of their children, a third of whom were under 16, who also worked. . . . In 1923, 52 per cent of a sample of 942 mothers who received grants in nine metropolitan areas were earning part of the family support" (Bell, 16).

[3] Those profiting from the labor of women and children are often disposed to abolish public assistance altogether. In 1954, a civic organization in Louisiana reported that groups hostile to AFDC "contended that public assistance results in reducing the unskilled labor supply in employment where women and children form a principal part of the labor supply" (Public Affairs Research Council, 6).

as we noted in Chapter 1. Employment training programs under welfare auspices provide one example, as shown by testimony given in 1967 at hearings convened by the Mississippi State Advisory Committee to the U.S. Commission on Civil Rights in Jackson. Black welfare recipients enrolled in Mississippi's "work experience" program, federally subsidized but under welfare auspices, were assigned to private entrepreneurs who, according to testimony, were told to "use them any way you can." As a result, women were given "work experience" in dishwashing and heavy cleaning, in hauling gravel and cutting grass.[4]

A similar situation was alleged by recipients testifying in Gary, Indiana, also before the U.S. Commission on Civil Rights. One recipient said of the welfare department's "domestic service training programs" that "it seems rather unnecessary for a Negro to go to school to get a certificate to clean up someone else's house."[5]

When mothers and children do get aid, they ordinarily get less than the aged, blind, and disabled, and this also encourages at least their partial involvement in the labor force. The Social Security Act of 1935 set $30 per month as the maximum state grant to which the federal government would contribute for each aged and blind person; but the maximum AFDC grant eligible for federal sharing was set at $18 per month for the first child in a family and $12 for each additional child. Within these maximums, moreover, the rate of federal reimbursement was set at half of state payments for Old Age Assistance, but only one third of state payments for AFDC. Since 1935, Congress has always

---

[4] For an account of these hearings, see the authors' "Mississippi: Starving by the Rule Book," 429–431. By now it should be clear that we are not addressing the question of whether women and children should or should not work. Our point is a very different one: that the relief system is shaped to ensure the availability, *on the employer's terms,* of those of the poor who may be required as laborers, whatever their age or sex. In the United States, as we shall presently note, relief policies are also designed to ensure that blacks are made more vulnerable than whites to marginal employment, reflecting racial differentiations in the labor market.

[5] U.S. Commission on Civil Rights, 1967, 18.

shown greater willingness to vote increases in the federal
share of grants for the aged, blind, and disabled than for
AFDC; and state-legislated limits on payments have generally reflected the same bias.[6]

Adapting Relief
to Regional Economies

We have so far spoken of relatively general features of the
American relief system. There are, however, wide variations among the states. In 1969 in the state of Mississippi,
for example, a family of four with no income received $69
per month; a comparable New Jersey family received $347.
When a father is present, even if unemployed, the family is
not entitled to any aid in Mississippi but can be given relief
in New Jersey. And, legal restrictions aside, if an impoverished woman and her children who apply for welfare in
Mississippi happen to be black, they will have to contend
with welfare officials who will try to embarrass, scold, or
frighten them into withdrawing their application; officials
in most Northern states are far less inclined to single out
blacks for vituperation and scrutiny.

These variations in relief practices are often said to reflect the vestigial influence of the English Poor Law, which
was based on several key principles: that relief should be
a local responsibility; that relief allowances should be less
remunerative than wages (the principle of "less eligibility"); and that "settlement" in the local community should
be a prerequisite for aid.

If relief practices are viewed as methods of enforcing low-
wage work, however, it becomes obvious that the old Poor
Law principles underlying our relief system are not merely
vestiges of an archaic tradition. They have an important
function in our economy, for they make it possible to shape

---

[6] Steiner, 18–47. For a further discussion of these biases against the
AFDC program, see Schorr, 3–15.

relief practices in accord with widely differing labor practices from region to region, state to state, and locality to locality. Thus, the principle of local responsibility ensures that local officials can vary eligibility criteria so as to mesh with local labor requirements. The "less eligibility" rule ensures that welfare grants can be kept from becoming competitive with wages, no matter how low the wages. And residence laws (the principle of "settlement") hold these locally differentiated arrangements firmly in place. In other words, the variations in relief practices, like the similarities, can best be understood by the economic functions they serve.

The best example of such regional adaptations in the United States, of course, is provided by the South. Moreover, the Southern case also reveals how relief policies can be used to support a caste labor system, one in which the subjugation of particular ethnic or racial groups (in this case blacks) serves to lower the price of labor generally. Since such variant features of the relief system in the South may be less well-known than the common features of relief in the United States, some detailed illustrations follow.

In the South,[7] where wage levels are lower than elsewhere, relief payments also have always been lower. In 1951, the average payment per person in the Southern region was only $14 per month, while all other regions had levels almost twice as high. At the extremes, a person in Mississippi got $5 per month, a person in California $36. Between 1951 and 1969, payment levels almost doubled everywhere; still, Mississippi paid $10 per person per month while Massachusetts paid $68.

---

[7] For convenience, we have adopted the regional groupings of states employed by the Bureau of the Census. In that classification, the Southern region includes a number of states which might be considered Northern, such as Maryland and Delaware. Some of these states have more liberal grant levels and less restrictive practices than other states in the Southern region. Hence our comparisons of regions tend to understate the differences between "Northern" and "Southern" practices. See Appendix, Source Table 1, for an enumeration of the states in each region.

TABLE I

Average Monthly Payment per AFDC Recipient [8]

REGION	JUNE '51	JUNE '60	FEBRUARY '69
South	$14	$21	$26
West	27	35	39
North Central	25	33	45
Northeast	27	35	53
National Average	22	30	39

These differences in grant levels vary directly with differences in wage levels. The average hourly agricultural wage in 1969 ranged from $1.01 in South Carolina to $1.78 in California; the state-by-state rank-order correlation between relief payments and agricultural wages was .77. In 1960, it was .84; and it was .75 in 1951. [9]

Other variations in welfare arrangements made possible by the "principle" of local responsibility can also be traced to regional variations in labor practices. For example, when the congressional amendment permitting federal reimbursement to the states for aid to unemployed fathers (AFDC-UP) was passed in 1961, a striking regional pattern emerged. All but four of the twenty-four states that subsequently implemented the program were in the North.

[8] Excludes AFDC-UP cases (i.e., unemployed parent cases permitted under the congressional amendment of 1961) and vendor payments for medical care. These figures were computed by obtaining the average payment per recipient in each state in a given region, summing the average state payments, and dividing the total by the number of states in the region. The alternative procedure is to aggregate all money payments in a region and then divide by all recipients in the region. Each procedure biases the result in the direction of either high-payment states or states with a large number of recipients. But both procedures show the same general differences among regions.

[9] Agricultural wage data were obtained from the U.S. Department of Agriculture and exclude payments in kind, such as room or board.

Moreover, the four exceptions (Delaware, Maryland, West Virginia, and Oklahoma) were among the more urbanized and industrial states of the South. The prevailing Southern sentiment against enacting AFDC-UP was probably expressed by a county welfare director in Alabama who opposed the program on the ground that "Negroes just do not want to work." [10]

When a particular racial group does the most menial work for the lowest wages, the relief system cooperates by reducing the amount of aid to that group or by closing off the possibility of any aid whatsoever. In the South, of course, it is primarily blacks who do the menial work and who have been denied relief, providing an especially powerful illustration of the economic functions of welfare regionalism. Under pressure from Southern congressmen, any wording that might have been interpreted as constraining the states from racial discrimination in welfare was deleted from the Social Security Act of 1935. The Southern states then proceeded to use the free hand they had been given to keep blacks off the rolls. In *An American Dilemma* (1944), Gunnar Myrdal noted the not-unexpected consequence of vesting authority for the administration of AFDC in the states:

Aid to dependent children is intended, primarily, for broken families with children. In view of the great number of widows and widowers in the Negro population, and its high divorce, separation, and illegitimacy rates, it is quite apparent that Negroes need this assistance much more than do whites. In 1937–1940 from 14 to 17 per cent of all recipients accepted for such aid were Negroes. In seven of the Southern states, however, the proportion of Negroes among those accepted for aid to dependent children was smaller even than the proportion of Negroes among all children under 16 years of age. The discrimination was particularly pronounced in Georgia, where, in 1940, 38 per cent of all children under 15

---

[10] U.S. Commission on Civil Rights, n.d., 15.

were Negroes, whereas the proportion of Negroes among those accepted for aid to dependent children during 1937–1940 was 11 to 12 per cent.[11]

On the basis of these and other data, Myrdal concluded that the black "is worst off in the rural South, where the most apparent racial discrimination is shown, at the same time as the general relief standards are very low."[12]

The low proportion of blacks on the Southern AFDC rolls resulted from the articulation of welfare practices with labor practices. As soon as the states began to implement AFDC programs, they instituted special provisions designed to keep blacks in the labor pool. In 1943, for example, Louisiana adopted the first "employable mother" rule requiring that all AFDC families with children seven years old or older be refused assistance as long as the mother was presumed to be employable in the fields. In her account of the AFDC program, Winifred Bell shows that such "seasonal employment policies emerged in areas where seasonal employment was almost exclusively performed by nonwhite families."[13]

Georgia enacted a similar rule in 1952 that permitted welfare officials to deny assistance to mothers with children over three years of age who were deemed to be employable if "suitable" employment were deemed to be "available." Suitable employment meant employment at any wage, and the Georgia rule explicitly prohibited county welfare departments from supplementing that wage, even when it fell below welfare grant levels. The rule also directed county

---

[11] Myrdal, 359. However, discrimination against blacks in access to benefits did not begin with AFDC. It was also characteristic of its predecessor, the Mothers' Pension program. "The only systematic study of the racial composition of Mothers' Pension caseloads was made in 1931 when reports were secured on approximately half the families across the nation. In 46,597 families 96 per cent of the mothers were white, 3 per cent were Negro, and 1 per cent was of other racial extraction. About half the Negro families lived in two states: Ohio and Pennsylvania" (Bell, 9).

[12] Myrdal, 357.

[13] Bell, 46.

welfare boards to deny *all* applications and to close *all* existing cases of mothers who were deemed able to work during "periods of full employment"—that is, during periods of seasonal employment when, for example, many hands were needed in the fields to pick cotton.[14]

The first year for which exact data on the racial composition of the AFDC rolls are available is 1948. All that can be said with certainty of the earlier years is that there were substantially fewer blacks than whites on the rolls in the South. In 1948, blacks comprised less than one third of the rolls in seven Southern states. As a result of this disclosure, the federal government exerted some pressure for a relaxation of discriminatory practices—for example, by requiring the establishment of a formal application process, thus making it somewhat more difficult for welfare officials to brush off applicants by treating their requests as mere casual inquiries. Between 1948 and 1953 (when the next racial census of the relief rolls was taken), the proportion of blacks on the rolls rose by at least 25 per cent in eleven of the seventeen Southern states. But from 1953 to 1961, only two Southern states (Tennessee and West Virginia) showed a comparable increase in the proportion of blacks receiving aid.[15]

Even when black women did get on the rolls, however, they were kept under pressure to work at least part time— a pattern of discrimination that still persists. A national study of state welfare programs conducted by the Department of Health, Education, and Welfare (HEW) in 1961 showed that 19 per cent of black AFDC mothers worked as opposed to only 10 per cent of whites. The same study showed that about 24 per cent of AFDC mothers in the

---

[14] Arkansas adopted a "farm policy" in 1953, requiring able-bodied mothers and older children to accept employment whenever available. "The farm policy was responsible for between 38.6 and 58.6 per cent of all closings between 1953 and 1960" (*ibid.*, 107).

[15] For data on the racial composition of the AFDC rolls at different times, see Source Table 4 in the Appendix.

South worked compared to 8 per cent in the rest of the nation. Although this study does not cross-tabulate employment by race and region simultaneously, it is reasonable to assume that the higher proportion of working AFDC mothers in the South and the higher proportion of working black AFDC mothers in the nation adds up to a very high proportion of working black AFDC mothers in the South.[16] A second national study, in which every third case closed during a three-month period in 1961 was examined, lends support to the conclusion that black women are two or three times as likely to work, particularly in rural areas (which means in the South, for it is only there that rural areas contain significant numbers of blacks):

> Significantly more Negro than white homemakers were employed during the ADC period for each age grouping of children both in urban and rural areas. In urban areas from 30 to 55 per cent of the Negroes worked and in rural areas from 57 to 75 per cent worked when children were in various age groups. Among whites, 17 to 33 per cent in urban and 22 to 26 per cent in rural areas had some employment for differing age groups of children.[17]

In order to keep black relief mothers in the labor force, they are given less money by welfare, especially in the rural South: in effect, black women are confronted with the choice of either trying to earn the difference between what they are given and what white women are given or struggling to live on the smaller amount. Evidence from the national study of terminations shows this clearly. Thus, in

---

[16] HEW, 1965, Tables 48a and 48b (from which these percentages were extrapolated).

[17] Burgess and Price, 30; see also Table VIII, 251. Since the study was confined to families leaving the rolls, these results cannot be generalized with certainty to all welfare cases. But over-all, the results of various studies lead to the unmistakable conclusion that black AFDC women are more likely to be kept in the labor force. In this connection, Bell reports: "In 1958 of the ADC families in the nation with the mother in the home, 9.4 per cent of white mothers were employed as contrasted to 20.4 per cent of Negro mothers. In Louisiana the proportions were 9.8 and 28.9, respectively" (Bell, 231, n. 5).

1961, there were no differences by race in median AFDC payments per person in cities of more than 500,000 population. However, in cities of 50,000 to 500,000 persons, the median monthly AFDC payment to blacks was $24.40; to whites, $30.40. The most extreme difference occurred in rural farm areas in non-metropolitan counties, where the payments were $11.70 and $21.90 to blacks and whites, respectively.[18] (As with most reports prepared by or commissioned by HEW, the authors of this particular study fail to draw the obvious inference regarding racial practices from their data: namely, that Southern welfare policies discriminate against blacks. Thus they comment on the higher proportion of black AFDC mothers in the rural farm work force by suggesting that there is "a better opportunity for Negroes [to be employed] in rural areas."[19] There is indeed.)

That AFDC mothers are forced into very low-level jobs also emerges clearly from this study: "Only 8 per cent of the sample of ADC mothers . . . [were employed in jobs that were] . . . skilled, clerical, or white collar (11 per cent white, 4 per cent Negro). The remainder were concentrated largely in unskilled labor and service jobs."[20] Moreover, such low-level jobs were more preponderant in the South:

> Regionally, the Southeast had the largest group of mothers who were farm operatives, and the Southeast and Far West had the highest proportion of farm laborers. . . . Mothers whose usual occupation was "service worker" were found most frequently among Negroes in the Southeast (46 per cent) and the Southwest (44 per cent). . . .[21]

---

[18] Burgess and Price, Table 4.9, 74. Statistical reports issued by HEW show the same general pattern. In non-metropolitan rural farm areas, black AFDC families received an average payment in 1961 of $57 per month; white AFDC families received an average of $81 per month (HEW, 1965, Table 43).

[19] Burgess and Price, 78.

[20] *Ibid.*, 24.

[21] *Ibid.*, 25. These are two of the three sub-regions comprising the South.

There are many mechanisms by which Southern welfare departments deny or reduce payments to blacks, thus keeping them in the marginal labor market. The "employable mother" rule described earlier in this chapter has been more characteristic of states in the South than in the North and it has been applied discriminatorily against black women: when field hands are needed, Southern welfare officials assume that a black woman is employable, but not a white woman.

Federal surplus commodities are also sometimes distributed on the condition that the recipient be employed. Organizers affiliated with the "migrant ministry" program of the National Council of Churches in such places as Polk County, Florida, report that black (but not white) women are often refused surplus foods unless they are employed and produce a note confirming that fact from their employer, who is typically a fruit grower or cannery operator using extremely low-wage labor. Collusion with administrators of food programs assures these employers of a docile and exploitable labor supply. Whether such collusion is widespread in Southern agricultural areas cannot be said for certain—these matters are rarely investigated—but what evidence there is suggests the worst.[22]

The especially vigorous enforcement of man-in-the-house rules in Southern states is directed almost exclusively at the Southern black, a pattern of discrimination that is justified on the grounds of the alleged defects in black

---

[22] An observer of recent food-distribution practices in a Mississippi rural county reports that "to avoid relying on the . . . [black tenant farmer as a source of information about his eligibility for food programs], the welfare department usually demands of the tenant an affidavit signed by the planter, telling what the employee's income is. No [welfare] official will question the judgment of a planter concerning his tenants; it is the opinion of many poor people that their bosses state that their income is too high." Moreover, "on some plantations, it is said, the planter himself will purchase the stamps for his tenants and sell them to his workers as he sees fit." In any event, many tenants have to borrow the money from the plantation owner to purchase stamps, so the planter controls access to food programs whether or not he actually distributes the stamps (Dunbar, 47–48).

family life. In *An American Dilemma*, Myrdal observed that "according to popular belief in the South, few Negro low-income families have homes which could be called 'suitable' for any purpose . . . and since often practically all Negroes are believed to be 'immoral,' almost any discrimination against Negroes can be motivated on such grounds." [23] By 1942, more than half of the states, most of them in the Southern region, had enacted "suitable home" laws. Many mothers found "guilty" of violating social norms (usually, bearing illegitimate children) were permitted to keep their offspring but had to rear them without public aid, thus keeping these mothers in the labor force.

Evidence from the national study of terminations conducted in 1961 reveals the persistence with which these moral criteria are used as a way of forcing blacks to work. The highest proportion of working AFDC mothers were blacks who had been classified as being on the rolls for "socially unacceptable reasons"—that is, for having illegitimate children, or because the father had deserted or was imprisoned. No such differences in the rates of employment were found among comparable groupings of white AFDC mothers, leading the authors of this study to conclude:

> There may be more pressure brought to bear on clients of certain kinds of cases [i.e., black on the rolls for socially unacceptable reasons] to obtain work or some outside support to supplement ADC. There is no similar pattern evident for white cases . . . when one divides the "socially acceptable" from the "socially nonacceptable" crisis cases.[24]

Justifying these activities by fundamentalist principles of family life, Southern states especially have engaged in periodic campaigns to purge mothers and children from the rolls because of "unsuitable homes." In 1959, for ex-

[23] Myrdal, 360.
[24] Burgess and Price, 80.

ample, Florida undertook a strenuous relief clearance program of this sort: adverse reports were filed on 14,664 families, 91 per cent of them black. (Only 181 of these homes were declared unsuitable because the children were actually found to be neglected.) Roland A. Chilton, a university-based researcher investigating these events for HEW, subsequently reported that Florida's suitable home law "did in fact result in the loss of assistance to over 7,000 families with over 30,000 children when, presumably, all of the eligibility requirements for ADC were met but where one or more of the children was illegitimate . . . or where the welfare worker reported that the mother's past or present conduct of her sex life was not acceptable when examined in light of the spirit of the law." [25] Having thus dropped thousands of families from the rolls, the Florida relief system presented itself to the public in subsequent annual reports as a model of administrative efficiency and moral virtue. The mothers thus affected had little choice but to accept what work they could get, even at wages below Florida's AFDC levels of $15 a month per person. In 1960, Louisiana also struck 20,000 children from the rolls, most of them black, again on the ground that they were being reared in unsuitable homes, but HEW subsequently forced their reinstatement. [26] Although these laws were more prev-

---

[25] Chilton, 65.

[26] The federal supervision of public welfare has been lodged in HEW since its creation during the Eisenhower years. Like its predecessor federal agencies, HEW has usually adopted a more liberal stance than local welfare departments, but its authority is very limited, and what pressure it does exert on local agencies usually takes the form of offering financial incentives for professional innovation or conducting studies whose conclusions may serve to scold some local administrations. However, in 1960, in an uncharacteristically assertive action, HEW Secretary Arthur S. Flemming informed the states that they could not discharge families with illegitimate children from the rolls unless some other provision was made for the children (i.e., placement in an institution or foster home). Otherwise, cash assistance had to be continued. In 1966, Congress added the "Flemming Rule" to the Social Security Act. Since the cost of placing children is very high, this rule has greatly hampered the application of suitable home laws.

alent in the South, they also were enacted in some Northern states—Michigan, for example.

Such evidence, in short, suggests that various legal and administrative definitions of immoral, unsuitable, and unacceptable family life are used to force black women into marginal work in the South, either by excluding them from aid or by giving them lower payments than whites, while threatening to remove them from the rolls altogether if they do not work.[27]

These practices are not unique to the South. They have occurred in other areas where there is a similar need for marginal labor, as revealed during hearings convened by the U.S. Commission on Civil Rights in Cairo, Illinois, in 1966. Blacks, who comprised one third of the population, held virtually no jobs other than menial ones in either private enterprise or public agencies. Testimony also revealed that the relief system played a crucial role in keeping blacks at the bottom of the occupational order:

> *Reverend Cobb:* Mr. Chairman and The Commission . . . [I am an official of the local NAACP]. The state employment office has been contacted concerning hiring Negroes in [better jobs]. It is our feeling that the state office is cooperating in a program to hold the Negro in a certain status economically. We are sent to the fields by this office with the help or encouragement of the various departments of relief, and some political

---

[27] Although we have been stressing variations in regional and state practices, a further refinement of the principle of local responsibility occurs in those states which delegate the operation of public assistance to the county or city governments. In such states, wide variations in practice often result, with more punitive practices characterizing counties with a high proportion of blacks. A study in Virginia, for example, found that there was "preferential treatment of residents of predominantly white, rural counties (i.e., the proportions of the poor on the rolls were higher and they were given more money) in comparison with predominantly Negro, rural counties" (Schorr and Wagner, 51).

persons. I do not know of any white person on relief that has been sent to the fields at any time. I have reports from a member of my church who was a reliefer that when her grandson went to work in the field on advice from the Department of Relief, her check was reduced. On rainy days there was no supplement to make up for that amount of money that was lost because of bad weather.

Committee Member: I want to ask you another question. One of the reasons that people do not complain [about discrimination in getting jobs], you say, is because they fear reprisals from the department that handles their relief checks.

Reverend Cobb: Right.

Committee Member: Evidently there seems to be a general consensus that this department is indulging in intimidation against those relief recipients if they complain about discrimination in private industry. Would you say that there is, because of this kind of intimidation, would you say that there is an actual conspiracy?

Reverend Cobb: It appears that there is some type of organization between various agencies, and this is what people are afraid of.

Committee Member: You mean agencies and private industry?

Reverend Cobb: Various agencies of relief and possibly political machines.

Committee Member: Did I understand you to say that people on relief are ordered to work in the cotton fields?

Reverend Cobb: They have been in the past ordered to work in cotton fields and corn fields and any other farm work.

Committee Member: And is there certain wages that must be paid to these people when they are ordered to work? Is there a standard wage that must be paid to these people when they work that the department sets?

Reverend Cobb: No. They work for 50 cents an hour.

Committee Member: They work for 50 cents an hour?

Reverend Cobb: Fifty cents an hour.

Committee Member: Did I also understand you to say that only the Negroes on public aid are ordered to work in the fields?

Reverend Cobb: I know of no white person, my statement was that I know of no white person that worked in the field ordered by the Department of Relief.[28]

Mr. Jones: My name is L. V. Jones from out in the county. I am married and I have nine kids. My problem is providing for my wife and kids and myself. I is on farm labor during the summer, and during the winter I am on ADC, and in May every year, May, I get a letter that my grant will be cut off because, due to full-time employment. I mean they never comes out to check to see if my employment have started, they just send the letter saying your grant will be cut off. They don't know when my employment even starts, which everyone knows this year the month of May it rained practically all the month, but still I got the same letter, the same type of letter saying that I would be cut off due to full-time employment. I think that they should see if my work really have started before they cut me off, but they don't do it. I mean they cut me off each year completely.

Now I don't make, sometimes I don't make $20 a month, but they don't care. They don't ask you is that enough or nothing. When work is opened up I am supposed to go to work regardless whether I can get a job or not.[29]

---

[28] U.S. Commission on Civil Rights, 1966, 25–30 (abridged).

[29] *Ibid.*, 108–144 (abridged).

It remains now to note how the "principle of settlement" buttresses the economic functions served by the principles of "local responsibility" and "less eligibility." Residence laws—the contemporary term for traditional "settlement" rules—typically result in denial of aid to those who have not lived in the state for at least one year. This cements the relationship between a regional welfare system and a regional economy; the poor are clamped between the pincers of local wages and local welfare restrictions, for if they move elsewhere they may not find jobs, nor will they be eligible for public assistance. Migrant farm workers have been especially vulnerable to exploitation as a result of residence laws, since they were disqualified from public assistance in almost all states simply by virtue of their migratory occupation, and therefore had no choice but to accept the wages and living conditions dictated by farmers in each locale.[30] In this and other ways, then, the statutory

---

[30] Residence requirements for relief recipients were recently struck down by the Supreme Court. This and other recent changes, as we will note in subsequent chapters, suggest that welfare regionalism may be diminishing, partly because the economic interests that support it are less powerful than they once were. Today, local and regional economic interests are being overshadowed by the growth of national corporations which do not depend on unskilled low-wage labor since they have substantial ability to control prices and to assure profits whatever their labor costs. To these corporate interests, residence requirements and other exclusionary features of the welfare system have become largely a matter of indifference, and have recently even become a source of trouble, for Southern welfare restrictions have helped to force the Southern black poor to migrate, contributing to mounting disorders in the cities. Concern with the resulting "urban crisis" has led some corporate leaders to repudiate Southern welfare practices and to advocate a federally imposed national minimum payment intended to retard migration.

Residence restrictions have also come under attack by economic interests at other times in history. On occasions when labor becomes scarce in some sector of a national economy, for example, such restrictions may be seen as a hindrance to labor mobility. Thus a relaxation of residence requirements took place at the height of the industrial revolution in England, when William Pitt declared in the House of Commons that "the law of settlement prevents the workman from going to that market where he could dispose of his industry to the greatest advantage, and the capitalist from employing a person who is qualified to procure him the best returns for his advance." The Act of 1795 which followed prevented the local structure of the relief system—whether statutes peculiar to some states or those common to most—helps to maintain a low-wage labor pool.

REFERENCES

Bell, Winifred, *Aid to Dependent Children*. New York, Columbia University Press, 1965.

Brown, Josephine Chapin, *Public Relief 1929–1939*. New York, Henry Holt & Company, 1940.

Bruno, Frank J., *Trends in Social Work as Reflected in the Proceedings of the National Conference of Social Work 1874–1946*. New York, Columbia University Press, 1948.

Burgess, M. Elaine, and Price, Daniel O., *An American Dependency Challenge*. A Study made by the Institute for Research in Social Science of the University of North Carolina for the American Public Welfare Association. Chicago, The Association, 1963.

Chilton, Roland A., *Consequences of a State Suitable Home Law for ADC Families in Florida*. Tallahassee, Florida State University (Institute for Social Research), 1968.

Cloward, Richard A., and Piven, Frances Fox, "Mississippi: Starving by the Rule Book," *Nation*, 1967, 204, 429–431.

Dunbar, Anthony, *The Will to Survive: A Study of a Mississippi Plantation Community Based on the Words of its Citizens*. Atlanta, Ga., Southern Regional Council and Mississippi Council on Human Relations, 1969.

Mantoux, Paul, *The Industrial Revolution in the Eighteenth Century: An Outline of the Beginnings of the Modern Factory System in England*. New York, Harper & Row, 1962.

Myrdal, Gunnar, *An American Dilemma: The Negro Problem and Modern Democracy*. New York, Harper & Row, 1944.

Public Affairs Research Council, *PAR Report on Welfare No. 4*. Baton Rouge, La., The Council, 1954.

Schorr, Alvin L., "Problems in the ADC Program," *Social Work*, April 1960, 5, 3–15.

---

parishes from expelling strangers who *might* become a burden on the parish, as had been their practice, and thus partially removed what had become a formidable obstacle to the mobility of labor (Mantoux, 434).

Schorr, Alvin L., and Wagner, Carl, "Cash and Food Programs in Virginia." A Study for the Select Committee on Nutrition and Human Needs of the U.S. Senate, Washington, 1969 (mimeographed).

Steiner, Gilbert Y., *Social Insecurity: The Politics of Welfare.* Chicago, Rand McNally & Company, 1966.

U.S. Commission on Civil Rights, *Gary Midtown West Families on AFDC.* Testimony of the Indiana State Advisory Committee, December 1966. Washington, The Commission, 1967.

U.S. Commission on Civil Rights. Unpublished testimony by the Illinois State Advisory Committee on Civil Rights, during a hearing at Cairo, Illinois, June 10, 1966. The transcript is available at the Commission's offices in Washington, D.C.

U.S. Commission on Civil Rights, *Staff Report on Public Assistance in Alabama.* Washington, The Commission, n.d.

U.S. Department of Health, Education, and Welfare, *Study of Recipients of Aid to Families with Dependent Children, November–December 1961: National Cross Tabulations.* Washington, The Department, 1965.

U.S. Manpower Administration, *Barriers to Employment of the Disadvantaged.* 1968 manpower report of the President, including a report on manpower requirements, resources, utilization, and training by the United States Department of Labor, transmitted to the Congress April 1968. Washington, U.S. Government Printing Office, 1968. (Also issued as House Doc. 302, 90th Congress, 2nd Session.)

CHAPTER FIVE

Enforcing Low-Wage Work:
Administrative Methods

Relief practice is always more restrictive than relief law. If most of the poor are disqualified for assistance by statute, still others are barred as a result of agency procedures that constitute secondary barriers, fending off many of those who manage to slip through the more formal network of restrictive statutes. Administrative obstacles thus reinforce legal exclusions in ensuring that those who are or might be workers do not get aid.

Harsh relief practices serve to enforce work in another way as well. Some few of the very young, the old, or the disabled are allowed on the rolls even during periods of political stability. But once there, they are systematically punished and degraded, made into object lessons for other poor people to observe and shun, their own station raised by contrast. None of this happens because relief administrators are an especially hard-bitten lot, but rather because of the pressures that play on them and their agencies. The exigencies of their political environment force relief officials to design procedures that serve the economic ends of groups outside of the relief system.

A public agency will cater to a clientele that has some

political force, for that clientele can become a supporting (or threatening) constituency. The social security agencies which provide benefits for the families of retired workers, for example, can count on the support of organized labor. But the public agency whose clientele has no political force has to look elsewhere for a supporting constituency. So it is with relief agencies, or any of the "poor-serving agencies" for that matter, for their clientele lack conventional political influence. If relief agencies were to distribute benefits liberally, their poor beneficiaries could ordinarily afford them little defense against attack by outside groups. Meanwhile, the large farmers and factory owners who need cheap labor do have influence, and so it is they whom relief administrators must appease.

Moreover, it is not only employers whom relief administrators have to fear. The great majority of Americans, although they have no direct economic stake in the relief system, despise it. The relief agency is their whipping boy; it marks and makes visible the dependent poor, and it is made to take the blame for the existence of these poor. Thus relief agencies are regularly attacked for maladministration—that is, for indulging chiselers and malingerers.

These political perils are the immediate cause of harsh relief practices. To fend off public attack, relief administrators design policies and procedures which prevent many of the very poor who apparently qualify from getting on the rolls; they also prevent those who do get aid from obtaining all of the benefits to which they might be entitled; and they punish and degrade recipients as befits their socially defined station.

What has to be understood, however, is that the loathing of "reliefers" is not an accidental feature of American culture. It has deep roots in the two main tenets of market ideology: the economic system is open, and economic success is a matter of individual merit (and sometimes luck); those who fail—the very poor—are therefore morally or personally defective. Each belief reinforces the other. The fervor with which these beliefs are held is a mark of the highly developed capitalistic society in which the mass of workers are "self-motivated" to perform the work required of them by economic enterprise. In earlier stages of capital-istic development, these values were not widely inculcated, so that outright governmental coercion—including a penal-istic relief system that could indenture paupers—was re-quired to ensure the necessary labor resources. With the in-creasingly widespread diffusion and acceptance of mar-ket values by workers, the penalistic features of relief arrangements softened; what has always remained, how-ever, is the ritual degradation of a pariah class that serves to mark the boundary between the appropriately moti-vated and the inappropriately motivated, between the virtuous and the defective. The point is, then, that relief practices are not a mere reflection of market ideology; they are an agent in nurturing and reinforcing that ideology.

Keeping People Off the Rolls

Nothing so arouses public hostility toward relief agencies as increasing expenditures or signs of a growing class of "dependents." Indeed, the solution frequently proposed at such times is simply to abolish relief. Thus the Royal Com-mission of 1834 proposed to deal with the swollen English relief rolls by doing away with outdoor relief for the able-bodied and removing the administration of the workhouses from parish authorities. Toward the end of the nineteenth century in this country, when it became apparent that the welfare load had been left a little larger by each depression, officials in public and private charities took the view that the growing relief load was a sign that a too-liberal dole was encouraging pauperism. The solution widely adopted in the 1880's was to abolish public programs of outdoor relief, and that is precisely what was done in Philadelphia, Baltimore, St. Louis, Washington, D.C., Brooklyn, and, in 1898, New York City. Subsequently, philanthropists pointed to the fact that, in Brooklyn at least, the load on private charity had not increased as a consequence of the withdrawal of outdoor relief. The presumption was thereby confirmed that maladministration had somehow been to blame for the growing relief rolls.

Some eighty-odd years later, during a comparable period of rising rolls, attacks on relief agencies were mounted across the nation. One of the most notorious was Senator Byrd's (D-W. Va.) spectacular investigation of the District of Columbia welfare department in the early 1960's. As a consequence of his continued exposés, the welfare department "ran scared"—approval of new applications dropped from 39 to 28 per cent within a year, and terminations rose from 25 per cent in 1961 to 46 per cent in 1962, and then up to 53 per cent in 1963—allowing the Senator to proclaim on the floor of the Congress that because of his effort, the welfare department had reduced the welfare load by almost half. This reduction, he was at great pains to point out, did not reflect punitiveness toward the poor; rather, he contended, the rolls had been allowed to rise because of administrative laxity, a circumstance corrected because of his investigation.[1]

Always apprehensive about the possibility of such attacks, welfare officials resort to a variety of practices with the intent of warding off requests for aid. Welfare departments never conduct public information campaigns about the availability of legal benefits, for if people are ignorant of entitlements, many will not apply, and many of those who do can be arbitrarily brushed aside as ineligible. Several studies demonstrate that this is so: a survey of unwed mothers conducted by the Community Council of Greater New York in 1965 found that many who were in extreme

---

[1] Bell, 1968, 60–67.

financial straits had not applied for assistance either because they believed they would be found ineligible, or because they believed they would be given so little that it would not be worth the harassments of the application process, or because they had had previous humiliating experiences with the welfare department.[2] Another survey in 1965 uncovered pervasive ignorance in a large sample of low-income families in Detroit: of those families found to be in severe need but not on the rolls (i.e., 43 per cent in the sample studied), *half* did not know that financial assistance could be available; an additional 14 per cent thought that they would probably be ineligible; 13 per cent had actually been denied assistance; and another 8 per cent were afraid or ashamed to apply.[3]

It is not reasonable to attribute ignorance of a matter so critical to survival simply to lack of education among the poor. Government agencies have ways of explaining themselves to their constituencies when called upon to do so; but they can also choose to cloak themselves in secrecy. The Social Security Administration, for example, works vigorously to inform a broad public of entitlements to old-age payments, advertising on radio and in newspapers, and deploring the fact that some benefits go unclaimed. Similarly, a massive publicity campaign—financed from anti-poverty funds—was conducted several years ago to inform the aged of their rights under Medicare. By contrast, potential welfare recipients are never sought out; rather, they are fended off. Welfare statutes, for example, are elaborated into voluminous procedural manuals, often so complicated that they are not quite comprehensible even to those who administer them. In any case, these manuals are not released to clients, were any sufficiently skilled and assiduous to decipher them, even though, by law, the manuals are public docu-

---

[2] Sauber and Rubinstein, 108–110.
[3] Greenleigh Associates, 1965, 38–39.

ments. As a result, the poor do not know the regulations, and welfare officials are not disposed to do much instructing.[4]

A recent report on public welfare practices in six cities (Atlanta, Cleveland, Los Angeles, Minneapolis, New Orleans, and Philadelphia) pointed out that, in one city, receptionists were told by their superiors to ascertain whether an emergency need for money existed by "concluding the initial contact with the question, 'Do you have any questions?' or 'Is there anything you want to ask?' Only if the applicant speaks out of his need is he referred to a caseworker [for an immediate emergency grant of money]. No inquiry is made of his need." [5] This simple instruction obviously made it easier to avoid granting emergency funds.

Anyone who penetrates the information barrier must then survive a series of admission procedures that can best be understood as a bureaucratic design in deterrence. One device is the intimidation of applicants, accomplished in part by hostile and mistrustful treatment which leads people either to avoid asking for aid or to withdraw requests once made. A study of practices in various Virginia counties illustrates this process. In that state, there are two types of applications—signed and unsigned.

Unsigned applications are not a policy but an administrative device by which county agencies escape such audits [the state may conduct] . . . of their policies. . . . State regulations distinguish between regular applications and inquiries in these terms: "Any person requesting aid shall be considered as making an application even though he

---

[4] When antipoverty agencies in Baltimore found that many eligible families had not been receiving welfare aid and began to help them get it, the rolls rose dramatically. Queried about this by the press, the director of the Maryland Board of Social Welfare said that the rise "represented quite a dramatic increase" and that it was "possibly true" that a large number of people need relief but are not getting it. He went on to note, however, that "we would be bitterly criticized if we went out canvassing, so I don't think we ought to be in that position" (*Baltimore Afro-American*, p. 1).

[5] U.S. Welfare Administration, 32.

is obviously ineligible and withdraws his application during the initial interview. . . . An application is distinguished from any inquiry by the intent of the person making the request to receive assistance rather than information." (State Regulations. Volume II. Section 207.1)

The file called unsigned applications in Buckingham County contains information about numbers of people who at least came in wishing to apply. A woman with two young children, who is separated from her husband, asks about ADC. No application is taken, but she is advised to try to get back a job she had and to file against her husband for support. She says she will return and does not—an unsigned application.

In the Franklin County study, 13 unsigned applications were reviewed; the reviewer concluded that three of the people involved would have wanted to apply and were certainly eligible. The first case recorded in the follow-up study a year later is a man who withdrew his application. He explained: "She didn't come plumb out with it but made it plain they wouldn't help me. [So I] told her to drop it to save her from worrying about it and making so many trips to see me. And I was so mad at them." It is probably superfluous to add that the Welfare Rights Organization in Buckingham and the citizens' group in Franklin County, as well as similar groups elsewhere, complain *that more people are turned away informally than are formally denied assistance.* [Emphasis added.] [6]

A more intimate picture of intimidation and deterrence is available from the notes of a field worker who, for several months in 1966, observed the workings of the Lower Manhattan Welfare Center, one of three dozen or so district welfare offices in New York City.[7] An applicant for public assistance entered the Center past a uniformed guard to address a clerk seated at a desk, where she was given her

---

[6] Schorr and Wagner, 19–20.

[7] The observer was Richard M. Elman, who was employed at the time by the Research Division of Mobilization For Youth, the first antipoverty agency. Some of his observations were subsequently published in his book, *The Poorhouse State*. In this chapter, all references to the Lower Manhattan Center are based on his field notes.

first brief interview. The ostensible purpose of this "softening-up" interview was, as one case investigator described it, to determine whether the person had come to the right office for the right type of assistance. But workers seemed to consider it their duty to shake the applicant's credibility, for the interview consisted of challenging the applicant to produce proof that she did not have an actual or potential source of income.

Unemployed men rarely got further than this desk, especially if they were single, despite the fact that they might have been eligible for "home relief." Instead, it was accepted practice for the initial interviewer to deal with such men as bums, dispatching them to the Municipal Shelter with a voucher for a meal and a night's lodging.

Those who got past the interviewing clerk were assigned a number and allowed to pass around the clerk's desk into a "bull pen" surrounded on all sides by the glass-walled cubicles of the "intake" investigators. The "bull pen" looked like the waiting rooms of many public hospitals and unemployment offices: rows of folding chairs packed together, harsh lights, dingy walls. An investigator paraded down the aisles between the squares, barking out numbers. When an applicant's number was finally called, she went behind a partition to talk with an intake investigator.

The major premise of all welfare interviewing is that "mere unsubstantiated assertions of need" are never sufficient to establish eligibility. Accordingly, the worker proceeded to elicit the prospective client's history a second time in more exhaustive detail: *When was the last time you worked? Where? Who was your employer? How much did you earn? Why did you leave? Do you belong to a union? Do you have any bank accounts? How are you living at present? Do you own a car? A TV set? Is there insurance? Are there relatives? Where did you get that gold watchband?*

Applicants were not permitted to certify to their pauper status but had to prove it repeatedly by completing elaborate forms, by providing such documentation as birth and marriage certificates, records of prior residences, and places of prior employment. Afterwards there were long waiting periods during which, presumably, further investigations were going forward, including the questioning of neighbors and relatives. The New York City welfare manual in use in 1966 counseled the investigator to try to make contact not only with the applicant's legally responsible relatives (such as a husband), but with other relatives as well (brothers, aunts), for it was sometimes possible to harass or shame the latter relatives into accepting financial responsibilities for which they were not legally obligated.

The HEW study cited earlier reported cumbersome intake procedures in the six cities studied, aggravated by staff shortages and high staff turnover. Intake appointments were being "scheduled for from 3 days to 4 to 6 weeks ahead." The department in one city was so far behind that half of all applicants whose eligibility was established did not receive checks for over 60 days. In two cities, intake was closed during the day when interviewers' schedules were filled. People coming in after that time were told to return the next day for appointments. Several cities had generated "lists of things the applicant needs to accumulate as records to verify eligibility" (e.g., marriage and birth certificates, rent receipts, records of prior places of employment and earnings).[8] The report modestly concluded that applicants in some cities were being required "to assume too much responsibility for substantiating their eligibility." [9]

Out of frustration, fear, or discouragement, some applicants fall by the wayside at each point in this bureaucratic obstacle course. A typical case is that of Mr. B, a forty-year-old Puerto Rican who was living with his wife and baby in a tiny three-room walkup. Since coming to New York in 1948, Mr. B had been steadily employed, but

[8] U.S. Welfare Administration, 2–5.
[9] *Ibid.,* 4.

he had never been able to earn more than the minimum wage. When laid off by his employer, Mr. B thought that it would be for only a few weeks, so he did not immediately apply for unemployment payments. After two weeks, he was penniless and went to the unemployment office, only to be told he would have to wait another two weeks for his first check. In the hope of obtaining emergency assistance, Mr. B then went to the Lower Manhattan Welfare Center where, after waiting all morning, he was told to come back the next day with a letter from his former boss stating that he had been laid off. He was also told to look for work. When he returned the following day with the letter, he was again urged to look for work. When he asked what he should do meanwhile to pay his bills, he was asked: "Didn't you save anything at all?" Mr. B did not return.

Whether those who persist finally receive aid depends upon the moral arithmetic of the investigator who has the task of subtracting those who are deserving from those who are not. Many of the applicants who meet all eligibility requirements are arbitrarily turned down. (To justify such decisions, the New York City welfare manual moralized that the withholding of assistance is often as important as the giving of assistance, for dependency is unwholesome and should be discouraged.) For example, until the mid-1960's half of the applications for relief made in Philadelphia were rejected, and welfare rights lawyers estimated that half of the rejections had not been justified under existing statutes. Earlier, in 1962, the Moreland Commission on Welfare—a New York State legislative commission—drew a similar although very cautiously worded conclusion when surveying the grounds for rejections in New York City, noting that in those cases in which reasons had not been verified, "there is some evidence that closings are arbitrary." [10] The Commission observed that families without income were denied assistance for such vague reasons as "other" or

[10] Greenleigh Associates, 1962, 57.

"failure to comply" with departmental regulations. Its view of these findings is suggested by this concluding comment: "Either the reasons for denial are unreasonable or contrary to policy, or there is carelessness or inaccuracy in recording reasons. . . ." [11] Even the *official* reports required by HEW from state-operated "quality control" programs reveal much larger errors in the direction of keeping eligible people off the rolls than in permitting ineligible people on the rolls. A recent independent study of several counties in Virginia provides a case in point: "In the year ending March 31, 1969, 7.3 per cent of ADC cases receiving assistance . . . showed errors, they should have been found ineligible. Of those denied ADC, 13 per cent were actually eligible and should have received assistance. . . ." [12]

Those who are lucky enough to get on the rolls may find themselves cut off at any time, even though they are without the income to maintain themselves. Arbitrary terminations are numerous and go far toward keeping the rolls down. [13] The New York City Community Council reports, for example, that in a sample of impoverished female-headed families, only 12 per cent had received assistance continuously for eighteen months following childbirth, and 56 per cent had had their cases closed at least once during that period, although many experienced persisting financial need. [14]

A similar pattern of arbitrary closings has been revealed in nationwide studies. The national study of terminations conducted in 1961 showed that 34 per cent of the closed cases were still in need of income by welfare standards, and

---

[11] *Ibid.*, 58.

[12] Schorr and Wagner, 11–12. In general, Schorr and Wagner show that "quality control" reporting systems fail to protect the interests of actual or potential recipients.

[13] For the nation, in 1961, it was found that 17 per cent of all AFDC cases had been on the rolls less than six months, 15 per cent for six months but less than one year, and another 17 per cent for a year but less than two years. Terminations, in other words, are very frequent (Mugge).

[14] Sauber and Rubinstein, 102–104. In addition, 10 per cent of the sample had applied for public assistance and had been turned down.

12 per cent of all cases (8 per cent of whites and 21 per cent of blacks) had been closed for what were noted in agency records as "other reasons." Upon examination, the most important of these "other reasons" turned out to be "unsuitable home" (39 per cent). Blacks closed out under "other reasons" were especially vulnerable to termination on "unsuitable home" grounds (44 per cent compared to 24 per cent for whites).[15]

Some terminations are the result of administrative errors in a system burdened by fantastic paperwork and haphazard procedures. Other cases are closed as a means of disciplining obstreperous families, for when these families ask to have the matter reopened, as they usually must, they are likely to be more compliant. Some cases are closed because the investigator has noticed a new couch or other items of furniture and suspects that the family is fraudulently concealing a source of extra income. Even if the explanation is satisfactory (such as having saved money out of the food budget), a termination may still result. Three Forsyth County families recently sued the North Carolina Department of Social Services for cutting them off the rolls because they owned color TV sets. One family had won its set in a grocery store contest; another had been left its set by a relative at death so that no possible question of undeclared income could be raised.[16]

To support its contention that "observations in the offices and evaluation of the handling of clients . . . reveal an attitude of annoyance and disregard of the human factors, and in many cases almost an 'adversary' rather than a 'helping' relationship," [17] the Moreland Commission cited the following examples from its study of a sample of terminations throughout New York State:

In one case the reason for closing was "refused to comply." According to the former recipient, the welfare de-

---

[15] Burgess and Price, 55 (Table 3.8) and 163.
[16] *New York Times*, January 11, 1970, 57.
[17] Greenleigh Associates, 1962, 45.

partment and the hospital had recommended that he enter the hospital for treatment of tuberculosis. When he refused to go to the hospital, the case was abruptly and arbitrarily closed. In another case with the same reason, the record reported that the client failed to keep an appointment with the caseworker. A later notation, however, records that the appointment was not kept because of serious illness: tuberculosis and emphysema. In another instance in which the reason given was "other," an OAA case was closed because a son who was a recipient in another category failed to keep a medical appointment.

In another case, "secured employment" was given as the reason for stopping assistance. The client earned $30 a week for himself and his family, much less than the relief budget. At the time the case was closed the recipient, who is Puerto Rican, was told that he could never receive public assistance again until he repaid the last check he received from the department. Even though the income is below the budget and supplementation is necessary, the client fears to return to the department.[18]

Interviews with clients and caseworkers at the Lower Manhattan Center in August 1964 turned up such examples as:

Mrs. T, a black woman with four children, lived in a Stanton Street tenement on her semimonthly AFDC payments of $105.70. One day her oldest child missed school. When the school social worker visited her, she said that she smelled whiskey on Mrs. T's breath and concluded that she must be neglecting her children. The Departmant on Welfare was notified and told Mrs. T that two of her children would have to be placed in a home if she expected to continue to receive benefits. When Mrs. T refused to allow representatives of Welfare to inspect her home without notice and interview her children, her case was closed.

Mr. G, a single man on Home Relief, received a letter telling him to report to Welfare the following morning to discuss his housing accommodation. When he arrived an hour late, he was severely chastised by his worker. Mr. G answered back and was then disqualified from further benefits for "obnoxious behavior."

---

[18] *Ibid.*, 57 (slightly abridged).

Several years ago, we conducted studies in a number of large Northern cities which showed that for every person on the AFDC rolls, there was another who was apparently eligible but not receiving assistance. Studies by others subsequently confirmed our initial findings.[19] Part of this pool was composed of people who erroneously believed themselves to be ineligible or who found relief abhorrent or fearsome and therefore did not apply for it. But part of it was composed of people who had applied and been capriciously rejected, or who had been capriciously terminated—mute testimony to the effectiveness of the administrative practices just described.

These practices are not merely the consequence of carelessness or inaccuracies inherent in a cumbersome bureaucracy. Rather, secrecy, intimidation, and red tape are adaptive patterns designed to inhibit completion of the application process and facilitate arbitrary rejections and terminations. Agency procedures are designed to make it easy and safe to reject or terminate cases but complicated and risky to accept them. The Moreland Commission noted, for example, that full factual evidence necessary to establish eligibility was collected in 97.4 per cent of the accepted cases, but in only 39 per cent of the cases which were denied assistance.

That full factual evidence must be gathered in order to accept clients, but not to reject them, is a matter of bureaucratic design. This is illustrated by an internal memorandum prepared by the New York City Bureau of the Budget in 1968, apparently at the request of Mayor Lindsay. It set out various options open to the mayor for economizing on welfare costs, among them extending waiting periods in order to create a backlog that would weary people and consolidating neighborhood welfare centers into a smaller number of district offices in order to make it more difficult for people to get to them and thereby to discourage ap-

---

[19] These studies will be discussed in Chapter 7.

plicants.[20] There is good reason to believe that long waiting periods and other such encumbrances do just that. A recent survey of eleven cities by HEW found that when people have to wait a long time for notification of eligibility, they are more likely to feel powerless; feelings of powerlessness, in turn, are apparently related to lower percentages of the poor on the rolls.[21]

Underbudgeting Recipients

Keeping people off the rolls is the main method by which relief administrations keep costs down and ward off public attack. Although it is less important, there is another adaptation that deserves mention—underbudgeting, or giving people less than they are entitled to.

One type of underbudgeting results because payments are often calculated on the basis of the ages of children, with older children being allowed more. Consequently, the family's budget is supposed to be increased annually—a process that, not surprisingly, often fails to happen, leaving thousands of families to live on smaller budgets than the regulations prescribe.

The administration of non-support payments provides

---

[20] Budget Bureau Recommendations for Savings in the Welfare Budget, March 24, 1969. In the language of the report: "To realize savings from administrative changes, the present administrative system must become more selective in offering welfare as a right. The administrative changes we propose are: . . . a new intake procedure which would send all TADC, unemployed HR and ADC (with no children below school age) to . . . an employment agency . . . before the intake interview . . . ; this proposal would attempt to . . . keep more welfare eligibles employed longer even at low levels . . . and would also hopefully have a deterrent effect on the rate of applications . . . ; the elimination of the seven outreach centers and at least seven of the regular welfare centers through consolidation . . . in order to . . . build up and maintain the maximum legal backlog between intake and final determination of eligibility." The actual consolidation of centers began in the fall of 1970.

[21] New York State Department of Social Services, 45–47.

another example. Women whose husbands have deserted them are commonly required by welfare departments to sue for non-support. Once a court has determined what amount the husband shall contribute, the assumption is often made that the wife will in fact collect the support payments from her husband, and that amount is then deducted in advance from the grant to the mother and child. As it happens, however, these contributions from husbands are frequently not made. Welfare regulations may take account of that eventuality by permitting the wife to make special application to the welfare department for an equivalent amount. Usually this must be done twice each month, and it may then take several months to process the forms and issue each supplementary check. What tends to happen in time, of course, is that many women fail to make these applications partly because of the red tape and partly because they are disparaged each week by welfare officers for not having persuaded their husbands to make the payments.

Many state regulations specify that "special grants" should be given to cover special expenses (e.g., to replace worn-out household furnishings or winter clothing). Until recently, for example, a recipient in New York State was entitled to two kinds of relief payment. The first was a semi-monthly check for food, rent, and miscellaneous items. In addition, the law prescribed that every recipient be maintained at a "minimum standard of decency" in heavy clothing and household furnishings. Thus each child was supposed to have an overcoat, hat, and galoshes, and his own bed. A family was also entitled to enough chairs so that all members could sit together to eat. "Special grants" of money to enable recipients to purchase these items were to be disbursed on an "as needed" basis. The trouble was that such grants were rarely made. A study conducted in central Harlem found that two thirds of the AFDC mothers interviewed had never been informed by their investigators of the availability of such funds.[22] In 1965, when there were more than 500,000 recipients in all federal categories in New York City, about 20 million dollars was disbursed, for an average of $40 per person. In a study we made at the time, we conservatively estimated that it would have cost an average of $100 per recipient to bring each family up to the standard prescribed by regulation. In other words, the department saved about $60 per person (or 30 million dollars) in that fiscal year alone.

Other sources reveal similar practices elsewhere. In the fall of 1968, for example, the Joint Committee on Social Welfare of the Massachusetts Legislature issued a report which, among other things, commented on the widespread ignorance among recipients regarding entitlements for furniture allowances. (The report was prompted by rapidly rising costs, especially in Boston, largely a result of successful mass protests to obtain such allowances by welfare recipients organized by the National Welfare Rights Organization in the spring and summer of that year.)

> After determination that the need for furniture exists, the recipient is given authorization to purchase the items at a store of his own choice based upon their estimate of cost. Until recently, the demand for furniture throughout the Commonwealth was moderate, without pattern and generally within bounds. The department's policy of granting furniture on the basis of need was met with general satisfaction by the recipients. *This was due in large part to the fact that the recipients were apparently unaware they were entitled to such items.* [Emphasis added.] [23]

The myriad ways in which recipients come to be denied full benefits was described in a recent study of county practices in Virginia:

---

[22] Gordon, 73–74.
[23] This report was mimeographed, untitled, undated, and unpaginated.

In the Franklin County study, 35 cases were reviewed to determine the accuracy with which payment was determined. In 23 cases, the level of payment was wrong. The errors are a catalogue of the possibilities open to local departments: The agency counted food and clothing contributed when it was not being contributed. The agency counted contributions from a relative who was not giving them. The agency counted all shelter, including utilities, as free, but the recipient was paying for utilities. The agency omitted two eligible children from the budget. The agency counted income from work after the recipient had stopped working. There were also errors in computation.[24]

Underbudgeting is not just a consequence of complex regulations, haphazard administrative procedures, and high staff turnover. The authors of a study of 766 AFDC recipients conducted during the summer and fall of 1967 in six Wisconsin counties conclude that "caseworkers tended to avoid [giving information about] areas which might lead to specific requests that would be costly to the agencies. . . . This finding parallels the findings [of an earlier] . . . study of the administration of AFDC budgets, through which it was discovered that very few clients made more than occasional requests for money grants to meet actual needs. *Either they were not advised about the availability of the grants or they were discouraged from making requests.*" [Emphasis added.] [25]

A form of underbudgeting that appears to be quite prevalent in the South consists of assigning an income value to various resources that a family presumably possesses (e.g., a "rent-free" shack on a cotton plantation), and reducing the monthly grant accordingly. If welfare statistics are to be believed, the unlikely conclusion emerges that Southern black AFDC families have more such resources than Southern white AFDC families, helping to account

---

24 Schorr and Wagner, 14.
25 Handler and Hollingsworth, 413.

for the substantially lower money payments made to blacks. A more likely explanation of such statistics, of course, is that Southern relief officials assign a higher money value to black resources than to white resources.[26]

Depriving AFDC families of full benefits exerts great pressure on mothers to stay in the marginal labor market— for example, as field hands or as domestic servants. In effect, relief agencies deduct potential earned income in advance. (And if recipients do find some work, for which they are ordinarily paid in cash and by the day, they may then try to conceal this fact from welfare officials who would otherwise typically deduct these earnings again—that is, twice.) [27] Administrative practices which lead to underbudgeting are thus similar in their work-enforcing results to a formal "employable mother" rule.

Socializing the Able-Bodied Poor by Degrading Relief Recipients

Market values and market incentives are weakest at the bottom of the social order. To buttress weak market controls and ensure the availability of marginal labor, an outcast class—the dependent poor—is created by the relief system. This class, whose members are of no productive use, is not treated with indifference, but with contempt. Its degradation at the hands of relief officials serves to celebrate the virtue of all work, and deters actual or potential workers from seeking aid.

---

[26] HEW, Tables 48a and 48b.

[27] Earned income, when reported, has traditionally been deducted from welfare payments. During the recent period of rapidly escalating welfare rolls, however, various "work incentive" schemes were proposed and inaugurated which permitted recipients to retain part of their earnings, with the rationale that in this way the recipients would be taught to become self-supporting. These schemes generally reflected the public's concern with rapidly rising welfare costs, a concern that temporarily overrode the more traditional concern with keeping recipient incomes below prevailing marginal wage levels.

It is not difficult to see why relief officials degrade their charges. The general public requires it, as evidenced by the general outrage when recipients show evidence of ingratitude or impenitence. To survive, relief agencies are therefore compelled to invent rituals of degradation and to subject their clientele to them.

A central feature of the recipient's degradation is that she must surrender commonly accepted rights in exchange for aid. AFDC mothers, for example, are often forced to answer questions about their sexual behavior ("When did you last menstruate?"), open their closets to inspection ("Whose pants are those?"), and permit their children to be interrogated ("Do any men visit your mother?"). Unannounced raids, usually after midnight and without benefit of warrant, in which a recipient's home is searched for signs of "immoral" activities, have also been part of life on AFDC. In Oakland, California, a public welfare caseworker, Bennie Parish, refused to take part in a raid in January 1962 and was dismissed for insubordination. When he sued for reinstatement, the state argued successfully in the lower courts that people taking public assistance waive certain constitutional rights, among them the right to privacy.[28] (The Court's position had at least the weight of long tradition, for the withdrawal of civil rights is an old feature of public relief. In England, for example, relief recipients were denied the franchise until 1918, and as late as 1934 the constitutions of fourteen American states deprived recipients of the right to vote or hold office.) [29]

That recipients are denied commonly accepted rights was dramatically illustrated by a recent district court ruling in Washington, D.C., in the matter of a group of AFDC

---

[28] But upon appeal, Parish won, and HEW has since ordered the states to desist from post-midnight raids.

[29] Delaware, Maine, Massachusetts, New Hampshire, New Jersey, Rhode Island, South Carolina, Texas, Virginia, and West Virginia, plus Louisiana, Missouri, Oklahoma, and Pennsylvania. In these last four states the loss of the franchise applied only to inmates of poorhouses or other charitable institutions (Heisterman and Keener, 43).

mothers who took the rare step of suing the welfare department for declaratory and injunctive relief against unreasonable searches, harassing surveillance, eavesdropping,
and interrogation concerning their sexual activities. The
court not only ruled against the mothers, but rendered the
opinion that welfare benefits are a gratuity; which of the
eligibles are actually to receive benefits is, the court held,
within the absolute discretion of administrative functionaries who may impose such requirements as they deem appropriate. During oral argument, the judge commented
that "any recipient has a perfect right to slam the door in
the face of the investigator. Of course, he runs the risk then
of being cut off the rolls."

Armed with this authority, relief administrators may
subject recipients to close and continuous surveillance.
Upon appeal, a three-judge federal panel ordered the case
noted above to be aired in full by a "fair hearing" under
the auspices of the welfare department. During the course
of that administrative hearing, the following testimony regarding surveillance procedures was elicited from an investigator who had formerly been employed by the welfare
department:

Q. How often were you refused admission to a recipient's
home?
A. Very, very seldom. Less than 1 per cent.
Q. After identifying yourself and requesting permission
to inspect the recipient's home, did you ever say that
he or she had the right to refuse entry?
A. Never.
Q. Why not?
A. It was always my understanding that they had to open
up their premises to inspection if they wanted welfare.
Q. What did you do then?
A. My partner and I then went through the house as fast
as possible. [Investigators always work in pairs.]
Q. How long did that usually take?
A. Five to seven minutes.
Q. Why did you hurry so?
A. The object was to go as far as you could before the

client objected. Usually we'd split up. One of us would keep the client busy talking and the other would move quickly through the rooms and closets.

Q. What if the client objected?

A. Then we'd leave. That's why we moved fast.

Q. Were there any other techniques you used?

A. Yes, we sometimes split up before entering a house, one of us going to the front door and the other to the back.

Q. Why was that?

A. If there was a man in the house, he'd leave by any means available—windows, fire escape, or out the back door.[30]

The threat of withdrawing benefits has been used by relief agencies to curb participation by recipients in public activities that might provoke the ire of powerful groups; thus clients are sometimes threatened if they participate in civil rights protests, if they lodge complaints regarding discrimination in housing or employment or education, or even if they fail to vote in ways that protect the agency. Caseworkers have been publicly charged in at least one formal hearing with distributing pre-marked ballots to recipients.[31] During the course of this particular hearing, convened in 1966 by the Civil Rights Commission in Cairo, Illinois, the fear of reprisals expressed by witnesses testifying to such abuses was so evident that a Commission member was moved to interrupt the proceedings as follows:

What I am about to say will not set well with possibly some officials in the various agencies and departments in the counties concerned at this hearing. I want to say this because I want to give some reassurance to these

---

[30] "Consent or Starve," 13.

[31] For a summary of these allegations, see U.S. Commission on Civil Rights, Appendix I. For another source of information on use of welfare benefits to curb protest, see Dunbar, 44. Dunbar reports allegations that in Mississippi "Welfare checks were cut off in the early 1960's as a means of stopping black people from registering to vote" as well as from participating in OEO programs that gave poor blacks some independence from the plantation owners.

people who have very courageously come out and testified at these hearings. This is the Advisory Committee
of the State of Illinois to the United States Civil Rights
Commission. It is the function of this Committee to
gather information for this Commission which will be
submitted to the President of the United States and to
the Congress of the United States. Any intimidation, any
reprisals against persons on welfare or against persons
who are in public housing is in direct violation of the
laws of the United States and any person so involved in
intimidation or reprisals will be subject to prosecution.[32]

Periodically the rituals of degradation are set forth for
public display through legislative investigations and newspaper exposés in which recipients are branded as sexually
immoral, as chiselers, and as malingerers. It is partly by
such public spectacles that popular definitions of relief are
formed. Several years ago in Newburgh, New York, city officials made wholesale accusations of illegitimacy and fraud
among recipients and proposed the not especially novel
remedy of forcing mothers into the labor market and removing illegitimate children from their "unsuitable"
homes. A similar spectacle was staged in 1962 by Senator
Byrd who forced District of Columbia welfare officials to
acquire nearly as many "fraud investigators" as "social investigators." The fraud investigators quickly put hundreds
of AFDC mothers under "parked car" surveillance and
"proved" a year later that close to 60 per cent were "ineligible" for benefits, chiefly because they appeared to have
contact with men. These allegations of immorality were, of
course, widely publicized.

Mass campaigns to purge the rolls of illegitimate children
also publicly define and degrade welfare recipients. And so,
in a more genteel and thoughtful manner, do the editorial
musings about illegitimacy and "the AFDC problem" by
such a newspaper as *The New York Times*. These definitions in the mass media constitute a contemporary (al-

---

[32] U.S. Commission on Civil Rights, 117.

though more benign) equivalent of the lash and iron once used to mark the pauper in the town square.

The array of activities relief agencies carry on in the name of re-equipping recipients for jobs (or, in an older vernacular, of putting paupers to work) is also an important source of degradation. Such rehabilitation programs are heavily emphasized by relief administrators, especially when a public attack is imminent. Thus, officials in HEW, threatened by the rising AFDC rolls, announced in an April 1969 memo to state welfare administrators:

> There is no more urgent and vital task facing us today than to assist increasingly large numbers of the nation's public welfare applicants and recipients to become economically independent. We must exert every effort to at least double in fiscal 1970 the total number of public assistance rehabilitations achieved in fiscal year 1968.

Similarly, in 1967, when the New York City Department of Welfare found itself predicting a budget approaching a billion dollars, it buried these unfortunate tidings in a public announcement regarding the launching of a few new day-care centers which, presumably, would permit mothers to become workers. Since the day-care facilities to free AFDC mothers for work or work-training are very expensive,[33] officials do not seriously believe that they will be developed on any scale. They persist in emphasizing day-care and job training programs, however, in order to appease public criticism by portraying the relief agency as guarding against

---

[33] Day-care costs run between $1,500 and $1,800 per child per year in most big cities and are even greater in some places. In New York City, for example, it costs about $400,000 to construct or refurbish a facility for 100 children; annual operating costs then run from $2,200 to $2,700 per child (*New York Times*, February 8, 1970, 68). However, in the absence of day-care programs, states and localities have wide latitude in determining the adequacy of alternative child-care arrangements: "A woman [in Virginia] was found ineligible [for welfare] on the grounds that she could work; her sister would be able to take care of her children. The sister has six children and an invalid husband; the applicant would be adding five children—two of them not yet in school—to her sister's household" (Schorr and Wagner, 18).

and exorcising the moral and personal defects that are the presumed source of poverty.[34]

The rehabilitation that results is not very impressive, but that is not the point. Since relief agencies by and large refuse aid in the first place to those who are suitable for work in the prevailing market, their efforts could not reasonably be expected to result in placing many people in remunerative jobs. (According to HEW's own figures, only 20,000 recipients were "rehabilitated" in fiscal 1968 out of a national AFDC caseload of about 1.5 million families—a success rate of 1 in 75.) In any case, the costs of training and day care being what they are, the rehabilitation process consists mostly of exhortation and condemnation. And that is the point. Just as the "friendly visitors" of old lectured poor widows on the values of hard work and the disgrace of charity, so New York State recently acted to require AFDC mothers to report at two-week intervals to the State Employment Office for interviews. If such rituals are not very effective in fitting a rural-bred mother into the urban job market, they are very effective in forewarning potential applicants for relief that they will be defined as "failures"— that is, as needing rehabilitation.

Of course, recipients must accept the treatment they receive from relief officials, for they depend on public aid for their survival. One of the welfare mothers who took the lawsuit against the Washington, D.C. welfare department referred to earlier was asked by the hearing officer why, during the several years that she had been on welfare, she had always opened her door to investigators. She answered simply, "I have my five children to feed."

Recipients must not only submit to this treatment, they come to endorse its premises. For example, even on those rare occasions when groups of recipients do rise up to

---

[34] In *The Making of Blind Men,* Robert A. Scott identifies a similar pattern in the behavior of agencies for the blind which, in order to secure public support, seek out and cultivate young, educable, and employable blind people as showpieces for potential philanthropists (Scott, 119–120).

protest their treatment by relief agencies—such as the demonstrations recently organized by the National Welfare Rights Organization—the work ethos is reaffirmed even as relief restrictions are condemned. Some AFDC mothers with four or five young children who picket welfare departments for MORE MONEY NOW! also carry signs proclaiming WE WANT JOBS! Among most welfare recipients, in short, the moral imperative to work—often no matter what the work, the wage, or the child-rearing obligations of the women who presume themselves to be employable—remains deeply felt.

Or consider this sweeping indictment of relief officials from the mouth of a recipient living in an urban ghetto:

> I think the welfare department is too soft, too lenient. They don't make investigations to see how the welfare money is being spent. If the workers went to the houses more often, they would be able to tell if the people are cheating. They could go to the home any time they want to, day or night. If the person isn't guilty, then they shouldn't care when the worker comes.[35]

The study from which this quote is taken showed that a majority of recipients endorsed such practices as midnight searches and budget counseling. Finally, these "respondents almost never (and most respondents never) referred to welfare recipients as 'we' but as 'they'." [6] Having set themselves apart from and condemned those in the same boat, recipients tend to identify with their oppressors, or so the results of another study (which showed that caseworkers failed to inform recipients of their entitlement to special grants) appear to suggest:

> Is the caseworker someone the respondents like, trust, talk to, and discuss problems with? Practically 80 per cent

---

[35] Briar, 46.
[36] *Ibid.*, 51.

> [of 766 recipients in six Wisconsin counties] expressed positive feelings toward their caseworkers. . . . High proportions of respondents said that they make a "special effort to stay on good terms with their caseworkers." Do the respondents think that their caseworkers have good reasons for what they do? *An overwhelming majority think so.* [Emphasis added.] [37]

When victims are induced to collaborate as victimizers, submission is assured. The most striking evidence is the almost total lack of appeals by welfare recipients. The Social Security Act requires that the states establish an appeals procedure (called "fair hearings") for recipients or applicants who believe they have been wronged. To secure a hearing, one fills out a form and forwards it to the state welfare department. A hearing officer is then appointed by the state and a hearing date is presumably to be set within sixty days.

Nationwide, there are ample grounds for appeals—grounds ranging from the deprivation of civil liberties to the deprivation of monetary benefits. But appeals have in fact been very rare. In 1964, when the over-all welfare rolls stood at about 500,000 persons in New York City, *a mere fifteen appeals were taken in an entire year.* Even considering that the poor are ill-informed about such procedures and that they have no money for legal assistance, this is still striking evidence of acquiescence. Nor is the situation different elsewhere. [38]

The main target of these rituals is not the recipient who ordinarily is not of much use as a worker, but the able-bodied poor who remain in the labor market. It is for these people that the spectacle of the degraded pauper is intended. For

---

[37] Handler and Hollingsworth, 411.
[38] Briar found that the same lack of appeals was characteristic of recipients on the West Coast.

example, scandals exposing welfare "fraud" have diffuse effects, for they reach a wide public—including the people who might otherwise apply for aid but who are deterred because of the invidious connotations of being on welfare. Thus, in the several years immediately before the Byrd attack in 1962, about 6,500 District of Columbia families had applied for aid annually; during the attack, the figure dropped to 4,400 and it did not rise for more than five years—long after the scandal had subsided.

The meaning which the label "reliefer" comes to have for the working poor is in no way better illustrated than by their widespread refusal to accept relief supplements to their low wages. In a number of Northern states and counties, fully employed men are eligible for supplementary payments from welfare agencies. Such programs—most of which were set up during the Depression and were then retained for residual groups that did not fall into any of the federal categories established under the Social Security Act—are paid for by the states or localities, usually under the name "general relief" or "home relief." Since relief payments under these residual programs are often scaled to family size, many large families with low earnings have incomes falling below established grant levels and are therefore entitled to supplements. In New York, for example, a minimum-wage worker with three dependents is entitled to a tax-free monthly relief payment of about $100; in Cleveland, the same worker would be entitled to about $70 monthly. And the payment increases with family size. But virtually no workers take advantage of these subsidies. During 1968 in New York City, for example, *approximately 150,000 families were eligible for wage subsidies* (according to the welfare department's own estimates), *but only about 15,000 families were claiming them.*[39]

---

[39] See the authors' "Workers and Welfare: The Poor Against Themselves," 558–562.

That few people know the welfare regulations only partly explains this peculiar situation, for even when poor families are informed of the funds available to them, they usually refuse to claim the payments. That the working poor are ready to forfeit such substantial sums is powerful testimony to the force with which the ideology of work and success, together with abhorrence of the dole, has been driven home to those who gain the least from their labor. It is especially powerful testimony considering that, while the poor shun "the dole," affluent groups profit greatly and regularly from public subsidies of many kinds.

The Constancy of Relief Doctrine

One final note. It is commonly believed that the infusion of professional values into the relief system is producing more humane practices. It is certainly true that professional doctrines are coming to supplant the older philanthropic tenets that once justified relief practices. But this amounts to a distinction without much of a difference; professional beliefs serve the same economic and political functions as philanthropic beliefs in guarding the system against claimants for aid, except that they may serve them better.

One of the most forthright discussions of the role of professionalism in the selection process is to be found in Winifred Bell's history of AFDC. In reviewing the state-supported Mothers' Aid programs which preceded AFDC, she notes that the main criterion of selection was the "suitability" of the home of the applicant, a criterion vigorously advocated and defended by the social welfare elites of the pre-Depression period. Indeed, some leaders of the social welfare profession opposed proposals for a national AFDC program precisely because of the possibility that "unsuitable" women might then obtain benefits. As to the consequence of applying "suitable home" criteria in the Mothers' Aid programs, Bell has this to say:

> The very vagueness of the "suitable home" eligibility conditions guaranteed their adaptability to local and regional mores, and, as the evidence shows, statutes rarely made any pretense of spelling out the meaning of "fit" or "proper" parents or "suitable homes." Local workers were relied upon to infuse the terms with meaning, and, in doing so, they tended to restrict the programs to nice Anglo-Saxon widows and to move separately but in concert to protect their young programs from Negro and unmarried mothers who might well attract criticism.[40]

If one imagines that the spread of professionalism has altered the course of relief practices since the days of Mothers' Aid, the results of a recent survey are sobering. Eleven cities were studied by HEW to discern the factors underlying recent caseload increases. Among other things, HEW found a negative relationship between professionalism and relief loads. The more professionally oriented the welfare staff, the lower the proportion of the poor who got relief:

> High scores on the professional orientation scale were given to caseworkers who belonged to professional associations, read professional journals, and held or were working toward the master's degree in social work. *There was a strong inverse relation between the measure of professionalism and the AFDC poor rate.* The lower the number of caseworkers with a professional orientation to the field of social work, the larger the number of poor persons using AFDC. [Emphasis added.] [41]

All in all, the doctrines and practices of scientific social casework which now dominate the relief system are in some

---

[40] Bell, 1965, 18–19.
[41] New York State Department of Social Services, 52.

ways less harsh than the earlier doctrines and practices of religious philanthropy, but there is nevertheless a close parallel between them. Where philanthropic doctrine traced the cause of poverty to moral defects, casework doctrine traces it to psychological defects. The older philanthropic treatment consisted of a strict regimen of individual surveillance and discipline, the contention being that poverty proved the existence of moral weakness; casework prescribes modern procedures of psychosocial diagnosis, "individualization," and counseling, as if by being poor the client proves his personality weakness and his need for professional treatment. (The professional associations that now stand as guardians of public assistance lobby insistently for greatly expanded funds for family counseling, literacy training, and, of course, vocational training.) If there is a real difference between the philanthropic and professional precepts that have variously justified relief practices, it is between invidious definitions of an essentially moral rather than a psychological kind. The degradation functions served for the society, however, are very much the same.

In summary, the structure of the American public welfare system meshes with and enforces the work system, not least by excluding potential workers from aid. The "fit" of the welfare system in a stable but diverse economy is assured by varying the pattern of exclusion in accord with regional differences in labor requirements. Furthermore, harsh relief practices also maintain work norms by evoking the image of the shamed pauper for all, especially the able-bodied poor, to see and shun. And so it is that if the justification given for welfare restrictions is usually moral, the functions these restrictions serve are typically economic. Those who exploit the cheap labor guaranteed by these practices can take comfort not only in their godliness but in their profits as well.

REFERENCES

Ayres, Philip W., "Experiments in Relief in Work," in *Proceedings of the National Conference of Charities and Correction*. Boston, Press of Geo. H. Ellis, 1892.

Bell, Winifred, *Aid to Dependent Children*. New York, Columbia University Press, 1965.

Bell, Winifred, "The 'Rights' of the Poor: Welfare Witch-Hunts in the District of Columbia," *Social Work*, 1968, 13, 60–67.

Briar, Scott, "Welfare from Below: Recipients' Views of the Welfare System," in Jacobus ten Broek, ed., *The Law of the Poor*. San Francisco, Chandler Publishing Company, 1966.

Brown, Josephine Chapin, *Public Relief 1929–1939*. New York, Henry Holt & Company, 1940.

Burgess, M. Elaine, and Price, Daniel O., *An American Dependency Challenge*. A Study made by the Institute for Research in Social Science of the University of North Carolina for the American Public Welfare Association. Chicago, The Association, 1963.

Cloward, Richard A., and Piven, Frances Fox, "Workers and Welfare: The Poor Against Themselves," *Nation*, 1968, 207, 558–562.

"Consent or Starve," editorial, *New Republic*, October 21, 1967, 157, 12–13.

de Schweinitz, Karl, *England's Road to Social Security: From the Statute of Laborers in 1349 to the Beveridge Report of 1942*. Philadelphia, University of Pennsylvania Press, 1943.

Dunbar, Anthony, *The Will to Survive: A Study of a Mississippi Plantation Community Based on the Words of its Citizens*. Atlanta, Ga., Southern Regional Council and Mississippi Council on Human Relations, 1969.

Dunning, Richard, *A Plain and Easie Method*. 1686. (Pamphlet in Columbia University Special Collections.)

Elman, Richard M., *The Poorhouse State: The American Way of Life on Public Assistance*. New York, Pantheon Books, 1966.

Gordon, Joan, *The Poor of Harlem: Social Functioning in the Underclass: A Report to the Welfare Administration*. New York, Office of the Mayor (Interdepartmental Neighborhood Service Center), 1965. (Welfare Administration Project 105.)

Greenleigh Associates, *Factual Data: Report to the Moreland Commission*. New York, Greenleigh Associates, 1962.

Greenleigh Associates, *Study of Services to Deal with Poverty in Detroit, Michigan*. New York, Greenleigh Associates, 1965.

Handler, Joel F., and Hollingsworth, Ellen Jane, "The Administration of Social Services and the Structure of Dependency: The Views of AFDC Recipients," *Social Service Review*, 1969, 43, 406–420.

Heisterman, Carl A., and Keener, Paris F., "Further Poor Law Notes," *Social Service Review*, 1934, 8, 43–49.

Hopkins, Harry L., *Spending to Save: The Complete Story of Relief*. New York, W. W. Norton & Company, 1936.

Marshall, Dorothy, *The English Poor in the Eighteenth Century: A Study in Social and Administrative History*. London, George Routledge & Sons, 1926.

Mugge, Robert H., "Aid to Families with Dependent Children: Initial Findings of the 1961 Report on the Characteristics of AFDC Recipients," *Social Security Bulletin*, March 1963, 26, 3.

New York State Department of Social Services. *The Administration of Aid to Families with Dependent Children in New York City, November 1968–February 1969*. Report of a joint review carried out by the United States Department of Health, Education, and Welfare and the New York State Department of Social Services. Albany, New York State Department of Social Services, 1969.

New York Times, April 7, 1969, January 11 and February 8, 1970.

Sauber, Mignon, and Rubinstein, Elaine, *Experiences of the Unwed Mother as a Parent: A Longitudinal Study of Unmarried Mothers Who Keep Their First-born*. New York, Community Council of Greater New York, 1965.

Schorr, Alvin, and Wagner, Carl, "Cash and Food Programs in Virginia." A Study for the Select Committee on Nutrition and Human Needs of the U.S. Senate, Washington, 1969 (mimeographed).

Scott, Robert A., *The Making of Blind Men: A Study of Adult Socialization*. New York, Russell Sage Foundation, 1969.

U.S. Commission on Civil Rights. Unpublished testimony by the Illinois State Advisory Committee on Civil Rights during a hearing at Cairo, Illinois, June 10, 1966. The transcript is available at the Commission's offices in Washington, D.C.

U.S. Department of Health, Education, and Welfare, *Study of Recipients of Aid to Families with Dependent Children,*

November–December, 1961: National Cross Tabulations. Washington, The Department, 1965.

U.S. Welfare Administration, *Operation Big City: A Review of How the Needs of People Coming to Public Welfare Agencies Are Met in Six Metropolitan Areas.* Washington, U.S. Department of Health, Education, and Welfare (Bureau of Family Services), 1965.

Winston, Ellen C., Foreword, in *A Constructive Public Welfare Program.* Washington, U.S. Government Printing Office, 1965. (Welfare Administration Pub. No. 9.)

PART III

Relief and the Urban Crisis

CHAPTER SIX

The Welfare Explosion
of the 1960's

During the 1950's the AFDC rolls rose by only 110,000 families, or 17 per cent. But from December 1960 to February 1969, some 800,000 families were added to the rolls, an increase of 107 per cent in just eight years and two months.[1] In the course of the 1960's, then, the nation ex-

---

[1] In this book, all statistics referring to AFDC pertain to "cases" (i.e., families) rather than to individuals. There are several reasons for using data on families rather than individuals. One is that Congress amended the Social Security Act in the early 1950's, permitting the custodians or guardians of AFDC children (e.g., their mothers) to be added to the case unit and to be provided for in the welfare grant. This provision added many more individuals to the rolls but did not increase the number of families on the rolls. Much more important, we are concerned in this book with the changing interaction between the welfare system and the poor. To examine such changes, we compare for different time periods such measures as application rates and acceptance rates, and these are family rather than individual measures. It is the family that does or does not apply for aid, and the family that is accepted or rejected. For understanding this interaction, changing definitions of who is to be included in a family unit are of little consequence, nor are changes in the family size of much significance.

In this and succeeding chapters, all statements and tables regarding "the welfare explosion in the 1960's" refer to the period from December 1960 to February 1969. At some points we refer to "the rise in the early 1960's"—that is, from December 1960 to December 1964—and at other points to "the rise in the late 1960's"—that is, from December 1964 to February 1969. The periods being compared are thus roughly equal, the one being four years perienced a "welfare explosion"; for all practical purposes, traditional restrictions collapsed and the relief money poured out. As costs rose, the relief system once again became a major public issue, a source of political controversy and conflict, and thus an object of proposals for "reorganization" and "reform." The remainder of this book will deal with the economic and political sources of this relief explosion.

Some Dimensions of the Welfare Rise

The relief rise was pervasive: even the rural counties of the South showed an increase of 34 per cent (see Table 1).[2] However (and this is important), the rises in some places were much greater than in others. By region, the rolls almost tripled in the Northeast and in the West, while the

---

and the other four years and two months. In the Epilogue, which was written while the book was in page proof, we comment on the welfare rises since February 1969.

[2] All the statistics on caseload changes in this chapter are taken from Source Tables 1 and 2 in the Appendix, unless otherwise indicated. Throughout this book, we have included cases enrolled under the AFDC-UP program unless otherwise indicated. There were 78,863 such cases in February 1969, representing 10 per cent of the combined increase in AFDC and AFDC-UP in the 1960's. Given our historical perspective, we would have preferred to omit these cases from the analysis, since the AFDC-UP program was not enacted until 1961. The difficulty is that although these cases can be separated in national, regional, and state tabulations, HEW does not report them separately for counties. Since the distinction between rural and urban counties is of some importance in our analysis, we are therefore obliged to include AFDC-UP cases for all other jurisdictions in order to remain statistically consistent. The national AFDC increase in the 1960's would be diminished only 10 percentage points if AFDC-UP cases were excluded. However, an unknown part of the AFDC-UP rolls is composed of families who were transferred from AFDC rolls, or who would have been admitted to the AFDC rolls in the absence of the AFDC-UP category. It can therefore be said with confidence that AFDC-UP accounts for something less than 10 per cent of the welfare increase in the 1960's (see Source Table 3 in the Appendix); see also footnotes 38 and 40 in Chapter 10.

rolls rose by 78 per cent in the North-Central area and by 54 per cent in the South as a whole.[3]

Among urban counties, the steepest increase (217 per cent) occurred in the 5 most populous ones—New York, Philadelphia, Cook County (Chicago), Wayne County (Detroit), and Los Angeles. A smaller upsurge took place in the 116 remaining urban centers (135 per cent). The rise was larger in Northern urban centers (175 per cent) than in Southern ones (121 per cent).

The nation's rural counties—many of which, especially in the South, experienced considerable outmigration of their poor—nevertheless had a rise of 60 per cent. The Northern rural rolls almost doubled (87 per cent), and Southern rolls moved up more modestly (34 per cent).

Another way to describe these increases is to ask: How many of the 800,000 additional families on the rolls in February 1969 were located in one region or another, in urban areas or in rural ones? Table 2 shows that many families in all parts of the country got on the rolls, although there were great variations by region. The Northeast and West accounted for most of the national increase (39 per cent and 26 per cent respectively). Seventeen per cent of the increase occurred in the North Central region. Finally, the South contributed 18 per cent to the national increase; this fact deserves special note, for the Southern rolls had not changed at all during the 1950's. It also deserves note because the welfare explosion is popularly believed to be a wholly Northern phenomenon.

Urban areas as a whole accounted for the overwhelming share of the national AFDC increases (70 per cent), but it was the "big five" urban centers that experienced the most

---

[3] The significance of the Southern increase is somewhat understated by the statistics because of regional differences in the enactment of AFDC-UP. A small part of the large Northern increase is due to AFDC-UP, for most of the Northern states enacted that program. However, most Southern states did not participate in AFDC-UP. Nevertheless, the Southern rolls rose by more than half.

TABLE I

AFDC Caseload Increase By Area [a]

	% Change 1950–1960	% Change 1960–1969 [b]	% of 1960–1969 Change Occurring After 1964 [c]
National Total	17%	107%	71%
Regions [d]			
Northeast	26	180	69
North Central	27	78	59
West	38	161	72
South	0	54	86
Deep South [e]	7	57	98
Other South	−3	52	81
121 Major Urban Counties [f]	35	165	71
5 Most Populous [g]	26	217	75
116 Remaining	41	135	68
78 Northern	41	175	70
43 Southern	13	121	80
All Less Urban and Rural Counties [h]	6	60	71
Northern	17	87	62
Southern	−3	34	93

[a] *Includes AFDC-UP. For further definitions, see Source Tables 1 and 2 in the Appendix.*

[b] *December of each year except February 1969.*

[c] *The periods being compared are approximately equal, the earlier being four years, the latter four years and two months.*

[d] *As defined by the U.S. Bureau of the Census.*

[e] *Louisiana, Mississippi, Georgia, Alabama, and South Carolina. The remaining 12 Southern states comprise the Other South, as noted in Appendix, Source Table 1.*

(Table notes continued at top of facing page.)

    t *A county with a main city of at least 100,000 persons. In
      1960, there were 121 such counties, and they contained 130
      main cities. See Source Table 2 for an enumeration of these
      counties and a discussion of definitions.*

    g *Counties with a main city of at least one million persons;
      New York City, which contains five counties, is treated as a
      single county.*

    h *Counties which do not contain a main city of at least 100,000
      persons. For convenience, we have referred to these counties
      as "rural" throughout this text. Strictly speaking, many are
      not rural, for they contain small cities. A more accurate but
      awkward designation would be "less urban or rural."*

---

dramatic rise. During the 1950's, these counties accounted for only 23 per cent of the national increase, while the remaining 116 urban counties accounted for two and a half times as much (57 per cent). In the 1960's, however, the "big five" counties contributed as much to the national increase as all the remaining urban counties in the nation combined (34 and 36 per cent, respectively).

Finally, rural counties contributed 30 per cent to the increase, although the contribution by Northern rural counties (22 per cent) was much greater than by Southern ones (9 per cent). (Still, it is worth remembering that the Southern rural rolls had fallen during the 1950's.)

We come now to the most striking feature of the welfare rise. To speak only of its magnitude and where it took place is to overlook an extraordinary fact: *that the rolls went up all at once*—by 31 per cent in the first four years of the decade, but by 58 per cent in the next four years. Stated another way, fully 71 per cent of the huge welfare increase during the 1960's took place in the four years *after* 1964 (Table 1). It was truly an explosion.[4]

---

[4] If AFDC-UP cases were excluded, the proportion of the national AFDC change in the 1960's occurring after 1964 would increase from 71 to 77 per cent, since 85 per cent of AFDC-UP cases were added (or transferred) in the three years immediately following congressional enactment of the program in 1961. See Source Table 3.

TABLE II

Area Contribution to the Welfare Explosion [a]

	% Contributed to the National AFDC Increase in	
	1950–60	1960–69
National Total	100%	100%
Regions		
Northeast	33	39
North Central	34	17
West	33	26
South	0	18
Deep South	.05	6
Other South	—.05	12
121 Major Urban Counties	80	70
5 Most Populous	23	34
116 Remaining	57	36
78 Northern	74	60
43 Southern	6	10
All Less Urban and Rural Counties	19	30
Northern	25	22
Southern	—6	9

[a] *See preceding table for notations and definitions.*

Among the regions, all but the North Central area experienced at least two thirds of their increases after 1964. Indeed, 86 per cent of the total Southern increase and an astonishing 98 per cent of the Deep South increase occurred after 1964!

Urban and rural areas show the same pattern (with the exception of Northern rural counties, where only 62 per cent of the increase took place after 1964). The rural South had an especially abrupt increase—93 per cent of the rise occurred after 1964. Any explanation of the welfare rise in the 1960's must account for this extraordinary precipitousness.

In summary, the welfare explosion occurred in all regions, and in both urban and rural counties. But the explosion was far greater in urban areas; and among those urban areas it was a handful of the most populous Northern cities that showed the largest rises. Finally, most of the increase occurred all at once, in just a brief period after 1964.

Some Explanations of the Welfare Rise

Of the explanations that have been advanced to account for the welfare explosion, three deserve mention here. One points to continued migration of the black poor from the South. Another attributes the increase to rising formal benefit levels. And the third fixes responsibility on the presumed deterioration of "the Negro family."

We believe that these explanations share a common defect that makes them at best incomplete. All are based on the extremely doubtful premise that *the relief rolls automatically grow when the pool of people eligible for relief grows.* Each of these explanations does, to be sure, point to a factor that increased the pool: the more poor people who migrate from Southern states with restrictive welfare systems to Northern states with more liberal ones, the larger the pool; the higher the formal benefit levels, the larger the pool of eligible families; and the more families without male heads, the larger the pool.[5] But relief-giving, as we

---

[5] Whenever benefit levels are raised, a new stratum of low-income families becomes qualified for assistance. Should such families apply for and receive aid, they would be given the difference between their existing income (which previously exceeded benefit levels) and the new benefit levels which then exceed their income.

showed in preceding chapters, does not increase simply because economic deprivation spreads; nor did it increase for this reason in the 1960's. The families who got on the rolls after 1964 were, on the whole, just as much in need of aid before 1964. A pool of eligible people had always been there; and although it grew for the reasons given above, it had also been growing for some time.

If these theories were valid, welfare increases should have occurred where the pool of eligible people was growing. In principle, for example, poor black families in Southern states with low payment levels and severe eligibility restrictions improved their chances of obtaining relief if they migrated to Northern states with higher formal benefit levels and fewer restrictions; some families may even have migrated for that reason. But the principle hardly worked out in practice during the 1950's. Indeed, the number of black families moving northward in the 1950's was greater than in the 1960's, yet the Northern regional increases were from three to seven times larger in the 1960's (Table 1). In the Northeast, for example, the rolls rose by 26 per cent in the 1950's, but by 180 per cent in the 1960's. New York and Los Angeles experienced great in-migration during the 1950's, not only by Southern blacks but by Spanish-speaking families as well; nevertheless, the rolls in these counties went up by only 16 and 14 per cent, respectively. During the 1960's, however, *the rolls in both counties quadrupled* (300 per cent and 293 per cent respectively), despite the fact that in-migration by blacks had slackened.[6]

---

[6] The slowing of black migration is evident from the following table, taken from the *Report of the National Advisory Commission on Civil Disorders*, 240:

Period	Net Negro Out-Migration From the South	Average Annual Rate
1910–1920	454,000	45,400
1920–1930	749,000	74,900
1930–1940	348,000	34,800
1940–1950	1,597,000	159,700
1950–1960	1,457,000	145,700
1960–1966	613,000	102,000

Not all of the Southern black poor were dislodged from agriculture in recent decades went North; many migrated to Southern cities. Although such migration might thus account for the decline in Southern rural rolls in the 1950's, it surely would lead us to expect an increase of more than 13 per cent in the Southern cities. The situation in the 1960's is even more puzzling: the rolls in the Southern cities jumped by 121 per cent, and that could be said to be a delayed response to in-migration; but such a speculation is made dubious by the fact that the Southern rural rolls also jumped, and this despite continued out-migration.

The upgrading of benefit levels obviously expands the pool of people who are eligible for assistance. However, even the most cursory examination of the relationship between this factor and changes in the welfare rolls reveals the inadequacy of this explanation. In the 1950's, the national average level of payment per recipient [7] rose almost by half, thus greatly enlarging the pool; but in fact the rolls rose a mere 17 per cent. In the South, furthermore, average payments went up by half but the rolls remained absolutely unchanged. During the 1960's, these patterns were reversed: a national increase of only one third in average payment was accompanied by more than a doubling of the rolls. In short, neither decade provides evidence to support the rising-payment-level thesis.

The record of individual states also casts serious doubt on this explanation. Between 1960 and early 1969, California increased its average monthly payment per recipient from $43 to $48—a change of 11 per cent. During the same period, California's rolls increased by 219 per cent. In

---

[7] It is impossible to measure formal benefit levels accurately because so many jurisdictions have systems of special allowances which may or may not be granted, and because of administrative variations in paying for such basic needs as rent. We will therefore examine changes in the actual amounts paid to recipients.

Georgia, the average payment rose by 4 per cent, and the rolls rose 138 per cent. North Carolina raised its average payment by 45 per cent, yet the rolls went up only 4 per cent.

Nor does the evidence from many individual cities bear out the thesis. The quadrupling of New York City's rolls could be explained by a series of substantial payment-level changes enacted by the state beginning in 1960; however, the rolls in Los Angeles also quadrupled although there was no significant upgrading of payment levels in California during the same period.[8]

Before we examine the adequacy of the family-deterioration thesis, it might be well to say a bit more about the thesis itself. This view of the welfare rise was put forward by Daniel P. Moynihan in a much-publicized report on "The Negro Family." Having noted that the number of individuals on the AFDC rolls trebled between 1940 and 1963, and that a disproportionate share of the increase was attributable to black families, he asserted that "the steady expansion of . . . [the AFDC] program, as of public assistance programs in general, can be taken as a measure of the steady disintegration of the Negro family structure over the past generation in the United States."[9]

---

[8] Lurie, 110 ff., also shows that this explanation does not hold.

[9] Moynihan, 14. How the expansion of "public assistance programs in general," as distinct from the expansion of AFDC alone, supports a family-deterioration thesis is far from clear. The proportion of blacks on the Aid to the Blind rolls in 1962 was only 30 per cent; 28 per cent of those on the Aid to the Permanently and Totally Disabled rolls were black in 1962; fewer than 25 per cent of the Old Age Assistance cases were black in 1965. Now these percentages are larger than the proportion of blacks in the general population, to be sure, but it is doubtful whether aspects of family structure explain the discrepancies. Among the more likely explanations are these: blacks have poorer health and fewer resources to care for themselves during illness than whites, so that more of them end up on the disabled rolls; blacks are also more likely to be employed in occupations which are covered neither by Social Security nor by private pension plans,

We find this explanation of the relief rise inadequate, but not because we dismiss the evidence showing that the black family has been weakened by uprooting, urban resettlement, and chronically high rates of urban unemployment. These forces have taken their toll, as they did of other dislocated groups in earlier periods of our history. (Indeed, we will return to the evidence on the erosion of the black family in Chapter 8, for we believe it does help to explain the welfare rise, albeit very circuitously. From our perspective, the weakening of the family signified a weakening of social control, especially over the young, and it was the young who were the most prominent in the disorders of the 1960's. Disorder, in turn, was a critical force in producing more liberal relief practices, or so we shall argue.) But Moynihan leaps to the conclusion that AFDC rolls rose simply because the changing structure of the black family increased the pool of families *presumably eligible* for relief; the rolls rose, in other words, as an automatic result of a growing pool of eligibles. That conclusion does not accord with the facts.

Until 1948, blacks did not appear on the AFDC rolls in significant proportions. Whatever their family structure, they were severely discriminated against prior to that time, especially in the South. Two changes then combined to increase their proportion on the rolls in the years immedi-

---

nor pay enough to permit families to save for retirement, thus forcing proportionately more of them than whites onto the old-age assistance rolls.

The statement that the rolls "trebled between 1940 and 1963" is true, but misleading. In 1940, the AFDC program had only just begun, and there were a mere 360,000 of America's poor families on the rolls. By using this base for comparisons with future years, Moynihan leaves the impression that subsequent rises were very large. As we have already noted, there was a brief upsurge in the rolls after World War II, but during the 1950's the rolls remained virtually unchanged. Moreover, to base changes in the rolls on the number of individuals—rather than families—introduces another source of bias, for the guardian or custodian (e.g., the mother) of AFDC children was not initially permitted on the rolls. When Congress made such persons eligible after 1950, the number of persons on the rolls increased to be sure, but the number of families did not.

ately after 1948, neither of which had anything to do with family structure. One was pressure by the federal government on Southern states to relax discriminatory practices, a circumstance that produced a sharp increase in the number of blacks who received aid in the South, especially between 1948 and 1952, as we noted in Chapter 4. The second factor was the steady migration of blacks to more liberal Northern cities, where they were less likely to be disqualified for assistance. These factors (or any other factors, for that matter) did not appreciably increase the *magnitude* of the national AFDC rolls between 1948 and 1960, a remarkable phenomenon on which we have already commented; however, they did significantly alter their *composition,* for the proportion of blacks increased from 31 to 40 per cent.

However worrisome the gradual AFDC rise in the 1950's, the rapid rise beginning in 1960 was a special source of alarm to Moynihan, for he thought he detected in this trend the basis for concluding that the black family had become so disorganized that "the present tangle of pathology is capable of perpetuating itself without assistance from the white world." [10] To arrive at this conclusion, Moynihan compared the trends in black male unemployment rates with trends in the total number of AFDC cases opened. From 1953 to 1958, he shows, the black male unemployment rate rose and the total number of new AFDC cases also rose, as if caused by the rising trend in unemployment. After 1958, the unemployment level slowly moved downward, but the total number of new AFDC cases inexplicably continued to climb. It was this failure of the relief rolls to decline in response to ostensibly improved economic conditions in the late 1950's and early 1960's that led Moynihan to say that the pathology of the black

---

[10] *Ibid.,* 47.

family had become so serious that it "may indeed have begun to feed on itself." [11]

The obvious question to which this conclusion leads is whether the absolute increase in female-headed families was as large as the absolute rise in AFDC cases. In a detailed examination of this question, Lurie found that even if all of the new female-headed families in the period between 1959 and 1966 had received AFDC assistance, only about 10 per cent of the AFDC increase would have been accounted for: "It is clear, then, that the rise in the number of families receiving AFDC cannot be explained by the rise in the number of poor families headed by females." [12]

Furthermore, how is one to reconcile recent AFDC increases in the rural South with an "urbanization leads to family deterioration" thesis? Even the urban data yield little support. The nation's 121 urban counties accounted for most of the recent increase, and at first glance this fact might seem to support the explanation, except that a major shift occurred among the urban communities that contributed to the welfare rise in the 1950's, as contrasted with the 1960's. In the 1950's, as we noted earlier, the "big five" counties accounted for only 23 per cent of the national increase; in the 1960's, however, they represented 34 per cent, or as much as the remaining 116 urban counties combined. A family-deterioration argument would have to explain why, during the 1950's, families were more likely to deteriorate in cities of less than one million persons, whereas in the 1960's the vulnerable families had shifted to cities of over one million persons. What such an explanation would be is not readily apparent.

Finally, and of great importance, none of these explanations, including the family-breakdown thesis, helps to ac-

[11] *Ibid.*
[12] Lurie, 131.

count for the striking fact that 71 per cent of the welfare rise in the 1960's took place after 1964. The extraordinary precipitousness of the Southern rise is clearly incompatible with all three of these theories, for the Southern rolls rose by just half, but virtually all of that increase (86 per cent) took place after 1964.

And so the puzzle remains, for if neither the rate of migration nor formal benefit levels skyrocketed after 1964, the rolls clearly did, and if family life among blacks did not suddenly collapse in those few years, many of the restrictive practices of the relief system clearly did. What must be explained, in short, is not why the pool of eligible families grew, although the existence of a pool of unemployed poor is one precondition for a welfare explosion; what must be explained is why so many of the families in that pool were finally able to get on the rolls.

In the chapters to follow, we shall argue, as we did in our discussion of the relief explosion during the Great Depression, that the contemporary relief explosion was a response to the civil disorder caused by rapid economic change—in this case, the modernization of Southern agriculture. The impact of modernization on blacks was much greater than on whites: it was they who were the chief victims of the convulsion in Southern agriculture, and it was they who were more likely to encounter barriers to employment once relocated in the cities, a combination of circumstances which led to a substantial weakening of social controls and widespread outbreaks of disorder. For if unemployment and forced migration altered the geography of black poverty, it also created a measure of black power. In the 1960's, the growing mass of black poor in the cities emerged as a political force for the first time, both in the voting booths and in the streets. And the relief system was, we believe, one of the main local institutions to respond to that force, even though the reaction was greatly delayed.

The relationship between increasing black power and the expanding welfare rolls is not altogether obvious. Great masses of poor blacks did not rise up in anger against a welfare system that denied them sustenance (although some did). Nor did the increased flow of public aid result from demands made by black political leaders; quite to the contrary, the expanding welfare rolls have often been as much a source of dismay to black elites as to white elites. Finally, there is a puzzling absence of liberalizing legislation. Legislative enactments in the years between 1960 and 1969 were intended not to put more families on the rolls, but to get them off via rehabilitation services (the passage of AFDC-UP is an exception).[13] Indeed, the puzzle deepens because some legislative enactments—particularly the congressional amendments of 1967—actually made the relief system more restrictive. Still, the rolls more than doubled. The politics of the welfare rise, in short, are anything but self-evident.

In our previous analysis of why relief restrictions collapsed in the Great Depression, we found that the critical factor was the growing volatility of those dislodged from the occupational order. Mass unemployment alone did not lead to the expansion of relief arrangements—not, that is, until unemployment had generated so much unrest as to threaten political stability. In other words, economic convulsions which also produce mass turbulence—whether riots in the streets or upheavals in electoral alignments— are likely to lead to the temporary liberalization of relief provisions.

Although unemployment during the Great Depression rapidly produced a political crisis and impelled the expansion of public aid, two decades passed before the unem-

---

[13] The Poor People's Campaign, a massive lobbying effort, did not even succeed in obtaining immediate and significant improvements in so minor a program as the distribution of surplus commodities and food stamps— a program funded through the Department of Agriculture and administered by local welfare departments.

ployment resulting from modernization and migration after World War II produced mass disorder, and so the relief rolls did not rise appreciably until after 1964. Agricultural modernization and migration to the cities brought blacks within the sphere of electoral politics, to be sure, but larger voting numbers alone did not produce concessions. It was not until this mass of unintegrated people finally became turbulent that both local government and the federal government began to register and react to their presence.

The welfare explosion occurred during several years of the greatest domestic disorder since the 1930's—perhaps the greatest in our history. It was concurrent with the turmoil produced by the civil rights struggle, with widespread and destructive rioting in the cities, and with the formation of a militant grass-roots movement of the poor dedicated to the combatting welfare restrictions. Not least, the welfare rise was also concurrent with the enactment of a series of ghetto-placating federal programs (such as the antipoverty program) which, among other things, hired thousands of poor people, social workers, and lawyers who, it subsequently turned out, greatly stimulated people to apply for relief and helped them to obtain it. And the welfare explosion, although an urban phenomenon generally, was greatest in just that handful of large metropolitan counties where the political turmoil of the middle and late 1960's was the most acute.

In other words, we shall argue that the expansion of the welfare rolls was a political response to political disorder. If many of the welfare restrictions described in Chapters 4 and 5 were not legislated out of existence in the 1960's, *their implementation in many localities (especially in the cities) almost completely broke down.* And that was very much a matter of politics. Moreover, it was a matter of black politics, or so we shall argue in the chapters that follow.

REFERENCES

Lurie, Irene, *An Economic Evaluation of Aid to Families with Dependent Children*. Washington, Brookings Institution, 1968.

Moynihan, Daniel P., *The Negro Family: The Case for National Action*. Washington, U.S. Department of Labor (Office of Policy Planning and Research), 1965.

U.S. Department of Agriculture, Economic Research Service, *U.S. Population Mobility and Distribution: Charts on Recent Trends*. Washington, The Department, 1969. (ERS-436.)

U.S. National Advisory Commission on Civil Disorders, *Report of the National Advisory Commission on Civil Disorders*. New York, Bantam Books, 1968.

CHAPTER SEVEN

Agricultural Modernization and Mass Unemployment

If it took the Great Depression, the most profound economic convulsion in American history, to break down temporarily the restrictions of the old relief system, it has taken the more prolonged economic convulsion in agriculture to break down the restrictions of the "reformed" relief system established when the Depression ended. This economic dislocation is the key to an understanding of the turbulence of the 1960's, and to a full understanding of the contemporary welfare explosion.

Unemployment in Southern Agriculture

No one would disagree that the rural economy of America, especially in the South, has undergone a profound transformation in recent decades. In 1945, there was one tractor per farm; in 1964 there were two. Mechanization and other technological developments, in turn, stimulated the enlargement of farm holdings. Between 1950 and 1969, 1 million farms disappeared; the 3 million remaining farms averaged 377 acres in size—30 per cent larger than the average farm ten years earlier. The chief and most obvious effect of these changes was to lessen the need for agricultural labor. In the years between 1950 and 1965 alone, "New machines and new methods increased farm output in the United States by 45 per cent—and reduced farm employment by 45 per cent." [1] In 1967, "the rate of unemployment nationally [was] about 4 per cent. The rate in rural areas average[d] about 18 per cent. Among farmworkers . . . underemployment [ran] as high as 37 per cent." [2] A mere 4 per cent of the American labor force now works the land, signaling an extraordinary displacement of people, with accompanying upheaval and suffering. The best summary measure of this dislocation is probably the volume of migration to the cities: over 20 million people, more than 4 million of them black, left the land after 1940.

Although modernization affected all agricultural areas, its impact was especially great in the South after World War II. One way to convey some sense of the severity of the ensuing disruption is to describe the conditions of unemployed black farm workers who remained in the South.

Humphreys County, Mississippi, is part of the rich delta region. Mechanization proceeded rapidly on the cotton-growing plantations of the area in the early 1950's. [3]

---

[1] U.S. President's National Advisory Commission on Rural Poverty, ix.

[2] *Ibid.,* x.

[3] All of the quotations in this chapter not specifically attributed to other sources are taken from an excellent but little-noticed report by Dunbar. (This report forms part of Dunbar's book *Our Land Too,* recently published by Pantheon Books.) Other reports from the cotton-growing sections of the South convey the same general picture. Writing on "The Southern Roots of Urban Crisis" in *Fortune* magazine, for example, Beardwood tells of this encounter: "Five miles south of Greenville, Mississippi, close to the Mississippi River, is a big flat cotton field owned by a white family. One day this summer [i.e., 1968], under a blazing sun, a group of Negro women and children were hoeing the weeds between the rows. Fifty yards away stood a row of wooden shacks, warping in the heat, alongside a sluggish creek, the only sanitary facility. 'The man pays but $3 a day,' said one woman, hoeing as she spoke. 'No, I don't know how much the children will get, but he said something. Maybe 60 cents the day, maybe more. It don't do no good to press him. We need the work, and he pays more than some people. Across there'—she pointed toward a

Tenant Farmer: There used to be a whole lot more people on the plantation than there are now. The machines started long back in '50. I believe it really started back in '53, '54. Then every year they begin to get more and more, more and more, and that begin to cut people down out of the pickin', you know. In other words, before that they were pickin' all the crop. Then after machines got in, they started pickin' ends, see. And so now, the biggest of 'em not pickin' none.

Before mechanization, tenant families lived on the plantations in shacks provided by the planters. In return, each family was on call to work as demanded by the planters at wages dictated by the planters. So little was paid that the tenant farmer was constantly in debt to the planter, who furnished money, goods, and services, especially during the winter months. These loans were deducted from the next season's wages. The resulting system of indebtedness kept the tenant in a literal state of indenture; the planter's power over him was virtually absolute. Still, the planter needed workers who could put in long and arduous hours during the periods of planting, chopping, and picking, so he had some incentive to see to it that his tenants had at least a minimum of food, housing, and medical care.

But with mechanization, only skilled workers were needed. "Poisons sprayed from crop-dusting planes have ended the demand for cotton choppers. Mechanical cotton pickers, looking insect-like with their large, awkward bins angling out above their tiny wheel base, have replaced

---

plantation on the far side of a highway—'the man pays $2.50 a day.' She and the husband have six children, five of them living at home, and one in Greenville looking for work. When the couple and their two sons, aged twelve and fourteen, are all working, the family's total income may be $70, 'but that is only at the planting and the harvesting, and maybe a few weeks of chopping in between.' Otherwise, the family lives on the husband's wages—a maximum of $50 a week, earned when the farmer needs him. Some weeks the family has no income at all."

hand pickers, except at the ends of the rows where the picker makes its turn and cannot reap cleanly for a stretch about 15 feet deep in the row. Here the women can still get a few sacks." The new machines are expensive, complicated, and varied—tractors, bulldozers, cotton pickers, and combines, not to speak of cotton gins. "Parts break down; engine belts snap; the machine jams." The introduction of machinery thus produced the beginnings of a skilled labor force. As a result, the availability of work for women and children declined sharply, and the burden of supporting a family began to fall wholly on the males; but even most skilled operatives have difficulty earning enough to keep their families from starving, for the basic condition of a labor surplus held wages down even for those who acquired the necessary mechanical skills. As for the families of the unskilled, many do starve.

After more than a decade of modernization, minimum-wage legislation was introduced. Previously, men had earned about three dollars a day; women and children earned less. The federal minimum-wage law enacted in 1966 set a floor of one dollar an hour for some workers, although many planters typically found ways of avoiding the law.[4] Despite the fact that all workers were not covered and despite evasions, the law nevertheless exerted pressure for

---

[4] "Agricultural workers in the U.S. are specifically excluded from most labor legislation. They do not have the right to bargain collectively, and only those who work for a farmer using more than 500 man-hours of hired labor in any quarter are entitled to the minimum wage.... In 1967 fewer than one worker in three in the South was entitled to the minimum wage. Not all of those entitled to that minimum have been getting it. Two months ago [early 1968], Roy Flowers, who owns a plantation in the Mississippi Delta, was permanently enjoined by a federal judge from violating minimum-wage, overtime-pay, record-keeping, and child-labor regulations. Among other things, the court found that Flowers had been charging his Negro workers $70 a month for shacks that should have been rented for no more than $5. In the first recovery of wages under 1966 amendments to the Fair Labor Standards Act, the judge ordered Flowers to pay 200 Negro employees $50,000. Last year, it should also be noted, the Agriculture Department paid Flowers $210,832 for not cultivating 4,000 of his 16,000 acres" (Beardwood).

greater labor efficiency—which led to more investment in machines and fewer jobs for the poor.

> *Tenant Farmer:* At first, the machines started throwin' people off the plantation, and after the wage law came along that made plantation owners buy more machines and put more people off.

Moreover, the use of machinery took away a major resource by which the tenant family previously managed to augment its meager wages:

> Until a few years ago, every family on a plantation was allowed a small patch of land to grow vegetables for their own use. Many tenants also raised hogs, chickens, and possibly a cow. Today only a few of the planters will allow even their full-time laborers to plant one or two rows of vegetables. For the rest a garden or coops or pens for poultry and livestock are impossible, because rows of cotton or soybeans now push up to the tenant's doorstep. In their drive to get the greatest possible yield from their land, the planters may force the tenants to move their toilets right up to their homes, so that every possible foot of land can be seeded and so that the machines can run straight down the rows without having to detour around the tiny, rickety privies. Even where space does permit the growing of a little truck, most tenants are prohibited from doing so because planters fear that weeds from the garden will spread to the cotton and bean fields, which they like to keep meticulously clean by spraying down poisons from the air.

In the wake of these events, the condition of black people worsened to the point of peril. There was some new industry in the area, but whites got the jobs. Planters either tore the shacks down so that people had to leave, or they refused to maintain them. "Of the families surveyed 76.6 per cent are troubled by rats in their homes, and 23.4 per cent of the families have killed snakes in their homes." Without adequate clothing, the children were often kept home from school. Subsistence farming had become a thing of the past. There was a time when pregnant women sucked clay and ate cornstarch or baking soda to fill themselves up; now most of the poor do so. "The black residents . . . do not eat well, they do not eat much, and they do not eat often." For obvious reasons, health problems were endemic. High blood pressure, diabetes, tuberculosis, amebic dysentery, and internal parasites became common problems. Running sores and scabs covered the bodies of most children in the summer.

> *Tenant Farmer:* This baby right here, he'll cough and go out of breath, and you can't disturb him. He'll go out of breath. . . . That child there, she complains right smart about her stomach. . . . I've got another boy here who looked like he just never would get well of his sores.

The poverty of tenant farmers had always been severe. Now that they had become economically superfluous, their poverty became desperate.

The Persistence of Southern Relief Restrictions

If relief systems existed to relieve suffering, they would have found much to do in the Southern rural areas during the 1950's. As it happens, the Southern relief system did nothing. Indeed, the traditional restrictive practices actually hardened. The sharp rise in the rolls after the close of World War II, when the AFDC program was still in the early stages of implementation, provoked antagonism in the South, and attacks on the welfare system mounted. Throughout the 1950's, one state after another enacted new laws and policies—such as employable mother rules, suitable home laws, and substitute parent rules—designed to stabilize or reduce the rolls. The 1950's also saw the eruption of campaigns to purge the rolls by expelling families with illegitimate children. As a consequence, despite deepening distress, the rolls in the South as a whole did not grow. The rolls in the Deep South states rose only by 7 per cent, and those in the states of the Other South declined 3 per cent. The urban counties of the South rose by a mere 13 per cent, and the rolls in the rural areas fell by 3 per cent. Judging from these figures, one would suppose that the Southern economy had also remained stable. But nothing could be further from the truth.

We described the general character of the relief practices that prevailed throughout the South during the 1940's and 1950's in Chapters 4 and 5. But even as late as the mid-1960's, there had not been much improvement. This was revealed by the Mississippi State Advisory Committee to the U.S. Commission on Civil Rights, which convened hearings in Jackson, Mississippi, in 1967.[5] The grand ballroom of the King Edward Hotel was filled with 800 black poor, and their chief spokesman was George A. Wiley, who headed the newly formed National Welfare Rights Organization (NWRO).

The proceedings began with formal testimony from a number of welfare recipients. Many complained that they received much less than the maximum public-assistance grant. The average payment to a family of four in the state was $36 a month; the legal maximum was $50. Many families who appeared to be eligible had been denied benefits. In some cases, grants were erratically reduced; a family received $38 one month, $20 the next, and then, perhaps, nothing at all. Each story of aid denied revealed a family close to starvation and then cast into it. The Committee seemed incredulous. One member asked: "How is it they

---

[5] These proceedings were observed and reported by the authors, 1967.

don't die?" A young law student working with NWRO replied, "They do die, slowly."

Many of the tales were of intimidation and harassment by welfare officials. A woman testified that in her county the welfare director sends the monthly checks to the local storekeeper (his wife), presumably as payment against the recipients' accounts. People who protested this practice were cut off the rolls. Other women claimed that they were threatened with the loss of their meager allotments if they were said to have "consorted" with men.

The second day's session opened with testimony from two state relief officials. One explained that some mishaps were inevitable in a department with 1,500 employees, and that grievances would be looked into and any errors quickly corrected. Still, he assured the Commission, the system was generally lawful and just.

A second official said that the problem was money, and he was caught between "the devil and the deep blue sea." Mississippi, he noted, is the poorest state in the nation, but it ranks far from the bottom in the proportion of the state budget that goes for welfare. He had to deal with the legislature, and the legislature did not like promiscuity. *He* knew that only 20 per cent of the children on welfare were illegitimate, but the legislature did not.

In response to the demand that the poor be given access to manuals describing criteria of eligibility, welfare officials replied that the regulations were set forth in nine different volumes which could be distributed only at great cost; moreover, changes were continually being made, so that manuals quickly became outdated. In any case, the officials maintained, the poor wouldn't be able to understand the manuals. Even when the rules were explained to them again and again, they couldn't get them straight, and the manuals would only compound their confusion. Poor people, the officials summed up, should have greater confidence in the skill and good faith of welfare personnel.

Edward Sparer, an attorney cooperating with NWRO, pointed out that only one of the nine volumes of the welfare code and a small section of another dealt with eligibility for public assistance. He offered to compile a simplified manual if the welfare department would produce and distribute it. The officials demurred. (Sparer had, in fact, already produced a simplified manual, and it was being distributed by the NAACP Education and Legal Defense Fund.)

The chief of the federal Bureau of Family Services also testified: progress was being made, he assured the Committee. When asked to describe what federal authorities were doing to oversee welfare practices in Mississippi, he referred to federal "quality-control" programs in which samples of cases are reviewed regularly—but by *state* personnel. Everyone makes mistakes, he said, and the disputed cases would be looked into.

Many recipients had come to the hearings to protest the fact that Mississippi counties were switching from the surplus food distribution program to the food stamp program, thus forcing many people toward starvation. According to the Food Stamp Act of 1964, a locality had to choose between these two food-distribution programs; it could not have both. In one program, surplus commodities were distributed free to those declared eligible. (A year earlier, thousands of people in Mississippi had been sustained on free cornmeal, flour, and lard, the answer to the mystery of why they did not die.)

Under the alternative program, recipients were allowed to buy food stamps, receiving a bonus graduated according to income level. Thus a family of four with a monthly income of $60 could purchase food stamps for $18 that were worth $60 in a store. In principle, the food stamp program is superior, for stamps can be used to buy a variety of products, whereas participants in the surplus commodities program are limited to the food available in surplus. For obvious reasons, local merchants considered it superior as well. And so it was that the surplus commodities program was being suspended in one Mississippi county after another in favor of the food stamp program. However, when a county switched to stamps, participation typically fell off sharply, for many of the very poor either received no money from welfare to enable them to buy stamps, or received such low grants that there was never sufficient cash on hand for the stamps (which had to be purchased on a lump-sum basis once a month for an amount that was often as large as the welfare check itself, so that buying stamps left little or nothing for rent, clothing, and other expenses).[6] Moreover, merchants had instituted a two-price system—charging higher prices to families buying with food stamps.[7]

That the Southern rural relief system did not respond to the dislocation of people from agriculture is no surprise. Relief restrictions continued to serve an economic function; while agricultural modernization meant that less marginal labor was needed, it did not mean that none was needed. Low-paid workers were still required, and a substantial improvement in formal benefit levels, or a marked easing of access to benefits, would have put the availability of that cheap labor in doubt. This point is revealed quite clearly by looking at farm wages. In 1964, for example, non-white farm workers in the Southern region worked an average of seventy-seven days for total average annual earnings of $502.[8] The relief system continued to be managed in a way that accorded with this extremely low wage structure.

---

[6] In the first comprehensive account of the politics of the food distribution programs, Kotz (55) reports figures on the decline in participation following the change from commodities to stamps: "As counties throughout the nation changed from free commodities to food stamps, participation . . . fell off by 40 per cent; more than one million persons, including 100,000 in Mississippi, were forced to drop out of the food aid program."

[7] For a discussion of this two-price system, see Dunbar, 44 ff.

[8] Economic Research Service, Table 7.

But even if no marginal labor had been needed, there still would have been little reason to expect a response from the relief system. By becoming economically obsolete, people also became objects of indifference. No one cared, especially the planters who ruled the institutions of the cotton economy, which included the relief system:

> The planter is out to make money, and, viewed in this way, he is coming of age [by mechanizing]. The last years in the Delta have seen tenants go homeless, truck patches on plantations prohibited or restricted, people dying or being permanently disabled because the planter would not send for a doctor, plantation huts being allowed to fall into complete disrepair, women and children by the thousands left with no way to earn money, women forced to do work for which they are physically unsuited in order to save their families from being told to move out, and countless other shameful events. This has happened, I think, not because the planters have decided to starve the black man out of the Delta, as some have said, but rather because the planters no longer care, except as it affects their own operations, what happens to the tenants on their farms; or, in a larger sense, they do not care whether the black man in the Delta starves or not.[9]

It must be said that indifference toward the plight of displaced black agricultural workers turned out to serve the rural South well, for it helped to rid that area of surplus

---

[9] Although indifference, rather than deliberate policy, may explain the fact that Southern relief practices had the consequence of forcing migration, it should be noted that history records other instances in which relief practices have been deliberately designed to induce migration or emigration. One prominent example was the deference shown landlords' interests by relief-givers during Ireland's "Great Potato Famine" in the 1840's. With millions starving, the provision of emergency food was restricted to tenants who occupied less than a quarter acre of land. "Ostensibly . . . [this restriction] was designed to prevent the well-off competing with the needy for soup. But at the time, possession of one, or even ten acres, was no guarantee of means. The choice for starving tenants lay between their survival or their holding; if they chose soup, that suited their landlords, who by this time were anxious to clear their property of useless, non-rent-paying tenantry, and convert it to pasture. Deprived of their land, the peasants' only resource was emigration" (Inglis, 139).

workers through migration.[10] The persistence of restrictive relief arrangements was crucial in promoting that process. The choices afforded the poor were starkly clear: work or starve; if there was no work, migrate or starve.[11]

The Absence of Disorder
in the Rural South

In accounting for the rigidity of the rural Southern relief system, it is important to see that it was free from any pressure by the poor themselves. During the Depression, the votes and volatility of dislocated workers were critical forces which led to the collapse of restrictive relief practices. Although neither of these forces emerged in the rural South, some of the preconditions for mass disorder were present. Perhaps the most important was the almost total disintegration of traditional patterns of social relations, a condition that has given rise to mass volatility throughout history. A vivid sense of the decline of community and the rise of uncertainty which modernization produced was caught by Dunbar:

There is nothing predictable now about life on the plantation. No man knows if his home is secure, or if he will be given enough work to support his family. He does not know if he will be placed in a hospital if he is hurt on the job. He has no idea what he will do when he becomes

[10] This point was made by the President's National Advisory Commission on Rural Poverty, for the poorest counties lost more than a fourth of their population through migration between 1950 and 1959. "In the Deep South, for example, a mass migration of Negroes, mainly to Northern industrial centers, has helped reduce Southern rural poverty at the expense of cities" (6).

[11] With the very gradual breakdown of voting barriers in the past few years, restrictive welfare practices have also come to serve an important political purpose, for in some localities Southern blacks have been developing sufficient political power to threaten local white hegemony. Forced migration substantially reduced that long-term political threat. In 1940, for example, Mississippi had thirty-nine counties that were more than half black; it had only twenty-eight in 1960.

too old to work. If he falls into debt to the planter, he does not know if he will be given enough work to get in the clear. He can no longer expect the planter to give him materials with which to repair his house. If he owes the planter or cannot accumulate any savings, he has no way to leave the plantation. If he can contemplate leaving, he, who has never been 100 miles from Louise, must face a move to Chicago, which he has seen on television but does not really believe in. And what will he do in Chicago? The plantation world is all uncertainty, and the tenant farmer is economically and politically unable to make it any less so.

But if these conditions ordinarily would have tended to produce disorder, other conditions militated against it. For one thing, the dislocation of workers from agriculture was gradual rather than precipitous. There was no moment at which huge numbers of workers simultaneously became unemployed, a distinction of some importance in comparing the economic modernization of the 1960's with the economic collapse of the 1930's. Furthermore, the unemployed in agriculture have been dispersed rather than concentrated, a condition that usually works against the emergence of disruptive crowd behavior. Only when the unemployed rural workers had migrated to the central cities, where they were concentrated in the ghettoes, did turmoil erupt.

Moreover, there was one expectation that lost none of its predictability in the rural South: that coercive force would unfailingly be wielded to deal with any who participated in protest. Despite modernization, rural elites still retained near-feudal powers of life and death. Blacks were subject to violence and terror, without any recourse to law-enforcement agencies. In an economy characterized by a vast surplus of labor, the planter could cut off the dissident or disorderly from even the most occasional work; he could also dispossess families on the spot, leaving them with nowhere to go. Moreover, as we have said, the planter controlled access to relief benefits, to food stamps, to surplus commodities. Thus Dunbar notes that the black engaged in protest activity

> has always been extremely vulnerable to the loss of his livelihood and has generally been the first to feel the wrath of the white community, though it is now a little easier to take that risk because a skilled worker can usually find work. Still, a planter with only one tenant and no prospect of running up on another would force that family to move in a minute if he heard that any member of it was engaged in what he considered to be "radical activity," which could range from registering to vote to joining the NAACP.

Probably the chief factor that counteracted a strain toward volatility was the option of migration. Those sectors of the population that might have been more prone to dissidence and disorder—the younger people and the somewhat better educated—were also the ones most likely to leave.[12] What this meant was that the responsibility for containing the disruptive potential of this agricultural revolution finally fell, as has often been the case in the past, to the cities.[13]

Unemployment in the Cities

The historic sequel to displacement from agricultural economies has been migration to the cities. In the United States, the trek began early in the twentieth century, but was interrupted and even temporarily reversed during the Great Depression, when there was no work to be had in the

---

[12] Differential migration by age is, of course, a general characteristic of rural poverty areas. "In 1965, among low income families in [rural poverty] areas, one of every four heads of household was 65 years of age, or older. Contrast this with rural areas with adequate incomes. There, only about 7 per cent of the heads of households were as old as 65" (U.S. President's National Advisory Commission on Rural Poverty, 7).

[13] But not always. In Chapter 1, we discussed several periods of disorder in the English countryside. However, the serious outbreaks during the first half of the nineteenth century followed more than a century of rapid population growth, with the result that the agricultural population was more densely concentrated than at any earlier period in English history.

cities. With the outbreak of World War II and the promise of jobs in the urban defense industries, the movement to the cities resumed. Six million people left the land between 1940 and 1945.

World War II also created a huge demand for agricultural produce, greatly accelerating mechanization and other technological developments. With the end of the war, large agricultural surpluses developed, foreshadowing mass unemployment and migration. Moreover, the fall in the market for farm products led to pressure for increases in federal subsidies which spurred mechanization and took land out of production, thus accelerating the displacement of labor. Meanwhile, smaller and marginal farmers were left to go bankrupt and be swallowed up by the larger mechanized farms. In the years after 1945, agricultural unemployment steadily increased, and an additional fourteen million people left the land.

The twenty million Americans who left the land after 1940 represented two thirds of those who had earned their living in agriculture. This vast movement took place in less than three decades, marking it as one of the greatest mass dislocations in United States history and making it comparable to the movement of twenty-two million immigrants to American shores between 1890 and 1930, a period of four decades.

Southern blacks were especially vulnerable to agricultural modernization after World War II. In 1940, only half of all blacks lived in urban areas (as classified by the U.S. Census); the figure reached 62 per cent in 1950, 73 per cent in 1960, and 80 per cent in 1965. Fewer than 5 per cent of America's 22.3 million blacks now work the land. In just a few decades, they have become an urban people— more so, it happens, than whites, for 73 per cent of blacks resided in urban areas in 1960, compared to only 69 per cent of whites.[14]

---

[14] Center for Research in Marketing, 8.

If blacks are now an urban people, they are also becoming a Northern people. Between 1940 and 1966, a net of 3.7 million blacks left the Southern region.[15] About half of all blacks now live in Northern areas, and migration is continuing. By contrast, a large proportion of the white agricultural workers displaced by modernization already resided in Northern states. Moreover, whether bred in the rural areas of North or South, white migrants tended to move toward villages, towns, and smaller cities, often within the same state or county from which they originated, while blacks tended to move to the largest Northern cities. Since these white migrants did not have to face racial discrimination, and since they were relatively acculturated to the communities into which they were moving, it is probable that they were more easily absorbed into new occupations.

The economic experience of blacks in the cities during the 1950's was, in general, one of severe unemployment and underemployment. At the close of the Korean War, the national non-white unemployment rate leaped from 4.5 per cent in 1953 to 9.9 per cent in 1954. By 1958, it had reached 12.6 per cent, and it stayed between 10 and 13 per cent until the escalation of the war in Vietnam after 1964.[16]

These figures pertain only to people unemployed and looking for work. They do not include the sporadically unemployed or those employed at extremely low wages. Combining such additional measures with the official unemployment measure produces a "subemployment" index. This index was first used in 1966—well after the economic recessions that characterized the years between the end of the Korean War and the escalation of the war in Vietnam. Were subemployment data available for the "Eisenhower recession" years, especially in the slum-ghettoes of the

---

[15] See Chapter 6.

[16] Bureau of Labor Statistics, 1969, 11. Blacks constitute about 94 per cent of non-whites. In general, the white unemployment rate was half that of the non-white rate throughout this period.

larger central cities, they would surely show much higher rates than prevailed in 1966. In any event, the figures for 1966 revealed a non-white subemployment rate of 21.6 per cent compared with a white rate of 7.6 per cent.[17]

But these are national figures. What of the central cities to which so many of the black poor moved? In 1966, during a war boom, the Department of Labor studied unemployment rates in the predominantly black slums of selected cities for the first time, and found the average to be about three times (9.3 per cent) the national average (3.5 per cent). The subemployment levels were astonishing: [18]

Average subemployment, nine slum-ghetto areas	33%
Boston (Roxbury area)	24
New Orleans (several contiguous areas)	45
New York City	
Central Harlem	29
East Harlem	33
Bedford-Stuyvesant	28
Philadelphia (North Philadelphia)	34
Phoenix (Salt River Bed area)	42
St. Louis (North Side)	39
San Francisco (Mission-Fillmore)	25

These high levels of unemployment and subemployment were the result of a variety of factors. Many of the migrants, being a rural people, were ill-suited for jobs in modern industry; and whatever their skills, racial discrimination worked to restrict access to many kinds of employment. Furthermore, blacks were much more likely than whites to have migrated to central cities that did not consistently share in the nation's rate of economic growth. In 1960, there were seventeen cities that contained at least 100,000 blacks. Of these, the six that "showed less employment gain than the national average of 7 per cent between 1963 and 1965 ... included such places of heavy Negro immigration as New York, Chicago, Philadelphia, Baltimore, Newark,

[17] *Ibid.*, 17.
[18] Bureau of Labor Statistics, 1967, 97.

and Los Angeles." Furthermore, "in the two cities having the largest Negro population in their region, as well as substantial Negro immigration—Los Angeles and New York—there was no increase in manufacturing employment." Finally, "six of the cities showing an employment gain of at least as much as the national average were in the South, where Negroes are not yet readily employed outside of service and laboring jobs." [19] For varied reasons, then, the official non-white employment rate has continued to be at least twice as high as the white rate.

The Persistence of Relief Restrictions in the Cities

Once again, if relief systems existed to reduce economic hardship, then the impact of migration and unemployment upon the urban welfare rolls in the 1950's should have been dramatic, especially in the Northern cities. Payment levels in Northern areas were much higher than in the South, so that even migrating families that managed to earn some income in the cities would still have been eligible for supplementary aid. There were also fewer restrictive rules in the North than in the South.

As a result, Northern welfare departments accepted a higher proportion of those who applied for aid. In 1960, for example, the Southern region granted assistance to 48 per cent of those who applied. The rates were 57 per cent in both the West and North Central regions and 63 per cent in the Northeast. At the extremes, Texas admitted only 34 per cent while Massachusetts admitted 80 per cent. Stated another way, a family migrating from Texas to Massachusetts in the late 1950's improved its chances of getting on welfare almost threefold.

But the expected did not happen. As we noted in Chap-

---

[19] Bureau of Labor Statistics, 1968, 17.

ter 6, the Northern rolls rose during the 1950's, but scarcely as much as might have been anticipated considering that millions of the poor were migrating. How a good many of these newcomers to the cities managed to survive is far from clear. Many migrants found jobs, but many did not, or found only irregular and poorly paid employment. Without adequate income, families had to live by doubling up with friends or relatives, spreading the income of a few among many. Some had to "hustle," turning to the slum and ghetto underworld for income. But one point is beyond dispute—they got very little assistance from public welfare.

This said, it must also be noted that what little the poor did get was gotten in the cities. Although the AFDC rolls rose by only 17 per cent in the 1950's, 80 per cent of that increase occurred in the 121 major urban counties. In some of these counties, the rise was substantial. In the six urban counties of New Jersey, for example, where the black-population increases ranged from 64 to 150 per cent between 1950 and 1960, the welfare rolls either doubled or tripled during the same period. In Chicago, the rolls rose 83 per cent.

On the whole, however, the relief response to these displaced people remained minimal. In America's "big five" urban counties, which experienced black-population increases ranging from 39 to 97 per cent during the 1950's, the welfare rises were relatively insubstantial (except in Chicago): in Philadelphia, the rolls rose by a mere 4 per cent; in Los Angeles and New York, by 14 and 16 per cent, respectively; and in Detroit, by 43 per cent. (New York and Los Angeles were also receiving large numbers of impoverished Spanish-speaking migrants during the same period.)

But the flow of poor people to the cities did not slacken because public aid was withheld. They continued to come, and many continued to be unemployed or underemployed. As a result, a large mass of impoverished people built up in the cities. We began to try to estimate the magnitude of this pool in 1960. In conjunction with the planning of

Mobilization For Youth, the forerunner of the antipoverty program, we conducted a survey of one thousand families drawn at random on the Lower East Side of Manhattan. Fourteen per cent of the total sample had been on the AFDC rolls at some time during the year preceding the survey; however, an additional 13 per cent of the total population reported income below the prevailing welfare schedules for food and rent. In other words, only half of the eligible poor on the Lower East Side appeared to be on the rolls.[20]

Little wonder, then, that when the rolls did go up sharply in the 1960's, the beneficiaries turned out to be residents of some duration (and not recent in-migrants, as is so commonly believed). A number of studies reveal this clearly. One, conducted in Baltimore in 1966 (where the AFDC rolls had trebled in six years), showed that only two tenths of 1 per cent of the caseload in that city consisted of people who had resided in the state less than one year before receiving assistance; only 6 per cent had lived in the state for less than five years before getting on welfare, and that percentage had been declining steadily.[21]

The implications of the accumulated evidence thus seem clear. Whether in the North or South, the relief system did not respond to the deprivation generated by one of the greatest economic upheavals in our history. The experience of the 1950's, like the experience in the early years of the Great Depression, again shows that the relationship between widespread economic deprivation and the expansion of relief arrangements is neither direct nor simple. Economic convulsions may thrust large numbers of families out of the occupational system and into near-starvation, but this condition alone is not sufficient to produce concessions in the way of relief. But if economic dislocation

---

[20] Other studies subsequently confirmed this finding. See Greenleigh Associates, January 1965, 22, and March 1965, 38-9; and Albin and Stein, 310-311.

[21] Maryland State Department of Public Welfare, 19.

also produces disorder and turmoil which lead to a political crisis, government may respond by allowing the relief rolls to expand. There was no political crisis in the 1950's, but there was in the 1960's.

REFERENCES

Albin, Peter S., and Stein, Bruno, "The Constrained Demand for Public Assistance," *Journal of Human Resources,* 1968, 3, 300–311.

Beardwood, Roger, "The Southern Roots of Urban Crisis," *Fortune,* August 1968.

Center for Research in Marketing, Inc., *The Negro Population: 1965 Estimates and 1970 Projections.* Peekskill, N.Y., The Center, 1966.

Cloward, Richard A., and Piven, Frances Fox, "Mississippi: Starving by the Rule Book," *Nation,* 1967, 204, 429–431.

Dunbar, Anthony, *The Will to Survive: A Study of a Mississippi Plantation Community Based on the Words of Its Citizens.* Atlanta, Ga., Southern Regional Council and Mississippi Council on Human Relations, 1969.

Greenleigh Associates, *Report of the Diagnostic Survey of Tenant Households in the West Side Urban Renewal Area of New York City.* New York, Greenleigh Associates, January 1965.

Greenleigh Associates, *Study of Services to Deal with Poverty in Detroit, Michigan.* New York, Greenleigh Associates, March 1965.

Inglis, Brian, *The Story of Ireland.* London, Faber & Faber, 1956.

Kotz, Nick, *Let Them Eat Promises: The Politics of Hunger in America.* Englewood Cliffs, N.J., Prentice-Hall, 1969.

Maryland State Department of Public Welfare, *A Report on Caseload Increase in the Aid to Families with Dependent Children Program, 1960–66.* Baltimore, The Department, 1967. (Research Report No. 2.)

Schorr, Alvin, and Wagner, Carl, "Cash and Food Programs in Virginia." A Study for the Select Committee on Nutrition and Human Needs of the U.S. Senate, Washington, 1969 (mimeographed).

U.S. Department of Agriculture, Economic Research Service, *The Hired Farm Working Force of 1964.* Washington, The Department, August 1965.

U.S. Department of Labor, Bureau of Labor Statistics, *The Negroes in the United States: Their Economic and Social Situation, June 1966.* Washington, U.S. Government Printing Office, 1968. (BLS Bulletin No. 1511.)

U.S. Department of Labor, Bureau of Labor Statistics, *Recent Trends in Social and Economic Conditions of Negroes in the United States, July 1968.* Washington, U.S. Government Printing Office, 1969. (BLS Report No. 347.)

U.S. Department of Labor, Bureau of Labor Statistics, *Social and Economic Conditions of Negroes in the United States, October 1967.* Washington, U.S. Government Printing Office, 1967. (BLS Report No. 332.)

U.S. President's National Advisory Commission on Rural Poverty, *The People Left Behind.* Washington, U.S. Government Printing Office, 1967.

CHAPTER EIGHT

Migration and the Rise of Disorder in the Cities

So far the main facts are indisputable. A large mass of economically obsolete rural poor were redistributed to the cities, particularly to Northern cities. Very large numbers of these newcomers (especially blacks) were not absorbed into the urban economy but were left to subsist on incomes well below established welfare payment levels. Only a small percentage were admitted to the welfare rolls during the 1950's.

Why did the AFDC caseloads rise so rapidly in the 1960's, especially after 1964? As outlined earlier, we believe the explanation to be the increasing political trouble caused by blacks—trouble in the streets, and trouble at the polls. Although we shall discuss each of these political disturbances in a separate chapter, they are, of course, intertwined. They occurred more or less simultaneously, for as mass disorder among urban blacks mounted, so did the number of black voters. Moreover, each of these forms of political influence was heightened by the existence of the other. Disorder among some blacks (such as civil rights protests) alerted and activated many others, leading them to shift their voting allegiances. White voting blocs also became aroused by black turbulence, leading some to defect from their traditional parties and leaders. It was partly the electoral repercussions of disorder that forced political leaders to cope with the disorder itself. In this chapter, the rise of disorder will be discussed; electoral repercussions are the subject of the next chapter.

The Weakening of Social Control

If the blacks remaining in the rural South were still subject to a near-feudal pattern of control, those who migrated were freed from it. They were also cut loose from their own traditional institutions—especially from their churches and from the established patterns of community relations that shape and direct people's lives.

The potential for disorder unleashed by these break-downs might have been moderated if the institutional structures of the city had absorbed and integrated the new-comers. What the institutions of the city offered instead was resistance, which worsened the strains toward disorder.

There were several reasons for this resistance. For one, the host institutions were confronted by very large numbers: some 4 million blacks came to the cities in less than three decades, and they tended to concentrate in the largest cities. (White rural migrants, by contrast, tended to disperse among smaller cities, towns, and villages.) [1] By 1960, half of the blacks in each of the six cities with the largest black populations (New York, Chicago, Philadelphia, Detroit, Los Angeles, and Washington, D.C.) had been born elsewhere, chiefly in the South.[2] Sheer numbers made the task of absorption formidable.

---

[1] In 1965, about 33 per cent of all blacks lived in America's twenty largest cities, compared with only 13 per cent of whites (Center for Research in Marketing, 1).

[2] Bureau of Labor Statistics, 1968, 15.

Further, the institutions of the city—not least the economic institutions—were dominated by whites who resisted the newcomers. The grossest forms of racial discrimination persisted, indeed hardened, in many occupations which unskilled and semi-skilled blacks might otherwise have entered (as a prime example, the construction industry). Meanwhile, automation wiped out thousands of other low-skill jobs. To make matters much worse, the years after the Korean War were marked by periodic recessions and rising unemployment. High labor demand would have eased the transition to the cities and thus modified the strain toward disorder, for the occupational role has been the main agency of social control throughout history. But blacks came to the cities during a period when jobs were scarce.[3] Even those who did get work often remained in financial straits. Many found their wages too small to support a family in the expensive urban environment. Others were employed only sporadically, never sure from week to week when there would be another paycheck. In prosperous 1963, for example, "29.2 per cent of all Negro men in the labor force were unemployed at some time during the year. Almost half of these men were out of work 15 weeks or more." [4]

The consequences of migratory upheaval followed by persistent unemployment and subemployment were predictable enough. Especially important, the structure of the family system eroded, further weakening the already shaky structure of social control in the ghettoes. Men who are chronically unemployed will mate like other men, but they

---

[3] Comparing the circumstances of European immigrants to those of blacks, one observer had this to say: "For one thing, the United States has far less need for unskilled labor today than it had when European immigrants were flooding our shores. . . . The gap is widening between Negro education and training, on the one hand, and the requirements of the labor market, on the other. . . . The Negroes' economic position has actually deteriorated over the last ten years, relative to that of whites" (Silberman, 40–41).

[4] Moynihan, 21.

are not so likely either to marry or to sustain a stable relationship with women and children. Year by year, the proportion of black female-headed families grew, rising from about 19 per cent in 1949 to almost 27 per cent in 1968.[5]

The erosion of the family was far greater in the cities than in rural areas. In 1960, 23.1 per cent of urban black families were headed by females, compared with 11.1 per cent in rural farm areas. In the Northeast and West, the differences were especially striking: 24.2 per cent and 4.3 per cent respectively in Northeastern cities and rural farm areas; and 20.7 per cent and 5.5 per cent respectively in Western cities and rural farm areas.[6] These proportions increase considerably if one looks at only the poorest stratum of blacks within the cities. Although precise data are not available, it is likely that the proportion of female-centered families among the ghetto poor of the larger cities ranges well above half.[7]

The weakening of the family as an agency of social control was crucial for the young.[8] And it was the young who were especially prone to disorder in the cities. In any circumstance, teenagers and young adults are the most volatile age group because they are partly loosed from the family system but not fully absorbed into the occupational system; compared with older groups, moreover, they are much more sensitive and vulnerable to social change. Two simple measures suggest the seriousness of family break-

---

[5] A slightly greater part of this increase occurred in the 1960's: between 1960 and 1968, the proportion of non-white households headed by females increased from 22.4 to 26.4 per cent (Bureau of Labor Statistics, 1969, 22).

[6] Moynihan, 17.

[7] For the nation as a whole, including rural areas, where there are proportionately fewer female-headed black families, 42 per cent of black families with incomes under $3,000 were headed by females in 1966 (Bureau of Labor Statistics, 1967, 71).

[8] We make no judgment about the relative merits of different family systems, female-headed or otherwise. Our point is a different one—that *any* type of family system undergoing rapid change is likely to be at least temporarily less effective as an agency of social control.

down and unemployment for the urban black young. In a study of Harlem conducted in the early 1960's, it turned out that "only about half of the children under eighteen... [were] living with both parents, compared with 83 per cent in New York City as a whole." [9] At the same time, black young people also found themselves confronted by shrinking occupational opportunities. In 1948, 7.6 per cent of non-white male teenagers were unemployed; by 1963, the figure had risen to 25.4 per cent.[10] In some ghettoes, it ranged upward to 50 per cent.

The litany of urban disorders in the wake of declining occupational and family controls is by now familiar: rising rates of gang delinquency and other forms of juvenile delinquency, such as school vandalism; spreading drug addiction; an alarming increase in serious crimes, such as armed robbery and burglary. Eventually, of course, disorder took the form of widespread rioting, and the rioters, too, were predominantly young, single, and marginally related to the occupational structure.[11] They were unmistakably unintegrated.

---

[9] Clark, 47.

[10] U.S. Bureau of Labor Statistics, 1968, 83–84.

[11] Although rioters were not more likely to be unemployed than non-rioters, they were more likely to have been periodically unemployed, according to the *Report of the National Advisory Commission on Civil Disorders* (132). This report contains a detailed description of the characteristics and attitudes of rioters and non-rioters.

The reader should be aware that our interpretation of the ghetto disturbances in the 1960's varies sharply from prevalent views, mainly in the great weight we give to the breakdown of regulatory institutions (especially to the breakdown of work patterns) in accounting for disorder. Others have tended to ascribe the disturbances either to the injustices suffered by blacks or to the thwarting of their expectations, which had presumably risen with the trek north. Neither condition seems to us a sufficient explanation. Throughout history, most people have suffered at the hands of a few; if this is what is meant by injustice, it surely does not account for what have been rare moments of rebellious behavior; in effect, such an explanation attributes occasional events to ever-present conditions. Nor does it seem to us that thwarted expectations among the poor account for recent disorders. The evidence suggests that it was among segments of the black middle class, rather than among the black poor, that expectations rose sharply after World War II. However, rising expectations, as we shall subse-

The Weakening of Legitimacy

In the 1960's, disorder worsened substantially. Moreover, it came to be directed outward, at the white world. Street crime spread beyond the ghettoes and made many areas of the cities unsafe. The roving gangs of black youth who in the 1940's and 1950's fought one another for control of sections of the ghetto now attacked whites on the streets. Teachers in ghetto schools were assaulted with much greater frequency; so were public welfare caseworkers making "home visits" in the ghettoes. The police found it dangerous to make arrests on ghetto streets, for they risked the anger of crowds that gathered to protest. When the riots broke out, mobs of young black did not simply loot and burn indiscriminately; they often selected white establishments, and they engaged policemen, firemen, and National Guardsmen in pitched battles, sometimes even in gun battles.

The main conclusion to be drawn from an appraisal of the disorder of the 1960's is that old patterns of servile conformity were shattered; the trauma and anger of an oppressed people not only had been released, but had been turned against the social structure. Disorder, in short, had become at least partly politicized. Both the rising magnitude of the disturbances in the 1960's and the fact that the disturbances came to be directed against whites probably owe much to this process of politicization.

There is nothing in the process of social disintegration as such that would account for the politicization of poor blacks in the nation's ghettoes during the 1960's. The weakening of occupational and familial roles may engender many forms of disorderly behavior, but that behavior is

---

quently note, probably did have something to do with the emergence of civil rights activism in the black middle class, and that in turn redounded on the black poor, politicizing the disorder created by the weakening of community and occupational controls.

ordinarily apolitical. When people violate social norms, it does not follow that they have changed their views about what is right and what is wrong, nor does it follow that they will strike out against the larger social structure. Rules may be broken simply because people find it impossible to do otherwise (as when fathers abandon families because they cannot support them), or because conformity is so poorly rewarded (as when people quit work because the pay is so low), or because nonconformity evokes so few sanctions (as when crimes by blacks against blacks are more or less ignored by the police). The acceptance of social rules as just and proper is itself a constraint on deviant behavior, to be sure; but if these sentiments find no support in the conduct of daily life—if conformity yields no rewards and nonconformity no sanctions—then they alone may be an insufficient force to regulate behavior. Social rules lose saliency; to acknowledge their legitimacy is to impute moral validity to abstractions.

Under these conditions, disorder may occur just because of its intrinsic values: it may yield profit, as in much crime; or provide escape from the boredom and frustration of daily life, as in much drug addiction; or drain off rage, as in much violence. A society can retain its legitimacy, in other words, and still lose control over large masses of people simply because the structures that ordinarily regulate behavior have weakened or collapsed.

Sometimes, however, the events that create disorder are accompanied by repudiation of the rules; disorder is then likely to spread and worsen, for the disorderly act comes to be defined as morally proper, as the appropriate response of a victimized group toward the victimizers. The difference is an important one: people may stop working because for one reason or another they are unable to work, or they may repudiate the obligation to work, as the young black does who remains idle on the ground that blacks are denied any but the most menial jobs. Thievery is one way of surviving;

but it may sometimes come to be justified on the ground that whites have always stolen from and exploited blacks, so reparations are due. To the extent that such a transvaluation took place in the 1960's, worsening disorder, the question is why?

The main cause, we suspect, was the denunciatory climate created by the civil rights movement. Between 1955 and 1965, various groups coalesced to repudiate American racism in the most unambiguous terms. As civil rights activists arose to attack caste arrangements in the South, similar groups mobilized in the North to attack discrimination in employment, in housing, and in education. The main legislative result was the enactment of the Civil Rights Act of 1964 and the Voting Rights Act of 1965, neither of which had much direct impact on poor blacks in the Northern cities. But the dramatic and prolonged struggle that led to the legislation probably *did* have the consequence of politicizing and alienating people, especially the young, in the black ghettoes.

The emergence of civil rights as a major national issue very likely owes much to the changing posture of various white elites.[12] During the 1940's and 1950's, men in the

---

[12] The role of elites in precipitating the breakdown of legitimacy has often been noted. Edward C. Banfield, for example, has this to say about the origins of the violent draft riots of 1863: "How did the mass of rioters come to have this feeling of moral immunity? Partly from the presence among them of a few leaders who did have political ideas or were at any rate motivated mainly by righteous (as they thought) indignation. (A longshoremen's association had been organized the month before and its 300 or so members seem to have been in the vanguard of the rioters.) Partly from the failure of the authorities to take stern action against them, a failure that seemed to imply some degree of assent. (The Archbishop's refusal to address the rioters in the first days of the riot seemed particularly significant.) Partly—and this I believe to have been the main part—from having for months been told by leading politicians that they were victims of outrageous injustices and were therefore likely (was this prediction or invitation?) to rise in righteous wrath. (Consider, for example, the words of Governor Seymour: 'One out of about two-and-a-half of our citizens is destined to be brought over into Messrs. Lincoln and Company's charnel house' and his warning—or was it a suggestion?—a few days before

highest places in business, philanthropy, and government began to speak out against racial discrimination. The new posture can probably be traced to changes in the economic role of blacks, changes that undermined the traditional economic uses of racism and also meant that discriminatory attitudes and practices were beginning to create economic and related problems of their own.

The stakes of large-scale corporate enterprise in domestic racism have been declining since the Depression. Before that, racism ensured a surplus of cheap black labor which was used against white workers, chiefly to undermine wage levels. It was also used against whites more directly, for blacks were hired as scabs and goons to impede unionization; the history of labor violence in this country has also been a history of racial violence.

Since World War II, however, the accelerated development of machine technology and the growing ability of corporations to manage markets have made low wages a relatively less important factor in profits, at least for large-scale enterprises. Accordingly, racism is also less important, for many corporate enterprises have less incentive to depress wages. As for inhibiting unionization, it has become clear that by helping to discipline the labor force, large-scale unions dominated by "bread and butter" concerns perform a useful function for mammoth industrial organizations.

But even as corporate stakes in domestic racism declined, corporate stakes in blacks as workers also declined. In recent decades, industry has come to require an increasingly skilled labor force. This change occurred just as unskilled blacks reached the cities in large numbers from the fields of the South, with the result that Northern industrial elites

---

the riot that 'the bloody and treasonable and revolutionary doctrine of public necessity can be proclaimed by a mob as well as by a government.') As Orestes Brownson wrote, the draft rioters 'only acted out the opinions they had received from men of higher religious and social position than themselves' " (Banfield, 57).

were becoming as indifferent to black labor as Southern agricultural elites already were.

But corporate elites could not long remain indifferent to unemployed and underemployed blacks as a source of disturbances in the cities. The disturbances had partly to do with outright disorder in the ghettoes, such as rising crime rates. Far more disruptive, however, at least at first, were the reactions of urban whites who panicked at the black "invasion." To be sure, the streets became less safe and the public schools seemed to deteriorate. But these changes were greatly exaggerated by the fear that the mere presence of growing numbers of blacks on the streets and in the schools evoked. Whether the dangers were real or imagined, however, more and more middle-class whites joined the exodus to the suburbs as the ghettoes enlarged, forcing economic enterprises to follow or risk being stranded in a central city without affluent customers. Taken together, black disorder and white panic were costly, and they threatened to become more costly, not least because they endangered the great property investments in the urban core.

Religious and philanthropic elites were also disturbed by the changing population of the cities. Many churches and social welfare agencies followed the white middle class to the suburbs, but many remained in the cities, and for them the black poor posed a new reality. In some "inner-city" neighborhoods, blacks became the only constituency available to these institutions. Protestant leaders especially were impelled toward racial liberalism because blacks were predominantly Protestant and the strength of blacks within church councils had been growing steadily.

Finally, it was inevitable that some Northern political leaders would also be affected by these events, especially those who were susceptible to a mass of new black voters or who depended on corporate, religious, and philanthropic elites whose opposition to racism was hardening. Accordingly, some Northern political leaders began tentatively to advocate racial reforms (which mainly threatened the interests of Southern whites rather than those of Northern whites).

The effects of this growing climate of racial liberalism can be seen in events dating back to the 1930's: the congressional struggle (albeit an unsuccessful one) for an anti-lynching law in 1934 and 1935; efforts by federal administrators to see that Southern blacks got at least something from New Deal programs; a 1941 Executive Order prohibiting discrimination in employment; the appointment of a presidential Commission on Civil Rights in 1947, followed by strenuous efforts by some congressmen and senators to enact a civil rights law; the Supreme Court decision in 1954 declaring *de jure* school segregation unconstitutional; the passage of the first Civil Rights Act of the twentieth century in 1957, together with the ordering of federal troops into Little Rock in the same year.

There were also attempts to deal more directly with trouble in the cities by measures intended to facilitate the "assimilation" of blacks. Some of the larger foundations, especially those with national interests and perspectives, were the first to act on this view of the problem. In the late 1950's, for example, the Ford Foundation inaugurated a "Great Cities" program through which money was funneled to urban school systems for experimental programs designed to reverse the high rates of academic failure among black youth. Later, Ford funded "Grey Areas" projects in several cities to encourage local leaders to get together on plans for new approaches to "urban problems." Foundation money, in other words, was used in an attempt to activate local professional and political elites, and to induce them to be more responsive to the urban black populace.

Few of these events led to a direct and immediate improvement, if any at all, in the lives of poor blacks. But they did reveal that sentiments supporting traditional racial controls were weakening, at least among some elites. This was to have consequences far beyond the symbolic actions of the elites themselves.

As the legitimacy of many racist attitudes and practices came to be questioned by prominent Northern groups, organized protests began to spread in the black community, mainly among the new black middle class. It was they who launched the "direct action" phase of the civil rights struggle, attracting thousands of followers, black and white. This group was itself being shaken by economic changes, although in a very different way than the black lower class. Even while high rates of official unemployment and subemployment afflicted those at the bottom of the black community, better-educated blacks had come to be in greater demand than ever before as a result of the growing need for skilled manpower during and after World War II. Thus, "in 1966, 28 per cent of all Negro families received incomes of $7,000 or more, compared with 55 per cent of white families. This was 1.6 times the proportion of Negroes receiving comparable incomes in 1960, and 4 times greater than the proportion receiving such incomes in 1947." [13] However, "about two thirds of the lowest income group—or 20 per cent of all Negroes—are making no significant economic gains. . . . Half of these hard-core disadvantaged—more than two million persons—live in central-city neighborhoods." [14] In other words, two opposing income trends were at work in the black community: rising affluence in an expanding middle class, and persisting poverty in a shrinking lower class.

These opposing income trends suggest why protest developed first among blacks at higher income levels. As is often the case, ascending economic fortunes stimulated ambitions in this rising group which outpaced their actual rate of advance.[15] They were, after all, as well-educated as

---

[13] U.S. National Advisory Commission on Civil Disorders, 251.

[14] *Ibid.*, 252.

[15] As Alexis de Tocqueville was to say regarding economic improvement and the origins of the French Revolution: "It is a singular fact that this

the traditional black middle class, but they were younger, they tended to have slightly less prestigious occupations, and they had lower incomes. Various studies of the Southern protest leader who emerged in the 1950's show that he

> is the young, somewhat underpaid Negro professional. He is of the Negro middle class but his occupational position does not yet provide him with either economic security or a comfortable income. . . . Protest leaders, like leaders in general, are a group of a much higher class position than the subcommunity as a whole. But among their fellow race leaders their class position is relatively low. The "typical" protest leader is not the well-established M.D., but the struggling young optometrist.[16]

The civil rights activism of the past decade can thus be understood in part as a struggle by a rising group to consolidate its position in the middle class.[17]

Direct action, in turn, accelerated the process of racial liberalization. The new black protest leaders found ready support in the Northern white community, especially among the sons and daughters of the affluent, who went

---

steadily increasing prosperity, far from tranquilizing the population, everywhere promoted a spirit of unrest. The general public became more and more hostile to every ancient institution, more and more discontented; indeed, it was increasingly obvious that the nation was heading for a revolution.

"Moreover, those parts of France in which improvement in the standard of living was most pronounced were the chief centers of revolutionary movement" (175).

[16] Ladd, 255. See also Killian and Smith; and Burgess.

[17] Within this rising group, tendencies toward activism were strongly influenced by occupation and source of income. As economic conditions improved for some in the black community, it was possible for a growing number of entrepreneurs and professionals (e.g., physicians, dentists, ministers) to derive their incomes from the black community itself, thus reducing their vulnerability to white retaliation. Others, such as social workers, teachers, and civil servants, were much more dependent on the good will of whites. It was from those enjoying more "independent" sources of income that the protest leadership was mainly drawn, for in the South, if not elsewhere, it has been "a basic fact of life for Negroes . . . that one does not actively engage in the work of protest organization unless he is secure from economic sanctions" (Ladd, 254).

south in large numbers to join the freedom rides, the "Mississippi summers," the protests and the marches, there to be beaten, jailed, and sometimes killed. With many groups in the North aroused and sympathetic, various elites were even more inclined to repudiate publicly the nation's racist practices, and the movement won victories, first in the courts, and then in the Congress. Each victory— even each symbolic victory—demonstrated that America's caste system was not only illegitimate but vulnerable.

The resulting climate could not help but affect the mass of poor blacks, for even as they were freed from institutional controls, they were led to think of themselves as exploited and oppressed by white institutional arrangements. Under the impact of these combined influences, it is hardly surprising that unrest mounted among poor blacks. This unrest, in turn, redounded on some of the new activists, producing a rising tide of militancy among black leaders. Integrationist goals gave way to the raised black fist and the call for "black power," to an ideology that celebrated race pride and race anger and proclaimed the need for violent struggle against oppressive white institutions. All this heightened restlessness in the ghettoes.

With social controls weakening and delegitimizing forces at work, disorder in the cities continued to increase. School vandalism provides one example. Pitching rocks through school windows is a not unfamiliar form of juvenile delinquency, but in recent years it has become so widespread as to represent something more than the aimless sport of uncontrolled youth. In New York City, for example, 161,000 panes of glass were broken during 1959; ten years later, the figure had risen to 275,000 panes, an increase of 71 per cent. Other types of school vandalism showed similarly sharp increases. Fewer than 800 unlawful entries to schools were reported in 1959; 3,000 were reported in 1969. The number of fires set in schools also rose—from 109 in 1959 to 330 in 1969. Data on the color of those who committed these acts of vandalism are not available, but the acts themselves occurred disproportionately in ghetto schools.[18] The sharp increase in vandalism suggests not only that social controls over youth were weakening, but that youth were turning against the schools, deliberately making them a target of their anger and frustration.

In the same vein, comparisons of rioters and non-rioters reveal marked differences in attitudes toward economic and political arrangements. First, the rioters were much more likely than non-rioters to possess accurate information about the economic and political condition of blacks. They were also more resentful than non-rioters: "69 per cent, as compared with 50 per cent of the noninvolved, felt that racial discrimination was the major obstacle to their finding better employment." [19] Rioters were more likely to have participated in protest actions (such as civil rights meetings and demonstrations); their hostility to whites and their "pride in race" were significantly greater; they were more likely to be contemptuous of efforts by local government in their behalf; and they were less likely to feel that "the country was worth fighting for in the event of a major war." They were more knowledgeable about the political system even while they were much less likely to feel that traditional electoral arrangements afforded an efficacious channel to promote justice and equality for blacks. The rioters were, in short, far more politicized, alienated, and rebellious than their non-rioting contemporaries.[20]

The political transformation of a part of the black poor should not be exaggerated. There have been periods in our history when blacks erupted in activities that were more clearly insurrectionary—for example, the slave conspiracies during the first third of the nineteenth century: Gabriel Prosser's plan to capture Richmond, Virginia; the

---

[18] These figures were provided by the New York City Board of Education.

[19] U.S. National Advisory Commission on Civil Disorders, 133.

[20] *Ibid.*, 133–135.

plantation uprising around New Orleans led by Deslandes; Denmark Vesey's conspiracy to capture Charleston, South Carolina; or the Nat Turner rebellion in Southampton County, Virginia. The number of blacks who participated ran into the thousands, and although these efforts were usually betrayed and always crushed, they represented political action of a clearly insurrectionary kind.[21]

If the riots of the 1960's were not insurrectionary conspiracies, they still reflect a marked change from the relative passivity that characterized black reaction to white oppression in the years between 1880 and World War I. Throughout this period, blacks were kept terrorized by lynchings in the South and by mobs of whites (many of them unemployed) who periodically invaded ghetto neighborhoods in the cities of both North and South. An early example of these mob actions occurred in Cincinnati in 1829, when half of the black population was burned out and driven from the city.[22] Ghetto invasions became more frequent as black migration increased after the Civil War, and especially after the turn of the century. At least a dozen major incidents occurred between 1900 and World War I, a period of greatly accelerated black migration. For example, white mobs killed, looted, and burned the ghetto of Springfield, Illinois, with the result that several thousand blacks fled the city and had to be cared for in camps established by the state.

Blacks offered little resistance to these events. But that was to change, and the turning point was probably the Chicago riot of 1919. Racial controls had already been weakened greatly—by enlarging black numbers, by unprecedented job opportunities in war industries, and by the return of many black men who had served in the armed forces during World War I. In any event, the Chicago riot

---

[21] For a discussion of these revolts, see especially Franklin, and Aptheker.
[22] U.S. National Advisory Commission on Civil Disorders, 209.

saw armed bands of blacks defending their neighborhoods against white mobs and sometimes retaliating by invading white neighborhoods.

Beginning with the Harlem riot in 1935, self-defense against white incursions escalated into black aggression against the symbols and agents of white domination—notably the white police, merchants, and landlords. Although aggression has rarely extended beyond ghetto boundaries, policemen and firemen within the ghetto have been frequent objects of direct attack—in just two years between 1965 and 1967, for example, twelve law officers were killed and twelve hundred injured in the course of ghetto riots.[23] Looters and arsonists also tended to single out white establishments, although fires, even when set on white property, often raged out of control and enveloped black stores and homes as well.

Many of the riots during the 1960's were triggered by civil rights demonstrations, again suggesting that these riots had a distinctly political character. In 1961 and 1962, "freedom riders" and other activists were the targets of violence by whites in one place after another throughout the South, with, at first, little overt reaction by blacks. By 1963, however, white aggression began to precipitate a black response, usually taking the form of mass rioting, as in Birmingham, Savannah, and Charleston (S.C.). A predominant feature of these Southern riots was attacks on the police. On May 24, 1964, for example, blacks in Jacksonville attacked the police, assaulted other whites, looted and damaged property, and introduced the use of Molotov cocktails—all this in the wake of court convictions of black sit-in participants. The rioting which was to follow in the big cities between 1964 and 1968—such as New York, Newark, Los Angeles, Philadelphia, and Detroit—was far more widespread and destructive, and its political character was evident; it was

---

[23] However, white riots against blacks in earlier periods of our history resulted in a much greater loss of life. *

often precipitated by some real or imagined act of official brutality, the police were frequent targets, and the violence was not just aimless.

Finally, it should be said that the urban riots appear to have been most severe where social controls were weakest. One of the differences between cities that experienced serious riots and those that did not was the rate of increase of the black population. A precipitous population increase, especially if migration accounts for a significant part of the increase, probably provides a crude index of weakening social control, for the larger and more rapid the increase, the greater the social disorganization. Among the nation's fifty largest cities, nineteen experienced less than a doubling of their black populations between 1940 and 1960, and only three of these cities (13 per cent) had serious disorders; but of the thirty-one cities where the proportion of blacks at least doubled, twenty (60 per cent) had serious disorders.[24] What, then, was government's response to the rising disorder in American cities?

---

[24] In classifying the seriousness of disorder, we followed the criteria used by the "Riot Commission" (see the *Report of the National Advisory Commission on Civil Disorders*, 112–113). Our use of the term "serious" disorder includes both what the Commission calls "major" and what it calls "serious"—that is, violence lasting more than one day, with at least some fires and rioting, at least one sizable crowd or many small groups, and the use at least of the state police (in addition to the local police) to quell the disturbance. To obtain descriptive information on the disorders themselves, we relied mainly on the Civil Disorder Chronology in the 1967 *Congressional Quarterly*, the "Riot Commission" report, and newspaper accounts. No incidents occurring after the summer of 1968 were included. Our grouping of cities by "serious" and "minor or no" disorders follows:

Serious Disorders

Atlanta	Dayton	Oakland
Baltimore	Detroit	Philadelphia
Birmingham	Jersey City	Phoenix
Boston	Los Angeles	Rochester
Buffalo	Miami	San Francisco
Cincinnati	Milwaukee	Tampa
Chicago	Newark	Washington
Cleveland	New York	

(Footnote continued on page 240.)

Local Responses to Disorder

Considering that migration brought blacks into urban electoral politics in large numbers, the initial unresponsiveness of local government is remarkable (low rates of registration among blacks notwithstanding). In the areas from which they migrated, blacks were generally disenfranchised; in the cities, they became at least nominal participants in electoral politics. By 1960 at least one in five residents in our 50 largest cities was a black.[25] Some of these cities had few blacks (El Paso, example, had fewer than 10,000), but others (such as Newark, Cleveland, Detroit, and Philadelphia) were well on their way toward black majorities. But despite their growing votes, urban blacks got little from the urban political apparatus—not jobs nor housing nor health care nor even much by way of relief payments.

Indeed, it can be said that in some respects the circumstances of urban blacks worsened precisely because their numbers increased. As the central-city ghettoes, swollen by thousands of newcomers (as well as by a high birth rate), began to spill over into white neighborhoods, schools, parks, and hospitals, bitter resistance was generated among the older inhabitants of the city. The trouble was often publicly attributed to blighted housing or inferior schools; but its main source was white resentment of black incur-

---

Minor or No Disorders

Akron	Long Beach	St. Louis
Columbus	Louisville	St. Paul
Dallas	Memphis	San Antonio
Denver	Minneapolis	San Diego
El Paso	New Orleans	Seattle
Fort Worth	Norfolk	Pittsburgh
Houston	Oklahoma City	Toledo
Indianapolis	Omaha	Tulsa
Kansas City	Portland	Wichita

[25] Center for Research in Marketing, 9.

sions. Even the fiscal troubles of the city, while real enough, aroused intense political ire because rising costs were associated with the influx of the black poor.

That these feelings were so bitter was partly a result of changes in the style and method of urban politics. In the era of the political machine, a degree of consensus could be maintained by converting public goods into private favors to be divided among competing groups. What one group got ordinarily did not directly (or at least, not obviously) infringe on the interests of other groups. But with the growth of bureaucratically organized municipal services, whether in education, housing, law enforcement, or urban renewal, the policies controlling the allocation of these services became the grist of urban politics. Unlike private favors, public-service concessions cannot easily be divvied up; if schools or housing are provided for one group, it is usually at the expense of another, and it is usually obvious that this is the case. And so the allocation of municipal services among competing groups emerged as the chief focus of political conflict.

Confronted by seemingly irreconcilable group demands regarding the allocation and control of municipal services, mayors generally favored the various white blocs with which they were aligned, ignoring their new black constituents. New public housing, for example, was reduced to a trickle despite the availability of federal funds because the projects generated fierce opposition from whites who feared the invasion of the black poor. Other federal programs, such as urban renewal, were turned against blacks; renewal projects were undertaken in most big cities to deal with the black invasion through "slum clearance," by reclaiming land taken by the expanding ghettoes and restoring it to "higher economic uses" (i.e., to uses that would keep better-off whites and businesses in the central city). Seventy per cent of the families thus uprooted were black.

But with blacks becoming more disorderly and more demanding in the early 1960's, local government began to make some concessions. Urban renewal provides one example. By the early 1960's, black protests were mounting against "Negro removal" in the guise of slum clearance, and political leaders in some cities with large black populations became apprehensive. They did not halt the demolition of black neighborhoods, however, for that would have displeased the commercial and civic interests that benefited from urban renewal.

Instead, to conciliate blacks while still pushing forward with renewal projects, local officials began to implement new federal guidelines which required that relocation services and subsidies be provided to those who would have to be removed from the neighborhoods designated for clearance. In other words, although black votes and protests did not yet have sufficient force to prevent the destruction of their homes and the usurpation of their neighborhoods, they at least produced modest services and financial aid for some of those who were driven out.

During the early 1960's, as black voting numbers in the cities continued to build up and mounting unrest among blacks gave these votes some power, city governments responded a bit more. To have acceded to some of the demands of blacks—a halt to urban renewal, integrated schools, access to white neighborhoods, apprenticeships in white unions, and the like—would doubtless have spelled the demise of many political leaders tied to traditional white constituencies, so blacks got few concessions in these areas.

What they *did* begin to get was more relief benefits: more people began to apply for relief, and more of those who applied were admitted to the rolls. In all likelihood this happened because it was easier to give relief than to grant other concessions. The rising rolls were objectionable to whites, to be sure, but considerably less so than locating public housing projects in white neighborhoods or integrating schools or enforcing fair-employment statutes.

Urban politicians, in other words, permitted modest concessions in relief-giving as a means of placating the discontented.[26]

And so the urban welfare rolls began to rise during the early 1960's, especially in the North. The seventy-eight Northern urban counties where the welfare rolls had risen by only 41 per cent in the earlier decade experienced increases of 53 per cent in the next four years alone.[27] In many places, the rises were quite substantial. The rolls in Baltimore, for example, rose 128 per cent; in Hartford, 120 per cent; in Newark, 98 per cent; in Cleveland, 96 per cent; and in Kansas City (Kan.), 80 per cent.

Some Southern cities also began to respond. Civil rights agitation in the South reached a crescendo during this period: local whites repaid sit-ins, demonstrations, and boycotts with killings, jailings, burnings, and bombings. At the same time, and partly as a result of voter-registration campaigns by civil rights activists, blacks were beginning to emerge as a modest electoral force in the South. Even before the congressional enactment of voting-rights legislation in 1964 and 1965, black voter registration had risen sharply—by 800,000 between 1962 and 1964 [28]—and this

---

[26] Welfare programs are usually administered by the county, not by the municipality. But in larger cities, county programs are usually subject to the vicissitudes of city politics. Where the municipality includes a very large proportion of the county population, city politicians frequently run the county political organization as well, or at least have substantial influence in it.

[27] However, these increases are exaggerated because of the addition of AFDC-UP cases beginning in 1961. We estimate that about 29 per cent of the total national increase between 1960 and 1964 can be attributed to this new category (see Appendix, Source Table 3). Since most of the AFDC-UP programs were enacted in Northern states, the proportion of the increase attributable to AFDC-UP in that area may be as much as one third, and it may be even larger in the Northern urban centers. (This general statistical problem is discussed in Chapter 6.) Even without AFDC-UP, however, the rate of welfare increase in the early 1960's was greater than in the 1950's.

[28] Between 1952 and 1962, black registration increased only from 1 million to 1.4 million: in just the next two years, 800,000 additional registrants were added. (These figures apply to the eleven states that are

electorate was being alerted and activated by civil rights turmoil. Therefore, even as they publicly condoned repression of civil rights demonstrators, some Southern officials permitted a modest liberalization of relief policies. During 1960–1964, while the rolls in the South as a whole rose by only 7 per cent, the rolls in the forty-three urban counties showed an increase of 24 per cent.[29] In some cities, the rises were large enough to more or less offset the steep declines that had occurred during the 1950's. In New Orleans the rolls had fallen by 48 per cent in the 1950's, but they rose by 35 per cent between 1960 and 1964; in Atlanta, the rolls declined by 30 per cent in the 1950's but rose by 19 per cent in the early 1960's; in Savannah, the rolls dropped by 40 per cent in the 1950's and then rose by 50 per cent in just four years. In the light of the deepening distress of the black poor in the South, however, these rises were modest.

None of this should be taken to mean that welfare restrictions gave way in the early 1960's. As before, many families that applied for aid were turned down. Indeed, the rising tide of black migrants, and of white hostility toward them, led some jurisdictions to begin enacting new restrictions. In 1962, for example, New York State passed a "welfare abuses" act, a special type of residency law under which a person can be denied benefits if it can be shown that he came into the state for the express purpose of obtaining them. Although the New York law placed the burden of proof regarding motive on the local welfare department, the mere fact that an applicant came from

normally defined as Southern for purposes of political analysis, rather than to the seventeen-state census region that is used elsewhere in this book. The states omitted are Delaware, Maryland, Oklahoma, West Virginia, Tennessee, and the District of Columbia.) See the press release dated November 15, 1964, Southern Regional Council.

[29] Since only a handful of these states enacted AFDC-UP, these percentage increases are more substantial than they seem in comparison to the Northern urban increases, where AFDC-UP cases constituted a significant proportion of the increase in the early 1960's.

out of state was often used as prima facie evidence that he had migrated for the purpose of collecting welfare; consequently, many thousands of families were disqualified and given bus tickets back to their states of origin.[30] Despite a number of such efforts to impose new restrictions, however, a general pattern of liberalization did begin across the country. In the nation's 121 urban countries, the rolls rose 47 per cent in four years, compared to a rise of only 35 per cent during the entire preceding decade.

If the relief rise in the early 1960's coincided with the rise in disorder, this relationship was even more striking after 1964. As protests, demonstrations, riots, and other forms of disorder reached unprecedented heights between 1965 and 1968, the relief rolls climbed 58 per cent, having already risen 31 per cent in the preceding four years. The 121 urban counties showed an increase of 80 per cent after 1964; in the "big five" urban counties, the rolls more than doubled (up 105 per cent). And in the South the first significant rise in fifteen years, an increase of 43 per cent, took place after 1964.

At first glance, these data might suggest a simple and direct relationship between growing black turbulence, on the one hand, and greater responsiveness by local government, on the other. However, local government was also under pressure to conciliate blacks from quite another source during the 1960's; namely, the federal government. Even as many urban political leaders continued to fight a rearguard action against blacks on behalf of their white constituents, national political leaders were developing programs that represented concessions to blacks. The main significance of these new programs—especially the anti-

---

[30] Such practices were especially prevalent in New York City, where the city administration succeeded in turning away large numbers of "nonresident" families until a lawsuit initiated by antipoverty attorneys in 1964 compelled them to desist.

poverty program, which was initiated in 1964—is that they led to "reform" in the practices of local government. In other words, under prodding from the federal government, local government was made to revise some of its service policies so as to give more to blacks. Thus, as we shall presently see, it was the federal programs that washed away one local relief restriction after another, especially after 1964. To understand why the national government intervened in local service arrangements, it is necessary to examine the impact of both growing blocs of black voters and rising black disorder on national political alignments.

REFERENCES

Aptheker, Herbert, *American Slave Revolts*. New York, Columbia University Press, 1943.

Banfield, Edward, "Roots of the Draft Riots," *New York Magazine,* July 29, 1968, 55–57.

Burgess, Margaret Elaine, *Negro Leadership in a Southern City*. Chapel Hill, University of North Carolina Press, 1962.

Center for Research in Marketing, Inc., *The Negro Population: 1965 Estimates and 1970 Projections*. Peekskill, N.Y., The Center, 1966.

Clark, Kenneth B., *Dark Ghetto: Dilemmas of Social Power*. New York, Harper & Row, 1965.

de Tocqueville, Alexis, *The Old Régime and the French Revolution,* trans. Stuart Gilbert. Garden City, N.Y., Doubleday & Company, 1955.

Elkins, Stanley M., *Slavery: A Problem in American Institutional and Intellectual Life*. Chicago, University of Chicago Press, 1959.

Franklin, John Hope, *From Slavery to Freedom: A History of American Negroes*. Chicago, University of Chicago Press, 1956.

Killian, Lewis A., and Smith, Charles V., "Negro Protest Leaders in a Southern Community," *Social Forces*, 1960, 38, 253–257.

Ladd, Everett Caryll, *Negro Political Leadership in the South.* Ithaca, N.Y., Cornell University Press, 1966.

Moynihan, Daniel P., *The Negro Family: The Case for National Action.* Washington, U.S. Department of Labor (Office of Policy Planning and Research), 1965.

Silberman, Charles E., *Crisis In Black and White.* New York, Random House, 1964.

U.S. Department of Labor, Bureau of Labor Statistics, *The Negroes in the United States: Their Economic and Social Situation, June 1966.* Washington, U.S. Government Printing Office, 1968. (BLS Bulletin No. 1511.)

U.S. Department of Labor, Bureau of Labor Statistics, *Recent Trends in Social and Economic Conditions of Negroes in the United States, July 1968.* Washington, U.S. Government Printing Office, 1969. (BLS Report No. 347.)

U.S. Department of Labor, Bureau of Labor Statistics, *Social and Economic Conditions of Negroes in the United States, October 1967.* Washington, U.S. Government Printing Office, 1967. (BLS Report No. 332.)

U.S. National Advisory Commission on Civil Disorders, *Report of the National Advisory Commission on Civil Disorders.* New York, Bantam Books, 1968.

CHAPTER NINE

The Great Society
and Relief:
Federal Intervention

In the mid-1960's, welfare rights emerged as a national issue. A vast array of groups—social workers, churchmen, lawyers, civic organizations, public welfare employees, private foundations, activist students, antipoverty employees, civil rights organizations, settlement house and family agencies, not to speak of organizations of the poor themselves—began to batter the welfare system. What is not generally understood is that this upsurge of pressure was largely stimulated by the federal government through its Great Society programs.[1]

---

[1] The interpretation that follows of the origins and fate of the Great Society programs diverges sharply from other recent analyses, most notably those put forward by Donovan, Moynihan (1969), and Marris and Rein. Donovan, like several other political scientists who are cited below, approaches his analysis from the perspective of accepted interest-group theory, and is left concluding that the initiation of the programs is something of a puzzle, for no significant pressure groups were at work. He then, however, invokes the lack of active group support to account for the political troubles that subsequently beset the programs. Moynihan, on the other hand, ascribes the genesis of the programs to the ideas of professionals, mainly social scientists, who counseled federal officials—"those liberal, policy-oriented intellectuals who gathered in Washington, and in a significant sense came to power, in the early 1960's." He attributes the travails of the programs to the fact that these ideas were foolish, as were

Nor was this the first time that a national government had stimulated a relief explosion. During the 1620's in England, the Privy Council investigated the administration of parish relief and then insisted on improved relief arrangements, with the result that the rolls rose to unprecedented levels, in 1933, when the New Deal Administration launched a massive program of federally subsidized relief and required the states and localities to participate, the result was that millions obtained relief. Early in 1960, the federal government once again adopted a posture of concern for the poor (and the black), calling for institutional reform in the name of these "forgotten men."

But when the federal government intervened in local relief arrangements in the 1960's, it did so in a novel way —not by directly liberalizing the existing welfare system through legislative amendments to the Social Security Act, but indirectly, through a series of new measures (particularly the antipoverty program) which had the consequence of mobilizing pressure against local relief restrictions. In retrospect, federal intervention occurred along three main lines:

---

the politicians who were "taken in" by them. Marris and Rein have a similar view, though they are more sympathetic to the professionals. They trace the programs to a blossoming of reform idealism, mainly among professionals in the foundations, the universities, and the federal government. Once implemented, however, the Great Society programs are said to have foundered on the resistance of the local politicians and bureaucrats.

We ourselves do not believe that the stupidity or cupidity of particular political leaders or their "idea men" have much to do with the origin or fate of programs of such scale and duration. Nor do we believe that the initiation of these legislative measures can be ascribed to special-interest groups. Instead, we think that the Great Society programs were promulgated by federal leaders in order to deal with the political problems created by a new and unstable electoral constituency, namely blacks—and to deal with this new constituency not simply by responding to its expressed interests, but by shaping and directing its political future. The Great Society programs, in short, reflected a distinctively managerial kind of politics. Just what the problems requiring management were, and how the Great Society programs were designed to manage them, is the subject of this chapter.

The main points in the chapter were developed in a series of previously published articles by Piven (1967a, 1967b, 1968, and 1970).

—The establishment of new services, both public and private, that offered the poor information about welfare entitlements and the assistance of experts in obtaining benefits.

—The initiation of litigation to challenge a host of local laws and policies that kept people off the welfare rolls.

—The support of new organizations of the poor which informed people of their entitlement to public welfare and mounted pressure on officials to approve their applications for assistance.

This array of activities, we believe, had much to do with the abrupt welfare rise after 1964. As a result of mass protest, litigation, and new services—all focusing on welfare rights—relief agencies found themselves confronted with an unprecedented volume of applications and unprecedented pressures to approve the granting of benefits. In this chapter, we shall analyze the political problems that led the federal government to promulgate these programs; in the next chapter we will consider how the new programs, in turn, produced the welfare explosion.

The Electoral Repercussions of Migration and Disorder

In Chapter 8, we discussed the impact of black migration on city politics, and the modest consessions that local governments began to make in the early 1960's (especially with regard to relief benefits). Ultimately more important, however, was the impact of black migration on national politics. Urban blacks have been Democrats for almost four decades, but it was only in the aftermath of migration and urban turbulence that they began to exert significant influence on the national party, and in ways that literally tore the party apart.

A majority of the black vote went Democratic for the first time in 1936,[2] following the reorganization of the Democratic Party during the elections of 1928 and 1932, when an alliance was struck between urban ethnic groups in the North and the traditionally Democratic South. However, these black voters were located in the North, and they were a tiny minority of the general electorate; most blacks still lived in the South, where the franchise was generally denied them. And so blacks got little as members of the New Deal coalition. In 1935, some Northern Democrats fought a losing campaign for an anti-lynching law; in 1940, a Roosevelt-oriented Supreme Court declared the white primary unconstitutional; and in 1941 FDR established a token Fair Employment Practices Commission. But each such gesture toward blacks was resisted either by Southern Democrats or by the white ethnic leaders in the big cities, who succeeded in blocking moves for more substantial reforms, whether the right to vote in the South or the right to equal employment in the North.

However, agricultural modernization progressively strained and eventually disrupted this pattern of accommodation to the South. We have already observed that as masses of blacks were driven from the land, their voting numbers in the Northern cities increased. Moreover, blacks came to be located in states of the most strategic importance in presidential contests. In 1960, 90 per cent of all Northern blacks were concentrated in just 10 of the most populous Northern states—states with the largest number of electors.[3] To be sure, the electoral influence of Northern blacks was diluted by several factors: blacks were less likely

---

[2] Blacks, of course, had been Republicans, and staunch ones—a legacy of the Civil War. From 1868 on, blacks participated in Republican Party councils, and at certain junctures, as at the convention of 1912, have held the balance of power. In local politics, blacks were also Republicans, except in a few cities, such as New York, where Republicanism was futile (Gosnell, 8–10).

[3] California, New York, Pennsylvania, Ohio, New Jersey, Michigan, Illinois, Massachusetts, Indiana, and Missouri.

to be registered voters because they were younger than whites, and were more skeptical or apathetic toward the voting process; gerrymandering and other devices reduced the weight of urban black votes; and the black ghettoes often were not politically organized. Nevertheless black voting power in national elections grew steadily, if only because of the sheer weight of numbers, strategically concentrated. Eventually this voting power was to precipitate sharp and unmanageable divisions between the Southern and Northern wings of the Democratic Party, and between blacks and whites in Democratic cities. But the fragmentation of the Democratic Party was not produced by black votes alone; it was also the result of widespread turbulence in the streets.

One effect of black volatility was the dissolution of the North-South Democratic coalition. Despite efforts by national Democratic leaders to placate the South, agitation by blacks slowly undermined the allegiance of the Southern wing of the party. The first overt signs that the partnership was in danger of dissolving appeared during the presidential campaign of 1948. Early in February, President Truman, prodded by the insurgent third-party candidacy of Henry A. Wallace, gave recognition to the swelling numbers of blacks in the big Northern states by urging Congress to act on the recommendations of the President's Committee on Civil Rights, which had reported the previous year. Southern reactions were swift and angry, and Truman supporters moderated their stand, seeking a compromise civil rights plank in the party platform. But the convention voted a strong statement, and incensed delegates from Southern states bolted to form the States' Rights Party. An irate Georgia congressman summed up Southern sentiment in the declaration that "Harlem is wielding more influence . . . than the entire white South." In the subsequent election, four Deep South states—Louisiana, South Carolina, Alabama, and Mississippi—delivered their electoral votes to the States' Rights candidate. The South has not been "solid" since. Meanwhile, the black vote in California, Illinois, and Ohio provided the margin for Truman's victory.

Nevertheless, the convention of 1952 saw national Democratic leaders retreating from the civil rights question. After long-drawn-out intraparty struggles, they seated the Dixiecrat delegates without a "loyalty" pledge, and went on to adopt (in 1952 and again in 1956) a weak civil rights plank. During the campaign, Adlai E. Stevenson wavered, first coming out against "compulsory" fair-employment legislation, and then reversing himself to support this and other civil rights measures. As a result, although Dixiecrat states duly returned to the Democratic columns in 1952, South Carolina and Louisiana did so by very slim majorities, and elsewhere in the South the Republicans made big gains: Florida, Virginia, Tennessee, and Texas went for Eisenhower in 1952. Blacks, on the other hand, gave Stevenson 79 per cent of their vote.

Still, conciliation of the South remained the principal order of the day. Campaigning in 1956, Stevenson called for slow but deliberate efforts to desegregate. Even so, Louisiana and Kentucky joined Florida, Virginia, Tennessee, and Texas in voting Republican. And the black Democratic vote dropped to 61 per cent.

Shifting voting patterns—shifts that were being activated by the emergence of the civil rights movement—finally forced the Democratic hand. The Supreme Court decision on desegregated education in 1954 and the outbreak of the bus boycott in Montgomery toward the end of 1955 captured the attention of the nation, generating strong sympathy among many voters in the North and bitter antagonism among many in the South. The subsequent tactics of the civil rights movement exacerbated these divisions. The drama and high visibility of "direct action" and counteraction—of marches and demonstrations, which provoked bombings and jailings—helped to polarize regional sentiment. In this climate, civil rights proposals were championed by the Northern wing of the party. Such proposals represented concessions to urban blacks and their Northern sympathizers, and even though they failed to win legislative support, they aroused fury in the South.

As a result, the party's hold on the South began to slip. By 1960, the disarray in the Southern wing of the party had become plainly visible, for in the three previous presidential elections, only Georgia, Arkansas, and North Carolina had consistently given their electoral votes to the Democratic presidential candidate. The political consequences of modernization and migration were thus becoming clear. Efforts by the national Democratic Party to placate contending regional forces were no longer succeeding. In effect, the black migration northward did much to weaken the grip of the South on the Democratic Party, at least in presidential contests. For once the allegiance of the South could no longer be counted on, its capacity to thwart concessions to the growing mass of black voters diminished.

But the trouble was not only in the white South. As Southern support eroded, the political importance of the big cities in presidential contests magnified, but racial tensions interfered with the ability of urban politicians to produce the traditional ethnic and labor pluralities for the national party. In one city after another, racial strife led to polarization and division within the Democratic ranks. Local Democratic leaders in some cities became so threatened by cleavages in their constituencies that, to avoid further trouble, they simply ignored controversial national candidates and worked mainly to win local contests, a circumstance that severely hurt Stevenson in the campaigns of 1952 and 1956. Equally important from the perspective of national politicians, many local Democratic politicians made no attempt to stimulate participation by blacks or to get out their vote. All this could not help but be of concern to the national Democratic Party. With the South defecting, its ability to capture the presidency had come to depend on the cities, but the cities were ridden with conflict, their political functions often deadlocked.

The Democratic presidential candidate in 1960 was keenly alert to these urban troubles. Uncertain that he could resurrect Southern allegiance, Kennedy made a vigorous appeal to the black vote in the industrial states by campaigning on strong pledges to deal with civil rights and poverty.[4] As expected, the Democratic showing in the South was poor. The States' Rights Party won Mississippi and Alabama; Florida, Tennessee, Kentucky, and Virginia voted Republican. And although black skepticism toward the Democratic Party persisted, holding Kennedy down to 69 per cent of the national black vote, the ghettoes in a number of strategic Northern cities delivered overwhelming Democratic majorities, swinging several critical states to assure his election.

Despite the importance of the black vote, Kennedy did virtually nothing on civil rights during his first two years. He had won office, but narrowly, and his over-all legislative program was being throttled by the traditional coalition of conservative Republicans and Southern Democrats, which promised to grow more powerful in the midterm elections of 1962.[5] Accordingly, he signed an Executive Order bar-

---

[4] Theodore H. White writes of Kennedy's campaign plan: "He felt . . . that he must campaign personally for the big Northeastern industrial states. . . . These grand calculations worked. Of the nine big states, Kennedy carried seven: New York, Pennsylvania, Michigan, Illinois, Texas, New Jersey, Massachusetts. Nixon carried only two. . . . The most precise response of result to strategy lay, however, in the Negro vote. . . . In analyzing the Negro vote, almost all dissections agree that seven out of ten Negroes voted for Kennedy for President. . . . It is difficult to see how Illinois, New Jersey, Michigan, South Carolina, or Delaware (with 74 electoral votes) could have been won had the Republican-Democratic split of the Negro wards and precincts remained as it was, unchanged from the Eisenhower charm of 1956" (384–386).

[5] The Democrats' position in the Congress had been worsened by the election of 1960, which cost them twenty-one seats in the House, "all from the North, nearly all Liberal Democrats. . . . Without them [Kennedy] was more than ever dependent on the South . . ." (Schlesinger, 708).

Although avoiding a legislative confrontation over civil rights, Kennedy emphasized hiring blacks in federal jobs, and through his brother, he mobilized the resources and powers of the Office of Attorney General to

ring discrimination in federally subsidized housing, but
did nothing to implement it; he backed a bill to ease voter
literacy requirements, but sent no substantial civil rights
legislation to Congress. In the meantime, the Kennedy Administration began to cast about for other ways of strengthening its base in the cities.

It was no small problem. A way had to be found to prod
the local Democratic party machinery to cultivate the allegiance of urban black voters by extending a greater share
of municipal services to them, and to do this without alienating urban white voters. It was this political imperative
that eventually led the Kennedy and Johnson Administrations to intervene in the cities, and that intervention had
much to do with creating the welfare explosion.

The Federal Strategy in the Cities

What emerged, gropingly at first, and then in rapid-fire
order, was a series of service programs for the "inner city."
The best-known of these, no doubt because it created so
much controversy, was the "war on poverty," whose "community-action programs" were charged with fiscal misman-
agement and embezzlement and with encouraging demonstrations, protests, and even riots. But the antipoverty
program was only one legislative step—and not the first—
in a White House strategy to deal with political problems
in the cities; the over-all effort had begun earlier, evolved
slowly, and was modified, repeated, and enlarged throughout the 1960's.

In 1961, 10 million dollars was initially appropriated under the Juvenile Delinquency and Youth Offenses Control
Act for grants to "youth development" projects for the pre-

---

bring pressure against segregationist practices in the South. For a detailed
analysis of the activities of the federal executive branch in the civil rights
field between 1961 and 1965, see Fleming.

vention and treatment of juvenile delinquency in "inner
city" neighborhoods. In 1963 the Community Mental
Health Centers Act authorized the expenditure of 150 million dollars to promote what President Kennedy called "a
bold new approach" to mental illness by establishing community centers in the cores of the cities. A number of
further programs evolved under President Johnson. In
1964, Title II of the Economic Opportunity Act (the antipoverty program) allocated 350 million dollars to community-action programs which President Johnson said
would "call on all resources available to the community—
Federal and State, local and private, human and material"
to strike at poverty at its source, in the streets of the cities.
In 1966, Title I of the Demonstration Cities and Metropolitan Development Act called for a "comprehensive attack on social, economic, and physical problems in selected
slums and blighted areas through the most effective and
economical concentration and coordination of Federal,
State, and local public and private efforts . . . to develop
model neighborhoods in the deteriorated cores of the central cities." And lastly, after President Johnson announced
a new coordinated federal attack on the slums in a much-
publicized speech in Syracuse, the Neighborhood Service
Program was launched in 1967.

Although each of these measures was later modified in
response to feedback from the Congress and various constituent groups, each was launched as a distinct White
House initiative, and each was thrust upon a Congress and
a public that were at the outset virtually indifferent to the
specifics of the legislation.[6] In other words, the managerial

---

[6] The absence of interest groups pressing for new legislation of the
kind proposed by the Administration has been remarked upon frequently,
often with apparent amazement. Indeed, Moynihan saw in it a new and
higher stage in American political life, which he dubbed "the professionalization of reform" (1965, 6–16). The Economic Opportunity Act of 1964,
for example, was drafted by the White House and pushed through Congress, with relatively minor amendments, in less than six months—at a
time when there was little sign of any public concern with poverty (aside

powers of the presidency were used to forge programs to deal with the political problems of the presidency, and the publicity-making powers of the presidency were used to stir up the issues to justify the programs.[7]

Why this presidential initiative? The ordinary answers do not suffice. It has been said, for example, that the Great Society programs were needed to deal with one or another "urban problem"—crime, mental illness, poverty, blighted housing. But some of these problems were at least as prevalent in rural areas, and yet the programs were heavily weighted toward the cities. The funds allocated through OEO's Community Action Program (CAP) provide one example: "For the nation as a whole, CAP grants over the

---

from the concern for jobs expressed by the March on Washington in August 1963). The first congressional hearings on the legislation were held by the House Ad Hoc Subcommittee on the Poverty Program. The chief lobby to appear was the White House, which sent a parade of Administration officials, including seven cabinet officers, to speak in favor of the legislation. The only opposition came from groups traditionally and invariably opposed to welfare spending, such as the Farm Bureau Federation, the Chamber of Commerce, and a state division of the National Association of Manufacturers (Donovan, 73–74; Sundquist, 7; Levitan, 38–39; Graham, 256–259). Bibby and Davidson (236) write that "...Congress was asked not to draft the war on poverty, but rather to ratify a fully prepared administration program, and invited, though hardly encouraged, to propose marginal changes." The bill passed the House by 226 to 185; the Senate, 61 to 34.

Once the bill was enacted, the White House retained the initiative; the OEO legislation had been written to assure that it could. "The bill was deliberately drafted to grant the broadest possible discretion to the administrator. The nature of the community organization, the content of its program, the definition of the community itself, were all left vague. The states were given no role in community action.... Nor were the cities assured any role ..." (Sundquist, 27). Donovan comments that the old-line federal agencies dealt with OEO director Sargent Shriver warily, recognizing that he had a presidential mandate (30–31).

[7] For example, after President Johnson announced the war on poverty in January 1964, the news media were inundated by facts and rhetoric emanating from the White House on the plight of the impoverished one fifth of the nation—a group until then largely ignored—while a host of private organizations were enlisted to the war by the President (Graham, 243–244; 254–256). Very rapidly, poverty became a major newsbeat: "Fifteen or twenty Washington newsmen include OEO in their regular 'beat' and countless local reporters write about the antipoverty programs from time to time.... It has signaled the elevation of poverty to the status of a major public issue for the first time since the New Deal" (Levitan, 94).

first four years averaged roughly $97 per poor person. The comparable figure in the ten cities that received the largest grants was almost three times the national average. . . ." [8] These cities were New York, Chicago, Los Angeles, Philadelphia, Detroit, St. Louis, Washington, D.C., Boston, Atlanta, and Pittsburgh—that is, the largest urban centers in the nation. If the purpose was to deal with poverty, then the distribution of the poor, rural as well as urban, should have been the criterion for allocating OEO funds.

But this urban bias is only part of the puzzle. Whatever the problems that plagued the city or countryside, traditional federal programs already provided the vehicles, if not the funds, to help local governments (which presumably lacked the revenues and competence to cope with them). Legislation existed to relieve poverty (public welfare, Social Security, full employment), to build housing (public housing, federal mortgage insurance), and to redevelop slum neighborhoods (urban renewal).[9] Why, then, were these programs not reformed as necessary and augmented with substantially greater appropriations? [10] Why were programs that channeled money through state and

---

[8] Levitan, 120–121. That rural areas received what money they did probably resulted from the ongoing need to build broad support for the program. The original Administration design, for both antipoverty and model-cities legislation, was for "demonstration" programs located in key urban areas only.

[9] Not unreasonably, Congressman Robert Taft, Jr., put the following query to Sargent Shriver at the initial hearings on the Economic Opportunity Act: "I thought we had been working against poverty since the beginning of this country. I thought many of the programs, the Manpower Development and Training Act, vocational education, unemployment compensation, all kinds of measures of this sort, were trying to keep our economy strong. . . . Why, at this particular point, are we going ahead with a poverty program as such in a omnibus bill?" (House Education and Labor Subcommittee, 1964, as quoted in Sundquist, 6).

[10] In fact, some efforts were also made to reform existing programs. For example, urban renewal was modified so that it was possible to use federal subsidies to improve the ghetto instead of just demolishing it, and the public welfare program was amended so that the states were allowed reimbursement for unemployed fathers, as well as for rehabilitation services. As we argued earlier, however, these reforms were not usually administered by local governments according to federal intent.

municipal agencies superseded by measures that channeled funds directly to inner-city neighborhoods?

And how could programs so different from one another have been designed to deal with the same political problems? One of the Great Society programs presumably was concerned with juvenile delinquency, another with poverty, and still others with mental health and blighted neighborhoods—a veritable mélange of social maladies and programs to cope with them. But the diversity of labels is deceptive. These programs ostensibly had different functions, to be sure, but they carried them out in remarkably similar ways. Each program singled out the "inner city" as its main target; each provided a basketful of services; each channeled some portion of its funds more or less directly to new organizations in the "inner city," circumventing the existing municipal agencies which traditionally controlled services; and, most important, each made the service agencies of local government, whether in health, housing, education, or public welfare, the "mark"—the target of reform.

To understand the meaning of these similarities, one must go beyond legislative rationales to the political context within which the Great Society programs were launched. The language of the new statutes and policies referred to the "inner city," or to "slums," or to the "urban core." But these terms were only euphemisms for the ghetto, for it was ghetto neighborhoods that these programs were chiefly designed to reach,[11] and by tactics reminiscent

---

[11] "There was never any question about it," writes Earl Raab. "The early discussions of the program with city representatives, even before the [Economic Opportunity] Act was passed, indicated that the racial and ethnic communities would be chiefly involved. In discussing the problem of 'reaching the poor,' there were frequent references to the need to make contact with the NAACP, CORE, Mexican-American organizations, etc. And indeed, the target neighborhoods in the cities have turned out to be the racial and ethnic ghettoes, to nobody's surprise" (49). In his evaluation of the Economic Opportunity Act, Sar Levitan writes: "In a thousand different ways, black citizens have become the special objects and beneficiaries of antipoverty programs. . . . Negroes received greater benefits from the antipoverty programs than their proportion in the poor population would have indicated" (86).

of the traditional political machine. Local agencies were established, frequently in storefront centers. Professional staffs were hired which offered residents help in finding jobs, or in dealing with public welfare, or in securing access to a host of other public services. A neighborhood leadership was cultivated called "community workers" (close kin to the old ward workers) to receive program patronage.[12] This neighborhood leadership, in turn, became the vehicle for involving larger numbers of people in the new programs, for spreading the federal spoils. It made little difference whether the funds were appropriated under delinquency-prevention, mental-health, antipoverty, or model-cities legislation: in the streets of the ghettoes, many aspects of these programs looked very much alike.

New citywide coordinating structures, such as antipoverty councils and manpower-development agencies, were also created. Through federal requirements that the poor "participate," blacks came to staff and control many of these agencies, much as Italians or Irish or Jews controlled municipal departments. Through both neighborhood and citywide structures, in other words, the national administration revived the traditional processes of urban politics: offering jobs and services to build party loyalty.

But for the federal government to revivify the traditional processes of urban politics, it had to initiate a unique administrative arrangement: *the hallmark of the Great Society programs was the direct relationship between the national government and the ghettoes, a relationship in which both state and local governments were undercut.* It was this

---

[12] ". . . Approximate figures gathered from the [OEO] grant-funding data system showed that in fiscal 1968 about 68,500 nonprofessionals were employed on a year-round basis, with an additional 75,000 taken on during the summer. . . . Three of every four [community workers] were . . . employed only part time. The explanation given was that the CAA's tried to stretch their limited dollars to involve as many community residents as possible. Generally the poor were hired as neighborhood workers to provide outreach and referral services and to interest the neighborhood residents in the center and the community" (Levitan, 129).

shift in relations among levels of government that caused so much controversy. That state governments were not used by national Democratic administrations as the vehicle to reach blacks hardly requires explanation. A number of Northern states were controlled by Republicans, and in the South, the controlling state Democratic parties could hardly have been expected to cooperate in the implementation of new programs for the black poor. But city halls were also bypassed or undercut, including many in the big Northern cities that were traditional Democratic strongholds. That they too were circumvented, at least in the early years of the Great Society, is a mark of the concern felt by national leaders over the growing numbers of blacks in the cities, and over the failure of the urban political machinery to deal with them.

From the beginning of the Great Society programs, city government was defined as a major impediment by many federal officials, an obstacle to be hurdled or circumvented if federal funds were to reach blacks. The problem was solved by diverting a large portion of the new funds to a host of intermediaries other than local government, including private social agencies, universities, and new ghetto agencies created for the purpose, as well as by imposing specific guidelines for the use of those monies that were in fact funneled through established municipal agencies.[13] As one of the original antipoverty braintrusters, William F. Haddad, said: "We were trying to set up competing institutions for the traditional services of government."

Many of the early disputes over the Great Society programs grew out of these unique administrative arrangements, for local officials were hardly pleased to have substantial new sources of patronage and publicity escape their control. Still, the risk of antagonizing local political figures

---

[13] All of which was facilitated by federal grant formulas which required relatively small local contributions. The federal share covered 90 per cent of community-action grants, for example, and very few communities refused to make the token contribution of 10 per cent (Levitan, 120).

had to be run, for if the funds were simply given to local white ethnic political leaders, there was little reason to think that the black poor would benefit.

This was not the first time that shifting political alignments had led to federal action to undercut established relationships among levels of government, for the New Deal Democratic Administration also bypassed recalcitrant state governments which obstructed the flow of grants-in-aid to the white ethnic groups in the cities. But in the 1960's, the Great Society administration circumvented city governments in order to make sure that benefits reached ghetto voters, for by then it was city government that had become recalcitrant, obstructing the flow of services to the black voters massing in the ghettoes.

Giving blacks control over some new service agencies did not turn out to be the chief consequence of federal intervention in the cities, nor was it the main source of the controversy that ensued. The new programs progressively became the instrument with which the federal government attempted to prod municipal agencies (and the private social welfare establishment) into responding to blacks. If local white politicians were agitated at the outset because a great deal of patronage escaped their control, they became hysterical when the federal government permitted, and often encouraged, its new apparatus of local agencies to put pressure on municipal services themselves—pressure to get more for blacks. And that was no small reason for anguish, because services are the grist of contemporary municipal politics. Local political leaders depend on distribution of services to their traditional white constituents in order to maintain power. By interfering with the allocation of these services, with who got what, the Great Society programs shook up established relations among constituent groups in the city. That urban politicians and bureaucrats reacted with indignation is hardly startling.

The considerations which led the federal government to promote municipal reform are not difficult to see. Compared to ongoing programs in education, housing, or health, the Great Society agencies in the ghettoes were relatively insignificant and impermanent political instruments. For blacks to get more significant and permanent concessions, the existing service structures of local government, which controlled the bulk of federal, state, and local appropriations, had to be reoriented.[14] As it turns out, it was mainly—although not exclusively—welfare agencies that were reoriented.

Various tactics to produce municipal reform were attempted, at first under the banner of experiments in "institutional change." With that slogan, the Washington officials who administered the juvenile delinquency program (under Robert Kennedy's direction) required as a condition of granting funds that communities enter into a planning period during which they would prepare documents showing how they were going to "coordinate" their services according to a "comprehensive plan." "Coordination" meant simply that the numerous local officials from different agencies and departments had to get together and agree to do something about the ghetto ("slums, unemployment and juvenile crime could only be understood as the outcome of many interrelated social factors"); "comprehensive plans" meant that they would all agree to a federally supervised plan for delivering service to blacks ("remedies must

---

[14] On this point, Richard Boone, who helped to frame the OEO legislation and to administer the OEO program, has this to say: "The Economic Opportunity Act's architects were firm believers in *local community action* as basic to increased opportunities for have-nots. . . . In 1964 few believed the nation would endorse new systems of direct subsidy to the poor. And champions of community action did not believe a massive new public-employment program would be accepted by a reticent Congress. Further, they held that were such a program to pass Congress, its effect would prove marginal without basic changes in local administrative and accountability patterns. Hence, a continued championing of new policy and delivery systems locally" (5–6).

depend on correspondingly many-sided actions" [15]). But the mere existence of mimeographed plans for reallocating services did not turn out to be very compelling at the point of implementation, and so, as protests and disorder escalated in Northern ghettoes, the federal programs began to make use of another tactic to promote institutional change—"citizen participation." [16]

The controversy created by the Great Society programs in the cities is often attributed to this participatory feature—to the section of the Economic Opportunity Act that called for "maximum feasible participation of residents of the areas and members of the groups served." Actually, there is nothing especially notable about these words; some such participatory clause graces much federal domestic legislation, [17] just as token "representatives" grace many of the

---

[15] Marris and Rein, 93. John Wofford, who served on the President's Task Force on the War on Poverty and later became deputy director of the OEO community-action program, writes: "Although planning was viewed as one kind of community action, its purpose was the ultimate action itself—the initiation of programs that would directly and quickly benefit the poor. A long period of community planning could not be tolerated unless it was accompanied by some action" (76).

[16] Many commentators, viewing the Great Society as if it were an exercise in logic instead of politics, have treated the intermingling of these approaches as evidence of confusion. Thus Moynihan, in an article entitled "What Is 'Community Action'?," scolds the poverty program for its contradictory goals (1966, 3–8). And Marris and Rein lament "the intrinsic difficulty of reconciling ideals which led naturally towards very divergent solutions" (226). In fact, the evolution from planning to citizen participation reflected pragmatic adjustments to the obstacles encountered in attempting to induce a reallocation of local services. For a more realistic account of this transition by a federal official on the scene at the time, see Wofford.

[17] In fact, relying on the language of the legislation alone, many communities proceeded to implement the Economic Opportunity Act in the usual way, by establishing local boards made up of mayoral appointees and representatives of the traditional social welfare establishment. An OEO memo in April 1965 directed that all policy-making boards include at least one resident from each target area to be served by the program. Moreover, modest participation on policy-making boards was only the beginning. Subsequently, when ghetto leaders began to demand larger representation, top staff jobs, and virtual control of the neighborhood agencies created under the policy-making boards, OEO staff supported them;

public bodies charged with implementing legislation. Deference to "citizen participation" is important in legitimizing governmental action in the United States.[18] But the Great Society programs went beyond the customary rituals of legitimization.

Instead of token representation, the federal programs channeled funds directly to groups forming in the ghettoes, and they in turn often used these monies to harass city agencies. As we will show in the next chapter, community people, social workers, and lawyers were stationed in ghetto storefronts, from which they badgered housing agencies to inspect slum buildings or pried loose payments from welfare departments. Later, the new agencies began to organize the poor to picket public welfare departments or boycott school systems. Local officials were flabbergasted; one level of government and political party was financing the harassment of another level.

At least as disturbing to some white municipal politicians, "non-partisan" voter registration drives were launched in the ghettoes with Great Society program funds. To be sure, more black voters meant larger urban pluralities for the national Democratic Party, but for incumbent white municipal politicians, more black voters represented a new and threatening constituency in local contests.[19] To municipal leaders, it was incredible that voter registration in

---

indeed, ghetto leaders quickly learned to appeal to OEO in the struggles that erupted with the public and private social welfare establishment over control of operating programs.

[18] According to the Housing Act of 1954, for example, localities had to show evidence of "citizen participation" in order to obtain urban renewal funds, but all that this entailed was establishing a community-wide committee containing at least one representative of each civic group interested in the program. It certainly did not mean yielding influence or money to the poor who lived in the areas to be demolished. These residents did eventually come to "participate" by their vigorous protests, but this obviously did not happen under government auspices.

[19] The Mayor of Syracuse, being a Republican, was apparently not so much incredulous as indignant at what he considered "an exercise in helping Democrats rather than democracy" (Levitan, 114).

the ghettoes was being defined as a technique to combat juvenile delinquency or mental illness or poverty, and they were at great pains to say so. But as a device to promote a modest shift in the political balance between voting constituencies, it was not incredible at all.

Although little of this was mapped out in advance, neither was it accidental. Federal officials felt their way, step by step, as they evolved an approach to deal with political troubles in the cities.[20] When controversies flared up, the federal government attempted to conciliate urban leaders by drawing back a step or two, especially in cities where white ethnic-based political machines were still firmly entrenched. The executive staff of the seventeen big-city juvenile delinquency projects which preceded the OEO program suffered a startling occupational mortality as they ran afoul of city governments; in the end, most of these projects were allowed to collapse. But they were superseded by a similar system of agencies under the antipoverty program, and on a much larger scale. When mayors and local bureaucrats throughout the country then rose up in even greater indignation, the Administration retreated, terminating a few of the more abrasive projects and conceding new administrative guidelines that allowed for more control by local politicians. (In 1967, an irritated Congress passed the Green Amendment, requiring that local poverty agencies be designated by state or local governments. By that time, however, there were already signs that the federal strategy was taking effect; chastened by controversy, mayors and other local officials had already reached accommodations with the projects, and only a handful of localities

---

[20] Levitan comments that "OEO has taken to civil rights instinctively, but it is hard to say whether it fully recognizes the centrality of civil rights in its task.... Programs aimed at alleviating poverty are likely to produce increased political participation by the poor.... Articulate and activist representatives of the poor are bound to clash with merchants, landlords, welfare officials, and politicians" (88, 100).

made use of the option to widen their control over the new agencies.) [21] When the model cities program was subsequently designed, some of the more bruising conflict was avoided by providing that federal benefits be funneled to the ghetto via city government. But while local politicians and local bureaucrats were thus included at the outset, they were nevertheless subjected to the federal requirement that they negotiate agreements on redevelopment plans with ghetto residents before funds would be granted. Modified, and adapted, the Great Society approach went forward.

Some readers may question this analysis of the political impulses that underlay the Great Society programs. Other observers have said that neither Kennedy nor Johnson nor the Congress ever intended that the poor should gain much influence in these programs, much less that the programs should be turned against local government—that in fact it was all a ghastly mistake, especially because the resulting racial polarization presumably imperiled more substantial social-reform efforts (such as a massive employment program).[22] Moynihan, for example, says that his "recollection indicates that . . . [the provisions for maximum feasible participation were] intended to do no more than ensure that persons excluded from the political process in the

---

[21] Within eight months after the amendment became law, 792 of the 1,018 state and local governments affected had debated whether to take greater control of the community-action programs; only 3.2 per cent had chosen to do so (Levitan, 67).

[22] But it is our point that even if Congress had been of a mind to enact such far-reaching programs, their implementation would have foundered on resistance in the cities to giving blacks anything, as had been the fate of so many earlier federal programs from which blacks might otherwise have benefitted. What the Great Society programs did was begin to come to grips with the sources of this resistance by exerting various forms of pressure (including arousing the ghettoes themselves) on local government for the reform of its service systems—a point that critics constantly overlook.

South and elsewhere would nevertheless participate in the *benefits* of the community action programs. . . ."[23]

That agitation was deliberately intended to be a method of reform seemed clear to Nathan Glazer, who made this comment in 1965:

> One of the most characteristic enterprises we have seen proposed in the Community Action Programs to fight poverty consists of efforts to increase pressure on government bureaucracies. We are all acquainted with such programs; they organize the impoverished community to press its demands upon the schools, the housing inspection services, the police, and so on. . . . The best way to improve services is by attack from the outside, rather than by reform from the inside. When local government protests that federal money is used to attack it and its services, the federal administration will have to explain: but that is the only way to get you to do your job.[24]

Other participants in these events concur, pointing out that the federal staff that guided the Great Society programs from the Washington bureaucracies saw their task as the reform of local government. One observer says that OEO personnel at the federal level "operated on the assumption that the involvement of the poor in policy-making was necessary in order to redistribute power in the cities; without power redistribution, they believed, there would be no great improvement in the lot of the Negro poor."[25]

---

[23] Moynihan, 1969, 87. However, others feel that participation in benefits would not have occurred without community action in the ghettoes. Reviewing the consequences of the presumed "mistake" in North Carolina, John Strange concludes: "There is absolutely no evidence to indicate that, had there been no community action program in North Carolina, social opportunity programs would have been developed and implemented by state or local governments. . . . The evidence in North Carolina is that there was a preponderance of opposition to such activities before, as well as after, the development of community organization. Furthermore, where community organization did occur, local governments and political officials could, *if they desired to,* provide some new benefits for blacks and the poor . . ." (1969, 21–23).

[24] Glazer, 79–80.

[25] Donovan, 43.

Richard W. Boone, one of the antipoverty braintrusters often credited with transferring the "community action approach" from the juvenile delinquency program, where it began, to the antipoverty program, where it was played out on a much larger scale, explained the approach as follows:

It was an attempt to move administrative authority closer to people directly affected by federal legislation. Not only did it allow a bypass of states, it endorsed new administrative instruments at the local level, thus offering the opportunity to bypass traditional instruments of local government. Thus we find legislative language permitting new private, non-profit, local structures for policy and administration. This was sanctioned in the belief that many local governments were themselves unresponsive to the poor. Also suspect were private agencies traditionally identified as "serving" the poor. Concerns over neglect of the poor by public and private programs, their oppression by political design and the insensitivity of service systems were reasons for permitting, even encouraging, new conglomerate arrangements for policy and program.[26]

Robert Kennedy, testifying before a House committee, also suggested that the Administration's intent went beyond simply distributing some new federal dollars and services to the poor:

The institutions which affect the poor—education, welfare, recreation, business, labor—are huge, complex structures, operating far outside their control. . . . The community action programs must basically change these organizations by building into the program real representation for the poor. This bill calls for maximum feasible participation of residents. This means the involvement of the poor in planning and implementing programs: giving them a real voice in their institutions.[27]

The Economic Opportunity Act, Sargent Shriver told a Yale Law School audience in 1966, was "for the poor what the National Labor Relations Act was for unions. . . . It

[26] Boone, 3–4.
[27] House Education and Labor Subcommittee, 1964, 305.

establishes a new relationship and new grievance procedure between the poor and the rest of society." An early workbook for local communities prepared by Shriver's office suggested that a method of securing maximum feasible participation was "to assist the poor in developing autonomous and self-managed organizations which are competent to exert political influence on behalf of their own self-interest." [28]

If critics and commentators were later to claim that the thrust of the new agencies against local government came as a complete surprise, there were at least some big city mayors who had been wary from the outset. Testifying in the House in 1964, Mayor Wagner of New York City (who had already had some trying experiences with aggressive projects created under the Juvenile Delinquency Act of 1961, such as Mobilization For Youth, on Manhattan's Lower East Side), urged "very strongly that the sovereign government of each locality in which . . . a community action program is proposed should have the power of approval over the makeup of the planning group, the structure of the planning group, and over the plan." [29] Mayor Richard J. Daley of Chicago, who had also had experience with anti-delinquency projects, made his position on local control clear to the Congress: "We think very strongly that any project of this kind, in order to succeed, must be administered by the duly constituted elected officials of the areas with the cooperation of the private agencies." [30] Mayor William F. Walsh of Syracuse said simply: "If we could not have direct control of the program, we did not want it." [31] "I have a very definite feeling," Mayor Shelley of San Francisco remarked shortly after the antipoverty

---

[28] Community Action, III A.7.

[29] House Committee on Education and Labor, 1964, 728. Similarly, the U.S. Conference of Mayors and the National Association of Counties endorsed the original antipoverty bill with the proviso that CAP funds be channeled through an agency of local government (Levitan, 65).

[30] House Committee on Education and Labor, 1964, 768.

[31] *Ibid.*, 1964, 822.

program was established, "that this program is headed in a direction we don't want . . . it has the potential for setting up a great political organization. Not mine. Because I have had nothing to say about it." [32]

None of this is to deny that much of what happened under the auspices of the Great Society was both unintended and unanticipated. The objective was simply to reach blacks, to integrate them into the urban political system. The method was to offer federal funds to the ghettoes, and to use federal funds to create pressure for the reallocation of municipal services. That much was intended, and both the objective and the method were consistent with American political traditions.

But in reaching out to the "inner cities," the federal government was to become directly involved with a population that was extremely volatile and politically rebellious—not because it had been aroused by federal funds and federal rhetoric, as Moynihan and others would have it, but because of the traumatic dislocations it had suffered. It was often the most militant leaders rising on the crest of ghetto turbulence who grabbed the outstretched federal hand.

> The people who drew the concept of "participation" to its ultimate definition of political power were the local militants. And they were not generalized spokesmen for the poor: they were the Negro and Spanish-speaking activists left over from the civil rights movement. As a matter of fact, they tended to be the newer, younger, more militant, more chauvinistic wing of the old civil rights movement. . . .
>
> At first the erstwhile civil rights activists couldn't quite believe it. They expected treachery. But every time they screamed "no participation," the federal government held up the funds.[33]

---

[32] *San Francisco Examiner*, May 5, 1966, quoted in Kramer, 59–60.

[33] Raab, 52–53. Writing of the struggle for control of the poverty program in San Francisco, Kramer says that "the battle over representation of the poor was in reality a power struggle between the Mayor of San Francisco and a group of young minority-group spokesmen, most of whom

Even some agencies funded with quite pedestrian designs, such as day-care centers or family-planning services, found themselves forced to adopt aggressive postures and undertake agitational activity in order to maintain their credibility in the face of challenges by the militants, whose stature rose as the ghetto masses became more volatile.[34]

The federal government might have wished for calmer waters in which to launch its programs; but having set out to reach the ghettoes, it could not simply turn away when storms broke out—not, that is, without discrediting its entire effort and defeating its own political purposes.

> OEO found itself pulled in opposite directions. On one hand, increasingly militant reformers were demanding a radical shake-up of existing political and social-service practices. On the other hand, established political groups were alternately responsive and hostile. . . . To the extent that OEO insisted on "maximum feasibile participation" . . . it encountered hostility from City Hall and Congress. To the extent that it yielded to political realities and compromised, it faced rejection by the militants.[35]

In other words, if OEO had the problem of dealing with city halls and Congress, it had the even more difficult problem of dealing with the militants—for the ghetto populace was rumbling in the background.[36]

---

had leadership roles in prior civil rights protest activities. . . . The war on poverty became the successor to the civil rights movement by providing a sanction for middle-class ethnic activists to speak for the poor and to organize them as a constituency that might be used as pressure on community institutions" (Kramer, 25). As a matter of fact, nowhere was the conversion from civil rights to poverty program so evident as in San Francisco, where prominent CORE leadership quickly moved into top staff positions.

[34] Conversely, in slum communities which were not restless, where there was no such leadership, federal funds were left to be used by conventional social agencies to provide conventional services, and rarely became controversial. Kramer's description of the conservative community-action program in San Francisco's Chinatown is a good example (47).

[35] Levitan, 100.

[36] Adam Yarmolinsky, who served on the President's Task Force on the War on Poverty, writes that ". . . there is an irony in the failure of the original Task Force—this author included—to anticipate the violent reac-

Although the federal government did not fully anticipate and could not fully manage all of the varied activities it had set in motion, it nevertheless shaped the over-all course of these events, and in very traditional directions. If civil rights workers often turned federal dollars to their own purposes in the short run, in the longer run they became model-cities directors, or community-action executives— that is, they became government employees or contractors, subject to the constraints of federal funding and federal guidelines. In many cities the Great Society agencies became the base for new black political organizations whose rhetoric may have been thunderous but whose activities came to consist mainly of vying for position and patronage within the urban political system [37] (subjecting them, in

---

tion of poor people and poor neighborhoods to the opportunity to affect their own lives through community-action programs. In a community as sensitive to the problems of the distribution and transmission of power as Washington, the power potential—constructive and destructive—of the poor themselves was largely overlooked" (50).

[37] In North Carolina, especially in Durham, "community action, with special emphasis on participation and community organization, has ... channeled dissatisfaction and unrest into forms and issues which can be dealt with" (Strange, 1969, 29). Peter Bachrach, making the same point for Baltimore, places great stress on the morale-building effects of federally funded programs, which "provided black groups essential sources of power and conflict and decision-making arenas in which the struggle for power could be fought out in the open and *within the confines of the political system* [our emphasis]. One of the most significant power resources the government provided was a principle: that the poor should be involved in policy-making, in programs that affect them. The principle was important for two reasons: it generated conflict, which is an essential catalyst to politicize the poor, and it developed into an ideology embraced by the poor—an ideology that justified the demands of the poor to be heard and their claim to power." Over-all, Howard Hallman, who directed a Senate study of the Economic Opportunity Act, concludes that "... after five years, even though it has sometimes been misdirected, mismanaged and misinterpreted, CAP has a record of notable achievements in resident participation: Several thousand citizen organizations have been formed in urban and rural poverty areas. New leaders, numbering in the tens of thousands, have emerged from among the poor, near-poor, and minority groups, including many militants who now call the poverty program 'mickey-mouse' but who got considerable experience on the CAP payroll. Within the last four years, a new type of neighborhood institution—the

turn, to all the factional competition that system encourages). In some areas with large numbers of black voters, the leaders of these new organizations began to seek elective municipal office, thus vividly demonstrating how Great Society programs facilitated the channeling of blacks into the electoral system. For example, Newark's new black mayor, Kenneth Gibson, began his political career as vice president of the local community-action program.[38] In Boston (where blacks are a relatively small minority), the model-cities director gives his program credit for electing a city councilman. In New Haven, the Greater New Haven Black Coalition consists of forty-nine civil rights organizations and community-action agencies, over half of them funded by OEO. In 1969, the head of the Coalition resigned to run in the mayoralty primary; the new head directs an anti-poverty program. In Durham, organizers from the local OEO community-action agency collaborated with liberals in a successful takeover of the county Democratic machinery.[39] In Oakland, the black "Muleskinners Democratic Club" is based in the model-cities and community-action programs, and has its eye on the mayoralty. (Predictably, the community-action agency has recently become the political football in a struggle between the Republican and Democratic county committees.) [40]

Over a period of time, in other words, federal intervention had the effect of absorbing and directing many of the

---

community corporation—has come into being.... And the tripartite board of the community action agencies is one of the few places in today's polarized society that poor people, public officials, and civic leaders from the 'establishment' get together in a common endeavor" (Hallman, 11).

[38] Just how conventional Gibson's ascendancy was, at least as viewed by some groups, is suggested by the reaction of the business community to his victory. The Greater Newark Chamber referred to the election as "a new dawn for Newark" and the president of the Prudential Insurance Company, Newark's largest investor, wired his sincere congratulations (*New York Times,* June 18, 1970).

[39] Strange, 1968, 7.

[40] Cobb.

agitational elements in the black population. The process was not transparent and bold but richly intricate and confusing—as intricate and confusing as the traditional American political process itself, for it was that process which had been set in motion. From the perspective of integrating blacks into the political system, the Great Society was a startling success, and those who think otherwise will have to explain the accident that accounts for its political accomplishments. More important, however, those who regard these federal actions as unintended, as a mistake, will have to account for the reason the mistake was repeated and enlarged from one legislative program to another as the decade wore on.

The approach we are describing was a precarious one for a Democratic administration to undertake in its own strongholds. Since funds were to flow directly into black communities, there was every reason to expect a backlash from the urban white voters who were, after all, the stalwarts of the party. Several tactics served to avert this danger, at least for a time, and it was probably only because of these maneuvers that the Great Society programs were able to do as much as they did for the black poor—however little that may have been in the larger scheme of things.

One tactic was the emphasis on "community development." This concept was reassuring to whites; they understood it to mean that the assault would be on the "pathology of the ghetto," not on white stakes in neighborhoods, schools, jobs, or public services. The creation of separate citywide coordinating structures (e.g., antipoverty councils) also deflected white antagonism; blacks were to be conciliated with a measure of influence over entirely new structures rather than given greater control over traditional municipal agencies dominated by whites.

Perhaps most reassuring of all were the rationales put forward for the new activities. Juvenile delinquency, family deterioration, poor work habits, and welfare dependency among the black poor were, after all, precisely what many whites thought the "urban crisis" was all about. By promising to solve these problems, and to do so through black "self-help" projects within the confines of the ghettoes themselves, the programs not only conciliated blacks but appealed to whites as well, thus easing the way for federal intervention in the face of growing political divisiveness in the cities.

There were other reasons why the political interests at stake were not widely recognized, at least in the beginning. One was the large role played by various professionals, especially social workers and social scientists, who provided the rationales for the Great Society. Each measure was presented at the outset as a politically neutral "scientific cure" for a disturbing social malady.[41] Each concrete program that evolved was couched in the murky, esoteric terminology customarily used by professionals, a terminology that obscured the class and racial interests at stake, so that few groups could be certain who would gain from the new programs or who would lose, or what they would gain or lose.[42] Finally, the professionals and social scientists lent

---

[41] For a more detailed discussion of the political uses of professionalism in these programs, see Piven, 1967a.

[42] Earl Raab describes the rationales of the antipoverty program as "a kind of sociological surprise ball. Every few unwindings, some new thesis is exposed which changes the character of the whole package. But the package is so tricky that legislators, politicians, social workers, and various segments of the public tend to stop at the thesis which suits them best" (47). Ralph Kramer says that even the "maximum feasible participation" feature of the poverty program "was perceived in multiple and divergent ways by various groups with high stakes in the war on poverty . . ." (3). Whatever the intellectual awkwardness, the obvious political utility of the "sociological surprise ball" in obscuring political purposes from a larger public while at the same time appeasing different "in" groups has been entirely ignored by many who have criticized the Great Society programs for their diverse and contradictory goals. Moynihan went even further, accusing the Great Society braintrusters of stupidity: *"The government did not know what it was doing"* (1969, 170) [emphasis in original]; see also Moynihan, 1966, 3–8). For a description of the conceptual "surprise ball" that facilitated the launching of Mobilization For Youth, the Great Society's first community-action program, see Piven, 1968.

an aura of scientific authority to what might otherwise have been perceived as political rhetoric. By thus obscuring the fact that the federal government was about to give something to the blacks, opposition by white groups was deflected.

To be sure, some groups were wary from the beginning, especially the public and private agencies on whose terrain the federal government was venturing. Here again, professional definitions helped to assuage fears. Everyone was given to understand that there was no cause to worry that new service or administrative precedents were being established or imposed. Once the viability of a new policy or practice had been "demonstrated" by the federally funded projects, it would be up to the regular agencies to make appropriate changes in their own programs, and then the threatening "pilot" projects would wither away.[43]

Established agencies were all the more ready to accept these assurances because they were also given a piece of the action, a stake in the Great Society.[44] What some critics see as incredibly intricate networks of Great Society agencies held together by multitudes of subcontracting arrangements that bring tears of frustration to the eyes of auditors were merely the structural reflections of the politics of implementation, which required that many interested parties—municipal agencies, private social agencies, universities, new ghetto organizations, private corporations, etc.—be co-opted into the programs.[45] Professionals helped to justify these arrangements as well. Social problems were

---

[43] For a discussion of the political uses of the "demonstration" project, see Piven, 1967a, 6.

[44] For a case study of this process on the local level, see Piven, in press.

[45] A similar process, graced with the term "federal coordination," took place among the various federal agencies with a stake in the new programs. See, for example, Adam Yarmolinsky's account of the drafting of the Economic Opportunity Act, and the modifications imposed as a result of bureaucratic wrangling (34–51). Yarmolinsky attaches much importance to this process and little to the fact that the "community action" legislative design had already been prepared, and remained fundamentally intact despite the modifications (see Levitan, 3–47).

defined as "multifaceted," thus requiring "comprehensive" and "coordinated" solutions; to all appearances, the laws of science were dictating the politics of implementation. As for the professionals themselves, if they were politically useful, they were glad to be so, for federal intervention in the cities provided funds and authority for the expansion of professional interests as well.[46]

To say that such maneuvers helped to muffle and to delay conflict and so smoothed the way for federal intervention is not to say that conflict was avoided. Since an existing network of political relations was being undermined, conflict was inevitable. What was at stake was the allocation of local services, and as blacks began to demand more and to get more from public agencies, that was bound to be recognized—sooner or later.

In our discussion so far, we have focused on political troubles in the Northern urban Democratic strongholds and on federal efforts to deal with them. But black turmoil in the North produced concessions for blacks in the South as well. One concession was the franchise; once the Kennedy-Johnson regime emerged victorious from the midterm congressional election of 1962,[47] it lent support to civil rights legislation, leading to the passage of the Civil Rights Act of 1964 and the Voting Rights Act of 1965.

Although these measures were mainly a response to the black voters massed in the Northern cities, the legislation was also based on a reckoning of changing political align-

---

[46] Graham writes of the poverty program that "the social-service orientation, particularly the stress upon the 'reorganization' and 'total mobilization' of existing programs, is vigorously advocated by a well-organized and sophisticated lobby within the administrative branch." Moreover, "the social-service orientation of the War on Poverty is *job*-creating for the middle and upper classes" (235).

[47] The Democrats lost only two seats in the House and regained four seats in the Senate, a feat comparable to the New Deal victory of 1934 discussed in Chapter 2.

ments in the Southern states. As white defections in the South continued and spread, the hope of recapturing many of these voters waned, and so the Democrats had less to lose by enfranchising Southern blacks. Moreover, even without federal support, blacks were beginning to emerge as a modest electoral force in the South. They accounted for 11 per cent of registered Southern voters in 1962 and 14 per cent in 1964 (17 per cent by the end of 1969).[48] Legislation to accelerate the spread of the franchise could be expected to solidify black allegiance to the national Democratic Party and strengthen the Democratic vote in a number of border states that had teetered between the Democratic and Republican columns during the 1950's.

And so, prodded by demonstrations in thousands of cities and towns, North and South, the Democratic Party enacted the civil rights legislation of the 1960's. The movement of blacks northward, in other words, helped to get the vote for those blacks who remained behind. Displaced from the feudal plantation system, blacks were finally being incorporated into the electoral system, both North and South.

With electoral changes of such scale in process, the passage of civil rights measures was not a sufficient response. Southern blacks also wanted improved conditions of life, but under persisting caste arrangements, local governments were not providing services and resources. In some respects, therefore, the problem of reaching blacks in the South resembled that in the Northern urban areas, for the state and local Democratic parties in the South were entrenched, opposed to rising black aspirations, and hardly eager to reallocate services in order to cultivate black allegiance.

Accordingly, the strategy of the Great Society was also employed in Southern areas, although the powerful South-

---

[48] *Voter Education Project News*, November 1969, Vol. 3, No. 11. Atlanta: Southern Regional Council, 1969.

ern congressional delegation was watchful and was at least partly successful in curbing implementation of these programs in its homeland. Nevertheless, through legislative provisions permitting the federal government to bypass state and local governments, a direct federal relationship was established with black groups throughout the South. It was just this kind of relationship that came to be an issue in the prolonged controversy over the Mississippi Child Development Group, a "head-start" program which organized rural blacks to fight the white-controlled county political apparatus in that state on issues ranging from civil rights to sanitation services to getting families on the welfare rolls.

We noted earlier that the Great Society programs reoriented the activists of the Northern ghettoes. The same point can be made about the civil rights movement in the South. With the proliferation of OEO agencies, thousands of jobs were made available to civil rights workers, and many took them. Indeed, most of the welfare rights activity in the South was initiated by OEO staff members who had been affiliated with the civil rights movement in the early 1960's. The key welfare rights organizer in New Orleans in 1968, for example, was an OEO official, Isaiah Reynolds, who had won CORE's "Gandhi Award" in 1964 for his earlier civil rights work. Even more obviously than in the North, Great Society programs in the South channeled protest and turbulence, with the result that much civil rights activity became virtually synonymous with anti-poverty activity.

Our main point, then, is that to reach, placate, and integrate a turbulent black constituency, the national Democratic administration of the 1960's acted to help blacks get more from local government. To accomplish this goal, it reached past state and local governments—including Democratic ones—to stimulate black demands for services,[49] and in that process it directed rising black volatility into service protests against local government. In this way, the relatively limited funds expended through the Great Society programs acted as a lever in redirecting (and increasing) the monies that flowed through local agencies. By turning some of the benefits of these services to blacks, the apparatus of local government was put to work for the national Democratic party. Just how this happened in the arena of public welfare is the subject of the next chapter.

REFERENCES

Bachrach, Peter, "Non-decision-Making and the Urban Racial Crisis." Unpublished paper delivered at the meeting of the American Political Science Association, 1969.

Bibby, John Franklin, and Davidson, Roger H., *On Capitol Hill: Studies in the Legislative Process*. New York, Holt, Rinehart & Winston, 1967.

Boone, Richard W., "Reflections on Citizen Participation and the Economic Opportunity Act." Unpublished paper prepared for the National Academy of Public Administration's conference on crisis, conflict, and creativity, Warrington, Virginia, April 23–25, 1970.

Cobb, Paul, "Muleskinners Democratic Club." Unpublished paper released by the Oakland Black Caucus, Oakland, California, May 7, 1970.

---

[49] Although our main focus is on the stimulation of demand for relief benefits, the same point can be made about the demand for other services. Thus the authors of a study of the effects of the Great Society programs in Baltimore make this observation about the use of health services in the mid-1960's (prior to the enactment of Medicaid or Medicare): ". . . the medical care program and the use of clinics and other facilities by low income groups increased enormously in the State, to such an extent that the reorganization of out-patient clinical facilities was necessary in the entire hospital system. . . ." And they make the further interesting observation that the greatly increased utilization of health services represented, "if not an increase in health problems, *at least an increase in attention to health problems on the part of these people.*" [Emphasis added.] In this sense, then, the Great Society can be said to have promulgated programs that stimulated demands for a variety of local services (Maryland State Department of Public Welfare, 34).

Donovan, John C., *The Politics of Poverty*. New York, Pegasus, 1967.

Fleming, Harold C., "The Federal Executive and Civil Rights: 1961–1965," *Daedalus*, Fall 1965, 94, 921–948.

Glazer, Nathan, "Why Are the Poor Still With Us? Paradoxes of American Poverty," *Public Interest*, Fall 1965, 1, 71–81.

Gosnell, Harold, *Machine Politics: Chicago Model*. Chicago, University of Chicago Press, 1937.

Graham, Elinor, "The Politics of Poverty," in Ben B. Seligman, ed., *Poverty as a Public Issue*. New York, Free Press, 1965.

Graham, Elinor, "Poverty and the Legislative Process," in Ben B. Seligman, ed., *Poverty as a Public Issue*. New York, Free Press, 1965.

Hallman, Howard W., "Federally Financed Citizen Participation." Unpublished paper prepared for the National Academy of Public Administration's conference on crisis, conflict, and creativity, Warrington, Virginia, April 23–25, 1970.

Kramer, Ralph M., *Participation of the Poor: Comparative Case Studies in the War on Poverty*. Englewood Cliffs, N.J., Prentice-Hall, 1969.

Levitan, Sar A., *The Great Society's Poor Law: A New Approach to Poverty*. Baltimore, Johns Hopkins Press, 1969.

Marris, Peter, and Rein, Martin, *Dilemmas of Social Reform: Poverty and Community Action in the United States*. New York, Atherton Press, 1967.

Maryland State Department of Public Welfare, *A Report on Caseload Increase in the Aid to Families with Dependent Children Program, 1960–66*. Baltimore, The Department, July 1967. (Research Report No. 2.)

Moynihan, Daniel P., "The Professionalization of Reform," *Public Interest*, Fall 1965, 1, 6–16.

Moynihan, Daniel P., "What Is Community Action?" *Public Interest*, Fall 1966, 5, 3–8.

Moynihan, Daniel P., *Maximum Feasible Misunderstanding: Community Action in the War on Poverty*. New York, Free Press, 1969.

Piven, Frances Fox, "Participation of Residents in Neighborhood Community Action Programs," *Social Work*, January 1966, 11, 73–80.

Piven, Frances Fox, "Professionalism As a Political Skill: The Case of a Poverty Program," in *Personnel in Anti-Poverty Programs: Implications for Social Work Education*. New York, Council on Social Work Education, 1967a.

Piven, Francis Fox, "The Demonstration: A Federal Strategy

for Local Change," in George Brager and Francis Purcell, eds., *Community Action Against Poverty: Notes from the Mobilization Experience.* New Haven, College and University Press, 1967b.

Piven, Frances Fox, "Dilemmas in Social Planning: A Case Inquiry," *Social Service Review,* 1968, 42, 197–206.

Piven, Frances Fox, "The Great Society as Political Strategy," *Columbia Forum,* Summer 1970, XIII, 2, 17–22.

Piven, Frances Fox, "Federal Intervention in the Cities: The New Urban Programs as a Political Strategy," in Erwin Smigel, ed., *Handbook on the Study of Social Problems.* Chicago, Rand McNally & Company, in press.

Raab, Earl, "A Tale of Three Wars: (3) What War and Which Poverty?" *Public Interest,* Spring 1966, 3, 45–56.

Schlesinger, Arthur M., Jr., *A Thousand Days.* Boston, Houghton Mifflin Company, 1965.

Strange, John H., "The Politics of Protest: The Case of Durham." Unpublished paper prepared for delivery at the meeting of the Southern Political Science Association, Gatlinburg, Tennessee, November 1968.

Strange, John H., "Community Action in North Carolina: Maximum Feasible Misunderstanding? Mistake? Or Magic Formula?" Unpublished paper prepared for delivery at the meeting of the Southern Political Science Association, Miami, Florida, November 1969.

Sundquist, James L., "Origins of the War on Poverty," in James L. Sundquist, ed., *On Fighting Poverty.* New York, Basic Books, 1969.

U.S. House of Representatives, *Economic Opportunity Act of 1964.* Hearings Before the Subcommittee on the War on Poverty Program of the Committee on Education and Labor, 88th Congress, 2nd Session, March 17, 1964. Washington, U.S. Government Printing Office, 1964.

U.S. Office of Economic Opportunity, *Community Action Workbook.* Washington, OEO, 1965.

White, Theodore H., *The Making of the President 1960.* New York, Atheneum Publishers, 1961.

Wofford, John G., "The Politics of Local Responsibility: Administration of the Community Action Program—1964–1966," in James L. Sundquist, ed., *On Fighting Poverty.* New York, Basic Books, 1969.

Yarmolinsky, Adam, "The Beginnings of OEO," in James L. Sundquist, ed., *On Fighting Poverty.* New York, Basic Books, 1969.

CHAPTER TEN

The Great Society
and Relief:
Local Consequences

Before we begin our account of the ways in which the
Great Society programs increased the welfare load, let us
make it clear that we do not mean to suggest that national
political leaders intended the relief rolls to rise; in fact, we
suspect that public welfare was usually far from their
minds.[1] (Indeed, had they been asked, many would have

---

[1] But not always. Although most of the discussions among government
advisers apparently dealt with lofty strategies for "breaking the cycle of
poverty," their concrete examples were often about welfare. Writing in
1969, Adam Yarmolinsky recalled what had seemed to him in 1964 a
"model demonstration" of how maximum feasible participation of the poor
in the poverty program should work. The model he had in mind was a
project funded under the Juvenile Delinquency Act of 1961: "A woman . . .
had been visited in the wee hours of the morning by a welfare investigator
to see if she had a man in the house. She called her indigenous neighborhood worker—paid by the local community-action board—who came by,
took the investigator's name, and later filed a report on the incident, with
an eye to avoiding future recurrences" (49). Shortly afterwards, Sargent
Shriver also pointed the finger at the welfare system while testifying at
the first House hearings on administration of the antipoverty law. Presumably quoting a woman from Colorado, he said: "Poverty is having the
welfare investigators break in at four o'clock in the morning and cut off
your welfare check without an explanation—and then when you go down
and ask, they tell you it is because they found a pair of men's house slip-
pers in the attic, where your brother left them when he visited a month
ago. . . . Poverty is having a child with glaucoma and watching that eye

said their object was to reduce the welfare rolls by educating and training the poor.) The political circumstances of the 1960's made it crucial, however, that blacks get something in order to solidify their allegiance to the national Democratic Party, and in order to quiet them. As it turned out, welfare was the system that was made to do most of the giving—partly, perhaps, because black constituents needed money; more importantly, because it was easier to give welfare than to press for concessions that would challenge the interests of other groups in the cities. When the families who showed up at a community-action agency asked for housing because they lived in rat-infested tenements, or for more money for rent because they were dislocated by urban renewal, or for jobs, what were agency staff to do? They could not provide low-rent housing when none was being built or break down discriminatory housing patterns, or create jobs, or overcome discriminatory hiring practices. But it *was* possible to badger the welfare department into putting families on the relief rolls.

In other words, while the Great Society agencies often attempted to make gains for blacks in housing and health care and education and employment, resistance was stiff and sometimes virulent, for other groups in the cities had major stakes in these services and resources. But there were few other major groups in the cities with direct and immediate interests in welfare. (Giving welfare was also cheaper, at least in the short run, than building housing, for example.) Consequently, relief-giving turned out to be the most expeditious way to deal with the political pressures created by a dislocated poor, just as it had been many times in the past.

---

condition grow worse every day while the welfare officials send you to the private agencies, and the private agencies send you back to the welfare.... And they finally refer you but it is too late then, because your child has permanently lost 80 per cent of his vision ..." (House Committee on Education and Labor, 1965, 16–18).

Welfare Rights Services

Federal intervention, we said in the last chapter, proceeded along three main lines: establishing welfare rights services, promoting litigation, and nourishing grass-roots pressure by the poor themselves. Although most welfare rights services were sponsored by Great Society programs, there was one major exception—namely, the relocation provisions in the urban renewal program. These provisions, inaugurated in the late 1950's, were more vigorously enforced under Kennedy and Johnson than they had been before, and one consequence was that thousands of people were unearthed and referred to public welfare departments for financial assistance.

The city of Baltimore provides a dramatic illustration of this process. The relief rolls in Baltimore trebled between 1960 and 1966, accounting for about 75 per cent of the increase in the entire state of Maryland, and leading HEW and the Maryland State Department of Public Welfare to join in an investigation of the rise. Urban renewal and relocation services were, it turns out, an important cause. Some 14,000 units of low-rental housing had been destroyed over a ten-year period beginning in 1955, and equivalent numbers of poor households (with a median income of $2600) were forced to relocate. With their living arrangements disrupted, many families could no longer manage on their marginal incomes. For example, extended families (a mother with children living with her parents) were often forced to break up because the residences to which they were moved had less space; if their combined income was insufficient to pay two rentals, the mother and children were referred for AFDC benefits. For other families, adequate housing simply could not be found at rentals they could afford, so they were sent to the relief agency to obtain supplemental income. In the words of the report,

"Uncovering low-income families and forcing them to move eventuated in thousands of referrals by the Housing Agency to the Department of Welfare. . . . There can be no question but what the Urban Renewal effort during these years resulted in a substantial amount of 'case-finding' for the Welfare Department." [2] Thus the urban renewal agency solved its problems with the poor, not by modifying its clearance program, but by turning to the public agency that traditionally deals with the poor—public welfare.[3]

Baltimore is not an isolated instance; relocation agencies in other cities have also had to turn to public welfare. Considering the magnitude of urban renewal programs since the late 1950's, it is likely that many tens of thousands of eligible families in the cities have been led to apply for public assistance at the urging and with the help of relocation personnel.

The type of welfare rights service that became most prevalent in the 1960's was the "storefront service center," staffed by social workers, lawyers, churchmen, students, and slum dwellers themselves. Although other Great Society programs sponsored local centers, OEO's "community action agencies" (CAA's) sponsored most of them—perhaps one thousand in all. "The institution most closely identified with the CAA's was the neighborhood service center. As defined by OEO, neighborhood centers serve a definite target area, offering clients a variety of services or referring them to other facilities. . . . The centers' physical aspects range from small storefronts to large structures; their annual budgets range from a few thousand to more than a million dollars. . . . There were [one or more] neighborhood center programs in some 870 communities in 1968." [4]

Direct evidence of the impact of these services is avail-

---

[2] Maryland State Department of Public Welfare, 35.

[3] This situation was similar to the early New Deal period when relief was used to take care of some of the tenant farmers and farm laborers who lost their jobs as a result of new federal subsidy programs for farmers (see Chapter 3).

[4] Levitan, 128.

able from the Baltimore study mentioned earlier. The conclusion was reached that, in addition to relocation services,
the local OEO agencies were a major cause of the welfare
rise. The researchers analyzed the impact on the welfare
rolls one year after the first neighborhood service center
was opened: "From September of 1965 to September of
1966 . . . [the] AFDC caseload in [this particular anti-
poverty] area grew by 36.6 per cent; the total City AFDC
caseload, during the same period, increased by only 8.6
per cent. . . . All the [antipoverty] agency did . . . was to
make people aware of the availability of AFDC [and] to
stimulate the use of [it]." [5]

A more recent study examined the relationship between
antipoverty expenditures and AFDC caseload changes in
eleven cities, with the following tentative result:

> A statistically significant relation did exist between CAP
> expenditures and the *AFDC poor rate*—the higher the
> [per capita] expenditure the higher the rate [at which
> poor families were on the rolls]. Although there is no
> direct evidence, CAP programs may have helped the poor
> understand their rights under existing public assistance
> policies and may have lowered the amount of *personal*
> stigma recipients felt. There is evidence showing that
> CAP programs are associated with reduced feelings of
> helplessness. CAP expenditures per 1,000 poor persons
> were inversely related to powerlessness (the more a city
> received CAP funds, the fewer the number of recipients
> feeling helpless). [6]

The less helpless people felt in dealing with public agencies, this same study also tentatively concluded, the more
likely that a higher proportion of the poor were on the
rolls. [7] To understand just how these new services helped

---

[5] Maryland State Department of Public Welfare, 36. The antipoverty
area studied was not the same area where the large-scale urban renewal
clearance had occurred; the effects of the two programs were independent.

[6] Department of Health, Education, and Welfare, 48–49.

[7] *Ibid.*, 46.

expand the welfare rolls, we turn now to a description of
the activities carried out in two storefront centers—one in
New York City and the other in Chicago.

THE STOREFRONT ON STANTON STREET

Mobilization For Youth was the first Great Society agency.
It opened in 1962 on New York's Lower East Side, the precursor of seventeen such agencies established in sixteen
major cities in the early 1960's with federal anti-delinquency money.[8] It was later to become the model for
OEO's community-action agencies. To most of the adults
on the Lower East Side, MFY was symbolized by its storefront service centers, to which residents were encouraged
to bring their daily problems of living under the welfare
state. Later, these service centers—and centers like them
across the country—also helped give birth to a national
organization of welfare recipients.

The first storefront was opened on Stanton Street in a
neighborhood of dilapidated tenements and shabby stores
where some 14 per cent of the residents were already on
public assistance. Painted on the front windows of the storefront was: *Centro de Servicio al Vencendario . . . Neighborhood Service Center*; a sign lettered on the door said
Walk In! Those who did were encouraged by the staff to
tell about their problems as they saw them. Although the
people on Stanton Street had a lengthy charge sheet against
their generally hostile environment, most of their grievances had to do with lack of money—to pay their bills at
the grocer's, to placate the landlord who was threatening

---

[8] MFY's funds were supplemented by the National Institute of Mental
Health, the Ford Foundation, and the City of New York. For a good history of the evolution of the federal anti-delinquency program, see Marris
and Rein; for a rather muddled though more popular account, see Moynihan. MYF's original executive directors were: James E. McCarthy, administrative director; George A. Brager, program director; and Richard A.
Cloward, research director. An account of the activities in the storefront
on Stanton Street was published by Cloward and Elman.

eviction, to buy clothing so their children could go to school. To help them, the staff at the storefront mainly turned to welfare. As the months passed, hundreds of Stanton Street families learned through the neighborhood grapevine that the thing to do in the event of money trouble with the grocer or the landlord (as well as trouble of other kinds, such as a child suspended from school) was to come directly to the storefront.

Nearly two thirds of the people who found their way to the storefront during the first six months listed "insufficient income" as their principal problem. In more than half of these cases it turned out that they were eligible for public assistance but not receiving it; another third were already recipients, and their problems of "insufficient income" were often due to underbudgeting or delayed checks. Three years later—when the number of families seen at Stanton Street increased tenfold, the original storefront office had spilled over into two adjoining sites, and three other storefronts had been opened elsewhere on the Lower East Side—problems with public welfare continued to predominate.

As time passed, the center staff became skilled in fighting the welfare department. They totaled up scores of welfare budgets to detect underbudgeting; they placed telephone calls to a bewildering number of functionaries and sometimes accompanied families to see officials in person. They argued and cajoled; they bluffed and threatened. When a Stanton Street woman was charged with child neglect by the welfare department, a center worker presented evidence that the mother's childrearing efforts had been stymied by consistent underbudgeting for more than a year, and welfare was told that she would be provided with an attorney. "When I go to welfare," one Stanton Street staff member declared, "I don't wait around for the stall. If I don't get treated with respect, I start hollering for the supervisor, and then I threaten legal action." Another said of the welfare department: "Any way you cut it, they are the enemy." Staff members, in short, took sides with the poor:

> When I think that Mrs. Cortez hasn't gotten any money for her rat allowance, I sometimes want to throw up my hands and say: What difference does it make? [A New York City, welfare policy allowed slum families extra allowances toward their utility bill to offset the cost of keeping their light burning all night to drive away rats.] But when I realize that it isn't just the rat allowance . . . that it's a total system of oppressiveness and disrespect for people, why then I've got to get her that rat allowance. I've got to help her get as many things as possible.

And they did help them to get many things, which was what drew people to the centers.[9]

After a year, the agency hired two lawyers to back up these efforts by social workers; by 1964, four attorneys were employed. The attorneys challenged a great variety of welfare decisions. After successful litigation in 1964, the welfare department no longer invoked the Welfare Abuses Act as a matter of course (i.e., they stopped shipping recent migrants who applied for relief back South). Fear of legal action also prompted the department to abandon after-midnight raids on the residences of AFDC mothers. Actually the MFY lawyers litigated only a small percentage of the cases referred to them; the welfare department ordinarily preferred to settle out of court so as

---

[9] No statistics were ever completed by MYF's research division to measure the magnitude of the welfare increase that could be attributed to the storefront centers, as was done in Baltimore. An effort to compare caseload rises in the welfare district offices in the Lower East Side with caseload rises throughout the city had to be abandoned in 1964 because the welfare department had opened an additional district office in the MFY area a year earlier, and thousands of cases from offices outside of the MFY area had been transferred to offices located within the area, hopelessly confounding any interpretations of relative caseload changes. Instead, the research effort was limited to observing the work of center personnel as described here, and eventually to preparing estimates of the numbers of families in New York City (and in some other cities) who were eligible for benefits but not receiving them. These estimates are described in Chapter 7. The observer was Richard Elman.

to avoid precedent-setting rulings that would limit them in the future.

As time passed, however, storefront staff members began to feel frustrated by the need to deal with the same grievances over and over again—to take up the cases, for example, of each of hundreds of families who failed to get the periodic special grants for household furnishings and heavy clothing to which they were entitled. Instead, the center administrators began to think about group action; rather than bargaining separately on behalf of each of fifty clients for fifty separate clothing grants, why not bargain once on behalf of a group of fifty? This strategy, they reasoned, might also coerce welfare into making clothing and furnishing grants more routinely. And so, after three years of taking individual complaints, a community organizer was hired to work out of the center on Stanton Street,[10] and an MFY attorney was assigned to work with him. By the late summer and fall of 1965, the families that drifted into the Stanton Street center for help in making the usual applications for school and winter clothing were advised to go to a storefront next door to speak to the Committee of Welfare Families.

Although the Committee was new, group action was by no means novel on Stanton Street. Some of the Committee's initial group of AFDC mothers had participated in rent strikes and civil rights demonstrations sponsored by MFY. When the mothers were told that the Committee intended to organize people to act together against welfare, many were quick to respond. To begin with, each family was advised to make a survey of its winter-clothing needs and return the list to the Committee, which would then act as bargaining agent for all of them. Within a month, over ninety families had agreed to the procedure.

Bargaining for winter clothing went to the issue of what

---

[10] Sherman Barr was in charge of all of the storefront centers; Joseph Kriesler directed the storefront on Stanton Street; and Ezra Birnbaum organized the Committee of Welfare Families.

constituted a welfare entitlement. Every welfare family was budgeted a very small sum, included in their semi-monthly checks, with which to buy clothing. Invariably, these sums were used for ordinary living expenses, because grants for food and other necessities were low. The Department's official policy at that time was to allow additional grants for winter clothing of approximately $150 a year per family of four, but these grants were rarely made unless requested, and even then the investigators often allotted less than the prescribed amount.

In October 1965 the welfare centers in the MFY area began to receive letters from clients requesting clothing for their children—coats, snowsuits, coveralls, boots, scarves, and woolen skirts. All the requests had been certified by the Committee as being in accord with stated welfare policies. When there was no reply, a follow-up letter was sent, with copies to supervisory personnel as well. When there was still no reply, the Committee wrote the Commissioner of Welfare. When the Commissioner did not respond, a telegram was sent threatening mass picketing. The Commissioner replied by telegram the same day saying that he would be able to meet with the Committee on a given date and that in the meantime he would try to get information on each of the cases specified in the Committee's original letter. Of the subsequent meeting itself, the Commissioner said that it was the first between a top welfare official and a group of recipients in New York City since the demise of the Workers Alliance of America three decades earlier. He agreed that all Committee members who were entitled to winter clothing would receive it and acknowledged the bargaining status of the Committee by outlining formal grievance procedures.

In the days that followed, hundreds of Lower East Side families received checks from the welfare department for winter clothing. Word spread throughout New York City, and within six months tens of thousands of welfare families had joined in campaigns, which by 1968 had netted them several hundred million dollars. It was these drives, together with similar activity in a few other major cities, that provided the main impetus in the spring of 1966 for the formation of the National Welfare Rights Organization.

THE STOREFRONT IN KENWOOD-OAKLAND

Most CAA funds went, not to local public agencies, but to private organizations. Thus the Advisory Commission on Intergovernmental Relations [11] reports that 75 per cent of OEO's community-action programs were actually operated by private organizations—including new ghetto agencies (such as MFY), but also private social agencies (such as settlement houses and family services agencies),[12] churches, civil rights groups, universities, and the like. It was public funds, in short, that brought (or, more accurately, bought) thousands of voluntary groups into different phases of the antipoverty effort—including welfare rights. Until the antipoverty effort began, for example, the National Urban League had been concentrating mainly on problems confronting middle-class blacks; OEO grants turned the League toward poor blacks. In effect, the federal government used financial inducements to redirect and coordinate the activities of a vast segment of the private social welfare field, the legal profession, religious institutions, civil rights groups, and unaffiliated activists into a far-

---

[11] For a detailed description of the various administration bodies and types of agencies receiving OEO funds, see U.S. Advisory Commission on Intergovernmental Relations, 267, Table B-2.

[12] Most private social agencies had been engaged with the poor until the Depression years; then, with the development of public relief programs under the Social Security Act, and with the rapid spread of mental-hygiene concepts, many private agencies turned away from giving relief and other concrete services to the poor and began providing psychotherapy to middle-class families. (In this connection, see Cloward and Epstein, 1–54). The point is that OEO money did much to reverse that trend away from the poor in the field of private philanthropy.

flung attack on the public welfare system (and on other municipal institutions).

As a result, the advocacy services that had been undertaken in the new ghetto agencies were soon replicated by a variety of civic, religious, philanthropic, and civil rights organizations. One was Chicago's Kenwood-Oakland Community Organization (KOCO), which was formed in 1966 by a group of black ministers. Jan Linfield, a professional social worker, left her job in a private family service agency to work with KOCO. At our request, she recounted some of her experiences.

To start with, what has been most on my mind in the last week: A woman came into the office, an AFDC mother with no husband and two children, aged two and three. The story she told was not uncommon—her electric bill was supposed to be paid by the public aid department, but through some hangup it hadn't been taken care of and her lights were turned off a month ago. She'd called her caseworker numerous times, and his reply was the usual "I'll look into it." When I figured her budget, she had a deficit of $29.00; instead of the $133.00 a month to which she was entitled, she was only receiving $104.00. She paid $60.00 for rent, leaving $44.00 for food, clothing, and all other necessities for herself and her two children. I told her I would go with her to the district welfare office.

It was only as she was leaving that she told me that a week before she had had a baby at Cook County Hospital. As is the hospital custom, she and the baby were sent home two days after the delivery. This was just before her check was due. She had no money, and she had to "stretch the milk" (i.e., add water). Since the electricity was off, there was no refrigeration for what milk she had. The baby died at the age of four days. "It was all right when I brought it home," she said. And then she added, with practically no feeling, "Maybe it's better this way— I can hardly feed the two I have." Later she told me that she had to take her two-year-old to the clinic weekly because of "low blood," since the children hardly ever have meat to eat. She herself was "light-headed" most of the time.

When we went to the welfare office the next day, an

agency supervisor verified the fact that the woman's monthly check should be $133.00. The $29.00 had been deducted through a "clerical error," and had continued to be deducted for two months. When the error was discovered, the department sent the woman a check for $58.00, but she never received it. (As is common in the ghetto, this mother lived in a building that had no mailboxes. On the day her regular welfare check is due, she waits in front of the building for the mailman. Not expecting an extra payment, she had not taken this precaution, and no one knows what happened to the refund check.) The supervisor explained that the check could not be reissued until all the procedures for tracing missing checks had been followed, and that this would take several weeks. Furthermore, the client's monthly check, which had been due two weeks earlier, had been returned to the agency because of an incorrect address—another "clerical error." In spite of the urgency of this woman's situation—she was completely without funds and literally had no way of feeding her children—the supervisor said that there was no way the agency could give her any emergency money.

The only special thing about this case is that it resulted in a child's death. In other respects, the case is completely typical: bureaucratic procedures which are forever breaking down, and welfare recipients who have become so habituated to injustice that they are no longer able to react with anger when the grossest kinds of inhumanity are inflicted upon them.

When we first began knocking on doors in Kenwood-Oakland and talking to people about what they saw as their most pressing problems, it was apparent that welfare should be high on the list. Out of a population of 80,000, one third received public assistance; half of all families have incomes under $3,000, and 15 per cent of the adult males are unemployed. Once it became known that KOCO would help people with welfare problems, we were flooded with applicants, and have continued to be.

Many of these problems involve shocking violations of agency policy, abuses which are tolerated because welfare recipients are kept in ignorance of their rights. Not uncommonly, for example, a young woman pregnant by a man who has deserted her is told that she cannot be given assistance until she brings the father to the agency. She has no way of knowing that agency policy says only that she must cooperate to the extent of furnishing his name and last known address, so that the *agency* can try to locate him and attempt to collect child support. Applicants are left without assistance for months while they attempt to locate various documents verifying residence, parentage of children, legality of marriages, proof of past financial management, etc. The department obviously hopes that people will become so discouraged and frustrated that they will abandon efforts to obtain relief. This is precisely what happens in a great many cases.

The operating policy of the Cook County Department of Public Aid is to get every welfare recipient to take a job. Referrals to training programs or for employment are made indiscriminately; e.g., mothers with newborn babies or with families of four or five children are told to report to classes or to the employment office, under the threat (often explicit) that their checks will be cut off if they refuse. The department makes no provision for child-care for working mothers, apparently assuming that there are always relatives or neighbors who will babysit. How many children are left alone without adult supervision is an unknown statistic, but it is a large number.

KOCO's method of working with these problems is to inform people of their rights—the rights the welfare department never told them about—and to act as an advocate when people are having trouble with the welfare department. We train welfare recipients in the specifics of welfare policy so that complaints can be firmly founded. Perhaps more important, KOCO teaches recipients that they need not fear a welfare supervisor or be awed by the department's power—that people can fight back successfully.

The head of KOCO's welfare group, an AFDC mother with six children, has become an exceedingly effective negotiator with the welfare department. When I first met her, she was like most AFDC mothers, seeming to hold herself in very low self-esteem, and to regard other welfare recipients in the same way. Now she gives speeches, organizes protest demonstrations, and negotiates with public officials.

Such activities often involve great risk for welfare recipients. Recently ten members of KOCO's welfare com-

mission (seven AFDC mothers, two ministers, and myself)
staged a sit-in in our local district office to protest the
department's refusal to give emergency aid to a woman
with two small children who was facing imminent eviction. When we were still there a half hour after the office
had officially closed, an agency supervisor appeared, accompanied by the police. When ordinary arguments did
not prevail, they threatened the mothers with having
their children taken away from them. To these mothers,
with an aggregate of forty-four children, such a threat
was terrifying in spite of my assurance that the agency
could not carry it out. (Meanwhile, the district administrator had sent investigators to the homes of all the
mothers in the hope of being able to accuse them of
neglect for having left their children alone. This attempt
at intimidation was not successful, since all the children
were being cared for by older siblings or neighbors.) But
the women still refused to leave. They had strong em-
pathy with the mother who had no money to feed her
children and was about to be "set out on the street"; all
of them had, at one time or another, faced the threat of
eviction with no place to go. So we were arrested on a
charge of criminal trespass, and taken to the city lockup
in patrol wagons. The following day, after our release,
one of the mothers was visited by her caseworker at home
and told that if she ever again went to the district office
on any case other than her own, her check would be cut
off immediately. (These two incidents are the basis of an
action the American Civil Liberties Union is taking on
our behalf against the department on the ground that the
civil rights of these mothers had been violated.)

Fear is a serious obstacle in organizing a welfare union.
The first time we went to the district office we took along
eight people with grievances, and each went with much
trepidation. Neighbors and friends had told them—
"You'll really be in trouble if you make a fuss—they'll
cut you off and you'll be worse off than you were before."
Some of this group, however, had had applications pending for as long as six months (in spite of a state statute
that says all applications must be acted upon within sixty
days) and so had little to lose. On every one of these cases,
the agency acted very quickly to take the action we demanded. When we left the office that day, the eight
women had received a total of almost $900 in emergency

checks. We have had comparable results every time we've gone into the district office as an organized group.

The success of our first foray into the district welfare office spread quickly through the neighborhood, bringing a steady stream of people to us for help. But they are also afraid of us. Even those whom KOCO helps are often reluctant to become involved once their own grievance has been solved, for they are afraid to be identified with an organization known to be in disfavor with the welfare department. Even without a direct threat, they are highly susceptible to rumors and vague anxieties about what the welfare worker might do to them.

And in fact, most people on welfare do some things for which they can be terminated. Any family that receives any income whatsoever without reporting it to the agency runs the risk of being cut off, particularly if the caseworker is trying to find ways of reducing the family's allotment. The few dollars a child earns delivering groceries on Saturday mornings; a gift of clothing, even though it may be used; a cast-off television set or washing machine—all these are expected to be reported as "income," and to be deducted from future checks. Other people are afraid because of what they mistakenly construe to be agency violations. A common misconception is that the birth of a new baby out of wedlock will mean that the check will be stopped. I have known mothers who conceal their pregnancy and even conceal a new baby in a closet when the caseworker visits. But some do manage their fear and join our organization, and so far the organization has been able to protect them.

Before KOCO was formed, Kenwood-Oakwood had defied all efforts at community organization. It was a "non-community"—a collection of people living in geographical proximity but lacking any sense of common purpose or even of common problems. KOCO has taken some steps to change that. And it has helped to relieve some of the worst poverty by forcing the welfare department to help.

We have so far stressed the role of the federal programs in promoting advocacy services. The federal programs were also responsible for an information explosion in public welfare, and that too deserves note.

In the 1960's, organizations all over the country began to produce simplified welfare manuals for distribution in slums and ghettoes. The commmunity-action agencies themselves prepared handbooks in hundreds of cities and counties, and other organizations followed suit, partly in response to the demand for information created by the new advocacy services. Inner-city churches produced handbooks in Cleveland and Pittsburgh. The NAACP Legal Defense and Educational Fund made up handbooks for use in some Deep South states. Civil liberties unions brought out manuals in a number of places, such as Wisconsin and the District of Columbia. A comprehensive handbook for New Jersey was produced by the Scholarship, Education and Defense Fund. Recently, the National Urban League prepared and distributed handbooks for use in a dozen Northern states, each describing in detail the state general assistance programs under which fully employed but low-paid workers can obtain wage supplements. In Columbus and the District of Columbia, the first handbooks were prepared by settlement houses in 1966—and other settlement houses in other cities followed suit in subsequent years. A few family service agencies, especially in older surburban communities with central ghettoes, have also put such material together.

Beginning in 1966, the National Welfare Rights Organization stimulated the development of manuals in dozens of places, in part by distributing sample copies of manuals that had been prepared by various antipoverty agencies. At one point in New York City, three different comprehensive handbooks were available; one prepared by MFY, another by the Citizen's Committee For Children (a prestigious civic organization that had received a foundation grant for this purpose), and still another by the OEO-sponsored Center on Social Welfare Policy and Law at

Columbia University. At the same time, local groups all over the city had made up more abbreviated welfare rights manuals—some were really flyers, only three or four pages in length—so it could fairly be said that dozens of different welfare guides were circulating throughout New York's slums and ghettoes.

That a demand for information about welfare entitlements had been created is not difficult to show. The Southern California chapter of the ACLU prepared a manual in the summer of 1968, and within a short time 8,000 copies were sold to many different local organizations which had contact with the poor. Requests for more than one thousand copies were also received from public and private agencies elsewhere in the country. Indeed, even relief officials showed interest, for "state welfare departments as far away as South Carolina ordered [sample] copies." [13] After 1964, in other words, there was truly an information explosion, and that had much to do with the explosion of applications for welfare which followed.

Unfortunately, there are no available statistical data that would enable us to describe the pervasiveness of welfare rights activity in the nation's neighborhood service centers. The difficulty arises from the fact that welfare rights services were conducted under other formal program categories—such as employment training or preschool education.[14] From direct observation and a few published accounts, we do know that in some centers personnel did little else than handle welfare grievances, becoming specialists in dealing with welfare departments. In other centers, such activity was an incidental by-product of other pro-

---

[13] *Inside ACLU*, 1.

[14] The most prevalent programs in these centers were employment counseling and job placement; services in welfare, health, and education were next in popularity (Levitan, 129).

grams: For example, "Head-Start" teachers, who found their new pupils without adequate food and clothing sometimes responded by helping the family to get on the welfare rolls. A few even undertook to organize groups of welfare recipients that later affiliated with NWRO. The same can be said of social workers, employment counselors, lawyers, and other professionals working in the service centers, for great numbers of the poor people who came to them for help needed money, and public welfare was the only place to go for it.

It should be added that welfare rights did not have to be a primary activity in order to account for the welfare explosion; even if it had been the lowest-priority service in the centers, its magnitude still would have been unprecedented. About 15 per cent of CAA expenditures were devoted to neighborhood service center programs; in fiscal 1965, that amounted to 24 million dollars, and by fiscal 1968 the figure exceeded 132 million.[15] Translating these dollars into personnel, neighborhood service centers hired more than 100,000 professionals and community residents in 1968.[16] This horde of workers provided "outreach and referral" services and organized community groups. In the same year, applications for AFDC rose by 90,000—up from 998,000 in 1967 to 1,099,000 in 1968. On the average, if each of the service center workers reached and referred only one family to public welfare during the course of an entire year, the increase in applications would be largely explained.

Moreover, federally funded neighborhood services were as pervasively distributed throughout the country as the welfare rise itself. Although we have data only on the distribution of community action agencies and funds, not on service centers as such, we noted earlier that neighbor-

---

[15] *Ibid.*, 123.
[16] *Ibid.*, 129.

TABLE I

Regional Distribution of OEO
Community Action Agencies
April 1969

	NUMBER	%
National	963	100
Northeast	186	19
North Central	233	24
West	140	15
South	404	42
Deep South	121	13
Other South	283	29

Source: OEO
Notes: Coterminous United States; distributions by urban-rural were not available.

hood service centers were the most popular activity of community action agencies. Table I shows that these agencies were distributed in relatively equal numbers among the regions, except for the South, which had a disproportionate percentage (42 per cent).

All regions of the country also shared about equally in the distribution of community action funds (Table II). Urban areas got more, however, as we noted in Chapter 9; only about one quarter of CAA funds went to rural areas. But of CAA funds expended in rural areas. the rural South accounts for about two thirds (which probably goes far toward explaining why the Southern rural AFDC rolls, having declined in the 1950's, rose by 34 per cent in the 1960's, with 93 per cent of that increase occurring *after* 1964).

TABLE II

Total Dollar Effort for Community Action Agencies
by OEO and Localities
Fiscal 1968

	Millions of Dollars	%	% Urban Dollar Effort	% Rural Dollar Effort
National	1,120	100		
Urban	851	76	100	
Rural	269	24		100
Northeast	249	21		
Urban	220	20	26	
Rural	19	2		7
North Central	241	22		
Urban	196	18	23	
Rural	45	4		17
West	213	19		
Urban	189	17	22	
Rural	35	2		9
South	426	38		
Urban	246	22	29	
Rural	180	16		67
Deep South	156	14		
Urban	73	7	9	
Rural	83	7		31
Other South	270	24		
Urban	172	15	20	
Rural	98	9		36

Source: OEO, Community Action Agency Analysis Report as of
11/22/69.
Notes: Coterminous United States; columns may not total properly because of rounding; dollar effort includes a small proportion of money appropriated by localities as a condition of receiving OEO funds. In this table, we follow OEO's definition of urban: counties with a subdivision containing more than 10,000 persons.

Welfare Rights Litigation

While welfare restrictions were being battered from below, they were also being weakened from above. A series of judicial decisions in the 1960's had the effect of undermining some of the regulations by which the relief rolls have been kept down. For decades, reformers had lobbied unsuccessfully for legislative repeal of residence laws, man-in-the-house rules, and employable-mother rules. But in the 1960's these foundation blocks of the "poor law" were washed away by one court decision after another.[17]

The legal assaults that set this process in motion originated mainly with OEO's neighborhood legal services program. Lawyers know what they are paid to know, and until OEO funds became available very few knew anything about laws affecting the poor, least of all about the "poor laws." In the three years between 1966 and 1968, OEO spent about 85 million dollars on legal services—a very considerable sum, as the following comparison reveals. "One year after OEO was established, the budget of Legal Services was nearly double that of [all of the traditional] legal aid societies affiliated with the National Legal Aid and Defender Association (20 million dollars as compared with 11.7 million dollars)."[18] By fiscal 1968, OEO expenditures had reached 36 million dollars. Some 250 legal services projects were established which operated about 850 neighborhood law offices staffed by about 1800 attorneys.[19]

---

[17] The legal arguments which underpinned litigation against relief agencies were developed in substantial part by Jacobus ten Broek, a blind professor of political science at the University of California in Berkeley, who spent the better part of his career writing about what he called America's dual system of justice—one for the affluent, another for the poor. More recently, Charles Reich, a Yale law professor, expounded the view that social welfare benefits constitute a new form of property and should be accorded the same legal protections as property; his views also had considerable impact (see ten Broek and Reich).

[18] Levitan, 179.

[19] Exclusive of two additional groups: about 250 lawyers in a special OEO fellowship program, and the large number of law students enrolled

According to available evidence, only about 3 per cent of the activity in neighborhood legal services agencies was devoted to "state and local welfare," or about 8,000 cases out of the 282,000 cases taken in fiscal 1968.[20] However, these figures obscure a fact of great significance. In dealing with public welfare cases, OEO attorneys tended to eschew case-by-case assistance to families; instead, they promoted "institutional change through law reform" by taking "test cases" whose outcomes affected existing or potential welfare recipients as an entire class. "Class actions" were also litigated in some other areas (e.g., the rights of public housing tenants), but the most conspicuous legal victories by far were achieved in the public welfare field. A large volume of new law was made, and a large number of poor people were affected. Let us note briefly some of the better-known examples.[21]

On June 19, 1967, a three-judge federal court in Connecticut declared that state's relief residency requirements unconstitutional. The plaintiff had been on the AFDC rolls in Boston, moved to Hartford to be with her chronically ill mother, applied for welfare, and was turned down. An OEO legal services agency filed suit on her behalf. The majority of the court held that "the right of interstate travel also encompasses the right to be free of discouragement of interstate movement. Denying . . . even a gratuitous benefit because of her constitutional right effectively impedes the exercise of that right." During the next year, residence laws in more than a dozen states were success-

in VISTA. In the aggregate, there were probably about 2,500 lawyers and law students at work in neighborhood legal services agencies in fiscal 1968.

[20] Levitan, 184.

[21] Some of these cases deal with questions of civil liberties (e.g., midnight raids); others with the denial of benefits. However, one can overdraw this distinction. It is through abuses of civil liberties—such as Fourth Amendment protections against illegal search and seizure—that welfare departments harass welfare recipients and terminate them from the rolls; such abuses also deter others from applying for assistance. The point is that the violation of civil liberties is, in itself, a not unimportant means by which the welfare rolls have been kept down.

fully challenged in state or federal courts. In the spring of 1969, acting on an appeal from Connecticut, the United States Supreme Court held that relief residence laws violated the Constitution.

The Georgia "employable mother" rule was challenged and overturned by a suit on behalf of a group of AFDC mothers who claimed that the rule was used far more frequently to keep black mothers off the rolls than white women, thus violating the "equal protection" provisions of the Fourteenth Amendment. They also claimed that denying supplementary benefits to mothers who were employed for less money than they would get on welfare is contrary to the purpose of the AFDC program. The fact of whether a mother works, they further contended, is an arbitrary and capricious basis for classifying the beneficiaries of federal aid, also in violation of the equal-protection provisions of the Fourteenth Amendment. Finally, the plaintiffs asked for the right to rebut the presumption that they could get jobs merely because a welfare official said they were employable. They based their challenge on a prior ruling of the United States Supreme Court, to the effect "that a statute creating a presumption which operates to deny a fair opportunity to rebut it violates the due process clauses of the Fourteenth Amendment." In 1968, a three-judge federal court in Atlanta unanimously struck down the employable-mother regulation.

Man-in-the-house and substitute parent rules were dealt a lethal blow by the Supreme Court on June 17, 1968. The plaintiff was a black mother of four who earned a weekly salary of $16 as a waitress in Selma, Alabama. Her supplementary welfare payments were cut off after it was alleged that she consorted with a man; suit was brought by the Roger Baldwin Fund of the American Civil Liberties Union. In its unanimous decision, the Court held that "destitute children who are legally fatherless cannot be flatly denied federally funded assistance on the transparent fiction that they have a substitute father." The decision affected eighteen other states and the District of Columbia, all of which had some version of the man-in-the-house rule.

There is no way of measuring the exact impact of these major legal reforms on the welfare rolls; all that can be said is that it has been considerable. Persons knowledgeable in the public welfare field generally believe that at least 100,000 persons annually had been denied aid because of residence laws. Attorneys and welfare rights organizers in the South estimated that tens of thousands of families were denied aid under employable-mother rules. Once such rules were weakened or abandoned, approval rates rose, and the rolls grew. Litigation against Alabama's substitute-parent rule provides an illustration. As we noted earlier, court action was initiated in 1966, and after a series of appeals, the United States Supreme Court acted in June 1968. The effect of this continuous and much publicized course of litigation was startling: in Mobile, for example, the caseload rose from 1700 to 3100 (an increase of 82 per cent) in the brief period between June 1966 and February 1969.

Suits overturning exclusionary statutes, such as residence laws, have received a great deal of publicity, but successful challenges taken against arbitrary administrative procedures, although less publicized, may have done much more to expand the rolls. Welfare functionaries have always been allowed a wide range of discretion in deciding whether or not to give aid, and they have used that discretion to deter people from applying or to turn them down when they do apply or, if applicants get on the rolls, to cut them off arbitrarily. Legal action has gone far toward hampering these practices.

Arbitrary terminations, for example, have always been a conspicuous feature of the public assistance system. In 1967, a beneficiary under the Aid to the Permanent and Totally

Disabled program in Mississippi was abruptly notified that he was no longer medically qualified for assistance. No specific reasons were given, nor was a hearing held prior to the termination. The client, a thirty-year-old black man with a large family, quickly secured affidavits from prominent doctors confirming that his right hand had been amputated and that he had both pulmonary tuberculosis and sickle-cell disease (a type of anemia which leads to progressive weakening and, in this case, to a short life expectancy). The day before the court hearing, welfare officials visited the plaintiff to say that a mistake had been made and would be rectified. Nevertheless, the plaintiff insisted that the hearing be held, arguing that his benefits might be arbitrarily terminated at some later time unless the constitutional issues raised by termination procedures were ruled upon. Despite protests by attorneys for the state, the judge agreed that serious questions of due process were involved and held the matter over for trial.

This case was typical of many instituted elsewhere in the nation after 1964. One case finally reached the United States Supreme Court, and a favorable ruling was handed down on March 24, 1970. It asserted that welfare recipients have a constitutional right to a trial-like hearing, with trial-like constitutional safeguards, before officials may terminate benefits. During the proceedings, welfare officials warned that a favorable ruling could swamp the system with demands for hearings while ineligible people remained on the rolls. But the Court decided that the protection of recipients outweighed such fiscal and administrative problems.

Other traditional techniques of harassing welfare recipients have also come under attack. New York's highest court ruled several years ago that social welfare laws do not authorize the jailing of male welfare recipients who refuse to work under terms dictated by a welfare department. Any other interpretation, the court said, might result in violation of the Thirteenth Amendment and the Federal Anti-Peonage Act, which prohibit involuntary servitude. In situations where fraud is suspected, welfare recipients are often told that if they refuse to answer questions that might incriminate them, their benefits will be cut off. Recipients in several jurisdictions have successfully charged that this threat—frequently carried out—is a violation of the Fifth Amendment. Mass searches without warrants (e.g., midnight raids) have recently been declared unconstitutional, as we noted in Chapter 5 in connection with the Parish case in California. And a three-judge panel in New York, acting in a suit initiated by a Bronx welfare mother who was represented by David Gilman, an MFY lawyer and chief counsel for the New York City Coordinating Committee of Welfare Groups, declared in August 1969 that even daytime visits by welfare workers were unconstitutional unless warrants had been obtained. (The U.S. Supreme Court overturned this ruling in January 1971.)

Many procedural changes have been won without news-making court victories, often as a result of negotiation, backed up by the threat of court action, between attorneys and welfare officials. Such threats have forced welfare administrators to release official welfare manuals to lawyers, welfare rights organizers, and others. The same point can be made about efforts to establish the legal right of applicants or recipients to bring a "third party" to the interviewing cubicle—whether a friend, a welfare rights leader, or a lawyer. Welfare depatments have traditionally denied people the right to representation and thus deprived them of one means of challenging arbitrary and capricious decisions. A suit several years ago established the right to representation in New York, although most relief administrators elsewhere still resist under the pretext that they have a legal (a few even say a professional) obligation to "protect" applicants by holding transactions "confidential."

A more reasonable explanation of their motives is that welfare functionaries want to retain untrammeled discretion in dealing with the poor.

As these procedural safeguards multiplied, welfare departments found it increasingly difficult to restrict access to benefits, if only because the process of denial became so cumbersome. Just how cumbersome is revealed by this (abridged) exchange between Senator Byrd (D.-W.Va.) and District of Columbia welfare officials regarding the increased use of administrative hearings by welfare recipients:

Senator Byrd: How many fair-hearing officers have you had on the average each year from fiscal year 1962 through 1967?

Welfare Official: We did not have so many requests for fair hearings back then as we have at the present time.

Senator Byrd: Why do you have more requests now?

Welfare Official: The OEO neighborhood legal attorneys are requesting more fair hearings; at least they are encouraging recipients to request more fair hearings.

Senator Byrd: And what policies are questioned?

Welfare Official: Residency policies.

Senator Byrd: Substitute parent policies?

Welfare Official: Yes, the substitute parent policies, whether investigators should be allowed in homes without a search warrant, some of our decisions on resources.

Senator Byrd: You say fair hearings have increased. Could you be specific?

Welfare Official: Yes, Mr. Chairman. Within the past year and a half, we have seen a rather dramatic increase in the number of fair hearings. At the present time we are averaging four fair hearings a week. Each fair hearing may run anywhere from two to three hours. The fair hearing officer needs approximately anywhere from three to four hours to prepare his report which he submits to the

Director for the Director's decision. So on each fair hearing we have approximately, oh, say between five and eight hours of work on the part of the fair hearing officer.

It is not at all uncommon—let me put it this way, sir—it is extraordinary today to conduct a hearing without having an attorney, usually from Neighborhood Legal Services, representing the recipient or the appellant.

Prior to the advent of Neighborhood Legal Services, the reverse was true. That is to say, it was extraordinary to have an attorney at a fair hearing representing the appellant.

Senator Byrd: Have there been any changes in the complexity of the fair hearings?

Welfare Official: I must say, Mr. Chairman, that the complexity of the fair hearing has changed quite dramatically because of the presence of the attorneys representing the appellant.

The fair hearing process still remains an informal administrative review. It is not a legal procedure, even though the attorneys representing the appellants sometimes confuse themselves as to where they are, and act as if they were before a court of law.

They are splitting hairs, and it takes hours to split hairs, and even then they do not always accept the Department's position and the facts as we present them.

Not only that, if we rule in their favor they immediately want to go back and review every similar case.

Senator Byrd: Let me ask this question: Do you have to assign more investigators to a particular surveillance case, just to make sure that you have all your ends tied up and the facts clear and your record complete?

Welfare Official: That is right. Our cost of investigation I would say has gone up at least 25 per cent in the last two years because of this type of activity. We have to be able to thoroughly document anything that we do. This requires more time for a home visit or a report. We use three investigators now, two who go in the home, and another one who does not. This is necessary now.[22]

All in all, then, the legal assault on welfare departments contributed to the collapse of restrictions, partly by overturning major exclusionary statutes, but perhaps more importantly by instituting procedural safeguards that hampered the arbitrary exercise of discretion by relief officials. Rather than devote themselves to the difficult and time-consuming task of defending their decisions, welfare functionaries more often acquiesced, with the result that more people got on the rolls and they were not so likely to be terminated capriciously.

Just as OEO funds altered the practices of existing private social welfare agencies, so did OEO alter the practices of existing legal agencies. The impact on the National Legal Aid and Defender Association (NLADA) provides one conspicuous example. "Initially, OEO was confronted with a major policy decision: Should legal aid societies, where they existed, administer the Legal Services projects or should new agencies be established? The dilemma was not peculiar to this program; it was shared by practically all OEO efforts—the choice was between strengthening existing organizations and establishing new institutions." [23] NLADA, naturally enough, argued that its program should be strengthened. But OEO felt that NLADA affiliates were

---

[22] U.S. Senate, Committee on Appropriations, 1662–1670 (abridged).
[23] Levitan, 179.

dominated by conservative bar associations and business groups, thus making it unlikely that politically controversial advocacy would be undertaken (e.g., fighting wage-garnishment actions or suing public welfare departments). In the end, a compromise was reached, with some 40 per cent of OEO's Legal Services projects being administered by NLADA affiliates; the rest were administered through CAA's. But a price was exacted from NLADA: to qualify for funds, any affiliate was required to decentralize its operation to slum and ghetto neighborhoods and to undertake new and controversial areas of representation, including test cases designed to promote law reform.

The inauguration of hundreds of new neighborhood legal services under CAA programs, together with the new efforts in NLADA programs, had a far-reaching effect on the practice of poor law. Many private legal defense organizations soon shifted some of their resources into the poor-law field, including the NAACP Legal Defense and Educational Fund, the Scholarship Education and Defense Fund for Racial Equality (whose former chief counsel, Carl Rachlin, is also chief counsel for the National Welfare Rights Organization), and the American Civil Liberties Union (and its special division, the Roger Baldwin Fund). The Law Students Civil Rights Research Council began to recruit hundreds of law-student volunteers to work with welfare rights groups and to perform legal research for attorneys representing recipients.

Moreover, OEO created a new kind of legal personnel —non-professionals trained in specific facets of the law who were able to extend the reach of the neighborhood legal services programs. Hundreds of poor people were recruited and trained to perform various kinds of "lay advocacy" tasks. In 1964, for example, OEO established the Dixwell Legal Rights Association in New Haven for the express purpose of training such non-professionals. About four hundred graduates of the program have since been placed in neighborhood legal offices throughout the country, and

in other organizations, such as churches, as well. As part of
its program, Dixwell has produced and distributed about
a dozen different simplified manuals dealing with such
subjects as rights to welfare, to bail bond, to hospital care,
to urban renewal relocation subsidies, to public housing,
to bankruptcy proceedings (as a way in which poor people
can overcome indebtedness). Trainees are schooled in the
use of these manuals.

Miss Josephine Holley, a middle-aged black woman without a high school education, is a Dixwell graduate who was
hired by an Episcopal church in New Haven. In response
to an inquiry by us, she had this to say about her training
and work:

> I was unemployed after having a serious operation. My
> doctor told me not to do heavy work. It was very hard to
> get another type of job if you were not experienced in
> whatever job you were applying for.
>
> Someone told me about Dixwell Legal Rights and how
> they were helping people to get jobs. I went to Dixwell
> Legal Rights and took the three months' Training
> Course. The classes were great, very good instructors. I
> was softspoken and too easygoing and did not know how
> to speak up. Dixwell Legal Rights changed all of that
> with their method of teaching and being a little strict
> with me.
>
> As I went out in the field and saw how clients and
> people were being treated on welfare, and saw how
> people that were not on welfare that should have been,
> had applied for welfare and could not get it, it made me
> damn angry. I was from then on able to deal with any
> situation.
>
> Father R. Swartout of Saint Andrews Church was look-
> ing for someone, heard I was looking for a job and hired
> me. Father Swartout could see how I could help the
> people in this ghetto neighborhood as well as in the
> church.

Over a two-month period, Miss Holley's case log of
families asking for help showed the following entries, most
of which concerned public welfare:

Case 1.   Food stamps—State welfare
Case 2.   State welfare
Case 3.   Trouble with tenants' rent
Case 4.   An accident case
Case 5.   Hospital bill
Case 6.   State welfare
Case 7.   Welfare and food stamps
Case 8.   State welfare
Case 9.   City welfare and State welfare
Case 10. Public housing
Case 11. State welfare and public housing
Case 12. State welfare—husband in jail
Case 13. State welfare and rent
Case 14. State welfare and children
Case 15. School problem—enrolling daughter
Case 16. A problem with the teachers
Case 17. State welfare and doctor—illness
Case 18. Abandoned children—police called
Case 19. State welfare and homemaker
Case 20. State welfare and public housing
Case 21. Hospital bill—attachment on house
Case 22. State welfare for her and children, also sister and brother
Case 23. Lost welfare check; landlord rent
Case 24. Problem with son in school transferring
Case 25. State welfare and rent
Case 26. State welfare
Case 27. State welfare and school
Case 28. State welfare and a cardiac son
Case 29. City welfare and rent
Case 30. Hospital—depressed
Case 31. Landlord—furnace and code violations
Case 32. State welfare and mental patient
Case 33. State welfare and money for furniture
Case 34. Mother depressed
Case 35. State welfare (heart condition)

A typical case from Miss Holley's painstaking records (Case 28 above) reveals the nature of her daily work.

11/21   My client was referred by a friend that came in and said that my client was depressed, sick, and needs help financially. Her son is very sick too. My client is a private duty nurse who has become too disabled to work. She pays $120.00 per month for a 5 room apt. No heat, has to pay utilities. She has 3 children, ages 18-16-14. Donald, 18, is in jail. Tony, 14, is very sick with a heart condition. Client needs assistance from city welfare or state welfare very badly. I went to the city welfare and talked to the supervisor and she said that she would send someone to interview my client today, and later transfer her to state welfare. I also mentioned that my client needs transportation money for herself and her son to the doctor's office and hospital.

11/24   I called my client today to see how things went on Friday. She is very happy that the social worker from city welfare came out to see her after I left her house and gave her a voucher for food, and is paying her rent until the state takes over, and then they will get full benefits.

12/1   I called my client today to see how she is feeling. She isn't feeling too well today, neither is her son. They are on their way to the hospital for tests and examinations to see what is happening. My client also received $18.00 for $45.00 worth of food stamps for herself and her children.

1/12   I called my client to see if the checks were coming and she said they are. I also asked about her health and her two sons. Tony isn't feeling well and will have to go for an electrocardiogram on Jan. 28th. Donald is much happier in Sommers Jail than he was in Whalley Ave. Jail, and in good spirits. As for her, her arthritis is acting up and she can't hardly get out of bed.

Law schools themselves have been responsive to these new influences. "During fiscal 1967, OEO pumped more

TABLE III

*Distribution of OEO Neighborhood Legal
Services Attorneys, Fiscal 1969*

	NUMBER	%	% URBAN ATTORNEYS	% RURAL ATTORNEYS
National	1796	100%		
Urban	1084	60	100%	
Rural	712	40		100%
Northeast	631	35		
Urban	403	22	37	
Rural	228	13		32
North Central	394	22		
Urban	257	14	24	
Rural	137	8		19
West	394	22		
Urban	202	11	19	
Rural	193	11		27
South	377	21		
Urban	223	12	21	
Rural	154	9		22
Deep South	99	5		
Urban	52	3	5	
Rural	47	3		7
Other South	278	15		
Urban	171	10	16	
Rural	107	6		15

Source: OEO.
*Note: Coterminous United States; columns may not total prop-
erly because of rounding. In this table, we follow OEO's definition of urban: counties with a subdivision containing more
than 10,000 persons.*

than 2 million dollars into law schools for research, changes in curricula, and various projects dealing with the poor." [24] For example, a Center on Social Welfare Policy and Law was established at Columbia University to conduct legal research, advise attorneys in the field, and prepare briefs in test cases.[25] At Northwestern University School of Law, an Institute for Education in Law and Poverty was created which, among other things, publishes a monthly digest of current poverty-law cases and opinions—called the *Clearinghouse Review*—that is distributed to all OEO legal service attorneys and to other involved attorneys as well. Similar law centers and projects were established elsewhere in the country. The ferment also affected law school curricula—new courses in poverty law were introduced in dozens of universities, and some two thousand law students registered for them in the 1965-1967 academic years.[26]

Finally, like the service centers, OEO's legal services attorneys were distributed over a wide area (Table III). The largest proportion was concentrated in the Northeast, with the remainder roughly equally divided among the other regions; about 60 per cent of the services were located in urban counties, where the welfare rise was greatest.

Grass-roots Protest: The National Welfare Rights Organization

In the 1960's as in the 1930's, poor people banded together to attack the relief system. Just as unemployed groups sprang up during the Depression and eventually banded together in the Workers' Alliance, so in the late 1960's welfare rights groups began to appear and then banded to-

---

[24] Levitan, 188.
[25] The Center also received an initial grant from the Stern Family Fund.
[26] Levitan, 188.

gether in a National Welfare Rights Organization. In some respects, these organizations bear little similarity to each other; the Alliance was composed primarily of unemployed white men, whereas NWRO is composed mostly of black women who are, practically speaking, unemployable in today's market. But there are also striking similarities: each arose in a period of widespread social and political upheaval occasioned by profound economic dislocation, and each flourished by capitalizing on disorder to obtain public aid for masses of families in financial distress.

The first welfare protest groups originated in the OEO agencies, like the Committee of Welfare Families formed at the Stanton Street Neighborhood Service Center. But once such groups came into being, so did the possibility of building a national grass-roots organization through relief protests. Some independent activists came to see this.[27] One was Dr. George A. Wiley, a professor of chemistry who had joined the civil rights movement and became the associate national director of CORE. In the late spring of 1966, he

---

[27] Their interest was stimulated by a paper we circulated in late 1965 among antipoverty workers, organizers, and activists entitled "Mobilizing the Poor: How It Can Be Done." It called upon those who were working with welfare recipients, as well as other activists, to form a movement with the express purpose of getting hundreds of thousands of families onto the relief rolls, for we had by then conducted sufficient research to establish that only half of the eligible poor were on the rolls. We also reasoned that campaigns to double and triple the relief rolls would produce significant pressure for national reforms in the relief system, perhaps along the lines of a national guaranteed minimum income. Rapidly rising rolls would mean procedural turmoil in the cumbersome welfare bureaucracies, fiscal turmoil in the localities where existing sources of tax revenue were already overburdened, and political turmoil as an alerted electorate divided on the question of how to overcome this disruption in local government. To deal with these problems, we argued, mayors and governors would call upon the federal government with increasing insistency to establish a federally financed minimum income. This call for the mobilization of a nationwide drive against relief agencies was subsequently published in *The Nation* under the title "A Strategy to End Poverty." Our formulation came to be called the "crisis theory" of the welfare rights movement, and while it alone was surely not responsible for the rise of welfare protests, it probably did help to spread those protests and to give them direction.

left CORE to open the Poverty/Rights Action Center in Washington, D.C. Within several months, PRAC became the organizing vehicle for what was to become the National Welfare Rights Organization; and under Wiley's leadership, the organization has since burgeoned.

Wiley, with Edwin Day and later Timothy Sampson, began by making strenuous efforts to establish links with the scattered welfare groups that already existed around the country and to spur the staff of antipoverty agencies (as well as activists who were in limbo after the civil rights movement passed its peak) to concentrate on organizing in the field of welfare. The idea spread rapidly, especially among antipoverty staff. As new groups developed, Wiley established contact and urged them to affiliate with the national headquarters. In February 1967, 350 leaders representing 200 welfare groups in 70 cities of 26 states answered the call to attend the first national meeting. Participating groups ranged from "Mothers of Watts" to "Mothers for Adequate Welfare" in Boston; from Chicago's "Welfare Union of the West Side Organization," composed of unemployed black men, to Eastern Kentucky's "Committee to Save Unemployed Fathers," consisting of unemployed white miners. Most of the groups originated in antipoverty agencies, but some had been organized by churchmen, others by civil rights activists, and still others by Students for a Democratic Society. By 1969, NWRO claimed more than 100,000 dues-paying members in some 350 local groups.[28]

The new organization first came to national attention in June 1966. On June 20, Rev. Paul Younger and Edith

---

[28] The national chairman is an AFDC mother from Watts, Johnnie Tillmon; Beulah Sanders, recipient leader of the City-Wide Coordinating Committee of Welfare Groups in New York City, is a vice-chairman; initially, Etta Horn, a recipient leader in Washington, D.C., and Carmen Olivo, a Puerto Rican recipient leader in New York's Lower East Side, were also vice-chairmen.

Doering, welfare rights organizers who had been hired by the Cleveland Council of Churches, led about forty welfare recipients out of Cleveland on the first lap of a 155-mile march to Columbus to lobby with the Governor for an increase in Ohio's welfare payments. On the morning of June 30, when they finally reached Columbus, the forty marchers were joined by two thousand recipients and sympathizers from other towns in Ohio. On the same day in New York, two thousand recipients massed in front of City Hall to picket in the hot sun while swarms of their children clambered over the iron railings to play on the grassy squares of City Hall Park. Groups of recipients in fifteen other cities, including Baltimore, Washington, Los Angeles, Boston, Louisville, Chicago, Trenton, and San Francisco, also joined demonstrations against "the welfare."

By now NWRO is fairly well known, especially in Northern cities, where local groups have staged hundreds of demonstrations to protest various welfare restrictions. Thousands of welfare recipients and organizers have been jailed on charges from trespass to riot. In the South, storefront offices have been razed, and welfare rights leaders' homes have been fired into and burned. One of the largest demonstrations was mounted in conjunction with the Poor People's Campaign in the spring and summer of 1968. On May 12 of that year, Wiley and Coretta King, widow of the slain civil rights leader, led more than five thousand welfare recipients on a "Mother's Day" march through the riot-torn section of Washington, D.C. Perhaps the most widely publicized incident occurred in the fall of 1969, when one thousand recipients and university students took over Wisconsin's legislative chamber to protest a cutback in welfare appropriations.

Most day-to-day organizing across the nation has consisted of efforts to settle individual grievances. Organizers generally begin by preparing a simplified handbook of welfare regulations (which may first require staging a sit-in in order to get a copy of the official manual), and thousands of copies are distributed through welfare rights groups, churches, stores, and other outlets in the ghettoes. The handbooks alert people to the ways in which the system typically and often illegally rejects applicants or reduces benefits—e.g., by failing to increase payments as children grow older or to give special utility allowances in rat-infested areas so that lights may be kept on at night. Arbitrary terminations have been a constant subject of grievance work. The practice of summarily terminating people from the rolls without a written reason or an opportunity for a hearing led the welfare rights groups in Boston to stage a welfare department sit-in in the spring of 1967. When the police beat the demonstrators, they screamed from the windows of the welfare department, and for three nights widespread rioting erupted in the streets—the first major riot in the violent summer of 1967.

Welfare rights groups have also mounted large-scale campaigns to obtain certain benefits which many people are entitled to but few receive. As we pointed out earlier, for example, many welfare departments officially permit extra grants for special purposes, but people are rarely told about them and generally don't get them. Staging a "mass benefit campaign" requires less organizing effort than the laborious process of adjusting individual grievances and produces a far greater financial pay-off. School clothing lists, for example, are mimeographed and widely distributed in slum neighborhoods, together with an announcement of a forthcoming demonstration at the welfare center. When hundreds of people assemble with a common demand, welfare departments usually release the grants, especially in cities where public officials fear that repression will provoke outbreaks of violence in the ghettoes.

Campaigns of this sort in New York City included week-long sit-ins and forced some district welfare centers to close down.[29] As the system lost control over its discretionary giving, the costs of special grants zoomed from about $40 per recipient in 1965 to $100 in 1968. When the aggregate costs reached an annual rate of 100 million dollars, *The New York Times* was moved editorially to call these campaigns a "threat to [New York City's] treasury." To blunt that threat, state officials—responding to increased white antagonism toward welfare costs—abolished the special grant. But in the meantime, a great many people had got a great deal of money that they would not otherwise have received.

These campaigns were greatly aided by the contagious effects of successful welfare rights activity. In May 1968, for example, thousands of Puerto Rican mothers and children who were not affiliated with NWRO unexpectedly appeared in the South Bronx relief centers demanding money. After week-long sit-ins, checks were disbursed. Relief administrators attributed this avalanche of requests to a clothing grants campaign being conducted at the time by the City-Wide Coordinating Committee of Welfare Groups. But they were wrong. The relief offices were engulfed by this mass of people, it turned out, because a rumor of unknown origin had spread to the effect that a wealthy patrón had died and left 50 million dollars to the welfare department to be given to the poor. Nor could the rumor be dispelled. Within days, it spread to Spanish Harlem and then to Central Harlem, and the relief offices in those districts were flooded, forcing the check-writing machines onto a virtual twenty-four-hour schedule. These unplanned demonstrations were partly responsible for the fact that the cost of special grants, which had totaled some 3 million dollars in the same month a year earlier, reached 13 million dol-

---

[29] At one point during this period (the spring and summer of 1968), the welfare department established a special "war room" in its central headquarters, filled with telephones and staff members, in order to keep abreast of the dozens of simultaneous demonstrations in the city's far-flung district offices. These campaigns were led by Hulbert James; equally successful campaigns were led in Boston by William Pastreich.

lars in June 1968. For, except by calling the police and thus risking mass violence, how else was the welfare department to clear its offices and restore control?

NWRO's organizing activities, it should be pointed out, were conducted mainly to benefit people already on the welfare rolls, for NWRO is an organization composed of recipients. To keep their members interested and involved, NWRO organizers have been constantly under pressure to increase benefits for existing recipients rather than to find and organize the non-recipient poor for the purpose of getting them on the rolls. For this reason, NWRO's contribution to the rising welfare rolls has been largely indirect, the unintended effect of other activities. For example, slum and ghetto families who witness demonstrations over grievances or demands for special grants or for higher grants become more aware of their own rights and less fearful of applying for aid. This may be what HEW meant when, after surveying the causes of welfare increases in eleven cities, it drew the following conclusion regarding the impact of local welfare rights organizations (WRO's):

> There was evidence that the higher the number of AFDC recipients who belonged to WRO's, the larger the number of poor persons using AFDC, but the evidence was not statistically significant. However, the number of AFDC women who reported that they belonged to WRO's was very small in all cities. For example, only 4.1 per cent of all AFDC women in New York City, belonged to the local WRO. These small percentages could, however, lead to false conclusions. A slight increase in the number of WRO members might have a great influence on the attitudes of all AFDC recipients. To illustrate, there was a strong inverse relation between the percentage of WRO members and the number of recipients who felt helpless (the more WRO members in a city, the fewer the number of recipients who felt powerless).[30]

---

[30] U.S. Department of Health, Education, and Welfare, 49.

NWRO has also exerted some influence on acceptance and termination decisions, and that too contributed to larger rolls. Much welfare rights organizing occurred in the waiting rooms of local welfare centers with the intention of attracting new members from among those recipients who had come to negotiate grievances. But many of those jamming the waiting rooms were not recipients—they were new families hoping to get on the rolls. Welfare rights organizers have often given on-the-spot assistance to these potential recipients by helping them to negotiate the intake process. Moreover, the constant agitation in welfare centers by groups of recipients conducting campaigns for special grants has also led some welfare workers to take sides with applicants and intimidated many others. In this new climate, many intake workers, the "gate-keepers" of the system, have tended to make more liberal decisions. Acceptance rates rose sharply in the middle and late 1960's, and client protests were undoubtedly one cause.[31]

The close and continuing relationship between welfare organizing and OEO's agencies was vividly illustrated during NWRO's "hunger" campaign, conducted during the summer of 1970 in several Southern cities. After initial demonstrations organized to get people on relief and to obtain food stamps for them, Louisiana's Commissioner of Public Welfare, Garland L. Bonin, wrote on August 11 to Woodrow Dumas, Mayor of Baton Rouge, as follows:

> I am sure that you are familiar through Police Intelligence with the disruptive activity that has been going

---

[31] As this analysis makes apparent, NWRO's contribution to the welfare explosion would have been greater had it devoted fewer resources to organizing existing recipients and placed more emphasis on mobilizing the non-welfare poor to get on the rolls. NWRO, however, has generally considered it more important to build up its membership rolls than to build up the welfare rolls (on the dubious premise that poor people can develop political power through permanent membership organizations).

on for several days in connection with the local welfare office.

This drive has been headed by professional, National Welfare Rights organizers from out of state. The ordinary process of our local office has been disrupted and the services to needy citizens of this parish interrupted. I have been reliably informed both by the police and our local welfare office that officials of Community Advancement of East Baton Rouge Parish played a prominent part in these activities. I have been specifically advised that Mr. Jim Moss, with Community Advancement, Mr. Charlie Granger, Director of the South Baton Rouge Neighborhood Service Center, and Mrs. Ann Wilson, who works with the Valley Park Neighborhood Center, were in the office yesterday and were advising and counseling the demonstrators in their disruptive activity.

I am indeed greatly distressed and shocked that one public agency is actively engaged in attempting to destroy or disrupt the orderly activities of another public agency engaged in the same type of service to the people of this community.

A copy of this letter was sent to Charles W. Tapp, executive director of Community Advancement, Inc., an OEO agency in Baton Rouge, who replied to Commissioner Bonin on August 12 in the following terms:

I take exception to your letter of August 11, 1970, concerning this agency and the National Welfare Rights Organization. We have been working closely with the local Welfare Rights Organization for a long time. This is a matter of public information.

If you had taken time to call me, I could have given you the same information that you had to secure from Police Intelligence sources, as you put it.

Both you and I know full well that the welfare system has tragic shortcomings in Louisiana. I think you should face these shortcomings firmly and bring your prestige and influence to bear on reforms rather than fighting rearguard actions that you are bound to lose in the long run.

If any member of this staff has broken the law or has violated Federal regulations of the Office of Economic

Opportunity, then I will personally see that they are disciplined for such action. If, however, they are guilty of working with the poor in an attempt to bring about changes that will better the living conditions and the lives of the poor, then they are to be commended.

In many respects, the emergence of NWRO represents the most striking example one could give of the federal role in stimulating the welfare explosion. For what must be recognized is that the welfare poor came to form a coherent organization as a consequence of federal intervention in the cities—as a consequence of the Great Society social workers and VISTA volunteers who became the organizers of NWRO groups,[32] of Great Society lawyers who brought NWRO legal suits, and of the Great Society rhetoric and protection that made attacks on local welfare agencies first imaginable and then feasible.

If NWRO developed as a by-product of federal intervention in the cities, it later came to have quite direct relations with the national government. In 1968, the outgoing Johnson Administration granted NWRO more than $400,000 through the Department of Labor,[33] a sum roughly equivalent to the total amount raised from private sources after the organization was formed in early 1966. The money was ostensibly to be used to monitor the local employment programs for AFDC mothers, which had been mandated by the congressional amendments of 1967, in order to ensure that participation in training would be fully voluntary. However, federal officials were aware that a substantial part of

---

[32] At this writing, it is estimated that more than two hundred VISTA volunteers are engaged in welfare rights organizing throughout the country. They have been, by any measure, NWRO's chief organizing resource, although some organizing has been financed with private contributions, especially church contributions. The numerous recipient groups in Brooklyn, for example, were financed by the Catholic Archdiocese in that borough.

[33] Some local groups have also secured direct government grants, chiefly through OEO. For example, the New York City-Wide Coordinating Committee of Welfare Groups obtained an OEO grant of $25,000 in the summer of 1968.

the money would go toward strengthening local relief groups. The fact that the national government openly financed an organization of America's poor which was harassing local welfare departments provides a fitting epilogue to this extended discussion of the federal role in the welfare explosion in the late 1960's.

The Impact of the Welfare Rights Movement

It is not possible to calculate just how much each of the components of the broad-based, variegated welfare rights movement of the 1960's contributed to the doubling of the AFDC rolls. Legal services obviously had an impact, as did advocacy services in neighborhood centers, and organized protests by groups of recipients were influential in some places. Like most movements, this one was ubiquitous, and constantly changing. Once it had gained momentum, unexpected things happened. The press, for example, often played a large, if inadvertent, role. News coverage and documentaries on the movement alerted people to their rights and to the possibilities of obtaining them.[34] In the fall of 1967, the New York *Daily News*, which is read by millions of the poor in New York City, carried a three-part series on the clothing and household furnishings campaign being conducted by welfare recipient groups. By way of explaining the campaign to their readers, the authors of this series described the welfare regulations in great detail and acknowledged that most recipients were not receiving full entitlements; they even printed a half-page replica of the

---

[34] All of the major TV networks have recently produced one or more hour-long documentaries on welfare rights, carried at prime times. Most national magazines have also carried major stories, and some of these magazines reach the poor. Newspaper coverage—especially of protests and demonstrations—has been voluminous.

clothing and furnishings check-list being circulated by welfare rights groups.[35] For weeks thereafter, the welfare waiting rooms were filled with people carrying copies of the
page with the check list (much to the dismay of the *Daily
News* editors, one suspects, who were writing hostile edito-
rials throughout this period deploring the rise of a "new
'come-and-get-it' movement").

Taken as a whole, there is little reason to doubt that the
many-faceted welfare rights movement had a crucial impact
on the rolls. The report cited earlier on the causes of the
extraordinary AFDC rise in Baltimore reaches the same
judgment: *the rolls had risen primarily because families of
long-standing eligibility had been led to apply for public
aid in unprecedented numbers as a result of a great variety
of welfare rights activities.* Thus the report observed:

> When poor people are everywhere encouraged to make
> use of these resources [e.g., public welfare]—by publicity,
> by action workers on their own block, by teachers of their
> children in schools, by their doctors and by any social
> agency they happen to have contact with, a surge of re-
> sponse must be expected. It is the contention of this
> report that the increase of AFDC caseload reflects this
> response to the antipoverty effort, and that the poor fami-
> lies of this State through a combination of some changes
> in their alternative forms of maintenance and perhaps
> for the major part encouraged by the national effort to
> do something about poverty have responded to the use of
> public services, including welfare, in numbers heretofore
> unequalled.[36]

It is no exaggeration to speak of the poor applying for assistance "in numbers heretofore unequalled." Nationally,
applications rose from 588,000 in 1960 to 1,088,000 in 1968,

---

[35] The series, prepared by Michael Clendenin and Donald Singleton,
appeared on October 25, 26, and 27, 1967.

[36] Maryland State Department of Public Welfare, 36. The National
Welfare Rights Organization is not mentioned because it did not form
until the spring of 1966.

an increase of 85 per cent.[37] Moreover, the average annual volume of applications *after* 1964 was about 29 per cent larger than the average annual volume in the early years of the decade.[38]

---

[37] The use of data on applications is at best a treacherous business, owing partly to wide variations in what states define as an application and partly to the prevalent practice of counting cases transferred from one category to another as terminations in the one category and new applications in the second category. Despite these great problems in knowing what one is counting, we include data on applications—and the proportion of applications approved—as gross indicators of changes in the interaction of poor people and relief agencies. We have not, however, presented data on terminations, for these data are subject to even greater difficulties in definition and interpretation. In the final analysis, the firmest data are those pertaining to the rolls themselves.

[38] This figure understates the actual differences in application rates before and after 1964 for two reasons. First, the enactment of AFDC-UP in May 1961 led to the wholesale transfer of tens of thousands of cases into AFDC from other categories, especially from the general assistance category, as the states moved to take advantage of the new provisions for federal reimbursement. Pennsylvania, for example, was one of the first to do so. In April 1961, Pennsylvania received a total of 4,400 AFDC applications; in May, it received 18,000, an increase of more than 13,000 in a single month. Of these 18,000 applications, 14,000 were UP applications. The vast majority of the 14,000 UP applications were not new, but transfers from general assistance. (The practice described earlier maintains here: when a case is transferred from one category to another, it is counted as a termination in the first category and as a new application in the second.) That most of these 14,000 UP applications were transfers is evident from the fact that the general assistance rolls in Pennsylvania fell from 54,000 to 36,000 between April and May—a loss of 18,000 cases. The same inference seems warranted if one examines data from all ten of the states which inaugurated AFDC-UP between April and December 1961 (Connecticut, Delaware, Illinois, Maryland, Massachusetts, New York, North Carolina, Oklahoma, Pennsylvania, Rhode Island, Utah, Washington, West Virginia). In April, their aggregate general assistance cases stood at 212,000; by December, these rolls had dropped to 160,300, a loss of 51,700 cases. During the same period, the aggregate AFDC-UP caseload in these states rose to 48,044.

Second, the public welfare amendments to the Social Security Act in 1962 permitted states to claim 75 per cent rather than 50 per cent federal reimbursement for administrative costs in AFDC cases where rehabilitative services were given. Since the most casual contact between a caseworker and a family could be recorded as a "rehabilitative service," the states had little difficulty establishing a statistical basis for claiming a higher rate of reimbursement. To gain federal funds, many cases in other categories (e.g., a blind family with children or a disabled family with children) were terminated in those categories and opened in AFDC. Each transfer, however, represented an AFDC application received. Since most of these bookkeeping transfers occurred before 1965, the upsurge of appli-

TABLE IV
Average Annual Applications Received
(in thousands)

	1960–64	1965–68	% CHANGE
National	745	962	29
Northeast	226	280	24
North Central	135	149	10
West	148	285	93
South	236	247	5
Deep South	79	82	4
Other South	156	165	6

Source: Appendix, Source Table 5.

However, regional changes in the volume of applications varied markedly after 1964 (Table IV). In the West, the average annual volume virtually doubled after 1964,[39] while in the South there was virtually no change in applications from one time period to the next. These differences are at least partly attributable to regional differences in welfare rights activity. Southern storefront service centers were not so militant as those in the West or North; the distribution of welfare rights information was not so widespread; nor did locals of NWRO come to be established in the South on any scale. The poor, in short, were not acti-

---

cations from new families applying for assistance in the years thereafter is all the more dramatic.

[39] A substantial part of the increase in applications in the West occurred in California. That state's proportion of the total volume of applications received in the Western region increased from 62 per cent in 1960 to 72 per cent in 1967. Moreover, just one urban county—Los Angeles—accounted for a significant portion of the increased applications in California. Los Angeles contributed 15 per cent of the state's applications in 1960, but 28 per cent in 1967.

vated and mobilized nearly so much in the South, partly because the tradition of repression remained strong. The rolls rose in the South, to be sure, but not primarily because of increased applications, a point to which we shall presently return.

As the volume of applications rose, the proportion accepted also rose (Table V)—from 55 per cent in 1960 to 70 per cent in 1968.[40] In the Northeast, the acceptance rate reached 78 per cent, and in some Northern cities it exceeded even that level. Furthermore, the average annual acceptance rate after 1964 showed a 12 per cent increase over the average in earlier years. The largest shift after 1964 occurred in the South (16 per cent), and especially in the Deep South (23 per cent), a gain that accounts for most of the increase in the Southern rolls.

The Southern increase, we suspect, resulted mainly from legal services, the predominant form of welfare rights activity in the South. Much of the important litigation originated there, since the legal structure of the Southern welfare system was the most restrictive. When substitute-parent policies, employable-mother rules, and other restrictive practices were challenged, approval levels jumped, and the Southern rolls rose even though the volume of applications did not greatly increase.

The impact of changing application and approval rates on the welfare rolls was substantial, to say the least. Between

---

[40] The acceleration of the national acceptance rates would have been greater except for AFDC-UP activity in the early 1960's. As noted earlier, wholesale transfers of cases were made to AFDC from other categories in that period. Aside from artificially inflating the application rate, these bookkeeping transfers also artificially inflated the approval rates, for cases were not transferred unless already determined to be eligible for AFDC-UP. Of the 14,000 AFDC-UP applications recorded by Pennsylvania in 1961, for example, 13,000 were "accepted," yielding an approval rate of 93 per cent. Obviously, most of these applications were transfers from general assistance. Had they all been transfers, the acceptance rate would have reached 100 per cent. Once again, in short, our statistics understate the difference between the earlier and latter parts of the decade.

TABLE V
Average Annual Applications Approved

	% 1960–64	% 1965–68	% CHANGE
National	59	66	12
Northeast	66	73	11
North Central	62	67	8
West	59	67	14
South	50	58	16
Deep South	44	54	23
Other South	52	59	13

Source: Appendix, Source Table 5; calendar years.

December 1964 and February 1969, the rolls in the seventy-eight Northern urban counties exhibited a rise of 80 per cent (having already risen 53 per cent in the previous four years). In many cities, the rises were spectacular: Jersey City, 125 per cent; Kansas City (Kan.), 122 per cent; Flint, 114 per cent; Omaha, 113 per cent; Youngstown, 125 per cent; Milwaukee, 102 per cent; Oakland, 114 per cent; and Phoenix, 114 per cent. The greatest increases after 1964 occurred in the "big five" metropolitan centers where blacks had come to be concentrated; having risen 55 per cent in the early 1960's, these counties then jumped 105 per cent (the leaders, New York and Los Angeles, rose 137 and 145 per cent, respectively).[41]

---

[41] Just why the relief rolls rose earlier in some cities than in others is an interesting question. While there are doubtless a number of factors that bear on the question, we would guess that an important reason is differences in local political organization. Blacks may exercise greater leverage in cities where neither Democrats nor Republicans hold undisputed political hegemony. Or leverage may accrue to blacks when an established party

The consequences for the Southern relief system were also startling, especially in the Deep South states, where the AFDC rolls rose 57 per cent during the 1960's. All of that rise (98 per cent) occurred after 1964 [42]—after pressure from neighborhood legal services attorneys and from community action agency staff members resulted in many more applicants' getting on the rolls. In the remaining Southern states, the rolls rose 52 per cent, and 81 per cent of that increase occurred after 1964.

Nowhere is the evidence more striking than in the cities of the South that the size of the welfare rolls is not a response to the needs of the poor but a response to the trouble they make. During the 1950's, when the employment situation in Southern agriculture was rapidly worsening and migration was mounting, the AFDC rolls in eighteen of the forty-three Southern urban counties failed to

---

loses control because of internal fragmentation and defecting constituencies. (Moreover, blacks may benefit politically even though antagonism toward blacks has often been the chief cause of fragmentation.) In traditionally Democratic New York City, where blacks played a relatively insignificant political role, there was a negligible increase in the relief rolls during the 1950's (16 per cent) and only a modest increase during the early 1960's (68 per cent); then the Democratic coalition fragmented, and the massive defection of blacks assured the election of a Republican administration in 1966. Within two years, the rolls doubled.

Even among urban communities with entrenched political organizations, relief patterns may vary, depending on whether blacks are excluded or included. Chicago is famous for the stability of its political organization and for the absorption of blacks into it. It was the Chicago political machine that first brought blacks into electoral politics. Since 1882, at least one Chicago black has sat in the Illinois State Legislature; in 1915 the first black alderman was elected; by 1928, when blacks constituted only 7 per cent of the city's population, there were five representatives in the state legislature, and that year Chicago sent Oscar de Priest to the Congress, the first black representative since Reconstruction.

Chicago is also famous for giving and withholding relief benefits to engender political allegiance and to suppress political insurgency among the masses of newcomers to the ghettoes. And that may explain why Chicago's large relief rise of 282 per cent between 1950 and 1969 was so gradual: 83 per cent in the 1950's, 37 per cent in the early 1960's, and then 53 per cent after 1964.

[42] No part of this increase resulted from AFDC-UP, since none of these states implemented that program.

rise and even declined; in eight of these counties, the rolls dropped by at least 25 per cent—testifying to the rigidity of the relief system in the face of large-scale in-migration of destitute families. Sixteen of the Southern urban counties again showed either no change or a decline between 1960 and 1964 (although the declines were considerably smaller than in the 1950's).

All this was reversed in the late 1960's. The rolls declined or remained stable in only four Southern urban counties after 1964. The caseloads rose between 50 and 100 per cent in nineteen urban counties and at least doubled in twelve. Thus the rolls in Columbus, Georgia, fell by one third in the 1950's, showed little change in the early 1960's, and trebled after 1964. An almost identical pattern of changes occurred in Atlanta. In Birmingham, the rolls diminished by one quarter in the 1950's, rose 4 per cent by the end of 1964, but then went up by half. In New Orleans, the caseload went down by half in the 1950's and rose by one third in the early 1960's; after 1964, however, it more than doubled. All at once, in a mere four years, Southern relief restrictions collapsed.[43]

In summary, modernization, migration, urban unemployment, the breakup of families, rising grant levels, and other factors contributed to a growing pool of "eligible" families in the 1950's and 1960's. Nevertheless, the relief rolls did not rise until the 1960's. And when they did, it was largely as a result of governmental programs designed to moderate widespread political unrest among the black poor. One consequence of these programs was that the poor were sud-

---

[43] One of the ironies of the 1960's is that poor whites often benefitted as much as blacks from liberalized governmental responses to black votes and volatility. When the huge relief increases occurred, many whites who might otherwise have been rejected were accepted. Even now, blacks comprise slightly less than half of the AFDC rolls.

denly stimulated to apply for relief in unprecedented numbers (except in the South); another consequence was that welfare officials were suddenly stimulated to approve applications in unprecedented numbers.[44] The result was the relief explosion of the late 1960's. The terms in which that crisis must be explained are economic disruption, large-scale migration, mass volatility, and electoral responses—a sequence of disturbances leading to a precipitous expansion of the relief rolls.

We conclude, then, that because the 1960's were a time of profound disorder, both North and South, government responded with measures to ease that disorder. Blacks got a little more from some government agencies and suffered a little less at the hands of others, although, considering the magnitude of the political disturbances, it is remarkable to see how few and how modest these concessions were, and how often they turned out to be merely symbolic. Now that ghetto unrest has subsided (at least as of this writing), the liberalization of relief practices stands out, for without that concession the victims of agricultural modernization and of persisting unemployment in the cities would remain perilously close to starvation—as so many did in the late 1940's and the 1950's. And although the processes by which the relief expansion occurred were sometimes covert and circuitous, the moral seems clear: a placid poor get nothing, but a turbulent poor sometimes get something.

---

[44] The statements of welfare commissioners themselves are one measure of the changing climate. Instead of just reiterating how they were keeping ineligible families off the rolls, they began to speak of the large pool of families who were entitled to be on the rolls. Thus Mitchell I. Ginsberg, who became New York City's welfare commissioner in 1966, announced that "there are nearly as many eligible families *off* the relief rolls as there are on" (*New York Times*, May 18, 1967, 18). And James Dumpson, who had been commissioner of welfare in New York City during the early 1960's, had this to say in retrospect: "I was one of the people who was denying rights to recipients—not consciously or deliberately but because of my lack of insight into how these policies deny these rights" (*Long Island Press*, January 20, 1969, 3).

REFERENCES

Cloward, Richard A., and Elman, Richard M., "The Storefront on Stanton Street: Advocacy in the Ghetto," in George A. Brager and Francis P. Purcell, eds., *Community Action Against Poverty: Readings From the Mobilization Experience*. New Haven, College & University Press, 1967. (A condensed version of this article appeared in *Trans-Action*, 1966, 4, 27–35.)

Cloward, Richard A., and Epstein, Irwin, *Private Social Welfare's Disengagement From the Poor: The Case of Family Adjustment Agencies*. Buffalo, State University of New York (School of Social Welfare), 1965.

Cloward, Richard A., and Piven, Frances Fox, "A Strategy to End Poverty," *Nation*, May 2, 1966, 202, 510–517.

Elman, Richard M., *The Poorhouse State: The American Way of Life on Public Assistance*. New York, Pantheon Books, 1966.

Gosnell, Harold F., *Negro Politicians: The Rise of Negro Politics in Chicago*. Chicago, University of Chicago Press, 1935.

Levitan, Sar A., *The Great Society's Poor Law: A New Approach to Poverty*. Baltimore, Johns Hopkins Press, 1969.

Marris, Peter, and Rein, Martin, *Dilemmas of Social Reform: Poverty and Community Action in the United States*. New York, Atherton Press, 1967.

Maryland State Department of Public Welfare, *A Report on Caseload Increase in the Aid to Families With Dependent Children Program, 1960–66*. Baltimore, The Department, 1967. (Research Report No. 2.)

Moynihan, Daniel P., *Maximum Feasible Misunderstanding: Community Action in the War on Poverty*. New York, Free Press, 1969.

Reich, Charles A., "The New Property," *Yale Law Journal*, 1964, 73, 733–787.

ten Broek, Jacobus, *California's Dual System of Family Law: Its Origin, Development, and Present Status*. Berkeley, University of California (Department of Political Science), 1965. (Reprint Series No. 23.)

U.S. Advisory Commission on Intergovernmental Relations, *Intergovernmental Relations in the Poverty Program*. Washington, U.S. Government Printing Office, 1966. (Commission Report No. A-29.)

U.S. Department of Health, Education, and Welfare, *The Administration of Aid to Families With Dependent Children in New York City, November 1968–February 1969*. Report of a joint review carried out by the United States Department of Health, Education, and Welfare and New York State Department of Social Services. Washington, The Department, 1969.

U.S. House of Representatives, *Economic Opportunity Act of 1964*. Hearings before the Subcommittee on the War on Poverty Program of the Committee on Education and Labor, 88th Congress, 2nd Session, March 17, 1964. Washington, U.S. Government Printing Office, 1964.

U.S. House of Representatives, *Examination of the War on Poverty Program*. Hearings before the Subcommittee on the War on Poverty Program of the Committee on Education and Labor, 89th Congress, 1st Session, on examination of the facts which have developed under the administration of the act; hearings held in Washington, D.C., April 1965. Washington, U.S. Government Printing Office, 1965.

U.S. Senate, Committee on Appropriations, *District of Columbia Appropriations for Fiscal Year 1968*. Hearings before a subcommittee of the Committee on Appropriations, 90th Congress, 1st Session, on H.R. 8569. Washington, U.S. Government Printing Office, 1967. (Part II: *Federal Obligations, Loans and Interest, Public Welfare, Vocational Rehabilitation.*)

Welfare rights pamphlets printed. *Inside ACLU*, March 3, 1969, 1.

Yarmolinsky, Adam, "The Beginnings of OEO," in James L. Sundquist, ed., *On Fighting Poverty*. New York, Basic Books, 1969.

PART IV

Relief, Deindustrialization, and the War Against Labor: 1970–1990

CHAPTER ELEVEN

Poor Relief and the Dramaturgy of Work

In the Epilogue to the original edition, written in 1970, we said that the great expansion of relief beginning in the 1960s had, by the end of the decade, helped to mute protest and riots, and we predicted an imminent "shift from regulating civil disorder to regulating labor."[1] The Epilogue also contained some early evidence in support of that prediction. Since the present chapter takes up the evidence for the whole period since 1970, the Epilogue was omitted from this updated edition. But we wanted to preserve the prediction we made then:

> A great expansion of relief constitutes a "crisis" and pressure mounts to reorganize the system . . . in the name of reform. Similar episodes in the past suggest that such calls for reform signal a shift in emphasis between the major functions of relief arrangements—a shift from regulating civil disorder to regulating labor. For reasons we will explain, we are profoundly suspicious of the work-enforcing features of the reforms now being proposed.

---

[1] The Epilogue was entitled, "Relief and the Regulation of Labor."

The basis for our opposition is that when similar reforms were introduced in the past, they presaged the eventual expulsion of large numbers of people from the rolls, leaving them to fend for themselves in a labor market where there was too little work and thus subjecting them once again to severe economic exploitation.

In Chapter 1, we showed how labor regulating procedures were periodically activated in the pre-industrial world. And in chapters 4 and 5, we analyzed the initiation of such procedures during the 1940s and 1950s in the wake of the expansion of relief in the United States during the Great Depression. In this chapter we consider the work-enforcing campaign that evolved in the aftermath of the relief explosion of the 1960s.

The Turn to Labor Regulation

The civil disturbances which prompt the liberalizing of poor relief are often short-lived, and the expansion of relief is one reason why. This is the central meaning of our proposition that poor relief moderates disorder. A body of empirical research is now available on one aspect of this proposition—our claim that large relief increases are a response to disorder. Most of these studies (which will be discussed in a brief appendix to the next chapter) use quantitative techniques to determine which among different theories of welfare growth best fit the data, and the role of mass disorder receives considerable support. However, our related claim—that large relief rises in turn mute disorder—has so far been the subject of research in only one study. Kelly and Isaac found that annual increases in the AFDC rolls during the 1960s reduced black rioting in a "statistically significant and quite sizable" way, leading them to conclude that their findings "support the regulation function of welfare."[2]

---

[2]Kelly and Isaac, 219. These authors also found that rising federal expenditures for riot control diminished rioting.

As disorder subsides, elite preoccupation with work discipline comes to the fore. The better off (and, given our regressive tax structure, even the slightly better off) resent the costs of relief, and complain about the poor rates or tax rates. However, the deeper opposition results because employer groups fear that relief undermines labor discipline. Employers have always understood that by shielding working people from some of the hazards of the market, relief reduces the power of employers over workers. Moreover, for just this reason, the very *idea* of social provision is defined as dangerously subversive of market ideology. Because the stakes are high, struggles for social protection from below are always answered by resistance from above. Accordingly, once a measure of social peace has been restored following a large relief rise, employers press to restrict and reshape the programs. They exert themselves to lower benefits, to tighten eligibility criteria so fewer people can receive benefits, and to attach such punitive conditions to the receipt of aid that few people would willingly apply for it. Such measures are intended to compel workers generally to sell labor on whatever terms the market offers.

However, in the contemporary United States and in other rich industrial countries, social provision is no longer confined mainly to poor relief. A number of programs have been developed to provide income for categories of people such as the unemployed and the disabled who would once have turned to poor relief for subsistence. The turn toward labor regulation now includes these programs, since any form of extra-market income undermines labor discipline, whether relief payments or unemployment payments or disability payments. Our claim that "as turbulence subsides, the relief system contracts, expelling those who are needed to populate the labor market,"[3] thus has to take account of these programs. After the 1960s, as we will pres-

---

[3] See the first page of Chapter 1.

ently describe, efforts to slash programs for the unemployed and disabled were as vigorous as efforts to slash the poor relief rolls.

But poor relief still serves its traditional dramaturgical role. The degradation of relief recipients continues to be as virulent as when poor relief was the only form of non-market subsistence. Nor is the purpose of degradation—to exalt work, any work, at any wage—different. What did change is that the role of pariahs once played by the aged and infirm has come to be played by poor mothers, many of them minorities.

The intensity of campaigns to enforce work, and the specific forms they take, are influenced by economic context. In the United States in the period after the 1960s, efforts to reform relief developed in tandem with large-scale changes that worsened the conditions of work, and that posed acute problems of work discipline. As had happened so many times in market societies, traditional forms of employment were drying up, to be replaced by new jobs on less favorable terms. The problem that thus lent special urgency to work-enforcing reforms in relief policy in the 1970s and 80s was how to get people to accept lower wages, fewer benefits, and less job security.

These labor market changes were rooted in the decline of the American industrial sector as intensified competition from Europe and Japan, and later from newly industrializing countries, devastated the auto, steel, textiles, electronics, and machine tool industries in the United States.[4] Manufacturing employed less than 20 percent of the workforce in 1990, down from roughly 30 percent in 1960. Meanwhile, the service sector grew. But unlike jobs in the traditional industrial sector, many service jobs paid low

---

[4]Epstein, 145, reports that in 1953 almost 30 percent of manufactured exports in the industrialized West came from the U.S. By 1976, the U.S. share had shrunk to 13 percent. For several perspectives on the significance of internationalization, see Bluestone and Harrison; Magdoff; and Reich.

wages and provided few benefits. The terms of work in much of the service sector—and increasingly in the manufacturing sector—resembled those in the mass production industries a half century earlier, before the Wagner Act and the rise of industrial unions. For millions of people, work became less secure and less remunerative in the 1970s.

For a quarter of a century after World War II, American firms enjoyed unparalleled expansion, reflected in sharply rising profits, wages, and overall standards of living. By the late 1950s, economists could write books with titles like *The Affluent Society.* [5] But wages peaked in 1973, and then turned down. "Had the average wage continued to grow after 1973 at the rate it did from 1947 to 1973, toilers in 1992 would be earning almost $19 an hour instead of $10.56—a difference of more than $17,000 for full-time workers" that year.[6] Consequently, economists wrote books with titles like *The Deindustrialization of America,* [7] or *A Future of Lousy Jobs,* [8] or *The Age of Diminished Expectations.* [9]

There are large debates about the underlying causes of economic decline in the United States.[10] Some blamed business for years of failure to invest profits in research and development, and in new plant and equipment. Others blamed falling productivity on excessive labor costs. Still others pointed to a poorly educated workforce. Toward the

---

[5]Galbraith.

[6]Henwood, 628.

[7]Bluestone and Harrison.

[8]Burtless, 1990.

[9]Krugman.

[10]Falling productivity is treated by most economists as the main indicator of economic decline. Krugman, 12, notes the overall decline: "Over the first 70 years of this century, American output per worker rose at an average annual rate of 2.3 per cent. During the 1950s and 1960s that rate was 2.8 per cent. Since 1970, however, our economy has delivered average annual productivity growth of only 1.2 per cent. Had productivity growth [during the two decades since 1970] grown as fast as it did for the first 70 years of this century, our living standards would now be at least 25 per cent higher than they are." However, not all agree that productivity is the problem—for example, Block, 1987 and 1990.

end of the 1970s, a dramatic series of oil price shocks led some to blame the rising prices of Third World commodities. And then there were the high interest charges that corporations had to pay on the unprecedented debt incurred as a result of speculation in industrial assets during the 1980s.

We do not need to enter into this debate in order to understand the post-1960s labor regulating phase of the relief cycle. The salient point is that the peaking of the welfare explosion in the early 1970s coincided with a growing crisis in the economy, and with the mounting of a campaign by business to solve its problems of profitability by forcing workers to take less.[11] As this new class (and race) war on labor escalated, relief arrangements were converted into a weapon against workers.

Before developing this argument, we note that the United States was not alone in facing economic pressures beginning in the 1970s. Other Western industrial nations also experienced economic stress, and other governments and business leaders struggled to cope with the new economic conditions.[12] But they coped in different ways than in the United States, where disinvestment, speculation, and a broad-scale attack on social programs took place. The pattern in a number of other countries was to promote increased investment in new plant and equipment; to inaugurate active labor market policies, including the retraining of workers from industries buffeted by competitive pressures; and to place greater stress on innovation in technology and in the organization of production. These approaches apparently worked, at least for a time, not only

---

[11]The political mobilization by business in the late 1970s has been described by various analysts. For an updated analysis, including the mobilization to defeat labor law reform, see Akard.

[12]Magdoff, Table 2, 6, uses indexes from the Economic Report of the President, 1986 and 1991, to show a precipitous drop, beginning in 1970, in the annual increase in industrial production in the six leading industrial nations.

to shore up profits, but to sustain wage levels and maintain stable class relations.

What appeared to explain these more benign strategies is the complex of interrelated institutions which characterize nations with advanced welfare states: large and vigorous industrial and public sector unions, strong left political parties, and comprehensive income maintainance programs.[13] Because of the constraints created by these institutions, investors and government could not simply respond to problems of profitability by forcing workers to take less.[14] Moreover, these restraints on capital may actually foster overall economic growth.[15] The reasoning is that strong unions are able to restrain wage demands in favor of the collective gains yielded by higher rates of reinvestment, guided and guarded by left control of government.[16]

In the United States, corporate and government elites coped differently. One way was to shore up profits by closing plants and moving capital out of the old high-wage industrial regions and into low-wage regions here and abroad.[17] Another way was to turn to speculation—in real estate and in the financial markets, including mergers and leveraged buyouts of industrial assets.[18] By the 1980s, speculation reached frenzied heights, and the rash of Wall Street "insider trading" scandals was one result,[19] although

---

[13]Not all of these strategies were admirable. Some countries tried to expel "guest workers" in order to keep unemployment and social welfare costs down.

[14]Esping-Andersen.

[15]Lange and Garrett, 1986.

[16]Lange and Garrett, 1989; Hicks, 1988; Hicks and Patterson; and Hicks, forthcoming, which attempts to synthesize a range of neo-pluralist and neo-Marxist work on the impact of social democratic corporatist arrangements on growth. For a cross-national evaluation of the direct bearing of welfare state spending on economic growth, see Friedland and Sanders. See also Block, 1990.

[17]The classic study of deindustrialization is Bluestone and Harrison. Ginzberg and Vojta report that international investment by Americans increased twentyfold between 1950 and 1978, reaching $377 billion in 1978.

[18]See Block, 1992.

[19]See Barlett and Steele; Stewart; Phillips.

the elaboration of entirely legal forms of paper speculation was more important.[20] Predatory business practices in the multi-billion dollar defense contracting sector escalated, and widespread fraud helped bring about the collapse of the savings and loan industry.

Business also tried to shore up profits by cutting government regulation and taxation. Shortly after Reagan took office in 1980, a Republican regime backed by a temporarily unanimous business community rolled back environmental protections and workplace health and safety protections. Taxes on business and the better off were slashed, depriving the Federal Treasury of two trillion dollars by 1992 according to the chair of the Senate Budget Committee.[21] The tax burden was redistributed downward once again in 1983 when the "triply regressive" payroll tax for social security and medicare was raised.[22]

Most important for our argument, business tried to reduce labor costs by abandoning its postwar policy of accommodation with labor. Part of the strategy was to weaken union power in what Goldfield describes as "a growing offensive" by corporate America.[23] The threat of plant closings accompanied by capital flight struck fear in the hearts of workers. And new schemes for individualizing relations with workers proliferated.[24] Indeed, the 1970s saw the revival of an old American enterprise, the union-busting busi-

---

[20]A typical example was described in the *The Wall Street Journal* lead story of December 17, 1991. Joel Smilow, top officer of Playtex, parlayed an initial investment of $5.5 million into $186.5 million by taking his company through four leveraged buy-outs between 1985 and 1988, and he then began building an $8.5 million home on Long Island Sound.

[21]See *New York Times* Op-Ed by Senator Jim Sasser, February 2, 1993.

[22]Ornstein says that the payroll tax is triply regressive because "It has a flat rate: the same marginal tax rate for those who earn $1 as for those who earn $1 million. It has an earnings cap, so those who earn $10,000 actually pay a higher percentage of their earnings than those who earn $100,000. And it is a tax on earned income, wages and salaries, exempting income from interest and investments."

[23]Goldfield, 231; his book contains an excellent analysis of the decline of labor in the United States.

[24]Ferguson and Rogers, 84.

ness. These firms had prospered from the late 19th century up to the 1930s, providing private armies of thugs for hire to break strikes, such as the famed Pinkertons. (All told, the men under arms in private firms more or less matched the men under arms in the American army during those years.) However, when union-busting became a profitable specialty again in the 1970s, it was not mainly thugs to whom employers turned, but lawyers and public relations experts who used litigation and public relations tactics to defeat new unionization drives or to get established unions decertified.[25] Edsall says that "the strongest evidence" of this new adversarial posture was "the willingness of business to violate provisions of the National Labor Relations Act when fighting unions in representative elections." Illegal firings rose from 2,723 in 1970 to 8,592 in 1980, and back pay awards to workers rose more than tenfold, to $31.1 million during the same period, suggesting just how tough employers had become.[26] And this tough stance paid off handsomely for employers. In the 1960s, unions won most collective bargaining elections; in the 1970s, they began losing more than they won, and they were more likely to lose in larger bargaining units than in smaller ones.[27]

After Reagan smashed the air controllers strike following the 1980 election, the assault on unions intensified. By 1992, when the strike at the Caterpiller factory in Peoria, Illinois, by the United Auto Workers union collapsed in part because management threatened to replace striking workers,[28] it could fairly be said that corporate America had won its battle against unions.[29] Major work

---

[25]On the use of legal stratagems, see especially the data in Ferguson and Rogers.

[26]Edsall, 151–152. See also McCammon.

[27]*Ibid.*, 153–154. See also Ferguson and Rogers, 84–85.

[28]Goldfield, 231, also blames weak union leadership for the growing failure of strikes.

[29]South Africa is the only other major industrial nation that allows employers to fight strikes by replacing workers.

stoppages (involving 1,000 or more workers) dropped in 1991 to the lowest level since 1947, and 1991 was also the tenth year in a row that there were fewer than 100 major strikes.[30] Unions were forced to sign contracts with two-tier wage structures, and with pay increases that lagged behind the rate of inflation.[31] Overall, the percentage of unionized workers in the private sector fell from 29.1 percent in 1970 to 12 percent in 1990[32] (between 1970 and the mid-1980s, the proportion of unionized workers fell in only three of 15 other industrialized countries, and then only marginally[33]). "The right to strike is by no means meaningless in America," one analyst remarked, "but it is heading in that direction."[34]

With labor cowed, business could make enormous cuts in its permanent workforce, hire temporary and part-time workers, and slash wages and benefits. During the last four recessions, business eliminated jobs on an unparalleled scale. The Bureau of Labor Statistics reported that of those laid off in the 1973–75 recession who had held their jobs for three years, 51 percent lost their jobs permanently, 45 percent in the 1980 recession, 64 percent in the 1981–82 downturn, but almost all (85%) of those laid off lost their jobs permanently in the 1990–92 recession.[35] An average of 1,500 jobs were eliminated every day in 1992.[36]

At the same time, business turned to the hiring of "contingent workers"—part-time, temporary, and subcontracted employees—whose numbers grew rapidly after 1973.[37] By the 1990s, 30 million people—over a quarter of

---

[30]Hoerr, 109.
[31]See Harrison and Bluestone for an overall review of the concessions made by labor in this period.
[32]Brody, 33.
[33]Ibid.
[34]Hoerr, 108.
[35]U. S. Department of Commerce, July 1992.
[36]Dollars and Sense, November 1992, 23.
[37]See Tilly, 10.

the U. S. labor force—were "working in jobs outside the regular full-time work force. And while some are well-paid freelancers, most contingent workers are women and minorities clustered in low-wage jobs with no benefits."[38] They are six times more likely than full-time workers to receive the minimum wage, and a substantial proportion of them would prefer but cannot find permanent full-time jobs.[39] For business, the advantages of a contingent work force are obvious. By classifying workers as "part-time," "temporary," or "independent," employers can pay lower hourly wages and save on health and pension costs, and in many cases avoid payroll and unemployment insurance taxes. The use of contingent workers has emerged as "a permanent strategy for cheapening the workforce and weakening the bargaining power of labor. It threatens the economic security of all workers by dragging down wages and increasing wage-income inequality."[40]

And wages were indeed driven down. Non-supervisory personnel (who make up 81 percent of the workforce) suffered a real hourly wage decline of 15 percent between 1973 and 1992.[41] Overall, the proportion of full-time year-round workers who were paid wages too low to lift a family of four out of poverty grew from 12.1 percent in 1979 to 18 percent in 1990.[42] This was in part due to the erosion of the minimum wage. Between 1978 and 1981, the minimum wage was raised in a series of steps from $2.65 to $3.35. But it was not raised again for nine years, and then only to $3.80 in 1990, or 40% less than its real purchasing power in 1978, which brought it to the lowest level in real

---

[38]duRivage, 84.

[39]*Ibid.* See also Tilly, 10; and Callaghan and Hartmann.

[40]duRivage, 85.

[41]Data supplied by Doug Henwood, editor, *Left Business Review*, New York, New York. See also Bureau of the Census, March 1992, which shows that inflation-adjusted average hourly wages for non-supervisory personnel in the private market were lower in 1991 than in any year during the 1970s or 1980s.

[42]Bureau of the Census, March 1992.

terms since the mid-1950s. Even when the minimum was raised to 4.25 in 1991, it was still 30 percent less than the $5.54 required to compensate fully for inflation since 1978.[43] In the 1960s, the minimum wage was sufficient to lift a three person family with a fully employed worker out of poverty; by 1990, such a family fell short of the poverty line by more than $2,000.[44] Nor were minimum wage workers mainly teenagers: in 1988, 64 percent were 20 years and older, and two-thirds of these adults were women.[45]

The success of the campaign to lower benefits was also impressive. Medoff estimates that the proportion of those newly hired who got pensions fell from 43 to 38 percent between 1979 and 1990, and new hires who got health benefits dropped from 23 to 15 percent over the same decade.[46] Nearly four-fifths of all strikes in the 1980s were conducted to defend contractual health benefits,[47] and cuts in health and pension benefits continued into the 1990s.[48]

Finally—and much to the point of this book—an administration backed by a unified business community took office in 1980 and worked to enhance profitability by slashing social programs, including poor relief. The rise in spending on income transfer programs in the 1960s represented a downward redistribution of national income to which business organizations objected, claiming that the resulting taxes interfered with profitability. However, we think the more fundamental reason for the attack on these programs is that social benefits strengthen workers in labor market bargaining.

---

[43] *The Green Book*, 1992, Table 46, 601.

[44] Greenstein, 3.

[45] Extrapolated from Table 47, *The Green Book*, 1992, 601. Cutler shows that the decline in family income is due principally to changes in labor-market earnings, and he concludes that "macroeconomic growth is not the panacea for the disadvantaged that many have thought it to be."

[46] Medoff, Table 3, 7.

[47] See Moberg, 75, and Hoerr, 110.

[48] For example, see Mahar, May 11, 1992.

To see why, it is useful to remember a long-standing Marxist insight, that the unemployed constitute a "reserve army of labor" used by capitalists to weaken and divide the proletariat. Desperation pits the unemployed against the still-employed, thus weakening labor's market power. But income security programs reduce unemployment and temper desperation. They remove millions of people from the labor market, and protect other millions from the hardships of unemployment. The consequence is to tighten labor markets and diminish fear among those still in the market, and thus to strengthen workers in bargaining with employers over wages and working conditions.

Not surprisingly, programs with such potentially large effects generate conflict. Concern about the impact of public income maintenance programs (all such programs, not just AFDC) on wages became evident in the 1970s. Policymakers were troubled: unemployment rose in the late 1960s and early 1970s, but wages did not fall. This contradicted the common wisdom among economists that unemployment and wage levels vary inversely—a relationship embodied both in the reserve army thesis and in the neoclassical formula known as the "Phillips Curve" which was first published in 1958.[49] Post–World War II government macroeconomic policies were designed with this relationship in mind. Fiscal and monetary policies, by expanding or contracting aggregate demand and by raising or lowering the price of money, enabled government to control wage demands by manipulating levels of unemployment. Unionization and minimum wage laws modified but did not eliminate these effects.

For two decades following World War II, the unemployment/wages trade-off varied to order. Cyclical increases in

---

[49]See Phillips. This formula included prices, as well as wages. The broad debate in the economics profession over the validity of this formulation of a tradeoff between unemployment and inflation has been described and analyzed by Katznelson.

unemployment were matched by the expected fall-off in the rate of wage increases.[50] In the late 1960s, however, wages spiraled upward despite a 6 percent unemployment level. Barry Bosworth (who later headed Carter's Council on Wage and Price Stability) reported that "wage rate increases had actually accelerated slightly despite the high unemployment."[51] The problem persisted in the early 1970s: unemployment rose to the highest levels since the 1930s, and wages still did not fall.[52]

A good number of economic analysts concluded that the expansion of income maintenance programs in the late 1960s and early 1970s had insulated wages from the effects of rising unemployment. On the one hand, many of these programs absorbed the unemployed by allowing them to leave the labor market more or less permanently. Tens of millions of elderly people could stop working because of the extension of social security coverage to virtually all occupations, and because of the rise in benefits. The program for disabled workers also produced a sizeable drop in labor force participation: the number of recipients (excluding spouses and children) rose from 455,000 in 1960 to 2.49 million in 1975,[53] and many of the people who dropped out were of prime working age (more than a few of them, we suspect, older workers who were displaced as the industrial sector shrank). As for impoverished single mothers, they could apply for welfare; three million women were on the AFDC rolls by the early 1970s. The food stamp program, enacted in 1965, reached 16 million recipients of all ages by 1975, including the elderly poor, the disabled, and AFDC mothers, as well as a small number of working poor and some of those receiving unemployment compensation. Even striking workers could get food stamps.

---

[50]Haveman, 1978, 49.

[51]Bosworth, 62.

[52]See Duboff, for example.

[53]*1992 Green Book*, 65, Table 10.

At the same time, those of the unemployed who remained in the labor market and continued to search for work could obtain unemployment benefits, with important effects on the terms of employment they demanded. In the decades since 1935, unemployment coverage was extended to include 91 percent of all employed persons,[54] and benefits were liberalized, most importantly by congressional action extending the duration of coverage during periods of high unemployment. In the recession of 1973–4, when unemployment rose above 10 percent, the basic 26 week period of coverage was extended to 65 weeks (and many workers displaced from jobs by foreign competition also received benefits under the Trade Adjustment Assistance Act). As a result, two out of three of the unemployed received benefits during the prolonged 1973–4 recession. Almost all studies concluded that the availability of unemployment benefits increased the length of unemployment spells.[55] The unemployed could "prolong job search . . . refuse to accept work except at higher offered wages or cease active labor market participation" for a period of months, thus tightening the labor market.[56]

Taking all public income-maintenance programs together, the labor-market effects were large. The social programs reduced the total hours worked by *all* workers between 4.8 and 7 per cent.[57] And this is why mainstream economists began to recognize that income-maintenance programs had weakened capital's ability to depress wages and enhance profits by the traditional means of intensifying economic insecurity, especially by raising unemployment levels. As Fiedler put it, "A change has taken place in the

[54]*Ibid.,* 504.

[55]Danziger, Haveman, and Plotnick, 1981, review these studies. See also Feldstein; Garfinkel and Plotnick; and Mead, 1986, 72.

[56]Haveman, 1978, 46.

[57]See Danziger, Haveman, and Plotnick, 1981, 996, for the lower estimate, and Lampman for the higher one.

unemployment-inflation trade-off since the mid-1950s" because "the unemployed of today are subject to less economic pain" owing to "more generous income-maintenance programs."[58] As a result, Bosworth concluded that the unemployed "pose no threat to the employed."[59] And Fabricant recommended letting unemployment rise to "intolerable levels" in order to bring wages down.[60] In effect, the social programs had altered the terms of struggle between capital and labor. Still, this is more rediscovery than discovery. Government programs that distribute income in one form or another have always altered the terms on which people would work. This effect had been apparent since the emergence of "free markets" in which most people were forced to sell their labor in order to obtain subsistence. When people had an alternative means of subsistence, they were not as likely to sell their labor except under terms that improved their situation, and they were less likely to accept the most backbreaking or degrading forms of work. That has always been understood, whether relief took the form of bread and coal as was once the case, or the form of cash, nutritional supplements, housing subsidies, and health care as is now the case.

---

[58]Fiedler, 1979, 117; see also Fiedler, 1975. And see Bosworth, 69–70, for a similar conclusion. One of the ironies of the period is that research projects undertaken by liberals provided much of the empirical support for these contentions. The federal government sponsored a series of "guaranteed income" experiments presumably intended to test the feasibility of such schemes by evaluating their impact on incentives to work. Low-income families in the experimental groups were provided with income and were compared with control groups in several locations, including New Jersey, Seattle, Denver, rural Iowa, North Carolina, and Gary, Indiana. While the levels of experimental benefits varied between sites and among test groups, they were relatively generous compared to means-tested program payments. Not surprisingly (except perhaps to the researchers and their governmental sponsors), these generous benefits reduced work effort. In New Jersey, husbands reduced work effort by 5 per cent, and wives by 25 per cent; Seattle and Denver, which had more generous income supports, showed work effort reductions of 9 and 20 per cent by husbands and wives, respectively.

[59]Bosworth, 69–70.

[60]Fabricant, 165.

No wonder, therefore, that the social programs became a target of business criticism. The new tone was signalled at a series of meetings of the Conference Board, a forum of major corporate leaders, in the 1974 recession year. Leonard Silk and David Vogel attended the meetings and reported that business leaders felt themselves "engulfed by a rising tide of entitlement."[61] Consequently, as Domhoff reported, business leaders felt that the recession should be used to drive home the point that "People need to recognize that a job is the most important thing they can have."[62]

The main assault on the income programs began after Reagan's election in 1980 (although the attack on poor relief had begun earlier, as we will explain).[63] It was no easy matter to cut the programs, given broad public support for them.[64] In the drawn-out contest that ensued, the Reagan administration sometimes backed off, or turned to administrative subterfuge to achieve the cuts it wanted. For some programs, such as social security, the result was close to a standoff, at least in terms of short-run changes. Other programs suffered severe and lasting damage. Unemployment

---

[61]Silk and Vogel. During the 1970s, conservative intellectuals in Europe and the United States prepared the way for the business mobilization against the social programs with expressions of alarm about the dire consequences of the intrusion of popular economic demands into democratic politics. " 'Unrestrained appetite' has moved from the economic realm to the polity," according to Bell, with the result that economic expectations have been converted "into a range of *entitlements*" (emphasis in original), 23. Brittan, 130, offered a similar diagnosis of the British malady, where democracy was endangered by the "excessive expectations . . . generated by the democratic aspects of the system," which force politicians to incite an inherently incompetent electorate to want and demand more. Studies sponsored by the Trilateral Commission sounded the same theme. Thus, Crozier complained that European political systems were "overloaded" with participants and demands. And Huntington, 59, warned of the "danger of overloading the system" in the United States as a consequence of what he called a "dramatic renewal of the democratic spirit," expressed by the surge in participation and rising demands for equality.

[62]Domhoff, 279.

[63]For a general analysis of the impact of the Reagan cuts on the states and on the means-tested programs, see Nathan, Doolittle, and Associates.

[64]The evolution of popular ideology in the twentieth century supporting social welfare rights is described and analyzed in Piven and Cloward, 1985.

benefits, originally tax exempt, became partially and then fully taxable during the 1980s. Eligibility for benefits was sharply limited by raising the unemployment level required to "trigger" extended benefits, so that far fewer of the unemployed got benefits beyond the basic 26 weeks.[65] The result was a precipitous drop in coverage. Although 81 percent of the unemployed received benefits in April 1975, the proportion was driven down to 26 percent in October 1987—the lowest rate since the program was first introduced in the 1930s.[66] "For five of the six years from 1984 to 1989, the proportion of the unemployed receiving unemployment insurance benefits set a record low. No more than 34 percent of the unemployed received benefits in an average month in each of these years."[67] Even with the onset of recession in 1990, the figure only rose to 37 percent, and to 50 percent in 1991, the lowest levels in any previous year that included the start of recession.[68] "From July through October 1991, an average of 300,000 workers exhausted their benefits each month. Never before in the history of the unemployment insurance program, with data going back to 1951, have so many workers lost benefits without qualifying for more assistance."[69] The consequence was greater poverty among the longer-term unemployed.

The Comprehensive Education and Training Act was repealed, removing 400,000 people from public service jobs and returning them to the private labor market. The disability rolls were slashed. Social Security officials during the Carter Administration claimed that 20 percent of those on the disability rolls were in fact "ineligible," and Reagan officials subsequently struck 491,000 from the rolls, al-

---

[65]The intricacies of the changes are described and analyzed by Baldwin.
[66]*1992 Green Book*, 504.
[67]Greenstein, 7.
[68]*Ibid.*
[69]Baldwin.

though 200,000 were restored as a result of a court decision in 1986. Even so, the rolls have been kept down: the number of awards per 1,000 insured workers fell from an all-time high of 7.1 in 1975, to 2.9 in 1982, and only partly recovered to 4.5 in 1991.[70] Changes in the food stamp program—such as delaying various inflation indexing adjustments, and reducing maximum benefits—were estimated by the Congressional Budget Office to have saved $7 billion between 1982 and 1985, or 13 percent of what would otherwise have been expended.[71] (A number of these changes were subsequently reversed by Congress.) The food stamp participation rate was 9 percent of the population in 1983, fell off following the Reagan reforms, and then recovered to the same level in 1991 because many somewhat better-off families whose members lost jobs during the recession applied for assistance. But for the least-well-off families, the situation worsened: changes in procedures and new and confusing bureaucratic obstacles succeeded in cutting participation rates among the poor from a high of 65.6 percent in 1980 to 59.6 percent in 1991, and among the pre-transfer poor from 60.8 percent in 1981 to 55.7 percent in 1991.[72] Finally, work registration requirements were also introduced for those deemed suitable for work. And business interests, who had complained that the availability of food stamps for strikers gave them unfair advantage, succeeded in having strikers declared ineligible, unless they had been eligible before striking.

These cuts had their greatest impact on working conditions in the rapidly expanding service sector. Rothschild reported that more than 70 percent of all new private jobs created between 1973 and 1980 were in services and retail trades alone; and within these sectors, employment growth was concentrated in eating and drinking establishments,

---

[70]*1992 Green Book*, 504.
[71]*Ibid.*, 1637.
[72]*Ibid.*, Table 9, 1629.

which included the mammoth fastfood chains, and in health and business services, which included "services to buildings," such as offices and hotels.[73] This huge and expanding sector of the economy relied on a vast new "service proletariat"—an army of low-wage workers, the majority of them women and minorities, who cooked, served, and cleaned. The numbers of women workers expanded in the postwar period, for various reasons: rising rates of divorce left many women in poverty, forcing them to work; new ideas about gender led many to prefer work; and beginning in the 1970s, many married women took jobs in order to make up for the falling real wages of men. Labor force projections suggest that this trend will continue—63 percent of the growth between 1986 and 2000 is expected to be among women.[74]

The attack on the social programs occurred just as this large-scale movement of women into the labor force was accelerating. The resulting cut-backs in social programs that supplement wages, such as health benefits and food stamps, made this new service proletariat all the more vulnerable to onerous working conditions. And restricted access to unemployment benefits or disability benefits or AFDC benefits intensified the fear of being fired which underlies employer power.

The Reordered Class Structure

The spoils reaped by business in the war against labor were large enough to constitute a historic shift in the distribution of income and well-being in American society. Overall, the simultaneous growth of poverty and wealth was unprecedented in the twentieth century.[75] This was partly a simple

---

[73]Rothschild, 37.
[74]Fullerton.
[75]Krugman, 20.

and direct consequence of lowered taxes for the rich and social program cuts for poorer groups.[76]

Between 1977 and 1992, the poorest tenth lost 20.3 percent of its post-tax income. The top tenth gained 40.9 percent, the top 5 percent gained 59.7 percent, and the top one percent gained 135.7 percent.

And poverty increased. By the official measure, poverty had fallen from 22.4 percent in 1959 (39.5 million people) to a low of 11.6 percent in 1977 (24.7 million people). But then it rose to 14.2 percent in 1991 (35.7 million people), the highest level in a quarter of a century.[77]

Moreover, the official poverty measure greatly underestimated poverty. When the poverty line was first calculated in the 1960s, the average family spent one-third of its income on food, and the poverty line was set at three times food costs, adjusted for family size. But by 1990, food costs had dropped to one-sixth of the average family budget because other components—such as housing—had inflated at far higher rates. If the 1990 official poverty line of $13,360 for a family of four had been recalculated to reflect changes in the real costs of these components, it would have been about 155 percent of the official rate, or $21,700.[78] By that measure, poverty soared. From the same 22.4 percent in 1959 (39.5 million people), it fell to a low of 17.3 percent in 1972 (35.6 million people), and then rose to 25.6 percent in 1989 (62.8 million people)—or to almost twice the numbers shown by the official indicator.[79]

The most dramatic measure of the reordered class struc-

---

[76]A series of studies attempt to sort out the direct impact of changes in tax and income transfer policies on income distribution. See, for example, Blank and Blinder; Danziger and Plotnick; Danziger, Haveman, and Plotnick, 1986. And see Danziger, Gottschalk, and Smolensky, as well as Bradbury, for shifts in income distribution favoring the rich.

[77]Center on Budget and Policy Priorities.

[78]Schwarz and Volgy, 42; Chapter 3 contains a summary of different poverty calculations. See also Danziger and Gottschalk; and Jencks, 1992, 72–79 and 147–151.

[79]Schwarz and Volgy, table 6, 62.

TABLE I

Changes in Post-Tax Family Income, 1977–1992
(in constant 1992 dollars)

Decile Rank	Changes in Income
poorest tenth	− 20.3%
second	− 11.2
third	− 10.9
fourth	− 9.8
fifth	− 10.5
sixth	− 4.7
seventh	− 1.0
eighth	3.8
ninth	8.4
richest tenth	40.9
top 5 percent	59.7
top 1 percent	135.7
all deciles	9.1

Source: Congressional Budget Office.

ture was wealth accumulation—aggregate household assets, whether homes and other real estate, stock, bonds, paintings, jewelry, or yachts. Studies by the Federal Reserve show that between 1983 and 1989—the core Reagan years—the richest one percent of families increased their share of net private wealth from 31 to 37 percent, and they did so at the expense of all other social strata. The share of next richest 9 percent fell from 35 to 31 percent, and the bottom 90 percent lost one percent, from 33 to 32 percent.[80] In a characteristically opaque statement, Alan Greenspan, chair of the Federal Reserve, remarked of this finding that material distribution has become "more dispersed"; Claudia Goldin, the economic historian, put the data in perspective when she said that "Inequality is at its highest since the great leveling of wages and wealth during the New Deal and World War II."[81] Plainly, business won the war against workers.

The Role of Relief in Labor Regulation

Even as the class structure was being reordered between 1970 and 1990, attention was riveted on poor relief. Politicians running for reelection in the politically volatile 1970s and 1980s rushed to divert voter discontent over falling wage levels and new concentrations of wealth by focusing on welfare. They competed to define welfare as a principal national domestic problem—bad for the country, and bad for the poor. Politicians (and a good many intellectuals) denounced relief for draining public budgets and reducing work effort. And by allowing poor mothers to opt out of paid work, it sapped their initiative and induced disabling psychological and cultural patterns that entrenched their incapacity for work all the more. Deepening poverty ostensibly followed. In short, the new inequality in the United States could be traced to the "nonworking poor."[82]

Welfare, with its ancient connotations of pauperism, thus became the focus of unrelenting attack. No matter that AFDC was in fact a small program,[83] or that recipients were

---

[80]Relevant studies of wealth redistribution are summarized in *Dollars and Sense*, October 1992, 32.

[81]Both are quoted in the *New York Times*, April 20, 1.

[82]See the title of Mead's 1992 book.

[83]AFDC alone cost about one percent of both federal and state and local budgets in 1989. AFDC, coupled with Medicaid and social services, cost about

not valued by the market. Welfare was used to exemplify the way the full range of income-maintenance programs interfered with the labor market. And welfare recipients were made to symbolize the failure of character of *anyone* who opted out of the labor market by taking refuge in one or another of the income support programs.

The racial composition of the AFDC rolls facilitated the scapegoating of welfare recipients, since the majority of women and children on AFDC were blacks and Hispanics.[84] Race is a deeply divisive factor in American political culture. The post–World War II black movement was largely responsible for creating the political pressures which led to the expansion of social spending in the 1960s, as well as to the weakening of racial barriers in access to employment, housing, and education. Many of these gains activated and exacerbated white racism, and helped bring on a political backlash beginning with the election of 1968, and the ascendance of the Republican Party. The attack on welfare reflected these antagonisms and drew strength from them. In the process, white anger was deflected away from the new and pervasive economic insecurities and inequalities, and toward the welfare poor.

Historically, in the labor-regulating phase of relief cycles, poor law authorities reorganize relief arrangements to enforce work, both by expelling people from the rolls and by intensifying the degradation of those "impotents" allowed to remain on the rolls in order to reinforce work norms. In the past, the most common method of achieving this objective has been to shut down outdoor relief arrangements and to grant relief only in hell-holes called workhouses. That

---

4.2 per cent of the federal budget, and 4.9 per cent of state and local budgets. The proportion of food stamp expenditures going to AFDC recipients was about a half per cent of the federal budget. See the *1992 Statistical Abstract of the United States,* pages 355 and 357, Tables 561 and 565.

[84]In recent years, blacks and whites have each made up about 40 per cent of the rolls, and Hispanics 16 per cent.

was the solution in England in 1834. But the workhouse is no longer a politically feasible way to enforce market discipline[85]; by the late 20th century, popular beliefs in social rights, including "welfare rights," were more firmly held, and the potential for riots and electoral upheavals in defense of those rights persisted.[86] The less extreme alternative was to slash benefits in tandem with falling wage levels, to force more of the poor to accept the deteriorating conditions of market work by driving many of them off relief, and to subject those remaining on the rolls to "workfare" and other forms of ritualized degradation.

Justifying Labor Regulation

As in earlier periods, the introduction of labor-regulating measures was accompanied by a dirge of complaint attributing poverty and associated ills to relief. The claim that poor relief causes poverty is centuries old. As protest by the poor subsides, poor law commissioners, philanthropists, politicians, clergy, editorialists, and, more recently, social scientists, compete to advance what are purported to be new insights, presumably gleaned from the experience of the times, showing that the deteriorating conditions of the poor are owed to relief. The period after the 1960s was no different. Glazer argued that "Our efforts to deal with distress themselves increase distress."[87] Anderson concluded that the welfare system has "created a new caste of Ameri-

---

[85]However, imprisoning the poor—the U.S. has the highest incarceration rate among Western countries, more even than South Africa—could be construed as a partial equivalent of the workhouse.

[86]When we wrote *The New Class War* after the 1980 election, we thought the Reagan administration's professed goal of either abolishing or making deep cuts in various social programs would fail because of popular support for the programs. By the standard of the Administration's proposed reductions, the attack did fail; many of the cuts were resisted by the Congress, or were later reversed. Still, the cuts were deeper than we had predicted.

[87]Glazer.

cans . . . almost totally dependent on the state, with little hope or prospect of breaking free. Perhaps we should call them the Dependent Americans."[88]

The justification for these complaints is the coincidence of relief-giving and worsening poverty. The argument begins by pointing to a great increase in relief spending. Then the point is made that poverty worsened, as did family breakdown and out-of-wedlock births. And attachments to the labor force weakened. With these correlations established, the logic is obvious. Relief causes poverty by relaxing the discipline of the market, and by encouraging irresponsible family behavior. The central conclusion thus follows: so much more spent on relief, so much worse the poverty.

In this book, we interpreted these correlations differently. We argued that historical episodes of expanded relief-giving were preceded by sharp economic dislocations, resulting from cyclical market downturns or from the introduction of new forms of production. Market downturns left large proportions of the workforce unemployed and drove the wages of those still working below subsistence. Shifts in the market for goods and in methods of production had similar effects. Entire trades were destroyed when new machines and new ways of organizing production were introduced. In the United States, for example, many Southern rural people were left workless after World War II because of agricultural modernization, and were then left workless again in the cities to which they migrated because of the outward movement of industry to suburbs or Sunbelt, or to cheap labor regions abroad. Dislocations on this scale sometimes precipitate mass protest, and when they do, relief-giving is often expanded.

At the same time—and this is the crucial point—economic dislocations also produce widespread disorganiza-

---

[88]Anderson, 56.

tion. They wipe out the resources on which social life is constructed, as when enclosure eliminated the common lands in eighteenth-century England, or when agricultural modernization in the American South and highway and urban renewal projects in the cities after World War II (compounded in later decades by gentrification) displaced many poor and working class families from their homes and communities, or when deindustrialization in the wake of intensified global competition destroyed work and community in towns and neighborhoods throughout the United States. Under the impact of uprooting and migration, meaningful social life is ruined. The costs of these market developments for people at the bottom thus go beyond material hardship to the rupture of ties to place, kin, and community, and to the fraying of cultural patterns which make coherent social and personal life possible. And although the poor relief that is sometimes given at such times mitigates hardship, it does not repair the ruptures in social life that result from economic dislocation. Indeed, these disorganizing processes usually worsen, despite the wider availability of relief, precisely because the ruptures continue to go unrepaired. Symptoms of disorganization may thus spread among the poor, not because of the expanded availability of relief, but as a consequence of the socioeconomic dislocations which lead to the expansion of relief-giving in the first place. But since deepening poverty and accelerating disorganization coincide with the expansion of relief-giving, critics have little trouble producing the "proof" of their contention that relief is harmful to the poor.

In the 1960s, with the burgeoning of social science, it was not surprising that social scientists came to play a large role in intepreting the causes and consequences of increases in relief. Reams of reports were issued. Many were sponsored by business-funded "think tanks" as part of the attack on the welfare state (for example, the American Enterprise Institute was formed in 1970, the Heritage Foundation in

1973, and the Manhattan Institute in 1977). And other studies were conducted at universities with grants from government agencies trying to cope with the business attack. The welfare crisis, in short, led to a large research industry.

Except for new terminology, however, social scientists had nothing new to say; the attack on poor relief was scripted by a history going back to the sixteenth century.[89] The preoccupation of the research conducted in this period was with assessing the impact of expanded relief-giving on family structure, illegitimacy, incentives to work, and poverty.[90] Differences between liberal and conservative researchers were not as significant as their shared preoccupation with the perverse effects of relief. To be sure, liberal researchers demonstrated that conservative charges were overblown, and their remedies extreme. But liberals and conservatives could readily agree that poor relief generated "dependency," and that funnelling women into the labor force was the remedy. The liberal method emphasized education and training programs, and the provision of day care and health care services once women took jobs. The conservative method emphasized slashing the welfare rolls, or converting relief into mandatory work programs. Meanwhile, the institutional changes which weakened the occupational and life supports of the poor, and the role of dominant classes in promoting those changes, were typically ignored. The result, as we said in the original introduction to this book, is that "much of the literature on relief—whether the arid moralisms and pieties of nineteenth-century writers or the ostensible 'value-neutral' analyses of twentieth-century professionals and technicians—merely serves to obscure the central role of relief

---

[89]See Piven and Cloward, 1987a, for a discussion of the historical parallels with the contemporary relief debate.
[90]For an extended review of this research, see Piven and Cloward, 1987b.

agencies in the regulation of marginal labor and in the maintenance of civil order."

Slashing Benefits

One expression of the turn to work enforcement was lower benefit levels, a change which also sharply cut the number of families eligible for assistance. As wage levels began to fall in the early 1970s, welfare benefits threatened to become competitive with wages. A report to Congress on AFDC in New York City and ten other cities in 1969 had cautioned that "grant levels do seem to act as a disincentive to employment when they exceed wage levels."[91] Consequently, as wages eroded, AFDC payments were allowed to erode in tandem, thus preserving the "less eligibility" principle of the old poor law—that poor relief should pay less than the wages of the lowest laborer. The *New York Times* noted the coincidence between falling benefits and falling wages: "In 1991, a mother with two children qualified for an average of $7,471 a year in combined welfare and food stamp benefits. That is 27 percent less, accounting for inflation, than the amount two decades earlier . . . and the minimum wage is 23 percent lower than the average minimum wage during the 1970s."[92]

The erosion of benefits occurred entirely in the AFDC program, rather than in the food stamp program, which serves a wider range of constituencies, including the disabled and elderly poor. AFDC grant levels began to fall when protest subsided toward the end of the 1960s, as state legislatures generally stopped raising AFDC payments, or

---

[91]Committee on Ways and Means, 19.

[92]*New York Times*, June 8, 1991, A15. A word of thanks to Joe Davey for calling this to our attention, and for his useful comments on the debate over *Regulating the Poor*.

TABLE II.

Median State Monthly AFDC Benefit
(for a family of four with no other income)

Year	Payment	Constant 1990 Dollars
1970	$221	$739
1975	264	635
1980	350	552
1985	399	483
1990	432	432
1970–90 % Change	195%	−42%

even adjusting them for inflation. The result was that benefits lost 42 percent of their purchasing power between 1970 and 1990. By 1990, the maximum benefit was less than half the poverty level in a majority of the states, and less than a third of that level in a quarter of the states; for a family of three, the daily per capita benefit in the median payment state was $4.00.[93] (And as the nation entered recession in 1990, the pace of AFDC cuts actually accelerated.[94])

Food stamp benefits maintained their purchasing power, and partly offset AFDC losses. Food stamp benefits were made uniform nationally and indexed for inflation by Congress, beginning in 1972. In constant 1990 dollars, average monthly food stamp payments per person rose from $43.50 in 1972 to $61.50 in 1990.[95] Combining payments from AFDC and food stamps, the purchasing power of AFDC families was reduced by about 27 percent between 1972 and 1990.

---

[93]Center on Social Welfare Policy and Law, 3.

[94]See Center on Budget and Policy Priorities, February 1993, showing that state actions to reduce benefits in 1992 far exceeded cost-cutting actions in previous recession years.

[95]*1992 Green Book*, Table 12, 1639

Slashing Relief Rolls

After the 1960s, the welfare rolls were also slashed, enlarging the number of people looking for work and thus increasing the market pressures which force people to accept less desirable terms of work. In order to drive the rolls down, administrative methods had to be devised that would circumvent the bureaucratic and legal reforms of the 1960s. For example, the capacity of the relief system to fend off applicants had been weakened. Frontline eligibility workers—influenced by riots in the streets, by the demonstrations for "welfare rights,"[96] and by legal decisions affirming client rights—were more likely to use their administrative discretion to make liberal eligibility decisions. As a result, the proportions of applicants granted assistance gradually rose—from 55 percent in 1960 to 63 percent in 1970.

With the ebbing of protest, however, welfare reformers were presumably freed to institute measures to compel eligibility workers to interpret rules more restrictively. But they were partly hamstrung by new court rulings. Under the leadership of Edward Sparer, director of the Center on Social Welfare Policy and Law, a series of precedent-setting suits had been decided favorably by the U.S. Supreme Court. As we noted in the preceding chapter, "substitute father" and "man-in-the-house" rules were struck down in *King v. Smith*; durational residence laws were struck down in *Shapiro v. Thompson*; and the Court ruled in *Goldberg v. Kelly* that welfare recipients have due process rights entitling them to notice in advance, giving reasons for their elimination from the rolls, and an opportunity to rebut those reasons in a state hearing prior to the cut-off of benefits. Research has since shown that these decisions had last-

---

[96]See Piven and Cloward, 1977, Chapter 5, for a description and analysis of welfare rights demonstrations.

ing effects.[97] They were translated into federal regulations governing eligibility decisions, and national networks of advocates—especially anti-poverty legal services attorneys—stood ready to ensure compliance.

To neutralize the client rights which protest and litigation had created, existing federal regulations were repealed and new regulations promulgated following Nixon's reelection in 1972. Nixon had campaigned in part against welfare, claiming that his own mother had not been too proud to empty bedpans, and scorning McGovern's proposal for a guaranteed minimum income of $4,000 for a family of four. After the election, Nixon recruited top people from Governor Reagan's California welfare department, who were known for their innovative administrative tactics designed to keep people off the rolls. These officials had had bruising fights with California anti-poverty legal services personnel, who frequently managed to obstruct attempts by state government to slash social welfare costs, so they understood the importance of finding ways to cut the rolls that would survive court challenges.[98]

One part of the administrative strategy that evolved was to elaborate and lengthen the red-tape associated with getting and staying on welfare. And as the process of verifying eligibility became more intricate and complicated, the grounds for rejecting people because they "failed to comply" with department regulations rose exponentially. Existing federal regulations which protected against this sort of "verification extremism" by the states were repealed, in-

---

[97]Levy has since shown that these decisions were remarkably durable.

[98]After Reagan succeeded to the Presidency in 1980, he tried for two terms to destroy legal services by appointing like-minded conservatives to the board of the Legal Services Corporation, and he circumvented congressional approval by announcing his appointments during recesses. Still, Congress (led by Warren Rudman, Republican Senator from Vermont) defended legal services: when the legal services corporation slashed its annual budget requests, Congress raised them.

cluding a general regulation stating that the "verification of circumstances pertaining to eligibility will be limited to what is reasonably necessary to ensure the legality of expenditures," and local relief authorities were given discretion to ask for whatever additional documentation they wished (New York City subsequently created an 11 page application form). Previously, federal regulations instructed the states to "help applicants and recipients provide needed information" and to "obtain the information for them if . . . they themselves are unable to provide it." Or states could accept a substitute document, or even take a client's word regarding some factual condition. These regulations were also repealed in 1973. States were given 45 rather than 30 days to determine eligibility. And to insure that the states were motivated to implement these procedures, financial sanctions were imposed if "overpayment" or "ineligibility" errors exceeded a designated rate, a figure that was eventually fixed at three percent. By the mid-1980s, states had accumulated more than a billion dollars in penalties, although they succeeded in bringing enough pressure to keep the federal government from collecting.

As the application process became more cumbersome, fewer families were able to complete it, and more dropped out along the way, or were rejected for inadequate documentation.[99] Continuing eligibility verification procedures were similarly elaborated. Forms written in legalese were mailed out (as often as monthly) asking poorly-educated recipients with erratic mail delivery to fill in the blanks and

---

[99]For example, states could ask for letters from landlords and former employers, birth certificates, various documents substantiating how clients managed for two years before applying for assistance, and so on. The point is not that any one form is necessarily so difficult to get. It is that when the number of forms required is greatly increased, fewer clients will succeed in obtaining all of them.

provide documentation justifying the continuation of checks. Failure to return questionnaires, or to complete them properly, or to supply required documentation led to terminations. Nixon administration officials claimed that these new procedures were necessary in order to root out "fraud and abuse" which were ostensibly rampant. In this rapidly changing political climate, the message to eligibility workers was clear: saying "yes" had become risky, but saying "no" was safe.

In reports published by the Center on Social Welfare Policy and Law,[100] Casey and Mannix estimated that "there were about one million more procedural denials" in 1984 than in 1972, and that in 1984 "two-thirds or more of procedural denials (which represented about one-third of all denials) were denials to eligible families"—which meant that over two million children and one million adults were denied benefits for which they were eligible in that year alone.[101] The result was called "churning"—a process in which "eligible families have their applications rejected or their cases closed . . . and then reapply to gain or regain benefits"[102]—and it converted the welfare system into a revolving door. Churning also inflated application and acceptance rates, since those rejected during the eligibility process were often eligible and successfully reapplied, as did many of those already on the rolls who were terminated.[103]

---

[100]One searches in vain in the hundreds of social science research reports on AFDC that were published in this period for an examination of the regulatory and administrative changes that were used to drive the rolls down. Instead, evidence of changes in actual welfare practices was produced mainly by the anti-poverty legal services community.

[101]See Casey and Mannix, October 1988, for a summary of the federal administrative changes, and of their impact on the AFDC rolls. See also their report of December 1986, which contains extensive data in support of their claims.

[102]*Ibid.*, 10.

[103]Casey believes that most eligible terminees were able to reapply successfully because they had already established that they were eligible, and they knew how to negotiate the intake process. In his opinion, entirely new appli-

The great rise in rejections of eligible families was concealed by changes in the "quality control" system. This system, mandated by the federal government, required states to review samples of cases to estimate two error rates: those approved for assistance who were in fact ineligible, or eligible only for a lesser payment amount (the "ineligibility" or "overpayment" error rate), and those denied assistance for reasons not authorized under state law (the "denial" error rate). However, the denial error rate does not measure how many families are denied assistance who are in fact eligible, as the term might lead one to suppose. It is a measure only of denials which are not authorized under federally-approved state policy. The distinction is crucial. State law and policy authorize denials when agency requirements and procedures are not complied with fully, *even though the family is eligible.* For example, forms mailed to a recipient which are not delivered, or are not understood and returned, result in the case being closed because the form is not available in the case file. If the file is then inspected by a quality control worker, the decision to terminate will be upheld as authorized under policy because the form is missing—again, no matter that the recipient may in fact be eligible for assistance. It follows that if the procedures to be followed are multiplied, instances of "failure to comply" will multiply, case closings of eligible families will jump, and quality control reports will show that the closings were justified.

Moreover, state reviews under the Nixon administration did not measure denial error rates accurately, even by the limited criterion of whether they conformed with agency policy, because federal officials let it be known that they

---

cants were much more likely to be ensnared by the red tape, so they were more likely to be rejected at the point of initial application. If he is right, caseloads were kept down after the 1960s mainly at the expense of new families experiencing financial distress, and this at a time when poverty rates were rising. Personal communication.

were only concerned with ineligibility errors, and they threatened states with financial penalties if ineligibility errors exceeded three percent.[104] As a result, states reallocated staff, assigning more to ineligibility review than to denial review, and the rates of reported denial errors dropped sharply. In 1973, the official national denial error rate was 9 percent; by the mid-1980s, it was two percent (many states reported no denial errors at all).[105] Welfare advocates called foul, claiming that the true state of affairs was being obscured by a management review system biased toward exposing ineligibility errors rather than denial errors. Support for that contention was provided when the General Accounting Office reviewed denial error rates in the food stamp program, which had a quality control program modeled on the AFDC system. Two states were studied: the Illinois denial error rate was found to be 22.5 percent, or more than twice the reported rate of 9.1 percent; and Maryland had an actual error rate of 12.4 percent, although it reported a rate of only 2.2 percent.[106] The Department of Agriculture conducted a similar food stamp study in 21 states, and found denial error rates ranging from less than one percent to 23 percent, compared with official rates between less than one percent to 7 percent.[107] Henry Freedman (who succeeded Edward Sparer as director of the Center of Social Welfare Policy and Law in 1975) defined this combination of administrative changes as "the key to the federal strategy of driving the rolls down beginning in the mid-1970s."[108]

---

[104]Federal officials even dropped denial error review altogether for four years in the mid-1970s, but were forced to restore it under threat of a lawsuit by the National Welfare Rights Organization and three of its state affiliates, represented by the Center on Social Welfare Policy and Law.

[105]Casey and Mannix, October 1988, 13, and fn 33.

[106]*Ibid.*, 13.

[107]Cited in *ibid.*

[108]Personal communication.

Churning worked to lower the rolls. And so did cutting grant levels, by making fewer families eligible. Between 1970 and 1990, the proportion of people officially defined as poor who were receiving AFDC benefits fell sharply (Table III). The AFDC rolls included 58.5 percent of children in poverty in 1970 and reached an extraordinary 80.5 percent of poor children in 1973, a dramatic increase in the last three years of the welfare explosion. But by 1982, the proportion of poor children covered had been driven down to a low of 49.6 percent. The proportion recovered somewhat to 59.9 percent in 1990, although this was still a significant decline of 25 percent from the 1973 high. Data on AFDC coverage of all persons in officially defined prewelfare poverty, which first became available in 1979, showed the same downward trend. The ratio was 54.5 percent in that year, fell to a low of 40.6 percent in 1982, and then rose to 46.1 percent in 1990, for an overall decline of 15 percent since 1979.[109]

However, the campaign to drive the rolls down succeeded much more than these figures suggest because the official poverty line increasingly underestimated the extent of poverty, as we noted earlier. If the 155 percent adjusted poverty measure were used, the AFDC rolls represented a far smaller proportion of those in poverty than previously, and the campaign to enforce market discipline by slashing the rolls could be said to have succeeded.

We note, too, that some General Assistance programs, providing cash payments to more than one million single persons and needy families in 1990 who were not qualified for either AFDC or Supplemental Security Income, also got cut. Big industrial states made the largest cuts, all during recessions: Massachusetts in 1974 and 1991; Pennsylvania in 1982; and Michigan, Illinois, and Maryland in 1991 or

---

[109]*1992 Green Book*, Table 24, 663.

TABLE III

AFDC Families and Individuals, 1960–1990

(in thousands)

Year[a]	Families[b]	Individuals[b]	Individuals as % of Population	Child Recipients as % of Children in Poverty
1960	745	3,073	1.72%	NA
1965	975	4,022	2.08	NA
1970	1,909	7,429	4.07	58.4%
1971	2,532	9,556	4.86	69.2
1972	2,918	10,632	5.13	75.5
1973	3,123	11,038	5.08	80.5
1974	3,170	10,845	4.98	75.7
1975	3,342	11,067	5.17	71.6
1976	3,561	11,339	5.10	76.4
1977	3,575	11,108	4.94	74.2
1978	3,528	10,663	4.68	73.2
1979	3,493	10,311	4.52	68.0
1980	3,642	10,597	4.66	63.2
1981	3,871	11,160	4.74	59.2
1982	3,569	10,431	4.38	49.6
1983	3,651	10,659	4.51	50.1
1984	3,725	10,886	4.50	52.3
1985	3,692	10,813	4.47	54.4
1986	3,747	10,995	4.50	56.0
1987	3,784	11,065	4.45	56.4
1988	3,748	10,920	4.44	58.8
1989	3,771	10,935	4.35	57.9
1990	3,967	11,439	4.52	59.9
1991	4,362	12,567	4.89	NA
1992	4,692	12,636	4.95	NA

Source: *1992 Green Book*, Table 22, 660, and Table 24, 663.

[a]Average monthly number October 1 through September 30. 1992 figures estimated.

[b]Includes AFDC-UP; contiguous U. S. for 1960 and 1965; all U. S. thereafter.

1992. Pennsylvania, Michigan, and Illinois declared any "employable" persons completely ineligible; Pennsylvania limited aid to three months; and Maryland limited aid to those who could be expected to be disabled for at least 12 months (which meant they expected to be able to transfer these clients to the federal Supplemental Security Income Program). Follow-up studies found that many of those cut from the rolls had their utilities shut off, or were evicted, and that few found jobs.[110]

Poor Relief and Workfare Rituals

The churning process sifts and sorts the relief rolls, eliminating those with any possibility of surviving in the labor market. Even then, the shrunken relief system continues to play a role in regulating labor. Those who are of little or no use in the labor market are allowed to remain on the relief rolls, but they are treated punitively so as to affirm the importance of work. This was the meaning of the ritualized degradation of workhouse recipients.

With the workhouse no longer available, other rituals were devised. We first describe the workfare efforts that began to evolve in the late 1960s. Then we provide evidence that they were indeed rituals by showing that one work program after another was initiated despite repeated failures at placing welfare mothers in jobs. And we end by showing how these apparently failed programs in fact succeeded because they helped communicate meanings which reinforced labor discipline.

---

[110]Center on Social Welfare Policy and Law, February 1992 and September 1992.

Welfare-to-Work Reforms

A series of welfare-to-work programs were initiated beginning in the late 1960s.[111] **Work incentive** programs provided recipients with welfare supplements if they gained full- or part-time work. **Workfare** programs required recipients to "work-off" their grants by contributing labor to non-profit organizations or to government agencies (a scheme to which public employee unions and associations objected mightily) on the supposition that work experiences would prepare recipients to seek real jobs. **Job search** programs required recipients to look for jobs for a given number of hours each week, with supportive services sometimes provided, such as tutoring in how to identify potential jobs and how to conduct oneself in a job interview. **Education and training** programs were sometimes made available on the theory that lack of skills prevented recipients from becoming self-sufficient through work.

The first work incentive program was introduced in 1967. At the time, earned income was being deducted from welfare grants dollar for dollar, and proponents of reform reasoned that the resulting 100 percent tax rate discouraged recipients from working their way off welfare. The Work Incentives Now (WIN) legislation tried to remove this disincentive. In calculating continuing eligibility for relief among those who worked, a sum for work expenses was not counted against the welfare grant, nor the first $30 of monthly earned income as well as the next 1/3rd of earnings up to the maximum welfare grant level in the state, at which point people were terminated from the rolls. These earned income disregards were intended to be a

---

[111]There had been two earlier programs—the Community Work and Training Program, inaugurated in 1962, and the Work Experience and Training Program, which began in 1964—both of which failed. See Goodwin, 34.

bridge to self-sufficiency, providing working recipients with supplementary welfare benefits to enable them, over time, to improve their labor market position and eventually to work their way off welfare. With these inducements to offer, welfare departments were required to canvass the rolls for employable recipients, refer them for placement by state departments of labor, and supplement the wages of those placed. A variety of additional services or benefits were also provided, such as expenses for child care and transportation, as well as medical and dental care, and training. Not surprisingly, research evaluation showed that "subsidized employment is still likely to be more expensive than straight welfare."[112] Nor were many welfare mothers placed in jobs:

> Only about 10 percent of the 1.6 million eligibles were considered suitable for enrollment. Of all those terminated from WIN by April 1, 1970, only about 20 percent had jobs. Hence, the WIN program was successful in getting jobs for only about 20 percent of the 10 percent enrolled, or around 2 percent of the total eligible welfare population—and this during a period when welfare rolls for the whole country were rising by about 40 percent.[113]

In frustration, Congress enacted the "Talmadge Amendments" to the WIN program in 1971 requiring states to take more vigorous steps to register recipients for work by emphasizing immediate placement rather than training. But the job placement results were worse.[114] Federal regulations were then adopted in 1975 to restore the balance between training and placement, with results that were still no different. In the meanwhile, New York City initiated a work program for General Assistance recipients and paid them prevailing wages to work for the City; the program was abandoned in 1978 because "it was actually costing

---

[112]Goodwin, 25.
[113]*Ibid.*, 34.
[114]*Ibid.*, 25.

one-sixth more to run the welfare program with the jobs than without."[115] A similar scheme initiated at about the same time in Wisconsin was abandoned because work done by General Assistance recipients resulted in regular public employees being laid off, thus "creating unemployment among persons not receiving welfare and simply broadening the group who bear the burden of poverty."[116]

Meanwhile, with welfare costs rising, a very different initiative was undertaken by state and county officials beginning in the late 1960s: they mobilized to demand that the federal government take over full funding and administration of AFDC. Following the election in 1968, Nixon felt compelled to propose some sort of solution, not least because Republican governors, all of them in the North, where the rolls were rising the most, insisted on it. Consequently, in August 1969, Nixon proposed legislation for a "Family Assistance Plan" (FAP) that eliminated AFDC in favor of a broad national income support plan for all poor families.

The main provision called for a national minimum payment of $1,600 for a four-person family ($500 each for the first two persons, and $300 for each additional member). In order to be eligible for this income, family heads (whether on or off welfare) would have been required to work if they had no children under the age of six, keeping the first $720 of earned income, together with half of all additional earned income up to a gross of $3,920, at which point there would be no further subsidy.[117] The plan also called for federalizing the so-called "adult" relief categories (Old Age Assistance, and programs for the disabled). In October 1972, after two years of debate in the Congress, FAP went down to defeat.[118]

---

[115]Cooper and Nissenbaum.

[116]*Ibid.*

[117]See Moynihan, 230–31, for a description of the plan.

[118]See Piven and Cloward, 1977, 335–349, for an analysis of the demise of FAP.

Southern representatives played the key role in scuttling the bill. In deference to their persisting low wage labor system, Southern congressmen opposed any national minimum income standard, even one as low as $1,600 for a family of four. To be sure, economic modernization was under way in the South, but prevailing wages remained lower than elsewhere in the country, and agricultural and domestic wages were much lower.

Still, there were state and local fiscal strains to be dealt with. Part of the FAP plan on which politicians in both North and South could agree was to give fiscal relief to the states by federalizing the "adult" categories which provided benefits to the elderly and disabled. The result was the Supplemental Security Income (SSI) legislation, one of the most important social welfare reforms since the Social Security Act, and the welfare rise of the 1960s generated the fiscal and political pressures that led to its passage. As for the AFDC recipients whose rising numbers had prompted this reform, they would soon play the leading role in an unfolding dramaturgy of work.

By Reagan's election in 1980, the work incentive program had been discredited among conservative analysts. They alleged that poor working women were not using the 30 and 1/3 income disregards as a temporary bridge to full self-sufficiency; they were instead staying on welfare permanently, combining their earned income with welfare supplements. In reaction, the gross income limit for eligibility was dropped from 180 to 150 percent of the state's need standard, and the availability of income disregards was limited to four months by the Omnibus Budget Reconciliation Act of 1981 (benefits were also denied to any AFDC family with a member on strike).[119] The Department of Health and

---

[119]The gross income limit for AFDC eligibility was lowered to 150 per cent of the state's standard of need, making fewer working families eligible for wage supplementation; deductions for monthly child care costs were limited to $160; a standard monthly deduction of $75 was established for all other

Human Services subsequently reported that 408,000 families were terminated as a consequence of the new law, and 299,000 families had their benefits reduced.[120] Based on interviews in five cities one year later, the Government Accounting Office found that few of these families had been able to augment their income from additional earnings, so that most simply had less money.[121] The system was reformed again, with a shift toward slightly more generous incentives under the Deficit Reduction Act of 1984.[122] Nevertheless, subsequent employment success rates of welfare mothers were little changed.

At the same time, evaluation research suggested that poor labor market performance by AFDC women resulted from deficits in literacy and occupational skills. Title II-A of the Job Training Partnership Act of 1982 made funds available to private organizations to provide counseling, education, job search assistance, and other forms of support to prepare economically disadvantaged people for employment. The program was intended especially for people receiving any form of public cash assistance, and roughly 25 percent of the participants were AFDC recipients. Since the success rates were poor, the federal government authorized the states to experiment with "intensive services" for long-

---

work expenses; and the availability of the 30 and 1/3 earned income disregard was limited to four months.

[120]*1992 Green Book,* 704.

[121]*Ibid.* The average monthly income loss for single-parent working families was $186 in Memphis, $229 in Dallas, $180 in Milwaukee, $151 in Syracuse, and $115 in Boston. Many had no health insurance and had to forego dental and health treatment. It was also common for these families to run out of food before month's end, forcing them to rely on charities or to borrow from friends or relatives.

[122]The gross income limitation was raised from 150 to 185 per cent of the state standard of need, making more families eligible for wage supplementation; the $75 income disregard for work expenses was extended to part-time workers; and the $30 of the 30 and 1/3 income disregard was made available for eight additional months (or a year in all). Moreover, families who had lost medicaid eligibility because of the four month limit on earnings disregards were made eligible for nine additional months, and for six months more at state option. See *1992 Green Book,* 701.

term users of AFDC. Among the better known experiments were the Employment and Training Choices (ET) program in Massachusetts, the Training Opportunities in the Private Sector (TOPS) program in Maine, and the Options Program in Baltimore. These programs subsequently became the model for the work provisions of the Family Support Act of 1988, called Job Opportunities and Basic Skills (JOBS). States were required by October 1990, to begin phasing in a battery of intensive services, consisting of education, training, counseling, and job placement services. At least 55 percent of JOBS funds had to be spent on specifically targeted groups: (1) parents 24 years old or younger who had not graduated from high school; (2) parents who had been on public assistance for 36 months or longer; (3) older parents whose youngest child was within two years of reaching the age limitation for AFDC eligibility; and (4) one parent from two-parent families. Seven percent of these targetted groups were expected to participate on a monthly basis by 1991, and 20 percent by 1995. States were also required to extend Medicaid benefits for 12 months since some research showed that the loss of health benefits deterred families from leaving the rolls. In a preliminary evaluation of results, Jencks reported the "unexciting news" that there were "modest increases in welfare recipients' earnings," although nothing like enough to make them self-supporting.[123]

Workfare Failures

If one took the stated goals of the relief reformers at face value, they made little sense. The reason was obvious: there were too few jobs for unskilled workers, and many of them did not pay wages and benefits adequate to support fami-

---

[123]Jencks, 1992, 32.

lies. Indeed, had better paying jobs been abundant, the relief explosion of the 1960s would not have occurred in the first place.

Welfare work programs had also been tried in the 1950s, and they were also irrational, at least if one takes stated goals for granted. However, no one seemed to have learned much from them. In a 27-state survey of work relief programs for General Assistance recipients (who were mostly men), the federal Bureau of Family Services reported in 1962 that "work relief cannot reduce the public assistance rolls unless the economy produces additional regular jobs"—that is, full-time, year-round jobs with adequate wages and benefits. Work relief also requires "considerable additional funds because of increased administrative costs," not to speak of the way "work projects that are useful to the community tend to interfere with the employment of regular workers."[124]

Nevertheless, beginning in the late 1960s, work schemes proliferated. One or another method, or combination of methods, gained ascendance for a time, and failed. And then new schemes were devised, or past ones recombined, only to fail again. None of it seemed to make pragmatic sense. Unemployment averaged 4.4 percent in the 1950s, 4.7 percent in the 1960s, 6.1 percent in the 1970s, and 7.2 percent in the 1980s. The labor market was flooded with immigrants from Asia, from Mexico and other Central and South American countries. Confronted with an increasingly globalized world economy, corporations shed workers or closed plants and opened new manufacturing facilities in Third World countries with cheap labor. Later, with the end of the Cold War, defense industries began making workforce cuts. These and other developments contributed to abnormally high unemployment levels during the 1970s and 1980s, and to the longest recession of the postwar

[124]Cited in Goodwin, 34.

period beginning in 1990. There was no evidence, in short, that business required the labor of AFDC mothers.[125] What business did require was the more tractable labor force that results from intensified competition for jobs.

Those jobs that AFDC recipients could get paid too little and provided too few benefits. The AFDC rolls were composed in substantial part of unskilled women whose value in the labor market was at best marginal. Few of these women could command anything except the lowest wages, a problem that worsened rather than improved, especially in the 1980s when the minimum wage was allowed to fall much behind the rate of inflation. In a general review of research on work programs, Block and Noakes concluded that recipients typically could not find jobs which paid more than welfare.[126] Highly publicized stories of individual successes notwithstanding, a review of research conducted by the Center on Budget and Policy Priorities showed that work programs did not result in more than a handful of recipients achieving "a stable source of employment that provides enough income for a decent standard of living (at least above the poverty line) and job-related benefits that adequately cover medical needs."[127] Another general review, this time sponsored by the Brookings Institution, found that none of the programs succeeded in raising earnings by welfare mothers more than $2,000 above grant levels.[128] And Schwarz and Volgy concluded that, "No matter how much we may wish it otherwise, workfare cannot be an effective solution. Among the most important reasons for this is the absence of enough steady, decent-paying, full-time jobs to go around" because "low-wage employ-

---

[125]However, some business organizations thought otherwise. They foresaw a shortage of labor in the 1990s for low paid service jobs, and supported welfare reform for that reason. See the reports of The National Alliance of Business and The Hudson Institute in the cited references.

[126]Block and Noakes.

[127]Porter, 5.

[128]Burtless, 1989.

ment riddles the economy"—one in seven year-round full-time jobs in 1989, or eleven million jobs, paid less than $11,500 for the year, which was roughly $2,000 below the official poverty line for a family of four.[129]

The "adjusted" poverty line (155% of the official figure) showed conditions to be much worse; $21,700 for a family of four was almost three times the $7,904 annual earnings of a $3.80 per hour full-time minimum-wage worker that year. Overall, "eighteen million jobs available to fully employed workers paid less than three-quarters of the income" to meet this adjusted poverty line for a family of four in 1989.[130] Schwartz and Volgy interviewed a sample of nonwelfare families, some of whom had gross incomes at the adjusted poverty line, and found that even they could survive only by foregoing medical treatment and other necessities.[131]

If the 1980s are a precursor, the 1990s may see a growing number of low-paid jobs. According to the Bureau of the Census, there were 14.4 million (or 18%) of year-round, full-time workers 16 years of age or older who had annual earnings below the poverty level in 1990, up from 10.3 million (14.6%) in 1984, and from 6.6 million (12.3%) in 1974.[132] (The Bush administration tried to suppress these findings.[133]) There was no reason, in short, to think that most AFDC mothers would succeed in achieving self-sufficiency when growing millions of workers could not. In a study of the finances of welfare families, Jencks and Edin found that "single mothers do not turn to welfare because

---

[129]Schwarz and Volgy, 81 and 106.

[130]*Ibid.*, 81.

[131]Schwartz and Volgy; these interviews are dispersed throughout their book.

[132]U.S. Census, May 1992.

[133]Writing in *Barrons*, May 18, 1992, under the title, "Numbers Game: A Census Bureau Wage Report Takes Five Months to Surface," Maggie Mahar tells the whole story.

they are pathologically dependent on hand-outs or unusually reluctant to work—they do so because they cannot get jobs that pay better than welfare."[134]

Nor did the savings to government that resulted when AFDC women were placed in work programs come close to the administrative costs of operating these programs, including the costs incurred by cooperating agencies such as state employment services. Add to this the not insignificant costs of health care and child care for women who entered the various public work programs or who got low-wage jobs in the private market. The Congress was certainly not unmindful of this, as it showed by its endless squabbling over whether such benefits to working recipients should be funded at all, or for only four months, or nine months, or twelve months, or whatever. Jencks estimated that AFDC mothers working at the minimum wage would have to be given "free medical care and at least $5,000 worth of resources to supplement their wages," at a cost in excess of $50 billion, an expenditure which he agreed was unlikely to be made. (Kaus offered a similar dollar estimate for his recommendation for a WPA-like jobs program for the poor.[135]) Undaunted, Jencks recommended an incremental approach—"a few billion dollars in the first year, slightly more the second year, and so forth."[136]

Given scarce jobs and low wages, the result of work programs was predictable enough. They contributed to the "churning" or "revolving door" effect which had already been set in motion by the revised quality control system. Studies showed that "a substantial proportion of former recipients" who were working ended up reapplying for welfare because they could not survive on their earnings, even with wage supplementation, not to speak of deprivations

---

[134]Jencks and Edin, 1992, 204. See also Jencks and Edin, 1990.
[135]Kaus, 1992.
[136]Jencks, 1992, 36 and 39. See also Kaus 1992.

resulting from any "disruption in their income, such as a job layoff or an illness in the family."[137] Nevertheless, millions of dollars continued to be spent on one work scheme or another in an endlessly futile cycle.

Other professed goals of the work programs were equally irrational, if taken at face value, such as the unsubstantiated assertions that work would transform family structure, community life, and the so-called "culture of poverty." Kaus insisted that "replacing welfare with work can be expected to transform the entire culture of poverty," including family patterns, because "it's doubtful" that working women would "be willing to share their hard-earned paychecks with non-working men the way they might have been willing to share their welfare checks," so that "the natural incentives toward the formation of two-parent families will reassert themselves."[138] (Kaus presented no data to support the view that the source of a woman's income influences marriage rates.) Marriage rates might indeed have increased were jobs with adequate wages and benefits available to men, as well as to women on welfare who choose to work, but that would have required responses by business different from disinvestment, speculation, and a declaration of war against labor.

It was also doubtful that putting poor women to work would improve the care and socialization of children. Kaus claimed that, "If a mother has to set her alarm clock, she's likely to teach her children to set their alarm clocks as well,"[139] thus trivializing the real activities of most of these women. Many AFDC mothers with younger children get their children up every morning and, because of the danger in the streets, walk them to school, walk them home, and keep them locked up in their apartments until morning.

---

[137]Porter, xiv.
[138]Kaus, 1992, 129.
[139]*Ibid.*, 129.

Forcing these overburdened women to work would mean adding the market job to the exhausting job of maintaining a home without funds or services, and all the while surrounded by dangerous and disorganized neighborhoods. As we have said elsewhere, "Contemporary workfare reforms should be understood as a replay of a history of social-welfare initiatives in which intensely felt popular concerns with family are evoked to justify programs which shore-up labor-market discipline."[140]

Work was also advertised as the way to reverse the deterioration of community life. The minutes of a meeting of academics, intellectuals, and administrators who met in New York City after Nixon's election reported a consensus that the rising welfare rolls accompanied by rising violence and other manifestations of disorder proved that, "The social fabric . . . is coming to pieces. It isn't just 'strained' and it isn't just 'frayed'; but like a sheet of rotten canvas, it is starting to rip."[141] Converting AFDC to a work system was the remedy; work would restore the social fabric.

Removing women from their homes and neighborhoods would more likely shred the social fabric more. Putting mothers to work would deprive the poor community of its most stable element—of the women, for example, who have mounted campaigns to drive drug dealers from their housing projects and neighborhoods. Sally Hernandez-Pinero, the chairwoman of the New York City Housing Authority, commented on the social roles played by the 75,000 women living and raising children alone in the New York City projects. "Anyone with even a nodding acquaintance with these women knows them for what they are, the sanity of the poor community, resourceful survivors of abandonment, slander, and brutality. . . . In many poor communi-

---

[140]Piven and Cloward, 1988, 644.
[141]Cited in Moynihan, 76.

ties, they are the only signatures on the social contract, the glue that keeps our communities from spinning out of control."[142]

No social analyst explained convincingly why these women would contribute more to their communities by taking jobs flipping hamburgers. Nor did anyone explain why it would not be the better part of public policy to shore up income and social supports for women who are struggling to care for children under the jungle-like conditions of urban poverty. Instead, the family and community work performed by these women—like the family and community work of women more generally—was consistently ignored or devalued by critics of welfare.

Of course, many welfare mothers want to work,[143] and they should have the opportunity, together with training and supportive benefits, such as day care and health care, as well as wage income and supplemental welfare payments that would enable their families to survive in the market. Under such conditions, many would take jobs, and coercion would be unnecessary. As a realistic matter, however, such opportunities were not on the reform agenda. It was the rhetoric of work that was on the agenda.

Despite continued workfare failures, an aura of optimism continued to permeate the literature on welfare reform. Analysts were convinced that most welfare mothers could achieve self-sufficiency through work, and that benign consequences for family and community would ensue. The key to eventual success was finding the proper mix of programs

---

[142]From an unpublished speech at Columbia University in 1992. With thanks to Val Coleman.

[143]Polls in 1992 showed that 53 per cent of all women in the United States preferred to stay at home; this was true of 59 per cent of those with less than high school education, and 51 per cent of those with some college; and it was true of 64 per cent of married women (see *The Public Perspective*, 97). And Segal, 32, provides evidence that only a third of married women worked full-time throughout the year in 1992, and only 23 per cent of them had children under the age of three, even though they had a male partner to help juggle earner-parent roles.

targeted to those who could best benefit from them. As theories and policies proliferated—none of them gaining ascendance for long, since none of them succeeded in practice—the search went on and on for new strategies, or mix of strategies, that would produce the desired outcomes. And this was so, Schram points out, even though the research base which the reformers invoked to justify workfare legislation showed there would be few if any effects, leading him to conclude that these initiatives represented "symbols at the expense of substance."[144]

Workfare as Dramaturgy

If the reformers' claims did not justify their work programs, perhaps it was because another and unacknowledged dynamic did justify them. As we said in Chapter 1, once the threat of the unruly poor subsides, relief arrangements are reorganized in order to treat recipients in a manner that is "so degrading and punitive as to instill in the laboring masses a fear of the fate that awaits them should they relax into beggary and pauperism. To demean and punish those who do not work is to exalt by contrast even the meanest labor at the meanest wages."[145] This historically familiar drama was reenacted in the United States in the 1970s and 1980s, and perhaps even more boldly just because the terms of market labor were worsening. The pronouncements of one analyst after another revived this classical formula. Kaus wrote that we cannot promise welfare mothers who are forced to work that "they'll be rich, or even comfortably well-off" (and, he might have added, the society could not even promise them a living wage). But, he

---

[144]The quotation is from the title of Schram's 1992 article.

[145]See the first page of Chapter 1 in this book. For a powerful exposition of the way the degradation of "deviants" serves to reinforce societal norms, see Emile Durkheim's classic nineteenth century essay on *The Rules of the Sociological Method.*

went on to say, we can promise them *"respect"* because they "would have the tangible honor society reserves for workers."[146]

Degradation took other forms as well. Monitoring and excoriating the behavior of the poor, and conditioning access to benefits on changes in behavior, are as old as relief arrangements. Dramatic allegations that recipients are slothful, shiftless, promiscuous, criminal, and indifferent to the rules others value constitute rituals of public degradation. Conditioning benefits on approved conduct is the traditional remedy. Under Ohio and Wisconsin "learnfare" regulations, for example, AFDC benefits were cut sharply if AFDC children were truant. And New Jersey legislated a family grant "cap," which excluded payments for babies born to families already on welfare.

The degraded welfare mother was thus made to serve as a warning to all Americans who were working more and earning less, if they were working at all. There is a fate worse, and a status lower, than hard and unrewarding work. Welfare mothers were natural candidates for this labor-regulating role after the 1960s because of the changing gender and racial composition of the labor force. When the welfare system was enacted in 1935 as part of the Social Security Act, it was intended to support minor children being raised by mainly white widows who were not considered employable. And the states carefully crafted welfare practices in the 1940s and 1950s to ensure that none of the money given single women caring for children would find its way into the hands of men who were considered workers. Man-in-the-house rules, midnight raids, and related measures were all designed to avert that danger. But then women began entering the labor force in much greater numbers, taking jobs primarily in the service sector. And

---

[146]Kaus, 1992, 138–39 (emphasis in original). To imply that everyone who works is honored is ridiculous. Low-wage and unskilled workers receive hardly any honor. Honor is inherently scarce; if some have it, others don't.

with the rise of a predominantly female and minority service sector proletariat, the degradation of female relief recipients as a means of regulating labor became entirely
consistent with the historic uses of welfare to enforce market discipline.

Pressures for Reform Intensify

By the 1990s, the work-enforcing theme in anti-welfare
rhetoric had became grandiose. Moynihan announced to
the press that "just as unemployment was the defining issue
of industrialism, dependency is becoming the defining
issue of post-industrial society."[147] Mead wrote that "dependency" signals "the end of the Western tradition."[148]
By these accounts, rising unemployment, declining wage
levels, and disappearing fringe benefits need not have concerned anyone. "The old issues were economic and structural," Mead insists, and the "new issues" produced by
dependency "are social and personal."[149] Murray said "I
know how" to eliminate the problem of dependency: "You
just rip away every kind of government support there is."[150]
And Kaus justified such extreme measures by invoking a
grand historical parallel: "Underclass culture can't survive
the end of welfare any more than feudal culture could survive the advent of capitalism."[151]

Meanwhile, with the national press reporting that "dependency" had reached "epidemic proportions,"[152] Bush
and Clinton vied to excoriate welfare during the 1992 presidential campaign. Clinton proposed to limit time on welfare to "two years and off to work," either in the private

---

[147]*New York Times,* December 9, 1991, A13.
[148]Mead, 1992, 237.
[149]*Ibid.,* 211.
[150]*U.S. News & World Report,* October 5, 1992, 38.
[151]Kaus, 1992, 129.
[152]*Ibid.*

market or on subsidized community service or work relief projects. Moynihan hailed this as "a landmark for families," and called for creating "1.5 million jobs" for what would be "former" welfare mothers.

We do not know, at this writing in early 1993, what Clinton and the Congress will do. If they were actually to carry out a two-year cut-off under current labor market conditions, they would shortly find themselves debating the question of whether women unable to make it in the market should be readmitted to the rolls. (During the 1992 presidential campaign, Clinton claimed that 17,000 Arkansas residents had been successfully moved off the AFDC and food stamp rolls under a state jobs program between 1989 and 1992, although the administrator of the program subsequently acknowledged that "many people returned to welfare during that period."[153]) Otherwise, the streets would soon fill with homeless women and children, and the venerable body of theory and historical research which attributes riot and political disorder to insecurity about subsistence would once again be put to the test. It is hard to believe that national politicians will take that risk. More likely, they'll continue to contrive new variations in the dramaturgy of work.

When *Regulating the Poor* was first published in 1971, we warned that the rising clamor for "reform" presaged a turn toward work enforcement that would consist of efforts to slash caseloads and benefits, and to degrade recipients by forcing them to participate in spectacular workfare rituals. We therefore concluded in the Epilogue that

>   . . . *the explosion of the rolls is the true . . . reform*, that it should be defended, and expanded. Even now, hundreds of thou-

---

[153]*New York Times*, October 13, 1992, A5.

sands of impoverished families remain who are eligible for assistance but who receive no aid at all. [Emphasis in original.]

We still think so.

REFERENCES

Akard, Patrick J., "Corporate Mobilization and U.S. Economy Policy in the 1970s," *American Sociological Review*, 57, 5, 1992.

Anderson, Martin, *Welfare: The Political Economy of Welfare Reform in the United States.* Stanford, California, The Hoover Institution, 1978.

Barlett, Donald L., and James B. Steele, *America: What Went Wrong?* Kansas City, Andrews and McMeel, 1992.

Bell, Daniel, *Cultural Contradictions of Capitalism.* New York, Basic Books, 1978.

Blank, Rebecca M., and Alan S. Blinder, "Macroeconomics, Income Distribution, and Poverty." In Sheldon Danziger and Daniel H. Weinberg, eds., *Fighting Poverty: What Works and What Doesn't.* Cambridge, Harvard University Press, 1986.

Block, Fred, "Rethinking the Political Economy of the Welfare State." In Fred Block, Richard A. Cloward, Barbara Ehrenreich, and Frances Fox Piven, *The Mean Season.* New York, Pantheon, 1987.

Block, Fred, *Postindustrial Possibilities.* Berkeley, University of California Press, 1990.

Block, Fred, and John Noakes, "The Politics of New-Style Workfare," *Socialist Review*, 18, 1988.

Bluestone, Barry, and Bennett Harrison, *The Deindustrialization of America.* New York, Basic Books, 1982.

Bosworth, Barry, "Re-establishing An Economic Consensus: An Impossible Agenda?" *Daedalus*, 109, 3, 1980.

Bradbury, Katherine, "The Changing Fortunes of U.S. Families," *New England Economic Review*, July/August 1990.

Brittan, Samuel, "The Economic Contradictions of Democracy," *British Journal of Political Science*, 5, 1975.

Brody, David, "The Breakdown of Labor's Social Contract," *Dissent*, Winter, 1992.

Burtless, Gary, "The Effect of Reform on Employment, Earnings and Income." In Phoebe Cottingham and David Ellwood, eds., *Welfare Policy for the 1990s.* Cambridge, Harvard University Press, 1989.

Burtless, Gary, ed., *A Future of Lousy Jobs: The Changing Structure of U.S. Wages.* Washington, D.C., Brookings Institution, 1990.

Casey, Timothy J., and Mary R. Mannix, "Quality Control and the 'Churning' Crisis," Center on Social Welfare Policy and Law. New York, New York, December 1986.

Casey, Timothy J., and Mary R. Mannix, "Quality Control in Public Assistance: Victimizing the Poor Through One-Sided Accountability," Center on Social Welfare Policy and Law. New York, New York, October 1988.

Center on Budget and Policy Priorities, "Number in Poverty Hits 20-Year High." Washington, D.C., September 8, 1992.

Center on Budget and Policy Priorities, "The States and the Poor: Budget Decisions Hurt Low Income People in 1992." Washington, D.C., February 1993.

Center on Social Welfare Policy and Law, "Childhood Poverty and Public Transfers in International Perspective." New York, New York, May 1991.

Center on Social Welfare Policy and Law, "Impact of Termination of General Assistance Benefits for 'Employables' in Massachusetts, Michigan, and Pennsylvania," Publication No. 805. New York, New York, February 1992.

Center on Social Welfare Policy and Law, "No Relief for the Poor: 1992 State Cutbacks in AFDC, GA, and EAF," Part 1. Publication No. 167. New York, New York, September 1992.

Committee on Ways and Means, US House of Representatives, 91st Congress, 1st Session, *Report of the Findings of Special Review of Aid to Families with Dependent Children in New York City.* Washington, D.C., U. S. Government Printing Office, 1969.

Cooper, Mary A., and Ellen Nissenbaum, "Workfare: Unfair," *HUNGER, Newsletter of the Interreligious Taskforce on U. S. Food Policy.* Washington, D.C., June 1983.

Crozier, Michael, "Chapter II—Western Europe." In Michael Crozier, Samuel P. Huntington, and Joji Watanuki, eds., *The Crisis of Democracy: Report on the Governability of Democracies to the Trilateral Commission.* New York, New York University Press, 1975.

Cutler, David M., "Rising Inequality? Changes in the Distribution of Income and Consumption in the 1980s," *The American Economic Review*, 82, 2, 1992.

Danziger, Sheldon, and Peter Gottschalk, "The Measurement of Poverty: Implications for Antipoverty Policy," *American Behavioral Scientist*, 26, 6, 1983.

Danziger, Sheldon, Peter Gottschalk, and Eugene Smolensky, "American Income Inequality: How the Rich Have Fared, 1973–1987," *American Economic Association Papers and Proceedings*, 79, 2.

Danziger, Sheldon H., and Robert D. Plotnick, "Poverty and Policy: Lessons from the Last Two Decades," *Social Service Review*, 60, 1, 1986.

Danziger, Sheldon, Robert Haveman, and Robert Plotnick, "How Income Transfer Programs Affect Work, Savings, and the Income Distribution: A Critical Review, *Journal of Economic Literature*, 19, 1981.

Danziger, Sheldon, Robert Haveman, and Robert Plotnick, "Antipoverty Policy: Effects on the Poor and the Nonpoor." In Sheldon Danziger and Daniel H. Weinberg, eds., *Fighting Poverty: What Works and What Doesn't.* Cambridge, Harvard University Press, 1986.

Duboff, Richard B., "Full Employment: The History of a Receding Target," *Politics and Society*, 7, 1, 1977.

duRivage, Virginia L., "Flexibility Trap: The Proliferation of Marginal Jobs," *The American Prospect*, No. 9, Spring 1992.

Edin, Kathryn, and Christopher Jencks, "Reforming Welfare." Chapter 6 in Christopher Jencks, *Rethinking Social Policy: Race, Poverty, and the Underclass.* Cambridge, Harvard University Press, 1992.

Edsall, Thomas, *The New Politics of Inequality.* New York, W. W. Norton, 1984.

Epstein, Gerald, "Domestic Stagflation and Monetary Policy: The Federal Election and the Hidden Election." In Thomas Ferguson and Joel Rogers, eds., *The Hidden Election: Politics and Economics in the 1980 Presidential Campaign.* New York, Pantheon, 1981.

Esping-Andersen, Gosta, "Power and Distributional Regimes," *Politics and Society*, 1986.

Fabricant, Solomon, "The Problem of Controlling Inflation." In C. Lowell-Harris, ed., *Inflation: Long-term Problems. Proceedings of the Academy of Political Science*, 31, 4, 1975.

Feldstein, Martin, "Unemployment Compensation: Adverse Incentives and Distributional Anomalies," *National Tax Journal*, 27, 1974.

Ferguson, Thomas, and Joel Rogers, *Right Turn.* New York, Pantheon, 1986.

Fiedler, Edgar R., "Economic Policies to Control Stagflation." In C. Lowell-Harris, ed., *Inflation: Long-term Problems. Proceedings of the Academy of Political Science*, 31, 4, 1975.

Fiedler, Edgar R., "Inflation and Economic Policy." In Clarence C. Walton, ed., *Inflation and National Survival. Proceedings of the Academy of Political Science*, 33, 3, 1979.

Fullerton, Howard N., "Labor Force Projections: 1986–2000," *Monthly Labor Review*, Bureau of Labor Statistics, U. S. Department of Labor, Vol. 110, No. 9, September 1987.

Galbraith, John K., *The Affluent Society.* Boston, Houghton Mifflin, 1958.

Garfinkel, Irwin, and Robert Plotnick, "How Much Does Unemployment Insurance Increase the Unemployment Rate and Reduce Work, Earnings, and Inefficiency?" Discussion Paper 378–76. Madison, Institute for Research on Poverty, University of Wisconsin.

Garrett, Geoffrey, and Peter Lange, "Performance in a Hostile World: Economic Growth in Capitalist Democracies." *World Politics*, 38, 1986.

Garrett, Geoffrey, and Peter Lange, "Government Partisanship and Economic Performance: When and How Does 'Who Governs' Matter?" *Journal of Politics*, 51:676–93, 1989.

Ginzberg, Eli, and George J. Volta, "The Service Sector of the U. S. Economy," *Scientific American*, 244, 3, 1981.

Glazer, Nathan, "The Limits of Social Policy," *Commentary*, 52, 3, 1971.

Goldfield, Michael, *The Decline of Organized Labor in the United States.* Chicago, University of Chicago Press, 1987.

Goodwin, Leonard, *The Work Incentive (WIN) Program and Related Experiences.* U. S. Department of Labor, Employment Training Administration, Washington, D.C., 1977.

Greenstein, Robert, Director, Center on Budget and Priorities. Testimony before the U.S. House Committee on Ways and Means, March 13, 1991.

Harrison, Bennett, and Barry Bluestone, *The Great U-Turn: Corporate Restructuring and the Polarization of America.* New York, Basic Books, 1988.

Haveman, Robert H., "Unemployment in Western Europe

and the United States: A Problem of Demand, Structure, or Measurement," *American Economic Review,* 68, 2, 1978.

Henwood, Doug, "Clinton and the Austerity Cops," *The Nation,* November 23, 1992.

Hicks, Alexander, "Social Democratic Corporatism and Economic Growth," *Journal of Politics,* 50, 1988.

Hicks, Alexander, "Unions, Social Democracy, Welfare and Democracy," *Research in Political Sociology,* 5, 1992.

Hicks, Alexander, and William David Patterson, "On the Robustness of the Left Corporatist Model of Economic Growth," *Journal of Politics,* 51, 3, 1989.

Hoerr, John, "Is the Strike Dead?" *The American Prospect,* Summer 1992.

Huntington, Samuel P., "Chapter III—The United States." In Michael Crozier, Samuel P. Huntington, and Joji Watanuki, eds., *The Crisis of Democracy: Report on the Governability of Democracies to the Trilateral Commission.* New York, New York University Press, 1975.

Jencks, Christopher, "Can We Put a Time Limit on Welfare?" *The American Prospect,* Fall 1992.

Jencks, Christopher, and Kathryn Edin, "The Real Welfare Problem," *The American Prospect,* No. 1, Spring 1990.

Katznelson, Ira, "A Radical Departure: Social Welfare and the Election." In Thomas Ferguson and Joel Rogers, eds., *The Hidden Election: Politics and Economics in the 1980 Presidential Campaign.* New York, Pantheon, 1981.

Kaus, Mickey, "The Work Ethic State: The Only Way to Cure the Culture of Poverty," *The New Republic,* July 7, 1986.

Kaus, Mickey, *The End of Equality.* New York, Basic Books, 1992.

Kelly, William R., and Larry Isaac, "The Rise and Fall of Urban Racial Violence in the U.S.: 1948–1979," *Research in Social Movements, Conflict and Change,* Vol. 7, 1984.

Krugman, Paul, *The Age of Diminished Expectations: U. S. Economy Policy in the 1990s.* Cambridge, MIT Press, 1990.

Lampman, Robert, *Focus* 4, 1. Madison, Institute for Research on Poverty, University of Wisconsin, 1979.

Levy, Paul A., *Supreme Court Welfare Reform: Has It Lasted?* Unpublished Doctor of Social Welfare dissertation, Columbia University, 1990.

Magdoff, Harry, "Globalisation—To What End?" *Monthly Review,* 43, 9 and 10, February and March 1992.

Mahar, Maggie, "White-Collar and Blue-Collar Jobs are Vanishing," *Barrons,* May 11, 1992.

Mahar, Maggie, "Numbers Game: A Census Bureau Wage Report Takes Five Months to Surface," *Barrons,* May 18, 1992.

McCammon, Holly J., "Legal Limits on Labor Militancy: U. S. Labor Law and the Right to Strike Since the New Deal," *Social Problems,* 37.

Mead, Lawrence M., *Beyond Entitlement: The Social Obligations of Citizenship.* New York, Free Press, 1986.

Mead, Lawrence M., *The New Politics of Inequality: The Nonworking Poor in America.* New York, Basic Books, 1992.

Medoff, James, "The New Unemployment." Prepared for Senator Lloyd Bentsen, Chairman, Subcommittee on Economic Growth, Trade, and Taxes, Joint Economic Committee, April 1992 (Revised December 4, 1992).

Moberg, David, "Union Busting, Past and Present," *Dissent,* Winter 1992.

Moynihan, Daniel P., *The Politics of a Guaranteed Income.* New York, Random House, 1973.

Nathan, Richard P., Fred C. Doolittle, and Associates, *Reagan and the States.* Princeton, Princeton University Press, 1987.

Ornstein, Norman, "The Payroll Tax is Getting Out of Hand," *New York Times,* November 8, 1992, Section 3.

Phillips, A. W., "The Relation between Unemployment and the Rate of Change of Money Wage Rates in the United Kingdom, 1861–1957," *Economica,* 25, 1958.

Phillips, Kevin, *The Politics of Rich and Poor: Wealth and the American Electorate in the Reagan Aftermath.* New York, Random House, 1989.

Piven, Frances Fox, and Richard A. Cloward, *Poor People's Movements.* New York, Pantheon, 1977.

Piven, Frances Fox, and Richard A. Cloward, *The New Class War.* Revised and Enlarged Edition. New York, Pantheon, 1985.

Piven, Frances Fox, and Richard A. Cloward, "The Historical Sources of the Contemporary Relief Debate." In Fred Block, Richard A. Cloward, Barbara Ehrenreich, and Frances Fox Piven, *The Mean Season: The Attack on the Welfare State.* New York, Pantheon, 1987a.

Piven, Frances Fox, and Richard A. Cloward, "The Contemporary Relief Debate." In Fred Block, Richard A. Cloward, Barbara Ehrenreich, and Frances Fox Piven, *The Mean Sea-*

son: The Attack on the Welfare State. New York, Pantheon, 1987b.

Piven, Frances Fox, and Richard A. Cloward, "Welfare Doesn't Shore Up Traditional Family Roles: A Reply to Linda Gordon," *Social Research,* Winter 1988.

Porter, Kathryn H., "Making JOBS Work: What Research Says About Effective Employment Programs for AFDC Recipients," Center on Budget and Policy Priorities, Washington, D.C., March 1990.

Reich, Robert, "As the World Turns," *New Republic,* May 1, 1989.

Rothschild, Emma, "Reagan and the Real America," *New York Review of Books,* February 5, 1981.

Schram, Sanford F., "Post-Positivistic Policy Analysis and the Family Support Act of 1988: Symbols at the Expense of Substance," *Polity,* 24, 4, 1992.

Schwartz, John E., and Thomas J. Volgy, *Forgotten Americans.* New York, W. W. Norton & Co., 1992.

Segal, David, "Motherload," *The Washington Monthly,* October 1992.

Silk and Vogel, *Ethics and Profits.* New York, Simon and Schuster, 1976.

Stewart, James B., *Den of Thieves.* New York, Simon and Schuster, 1991.

The Hudson Institute, *Workforce 2000: Work and Workers for the 21st Century,* Indianapolis, 1987.

The National Alliance of Business, *Employment Policies: Looking Toward the Year 2000,* Washington, D.C., 1986.

The Public Perspective: A Roper Center Review of Public Opinion and Polling, September/October 1992.

Tilly, Chris, "Reasons for the Continuing Growth of Part-time Employment," *Monthly Labor Review,* March 1991.

U. S. Bureau of the Census, *Workers With Low Earnings: 1964 to 1990,* U. S. Department of Commerce, Washington, D.C., U. S. Government Printing Office, March 1992.

U. S. Bureau of the Census, *Annual Report on Poverty, October 1989,* U. S. Department of Commerce, Washington, D.C., U. S. Government Printing Office, 1992.

U. S. Department of Commerce, Bureau of Labor Statistics, *Issues in Labor Statistics: Recent Job Losers Less Likely to Expect Recall.* Washington, D.C., U. S. Government Printing Office, July 1992.

U. S. General Accounting Office, *Food Stamps: Reasons for Non-participation,* GAO/PEMD-89-5BR, December 8, 1988.

1992 Green Book, Overview of Entitlement Programs, Committee on Ways and Means, United States House of Representatives, Washington, D.C., U. S. Government Printing Office, May 15, 1992.

CHAPTER TWELVE

Poor Relief and Theories of the Welfare State

This book is about means-tested programs directed to the poor, and particularly about the archetypical American means-tested program, Aid to Families of Dependent Children. Means-tested programs exist in all industrialized countries, but in most places they have been overshadowed by programs that provide income supports or services to broad population groups, usually on universal or contributory principles, such as children's allowances, or pensions for the disabled or the old, or national health care programs.[1]

Given the continuing importance of welfare in the United States, other continuities with the poor relief politics of the past which we demonstrated in this book should perhaps not be surprising. As we have been at pains to show, the

---

[1]Some of these programs shore up income during biological exigencies; others during market exigencies; and some provide services deemed too essential to be left to market providers. The welfare state literature generally is plagued by theoretically significant definitional problems, such as the question of whether education is a welfare state policy, or whether non-governmental services and income supports are appropriately included in the definition.

dual imperatives of maintaining civil order and regulating labor which shaped the first poor relief systems in the sixteenth century still go far toward explaining the expansion and contraction of relief in the United States.

If *Regulating the Poor* offers a persuasive explanation of the dynamics of poor relief, we still need to know why it is that those dynamics continue to play a large role in the United States. Why do the politics of welfare in the late twentieth century continue to resemble the politics of poor relief in the nineteenth or eighteenth centuries? Why was "the great transformation" of nineteenth century market societies into welfare states which Polanyi thought had become literally essential to human survival impeded in the United States?[2] In the contemporary deluge of criticism of welfare and "dependency," this question is not even recognized. To the contrary, today's welfare critics mindlessly follow the scripts laid down by nineteenth century critics of a too liberal poor relief, apparently unaware of their historical precursors, and apparently not curious about why the current campaign against welfare is distinctly American.

We think the answer to the question of why the United States is still in a significant sense a poor relief state lies in the impact on popular politics of distinctive American political institutions. This argument is the burden of our closing chapter. We will develop it by reviewing the main theories that have been offered to explain the growth of the welfare state elsewhere. Taken together, these theories point to important elements of an explanation of the American pattern. It is true, of course, that this literature, like most academic work, is riddled with disputes. However, if we step back and view the literature as a whole, what is suggested is that several features of national political development combined to promote more broadly inclusive welfare state programs in other countries. Conversely, such a syn-

---

[2] Polanyi.

thesis also suggests how we might begin to understand the stunted development of American social policy. In other words, theories of development should also imply a theory of underdevelopment.

Social Security versus Poor Relief

Few academics studied the welfare state when *Regulating the Poor* was originally published over two decades ago, and most who did were located in the field of social welfare itself. Like professionals in other fields, they tended toward explanations that gave a large role in the evolution of welfare state programs to the ideas and activities of professionals themselves, as well as to their philanthropic forebears. These rather insular (and self-serving) interpretations paid scant attention to forces arising from the economy or the society or the polity, and a good deal of attention to the understandings and intentions of professional and philanthropic elites. *Regulating the Poor* was in part a critical response to this dominant view.

We stressed in our introduction to *Regulating the Poor* that "the key to an understanding of relief-giving is in the [disorder-moderating and labor-regulating] functions it serves for the larger economic and political order." Economic and political interpretations of social welfare were at the time not usual. But in the years since, social science theory and research on the welfare state has burgeoned, perhaps in belated reflection of welfare state expansion in the post World War II period. Most of this work is also preoccupied with the relationship of welfare state developments to underlying economic and political processes.

However, academic work on the welfare state focuses mainly on wider "social security state" programs, rather than on means-tested or "social assistance" programs.[3]

---

[3]See Myles, 1991, for the distinction between a social security and social assistance state.

The consensus underlying this work is that social security policies should be understood as an entirely different form of social provision than the old poor relief systems. The aid people received from poor relief programs was necessarily discretionary, and elaborately conditioned, presumably in order to determine the neediness and worthiness of particular supplicants. By contrast, the new policies are said to be characterized by the vesting of social rights.[4] They are often called citizenship *entitlements*, because they are rooted in law, embedded in bureaucracy, and supported by mass opinion and class or interest group organizations. They are, in other words, shored up by institutionalized politics. This distinction between programs has in turn become the basis for a distinction between countries, according to their relative reliance on social security or social assistance programs.

The distinction should not be overdrawn. All rich countries, including the United States, are social security states, in the sense that they all have a range of programs that provide income and services to broad population groups as a matter of right. And all countries also continue to rely on means-tested programs to shore up the income of at-risk groups, particularly those with weaker attachments to the labor force.

We also think the political dynamics which govern these programs are not entirely dissimilar. We suspect that the threats to political order that prompted poor relief expansion are more important in overall welfare state development than is typically recognized by the analysts who stress the distinctiveness of contemporary forms of social provision. Moreover, means-tested programs also reflect and encourage ideas about social rights. Even preindustrial poor relief was grounded in widely shared and tenaciously

---

[4]The definitive author on the emergence of social rights as citizenship rights is of course T. H. Marshall.

held ideas about rights. Thus, efforts to replace outdoor relief with the workhouse in England during the eighteenth century sparked recurrent protests because, as Tilly says, of an "implicit theory" that the community has an obligation to aid its poor.[5] And when the old poor relief system was in fact partially dismantled with the introduction of the New Poor Law in 1834, William Cobbett, a fiery journalist of the time, described the reform as a deep violation of the ancient rights of the poor, as nothing less than a smashing of the social contract.

> Among these rights . . . the right, in case we fell into distress, to have our wants sufficiently relieved out of the produce of the land, whether that distress arose from sickness, from decrepitude, from old age, or from inability to find employment. . . . For a thousand years, necessity was relieved out of the Tithes. When the Tithes were taken away . . . compensation was given in the rates as settled by the poor-law. The taking away those rates was to violate the agreement, which gave as much right to receive in case of need, relief out of the land, as it left the landowner a right to his rent.[6]

These qualifications notwithstanding, the broad distinction between the social security and the social assistance state is nevertheless useful and important, and it suggests that the American case requires explanation in theoretical terms. Social security programs are smaller here than in other rich nations, whether the measure is expenditures or proportion of the population reached.[7] And the means-tested or "social assistance" programs are larger. Esping-Andersen names this prototypically American kind of policy cluster the "liberal" welfare state. It is characterized

---

[5]See Tilly, 1978, 3–4.

[6]Cited in Thompson, 761.

[7]Kudrle and Marmor use an index developed by Peter Flora and his collaborators to measure coverage of industrial accident, sickness, pension and unemployment insurance in the U.S. and Canada compared with a number of European countries over time. The U.S. has always trailed badly.

by modest universal (or insurance) programs, and a reliance on means-tested programs.[8] And while Canada and Australia also fit this model, the United States is indisputably the polar type.[9] We turn then to a search for an explanation of the American pattern.

Theories of Industrial Society

Most of the work on the welfare state is framed by a master interpretation which analysts began to apply to the welfare state at about the same time that *Regulating the Poor* was first published. The master theory is structural-functionalism, which Giddens later called the "theory of industrial society."[10] While *Regulating the Poor* shares ground with theories of industrial society, it sets out to explain relief, not the welfare state. And it explains relief systems not as a response to industrialization, but as an even earlier response provoked by the political and economic problems of regulating labor that emerged as markets in labor emerged. Moreover, we argue that as these problems persist or recur in the United States, so do the strategies for coping with them that characterized preindustrial poor relief systems.

---

[8]See Esping-Andersen, 1990, 26–27 and 70–71. The United States spent 18.2 per cent of its total public social expenditures on means-tested programs in 1980. The average for OECD countries was 5.9 per cent.

[9]See Rainwater, Rein and Schwartz, 131–147, for data comparing the role of means-tested benefits in Sweden, Great Britain, and the United States. They estimate that fully 48 per cent of government transfers are means-tested in the United States, compared to 6 per cent in Sweden, and 20 per cent in Britain. See also Smeeding, O'Higgins, and Rainwater for a comparative overview relying on data from the Luxembourg Income Study. There are complications in assessing the significance of means-tested programs. In a number of European countries, means-tested expenditures are lower not because fewer people receive assistance, or because they receive less, but because they also receive income and services from programs that reach a wider population. In the U. S., the poor who receive means-tested benefits are more likely to rely on them as a primary source of income. Overall, the United States is least generous toward its poor, and its programs lift fewest recipients out of poverty.

[10]See Giddens, 718.

Theories of industrial society that purport to explain the development of broader welfare state programs are both similar to and different from *Regulating the Poor*. They are similar in that they locate the forces leading to the welfare state in the larger economy. They are different in that their leading assumption is one of modernization or progress. Thus, in the variant of structural functionalism known as the "logic of industrialism,"[11] attention is directed to the way economic growth and its demographic and social correlates, such as urbanization and the disruption of traditional systems of social support based in the family, the church, and the local community, generated new needs for state social provision. At the same time, industrialization also created the economic resources which could be tapped by the state, and the state developed enhanced organizational and extractive capacities, to meet these new needs. While the perspective allows for national variations, owing to cultural differences, for example,[12] or the peculiarities of national political organization,[13] the logic of industrialism nevertheless posits that the welfare state is ultimately shaped by systemic imperatives, and the system is industrial society.[14]

Marxist variants of the theory of industrial society also emerged, later aptly characterized as "the logic of capitalism." Like the logic of industrialism, the welfare state is viewed as the inevitable result of systemic imperatives, although the imperatives are generated by the capitalist organization of the economy rather than by industrialization. Thus, the welfare state is a response to problems—or needs—generated by capitalism, rather than by industrial-

---

[11]Kerr, *et al.*, coined the phrase, "the logic of industrialism."

[12]See for example Heidenheimer for a discussion of the role of religion in accounting for variations in welfare state development.

[13]See Flora and Alber.

[14]See Wilensky and Lebeaux; Cutwright, 1965 and 1967; and Wilensky, 1975.

ization as such. In the best known variant of this perspective, the problems or needs or functional imperatives arise from the accumulation requirements of big capitalists, or the political legitimation requirements of the state in the face of an economic system that constantly and inevitably renders many people surplus and unemployed or impoverished. The welfare state solves accumulation problems—at least in the medium run—by assuming some of the costs of "reproducing" labor power, in the form of education and health programs, for example. And it solves legitimation problems by providing public jobs or income transfers for the people who are made superfluous by the advance of capitalism.[15]

A feminist variant on structural-functionalist theories has also emerged in recent years which asserts that it is not the economy but the patriarchal family which is the master system creating the imperative needs which the welfare state satisfies. The broad conclusion is that welfare state programs can best be understood as enforcing or supporting the male-headed nuclear family, and enforcing or supporting women's several family roles as unpaid domestic laborers, as the providers of sexual and reproductive services, and as the consumers of goods and services produced in the market economy.[16] Additionally, welfare state programs are said to ensure that when women do participate in the labor market, they continue to be subordinated to men, and are concentrated in occupations consistent with their family roles.

Some early variants of the feminist analysis were not inconsistent with theories of industrial society which gave precedence to the economy as the driving institution. The family itself was seen as functionally related to the econ-

---

[15]See O'Connor; Gough; Offe, 1972.

[16]Various formulations of this argument can be found in Abramovitz; Brown; Fraser, 1987 and 1989; Shaver; Smith; Barrett; Holmstrom; Boris and Bardaglio; Eisenstein, 1981 and 1983; McIntosh; Polan; Wilson; and Ursel.

omy, through the role it plays in the reproduction of labor power. At the same time, the wrenching upheavals and intense exploitation associated with industrial capitalism undermined the family, weakening its ability to perform its reproductive functions. Social welfare programs that shore up the family are in this view also economically functional.[17] More recently, however, feminist work has challenged theories of industrial society with the argument that reproduction is at least partially autonomous from production,[18] and that it is the imperatives of reproduction and not economic imperatives that are the primary forces in the creation of social welfare programs. Linda Gordon, in a critique of *Regulating the Poor,* captures the main idea when she claims that "promoting the family wage system is a better overall explanation of the social control functions of the welfare state than has been previously offered."[19]

Cultural theories of social life are now ascendant in the social sciences, and in some hands, the discovery of culture, and its preeminent importance in the interpretation of social life, is treated as something of an intellectual revolution. In fact, culture has been an important element in most interpretations of the development of the welfare state. *Regulating the Poor* emphasizes the political and economic functions of relief-giving. But symbols and ideas play a large role in the realization of those functions. On the one hand, outbreaks of political disorder which may lead to the

---

[17]Marx, 252–253, himself was not oblivious to the distinctive and contradictory imperatives of production and reproduction. "Capital," he said, "cares nothing for the length of life of labour-power. All that concerns it is simply and solely the maximum of labour-power that can be rendered fluent in a working day."

[18]See for example Acker, 567, who says the "fundamental divide can be conceptualized, for our type of society, as a differentiation between production and reproduction, which is also an organization of gender."

[19]See Gordon, 23. See also Piven and Cloward, 1988, for our rejoinder.

expansion of relief giving are undergirded by ideas about social rights. On the other hand, periodic efforts to turn relief-giving to the purpose of work enforcement involve not only restrictions on aid, but efforts to change meanings by constructing elaborate rituals of symbolic degradation of those who subsist on the dole.

Culture also figures largely in theories of industrial society. Some analysts treat culture as the medium through which economic and demographic changes are translated into needs and hence into policy. Thus, in the hands of those who see the welfare state as a product of the developmental logic of industrialism, expanding ideas about social rights which undergird welfare state growth are viewed as an aspect of that logic, a natural and inevitable outcome of industrial development (and democratic arrangements) which helps to explain the translation of new needs and resources into welfare state programs.[20] A variant on this argument is that industrialization generates a tendency toward cultural homogenization, or a tendency toward "mass society," which fosters the incorporation of once marginal groups and communities by means of the expansion of welfare state programs.[21]

Others see the production of cultural dispositions as motivating welfare state growth. This tack is taken in an analysis descended from the Marxist tradition, which explains the construction of the welfare state primarily as a process of ideological domination. In Habermas' well-known formulation, just as the state intruded upon autonomous public spheres, so did the welfare state in particular "colonize" "the life world," with the consequence that democratic political capacities were suppressed.[22] A similar

---

[20]This is a reference of course to the influential argument of T. H. Marshall which posits that democratic ideas have developed according to an evolutionary logic embedded in capitalism and democracy.

[21]See, for example, Gronbjerg.

[22]See Habermas. See also Cohen and Arato for a similar argument.

theme in some feminist work also emphasizes the role of the welfare state in the production of meanings, although here the relevant meanings reinforce patriarchy by reinforcing traditional gender roles.[23] These interpretations fit broadly into structural functionalism in that the welfare state is said to generate cultural orientations which, at least in the medium run, reinforce a larger social system.

Academic disputes notwithstanding, theories of industrial society share certain basic orientations. All claim that welfare state programs emerge to solve problems or serve functions of a larger system, although the master systems are obviously different. All also share an underlying metaphor of evolution or modernization, positing that the expansion and elaboration of welfare state programs occurs in tandem with economic growth, or in response to the unfolding crises of a capitalist system, or to shore up a patriarchal family system. And structural-functionalist theories of this kind—Esping-Andersen calls them systemic theories[24]—are also satisfying for their sweep and coherence. However, as comparative research on the welfare state has accumulated, these systemic interpretations have lost force, largely because, taken alone, they do not do very well in explaining the differences among welfare states (and may not explain the commonalities either, as they appear to do on first reading[25]). These criticisms bear directly on our

---

[23]See for example Fraser, 1989, Chapter 7. From this point of view, the AFDC program contributes to the maintenance of the patriarchal family through the powerful rituals of degradation it enacts against women who violate the norms of the traditional family by giving birth and raising children without men.

[24]Esping-Andersen, 1990, 13–14.

[25]If the welfare state is a response to industrialism, or to capitalism, then it should not exist in countries that are not industrialist, or not capitalist. But there is some evidence that questions the correlation of welfare state development with either industrialism or capitalism. In the contemporary world, less developed and even very poor countries do inaugurate forms of social provi-

effort to explain the stunting of welfare state development, and the continuing importance of poor relief, in the United States.

There are two major problems. The first is that structural-functionalist theories fail to satisfy a reasonable temporal criterion. If welfare state programs are a response to systemic imperatives, then the "system" and welfare state initiatives should have an explicable temporal relationship to each other. The industrial or capitalist or patriarchal system should precede in time the programs which presumably satisfy its imperatives, although the system should not develop so long before the programs as to attenuate the claimed functional relationship. At any rate, time and chronology need to be taken into account, and as a number of analysts have pointed out, there are large empirical problems.

The first welfare states (Germany, Sweden, Austria) were at the forefront of neither industrial or capitalist growth, and the countries that were (England, the United States) never became leading welfare states, and have recently taken the initiative in dismantling at least some of the programs. Nor do variations in the patriarchal family, or in social changes which threatened its stability, seem to provide credible explanations for variations in timing. Moreover, while it is true that all industrial and capitalist and patriarchal countries eventually did develop welfare state programs, the relationship in time of these several developments is so widely variable as to itself demand explanation. As has often been pointed out, American "social security"

---

sion. See Quadagno, 1987, who makes this point, drawing on the work of Collier and Messick. Moreover, in a series of empirical tests of hypotheses derived from theories of industrial society, Myles 1984, 94–98, found no correlation between the quality of citizenship entitlements and the level of economic development, or the level of capital concentration, or the size of the dependent population. And even the most casual investigation makes clear that noncapitalist industrial societies have had large social welfare programs.

initiatives occurred half a century after the first programs were created in Imperial Germany.

The second main problem is that theories which derive the welfare state from systemic imperatives cannot account for variations among industrial and capitalist countries, not only in the timing of welfare state programs, but in the structure of the programs. They cannot account, in other words, for differences in what Esping-Andersen calls "welfare state regimes" among capitalist and industrialist and patriarchal societies.[26] This means they cannot account for large differences in the programs of different countries which may bear on the realization of "social rights," such as aggregate expenditures or "welfare state effort," or the scope of coverage, or the extent of reliance on private or employment-based social welfare programs, or the structure of administrative control, or the diverse revenue sources of the programs. Most important for our purposes, theories which cannot explain the differences among industrial and capitalist countries also cannot account for the persisting importance of means-tested programs—and the distinctive cycles of means-tested politics—in the United States.[27]

---

[26]Esping-Andersen, 1990.

[27]Structural-functionalist theories should also be able to show that the actual consequences of social welfare programs are broadly consistent with the functions attributed to them, at least over time. Feminist structural functionalism does not fare well by this criterion. Overall, the programs do not "enforce male breadwinning and female dependence" on male wages. True, earnings-related old age pensions make women somewhat dependent on men who are more likely to have had a regular work history, but it is hard to see how they are more dependent than they would be without pensions. Similarly, children's allowances make mothers a little less, not a little more, dependent on men, as does the American AFDC program. The AFDC program is frequently singled out for feminist analysis because its primary beneficiaries are women and their children, but the evidence does not bear out the view that it shores up the patriarchal family or traditional gender roles. A better case can be made that it does the opposite. By providing benefits mainly to families headed by women, and often on condition that there are no men present, it creates an incentive for two-parent families to break up, or not to form in the first place.

Political Theories

As some of the problems discussed above became apparent, a kind of consensus emerged that "something else is going on"[28] besides industrialization or capitalism or patriarchy. The something else is politics. Even in the abstract, it makes sense to think that politics matters in the translation of needs or systemic imperatives into public expenditures. The "needs" or imperatives posited by theories of industrial society as the motor of welfare state expansion are usually concentrated among classes or categories of people who do not control the economic resources which are also said to be essential. If some people have the needs, and other people have the resources, then needs (or systemic imperatives) have to somehow become the goals of real political actors who undertake real political actions, and who are capable by these actions of making an imprint on government policy even in the face of opposition from those who control resources.[29] And once politics comes into focus, it is immediately apparent that different societies enter industrial capitalism with different political institutions, which reflect different patterns of preindustrial political culture and organization, and which later come to nourish different patterns of welfare state politics. This political realm surely mediates and transforms the impact of industrial society on the welfare state. Perhaps it does more

---

And while the availability of benefits may allow some women to stay in the home, the program penalizes these women with stigma and low benefits.

[28]The phrase belongs to Noble, who emphasizes the impact of distinctive political institutions in accounting for the impediments to American social policy. His interpretation has been particularly helpful for the account we offer below.

[29]See Kristensen, 309, for a succinct statement of the argument that "socio-economic factors cannot in any direct or immediate way cause public-sector growth; they have to be transformed by the political and bureaucratic system to have any impact on public expenditures."

than mediate. Perhaps it also determines, influencing or even generating the forces that shape the welfare state.

Regulating the Poor offers an analysis of relief-giving that focuses on its functions in relation to both economy and polity. It also delineates the political conflicts through which these functions were realized. Poor relief was invented, and periodically expanded, to cope with widespread strife from below. And it was contracted or "reformed" in response to employer objections to an indiscriminate charity which intruded on labor market arrangements. While we use the language of *regulation,* we might also have used the language of *power,* because the stakes in these contests were clearly large. For those at the bottom, a more liberal poor relief meant survival; for those at the top, a too liberal poor relief would undermine their power as employers. But in the original edition of this book, we did not go much beyond this broad characterization of political conflict between those who depended on selling their labor and those who hired them. We did not attempt to develop a political theory to explain the different character of these contests in different polities. And without such a theory, we could not explain the distinctive features of the American welfare state.

While the emphasis on politics is an important advance, it is not quite the intellectual breakthrough it is sometimes presented to be. The theorists of industrial society in fact make more modulated arguments than the current round of critics allow, attributing a large, but far from determining, role to the processes they identify. Typically, industrial society proponents introduce qualifications to take account of distinctive national political cultures and institutions.[30] Still, theories of industrial society tend to subordinate the realm of politics, at least if we conceive of politics as some-

---

[30]It is worth reviewing Wilensky's 1975 book to be reminded of the densely mediated relationships he posited between welfare state effort and levels of economic development.

thing more than an intervening stage in the unfolding of a structurally determined outcome.[31]

The recent turn to the political has produced three main lines of analysis. Each identifies a different set of political institutions, and a different set of actors and processes, as critical in the evolution of the welfare state. The first approach we will consider points to the significance of class-based electoral organization. The second, or pluralist approach, emphasizes the influence of electoral-representative institutions and the voters and political parties they bring into being. The third approach focuses on the impact of state structures and state elites. Each of these perspectives is typically presented in the literature as an alternative to the others. We think, however, that a satisfactory explanation of the persisting poor law features of the U. S. welfare state depends on a more comprehensive theory that links together the main elements laid out in each of these competing perspectives. Working class political organization, electoral-representative institutions, and state structures all figure in the development of the welfare state. And they each help to shape the other over time, in an intricate mesh of interactive effects. In the United States, working-class organization was weak, electoral representative institutions were flawed, and state structures inhibited the translation of popular interests into policy. For just those reasons, the protest politics emphasized in the first edition of *Regulating the Poor* were important.

Underdevelopment and Race

Below we try to show how these several factors worked together to shape the American welfare state over time. We

---

[31]Steven Lukes, Chapter 1, argues tellingly that if structural constraints eliminate any latitude within which human actors can exercise agency, there is in fact no politics.

are developing a synthesis, drawing on the welfare state literature, much of it written in reference to more developed welfare states, to create a framework to explain the American case of underdevelopment. However, we do not pretend to have plumbed the limits of such an effort. We think the theoretical framework we sketch is illuminating, although far from complete. One reason is simply the nature of the endeavor; political interpretation is never exhaustive and therefore never finished. But another reason has to do with features of American political history which may be entirely distinctive, and thus escape attention in efforts to construct generalizable models of welfare state politics. The usual lists of such peculiar aspects of American history include: no feudalism, the open frontier, a uniquely individualistic ethos, ethnic divisions, rapid economic mobility, and so on. We leave the door open on the case for the impact of these or other peculiarities in shaping the American welfare state.

The argument we feel compelled to flag now is for the deep imprint of racism, and the complex political distortions it nourished, on the politics of the welfare state. Race has been one of the enduring issues of American politics, implicated in most of the great conflicts which periodically convulsed the United States, and also singularly important in the formation of everyday political identities. The political structures associated with a limited welfare state can only be fully explained by taking account of the tortured impact of slavery and institutionalized racism on the construction of the American polity. Thus, to anticipate our analysis, underdevelopment in the United States reflects the weakness of working class political organization. And the weakness of the working class in turn is traceable to constitutionally prescribed state structures which ensured a fragmented and decentralized party system, to the blunting of popular electoral influence by disenfranchisement, to the consequent construction of welfare state programs that in turn inhibited popular support for further improving or expanding the welfare state. Each of these dimensions of political underdevelopment is also marked by historic encounters with race and racism. The constitutional compromises which produced a decentralized and fragmented government and party system were imperative because the slave labor system was already established in the Southern colonies, and Southern elites feared the interference of a strong national government.[32] The disenfranchising movement that swept the states in the late nineteenth century began in the South as a movement to disenfranchise blacks (and succeeded as it did because poor whites were apparently ready to give up their voting rights in order to deprive blacks of theirs). And the sectional interests which blocked welfare state growth in the twentieth century were motivated to preserve the caste system of the South. With this in mind, we turn to theories of welfare state politics, and to their implications for the peculiarities of the American experience.

The "Democratic Class Struggle"[33]

One influential stream of contemporary interpretation has roots in Marxism, although unlike the "logic of capitalism" perspective, it does not focus on systemic requirements of capitalism, but rather on the class conflicts which emerge in capitalist relations. The understanding of what is at issue in welfare state politics is close to the classical Marxist understanding. Workers, organized and educated into class collectivities by their role in capitalist industries, seek protection from the vicissitudes of labor markets and human biology. Employers resist their demands, unwilling to pay the costs of such protections, or to concede protec-

---

[32]On slavery and the constitutional compromise, see Robinson, and Goldfield, 1990.
[33]The phase was coined by Korpi, 1983.

tions which would strengthen workers by shielding them from the market, or in Marxist terms, reduce the competitive force of the reserve army of labor. Welfare state programs are presumably forged in the vortex of these conflicting forces.[34]

In the contemporary "democratic class struggle" variant, the existence of classes and class conflict is taken as axiomatic, but the focus is specifically on electoral representative arrangements as the formative institutional context within which this conflict is played out. The class interests which originate in economic spheres are organized and expressed in political spheres where class-based political parties compete for state power using resources and strategies distinctive to electoral-representative institutions. The welfare state thus results from a sequence that begins with industrialization and the consequent emergence of an industrial working class whose numbers and concentration lead in turn to the formation of industrial trade unions. The roughly simultaneous development of electoral representative arrangements facilitates the formation of political parties based on this unionized working class. These labor-based parties, together with the union infrastructure which undergirds them, are the instrument through which the working class wins welfare state policies which modify the distributional inequalities of the market.[35]

To test these propositions, analysts have developed a

---

[34]*Regulating the Poor* is broadly consistent with this tradition. Although the focus is not exclusively on the industrial working class, class conflict is nevertheless posited as the motor of the functions attributed to relief. See also Piven and Cloward, 1985 and 1987.

[35]See Hibbs, 1977; Korpi, 1983, 1989, and 1991; Shalev, 1983; Esping-Andersen, 1985, 1990, and 1992; Castles; Myles, 1984. In its basic outlines, this "new political economy" reaches back to Eduard Bernstein's early advocacy of an electoral road to socialism which had a pervasive influence on European social democratic parties, and, perhaps especially on the Swedish Social Democratic Party. Sweden is something of a flagship for this school. See for example Korpi, 1983, 209, for a discussion of the Swedish concept of the reformist road to socialism in the interwar period.

variety of measures of class-based political power, including the numerical strength and degree of centralization of trade unions, labor party strength in the electorate, variable partisan alignments and cleavages, partisan control of the executive, and the strength of extra-parliamentary corporatist arrangements. They have also devised a wide range of measures of the welfare state, including measures of wage and income inequality and levels of unemployment, of public expenditure on social welfare programs or "welfare state effort,"[36] and even including some efforts to measure qualitative aspects of these programs.[37]

Using these complex models, a formidable array of comparative quantitative studies have examined the impact of various measures of working class strength in electoral representative institutions on measures of welfare state accomplishments.[38] The historiography assumed by the model

---

[36]There are nagging problems in developing satisfactory statistical measures of welfare state effort. One is that quasi-private pension and health systems play a large role in some countries, but are excluded from measures of public expenditure. See for example Shalev, 1988, and Stevens. The problem is compounded because such benefits are substantial in the United States and Japan, and these countries in turn carry enormous weight in making the case for the importance of working-class electoral organizations: they have weak unions and weak left parties, and are also the main welfare state laggards. Another problem is that different measures of welfare state success employed in different studies may well turn out to be trade-offs. Thus, where social democratic parties and centralized trade unions succeed in winning greater wage equality, it may be by sacrificing public expenditure programs, or vice versa. Thus van Arnheim and Schotsman, 351, conclude that in advanced capitalist societies, "the situation with respect to the possibilities for equality of income distribution . . . resembles that of a 'zero sum game'" where equality achieved by one set of policies is cancelled out by another set of policies.

[37]See, for example, Castles; Hicks and Swank, 1982; Friedland and Sanders; Myles, 1984.

[38]While cross-national statistical comparisons inevitably give the appearance of weighty scientific stuff, there are limitations in the method. For one, since the argument applies only to advanced industrial nations with democratic political systems, investigations of the interaction of an increasing array of variables is limited to a universe of perhaps 15 to 20 countries (usually the 18 OECD countries for which data are readily available), with results that can only be suggestive at best. Moreover, the case for treating European nations as distinctive cases grows weaker as the European Community takes on the

does not hold up well.[39] Welfare state development before World War II is not correlated with measures of working class electoral organization, as might be guessed from the forward role of strong and even monarchical states in initiating programs. Furthermore, parties of the center, and even conservative parties, sometimes played the role of welfare state proponents. However, a wide number of empirical studies do tend to buttress the general claim that, *in the contemporary period,* variations in the welfare state reflect variations in working class electoral strength.[40]

The implication of this argument for the United States is clear. One explanation for the distinctive pattern of the American welfare state—the narrower reach of the social security programs, and the persistence of means-tested programs and poor law political dyamics—may be the weakness of working class organizations in electoral politics. Certainly, a labor party did not develop here, and neither did an inclusive and centralized system of unions. This is, we think, part of an answer to our query about the sources of social welfare underdevelopment in the United States. Still, it is an answer that provokes a further question, and a very familiar one at that. What was it about American politics that prevented the emergence of a labor-based political party and a strong infrastructure of unions? And that question drives us back to dimensions of American politics which preceded and perhaps accounted for these organizational failures.

---

characteristics of a nation state. At some point, the reasoned basis for cross-national statistical comparisons will collapse.

[39]In fact, Korpi and Esping-Andersen, 1984, think the model may describe social policy development only in the post–World War II period, when working class unionization, and left voting, increased.

[40]However, Hicks and Swank, 1992, find that both center and left governments increase welfare effort.

Pluralist Interpretations

The pluralists propose an elaboration of the theory of industrial society to include the evolution of democratic institutions.[41] In effect, industrialization and its social and demographic concomitants generate demands for welfare spending, and democratic institutions facilitate the expression of those demands.[42] In this perspective the key political actors are voters, and the transmission of needs occurs through the action of citizens empowered by electoral/representative institutions. In one variant of the pluralist perspective, what matters are the diverse and competitive interest groups generated by economic growth and their organizational and numerical leverage on the one hand, and the extent of the incorporation of these groups in the polity through the extension of democratic rights.[43] Concretely, the emphasis is usually on the aged, who are numerous, who are voters, who are typically organized, and who therefore become the main beneficiaries of aggregate welfare state spending.[44]

---

[41]Pampel and Williamson, 1988, 1429, in fact say that what they call their "interest-group-politics" theory "may be seen as a political version of industrialism theory."

[42]See Janowitz, 75, for the argument that the post–World War II growth of the welfare state reflects the influence of pressure groups. See also Lenski for a consistent argument about democratic majorities and economic redistribution. For pluralist interpretations of the growth of the welfare state specifically, see Flora and Heidenheimer. See also Gronbjerg for a cultural variant of the pluralist interpretation. For a series of studies which examine the role of pluralist variables in accounting for interstate variations within the United States, see: Key; Lockard; Dye, 1966 and 1979; Gronbjerg; Gary; and Dawson and Robinson.

[43]This perspective is clearly indebted to T. H. Marshall who emphasized, however, the tensions between capitalist markets and the social rights which came to be associated with citizenship.

[44]A variant on the main lines of pluralist analysis has recently emerged among some feminist analysts, who claim that women—informed by family values and acting to defend family roles—were the main political actors in the forging of the American welfare state, thus making family concerns rather than

Other pluralist theorists focus less on interest groups empowered by democratic rights, and more on the process of electoral competition as the motor of welfare state expansion.[45] Political parties competing for state power, whether religious or conservative or labor parties, formulate policies that are responsive to the needs or demands of voter blocs. For example, politicians trying to win office strain to manage the economy so as to coordinate the business cycle and the election cycle, and Tufte claims that they also try to expand social security benefits in election years.[46]

There is clearly something to this perspective. Interest groups representing voter blocs do press for social welfare spending, and competitive political parties do sometimes promote welfare state expansion to win elections.[47] Still, there are a number of obvious problems as well. Historically, the countries which were welfare state leaders were not political democracies, but monarchies. Indeed, a number of analysts have argued that it was precisely the strength

---

economic concerns central in motivating welfare state innovations. See, for example, Gordon; Clemens; and Skocpol, 1992. And see Piven and Cloward, 1988, for our rejoinder to Gordon on these questions. We continue to be skeptical, mainly because women in the early twentieth century had few of what are usually considered political resources, including an organized mass base, significant economic power, or even the right to vote. True, women's groups were active in promoting a number of social welfare innovations early in the century—principally Mother's Pensions and the Shepard-Towner Act. Unfortunately for women and children, and for this feminist argument, not much came of these initiatives. Very few needy mothers and children actually got pensions, those who did usually got pitifully low grants, and the middle class women reformers quickly lost interest. For a description of the limited success of the Mother's Pensions programs, see Piven and Cloward, 1983. As for Sheppard-Towner, after a few brief years, the Act was simply allowed to expire. It is thus hard to see why Skocpol, 1992, Chapter 8, claims that these measures represent a key component in "the political origins of social policy in the United States," since she too concedes that these reforms came to little.

[45]See Schumpeter, and Downs.

[46]Tufte, 30.

[47]Hicks and Swank, 1992, provide data suggesting that electoral competition as such does not drive welfare state expansion, but rather that welfare spending effects depend on specific patterns of interaction between the party in power and the opposition.

of monarchical government in Germany which made these initiatives possible in a hostile political environment.[48] And parliamentary democracies such as Britain and France introduced social insurance programs later than the constitutional monarchies of Austria, Denmark, and Sweden.[49] These cases suggest at the very least that electoral/representative arrangements are not the only arena through which needs are expressed and resources claimed. Still, comparative studies among political democracies in the contemporary period, when welfare state programs have become larger and more important, do show the effect of such pluralist variables as the size of the aged population, levels of voter participation, and electoral competition.[50]

At first glance, the American experience seems to challenge the view that political democracy was important to the welfare state. The United States was the international pioneer in the extension of the franchise to white males and in broadening citizen access to office in the early nineteenth century.[51] If the pluralist view is correct, the United States ought to have been the pioneer in social welfare as well. But it was in fact the laggard.

It is not the pluralist model that is wrong in this case, so much as the inaccurate characterization of the history of democracy in the United States. The limiting of democratic rights here is another part of an explanation of our social welfare exceptionalism. Ironically, the early extension of

---

[48]See for example Flora and Heidenheimer, 37–80.

[49]Flora and Alber, 72.

[50]See especially the work of Dye, 1979; Pampel and Williamson, 1985 and 1988. Hibbs, 1987, and Cameron have been called "neo-pluralist." While the level of development of democratic political arrangements may help to account for variations in welfare state effort among capitalist and democratic countries, the theory must still answer the question of why nations that lack democratic arrangements may nevertheless have welfare states, and sometimes, as in the case of Eastern European states under communism, relatively large welfare states.

[51]Although, as we will shortly explain, effective access to the franchise was subsequently narrowed with the advent of industrialization.

the franchise may well have been one inhibition on democratic politics. In Europe, the winning of the male franchise, the growth of an industrial proletariat, and the emergence of labor parties, more or less coincided in the closing decades of the nineteenth century. In the United States, the early franchise meant that a mass party system developed before industrialization, and was therefore heavily freighted with the clientelist and particularistic modes of organizing voters which often characterize preindustrial parties.[52] By the time the industrial working class began to emerge after the Civil War, powerful political parties already existed which appealed to workers on the basis of ethnic, religious, and individual advantage, inhibiting the articulation of widely experienced needs associated with industrialization which underlies the pluralist model.[53]

The second and even more telling limit on democratic possibilities occurred in the United States just as democratic rights were expanding in Western Europe. During the closing decades of the nineteenth century, as industrialization accelerated, an elite-driven movement swept the country to disenfranchise the "discordant elements"[54] who were rising up in farmer protests, railroad strikes, and third party insurgencies. The effort was especially vigorous in the South, where the disenfranchisement of blacks was essential to the stability of the plantation economy and the serf labor on which it relied. There, new literacy and poll tax requirements, together with onerous personal registration procedures, were incorporated into state constitutions. And as the new conditions on the franchise were implemented, the entire black population in the South was disenfranchised, and most poor whites were as well.[55] A similar

---

[52]See Eisenstadt and Roniger on the conditions which encourage clientelism.

[53]See Bendix; and Piven and Cloward, 1988, Chapter 2.

[54]See McCormick, 295. For a discussion of the relationship between the suffrage and political mobilization, see Rokkan.

[55]See Kousser; and Rusk and Stucker.

reform movement swept the North, directed not primarily against blacks but against immigrant workers. The result was similar, albeit less total. Literacy tests that had been abandoned half a century earlier were reintroduced, in some states along with a poll tax. Residency requirements were stiffened, and laws allowing immigrants to vote if they declared the intention to become citizens were repealed. New and difficult requirements for personal and periodic registration were imposed, at first required mainly in the big cities, where the immigrant working class was concentrated. At the same time, the local parties, which might otherwise have worked to subvert these restrictions because of the threat they posed to the size of their voting base, came under direct attack by good government reformers who succeeded in stripping the state and local parties of much of their patronage with the establishment of nonpartisan and expert administrative agencies.[56] Together, these measures took their toll. Restrictive rules and procedures made voting difficult, and local parties had fewer resources to help voters through the process or, indeed, to mobilize voters at all. Voter turnout, which had hovered around 80 percent in presidential elections for most of the nineteenth century, fell steadily, to barely half of the electorate by the 1920s.[57]

The significance of these events for the subsequent course of electoral politics, and eventually for the welfare state, can hardly be overstated. Whatever the other obstacles, with the base of the voter universe constricted, political parties representing lower-strata farmers and workers could not grow. Nor were the major political parties as likely to fashion their appeals or their recruitment strategies to attract lower-strata groups. And without a political party to define the political world and thereby socialize

---

[56]On the reformers, see Weibe; Hays; Haber; Weinstein; and Shefter, 1978a.

[57]For a fuller analysis, see Piven and Cloward, 1988, Chapter 3.

workers, and to raise issues and identify alternatives, even the ability of people to recognize their own needs, which the pluralist model of welfare state development takes for granted, was inhibited, as of course was the legitimation of those needs and their expression in electoral competition.

In sum, the pluralist model of the welfare state, by highlighting the importance of votes, points by implication to the importance of limits on democratic rights in the United States.[58] The vote is the fundamental unit of pluralist politics, and the hindering of its exercise is surely part of the reason for the subsequent weakness of working class political organization and, as we will shortly demonstrate, the weakness of unions as well. But we think other features of the American political system worked in tandem with this pluralist debility.

State-Centered Interpretations

The state-centered approach to the politics of the welfare state begins with the premise that the main institution which structures the politics of social welfare is the state itself. From this perspective, governmental organizations and electoral-representative arrangements not only register and respond to political influence; they also help to shape political influence, by creating political resources, and by delineating the processes through which resources, and some resources more readily than other resources, can be used to try to exercise influence.

The recent rise of a state-centered school in interpretations of the welfare state focuses particularly on state bureaucracies. Accordingly, the main actors are state officials, usually bureaucrats and occasionally legislators, who take the lead in developing new initiatives in social policy.

---

[58]For comparisons of voter turnout levels in Europe and the United States, see Powell; and Piven and Cloward, 1988, Chapter 1.

These initiatives are in turn shaped and constrained by the preexisting structure of the state, especially by its bureaucratic capacities, and by patterns of fragmentation and competition within the state.[59] The initiatives of state actors are also limited by the policy heritage of a particular state, which constitutes a kind of repertoire of accepted practices and ideas.[60]

There has been a good deal of dispute generated by this variant of a state-centered perspective, much of it perhaps provoked by the inclination of its practitioners to assert the significance of state-centered factors to the exclusion of all else.[61] Nevertheless, the main thrust of the state-centered perspective—that the state itself constitutes a distinct orga-

---

[59]See Niskanen for the straightforward argument that state bureaucrats act to maximize state budgets. See Cloward and Piven, 1974, for the more general argument that welfare state bureaucratic decisions are driven by the imperatives of organizational maintenance. The current resurgence of the state centered approach is led by Theda Skocpol and her students. See, for example, Orloff and Skocpol; Skocpol and Amenta; Weir *et al.* Analysts in other schools have also tried to take account of state characteristics. See Stephens for a neo-Marxist analysis of the significance of political structures. See also Castles; and Huber *et al.*, 1991, on the influence of federalism; Cameron; and Wilensky, 1976, on the significance of tax structure; and Derthick, 1979, on bureaucracy.

[60]Problems arise, however, from the failure of state-centered analysts to be clear about the boundaries of the institutional domain they are analyzing, or the relative weight of state-centered variables within that domain, with the result that they seem almost capricious in asserting that events support a state-centered perspective. Thus, while they claim roots in a European tradition of theorizing about a grand state, they in fact ignore most of the state apparatus, except for selected state bureaucracies. At the same time, state-centered analysts episodically introduce aspects of the electoral-representative system into their account, under the expanded rubric of "political-institutional" analysis. And some of their arguments give such weight to reformers and their ideas as to be reminiscent of the view that professional and philanthropic elites deserve the lead role in the development of social policy. For example, Orloff, 6, thinks that the initiation of modern social provision "came in the coalescence of a cross-class coalition of workers, farmers, and middle classes under the political leadership of liberal political, intellectual and reform elites."

[61]See for example Therborn for a critique of the statists' depiction of key episodes in Swedish, British, and American history. And see Goldfield, 1987 and 1990, for a definitive critique on empirical grounds of the statist interpretation of American policy history in the 1930s. See also Domhoff, 1990.

nizational environment which informs the initiatives of political actors—seems to us indisputable. In fact, a state-centered analysis has long been at the heart of a main line of explanation of American political history generally.[62] The work of E. E. Schattschneider[63] is central in this tradition, and it is especially pertinent to the question of why working class influence in electoral politics was so limited. Schattschneider thought that popular influence in a formally democratic regime depended on strong parties, but that party organization in the United States was weak, and he pointed to the structure of the American state in explaining that weakness. The core of his argument was that the fragmented and decentralized structure of government that had been established under the Constitution ensured a fragmented and decentralized party system.[64]

Schattschneider singles out in particular the elaborate division of powers in the national government between the Congress, the presidency, and the courts, each of which was assigned distinct decision-making authority, and each of which was assigned different routes and different constituencies for accession to power. This structure, he says, was "designed to make parties ineffective . . . [because they] would lose and exhaust themselves in futile attempts to fight their way through the labyrinthine framework."[65] The invention of these arrangements in the eighteenth century reflected the founders' fear of the popular forces that could be mobilized by parties, at a time when radical democratic currents stirred by the revolution were strong, among a still-armed population. But the effects were enduring. The state structure that was created made it difficult to translate popular electoral victories into policy, not only in the eigh-

---

[62]See for example Huntington; Hofstadter; Bensel; and Keller.

[63]Sections of this discussion on the impediments to party development in the U. S. were originally published in Piven, 1991.

[64]Schattschneider, 1942.

[65]Schattschneider, 1942, 7.

teenth century but in the twentieth.[66] Divided powers, by fracturing the authority of the central government, created lasting impediments to coherent national party organization, and to the popular influence that could be realized through party organization.

The fragmentation of national authority was matched and complemented by the decentralization of governmental powers that was also incorporated into the Constitution, and which also had a large impact on the character of political parties. There were, to be sure, powerful reasons for centralizing government authority in the precarious post-revolutionary period, including the alarming insurgency represented by Shay's rebellion, the financial threat posed by radical initiatives in the state legislatures regarding currency and debt, and the threat of military aggression from expansionary European powers once the colonies were stripped of the British military presence. But there were also powerful forces working against centralization. The Constitution was necessarily a compromise between colonial elites from regionally distinct economies and societies who were afraid of the interferences of central authority, as was famously signaled by the provisions to limit but protect slavery embodied in the Constitution. The more general compromise, and it had lasting effects, was to decentralize power structurally. This was done in two ways. First, the authority of the new national government was limited to constitutionally specified policies, thus leaving an enormous reservoir of unspecified power to the state governments, and to the local governments chartered by state legislatures. Second, the system of electoral representation was designed to give large weight to regions as opposed to persons, both in representation in the Senate, and in the arrangement of the electoral college through which the President was chosen.

---

[66]See Lipset and Rokkan, 1967, 31–32.

Decentralization thus had its roots in sectional economic differences which have always marked American politics (particularly the distinctive economy and society of the Southern section).[67] Regionally distinct economies were protected, however, and sectionalism was nurtured, by a political system which lent sectional interests weight in national government, with, as it turned out, lasting implications for American political parties, and for working class political influence. Most important for our purposes, the decentralization of government authority made decentralized state and local parties that jockeyed for control over subnational governments far more important.[68] And decentralization also made these parties relatively autonomous from the national parties, for they could be sustained over time by the resources and authority of state and local governments, no matter the partisan complexion of national government.

The decentralizing of government power also nourished the local clientelist political organizations for which the United States is renowned, and which marked working class politics, particularly during the first decades of industrialization. Decentralization meant that local government did many things, and these activities in turn yielded the patronage resources which were then used to organize the nineteenth century artisans and laborers in the immigrant wards of the cities.[69] This is why ethnic-based local political ma-

---

[67]Other nations also formed through an initial compact between distinct regional governments. Elsewhere, however, these regional authorities gradually lost ground to an enlarging central government. In the United States, while the scope of national governmental power has increased, a vigorous federalism persists, and it persists in part because American politics has developed in a way that is dependent on decentralized policy structures.

[68]Griffin, 1991, 673, perhaps overstates the problem when he accounts for the absence of issues and program in the national parties that emerged in the first half of the nineteenth century by the simple fact that there were no important issues the national government could resolve.

[69]On clientelism and working class politics, see Bridges; Oestreicher; Piven and Cloward, 1988, Chapter 2; Shefter, 1978b.

chines became so important in the history of the United States. And ultimately, these clientalist parties inhibited national working-class electoral organization.

Decentralization meshed with the fragmentation of national authority to make parties ineffective as instruments of popular influence.[70] In particular, the weighted influence of sectional interests in the Senate and in the electoral college, later matched by internal arrangements in the House which privileged strong state and local parties by making seniority the criterion for committee headships, gave the chieftains of sectionally based state parties, and the bosses of clientelist city parties, something like a veto power over national policy. That veto power was regularly used to block welfare state initiatives. It was also used to block other policies which might have promoted more coherent national parties at the expense of decentralized power blocs.

Finally, a fragmented and decentralized state also nourished interest group politics, even as it inhibited the party development which might counter interest group influence. Because parties need to mobilize votes in their quest for state power, they are to varying degrees responsive to popular grievances and hopes. Interest groups are not.[71] Well organized interests are built out of the concentrated resources generated by social and economic inequalities, and they proliferate particularly for the singleminded pursuit of economic advantage. And interest groups flourish in a governmental system with more points of exposure to well organized groups with the resources and tenacity to pursue influence.[72] In the American constitutional system, interest

---

[70]Derthick, 1992, makes the additional point that the fragmentation of governmental powers in the federal system lent the non-elected judiciary great authority, thus further inhibiting popular influence.

[71]On this point, see not only Schattschneider, 1942, but Dahl.

[72]Katznelson, 323, has recently suggested a similar argument, pointing to key features of the American state in explaining the distinctive features of American social policy, including "decentralization and federalism, an institu-

groups could operate in the several branches of government, or at different levels of government, to promote the policies they favored or to block policies they opposed. In welfare state politics, that meant employer interests could influence policy at multiple points, in the formulation of national legislation and bureaucratic regulation, and in the case of AFDC and general relief, through state enabling legislation and state and local bureaucratic implementation as well. Furthermore, since the very structural arrangements which exposed the state to well-organized interests also ensured the fragmentation of the national parties, and their consequent lack of a strategic or programmatic center, there was little resistance from party leaders to the demands of organized interest groups.[73]

It is widely agreed that the potential for democratic political influence in mass societies depends on the activities of parties which mediate the relationship between citizens and government. It is parties that presumably articulate popular hopes and discontents, generate policy and candidate alternatives, and organize citizen-voters for one or another of these alternatives. When this does not happen, citizens are atomized and ineffective, and interest groups hold sway. The fragmented and decentralized American governmental structure thus worked to create parties that were uniquely

---

tionally constrained presidency, a porous central bureaucracy, catchall party organizations, a highly autonomous Congress, and the importance of law and the judiciary in policy making and implementation."

[73]Other features of the American constitutional system were also important in shaping the party system. Perhaps most important, single member districts made it difficult for third parties to succeed, unless their strength was regionally concentrated, in which case they might win the district majorities and representation in state legislatures or the Congress which made survival more likely. This fundamental encumbrance on third party efforts was gradually shored up by the elaboration of state laws which impeded ballot access by challengers. Two party systems are often extolled for the moderation they presumably encourage, as competition forces contenders toward the center. But a two party system also tends to be conservative, if only because party managers trying to hold together large and unwieldly majorities avoid issues which threaten conflict and cleavage. See Piven and Cloward, 1993.

ineffective in filling what Dennis Wrong has called this "creative and synthesizing" role.[74]

The theorists of the "democratic class struggle" place great weight on the role of labor or socialist parties in the politics of the welfare state. In some Western industrial countries, labor or socialist parties emerged which played an important role in articulating working class experience and forging a working class culture, and then in pressing for the working class interests which the party had helped to create. There was no labor party to play that role in the United States. The American experience suggests, however, a broader generalization. Not only did the United States lack a labor party, but it lacked strong national parties of any ideological stripe capable of holding sectional and interest group influences in check. The consequences for the American welfare state were enormous.

Weak Parties and Working Class Politics in the United States

The classical question is of course "why no labor party in the United States?" The larger question, we think, is why no strong national party of any kind came to serve as a vehicle for labor interests and aspirations.

The fateful and illuminating moment occurred in the 1930s, when the transformation of the Democratic party into a party of labor seemed possible. That transformation, and the enacting of national welfare state programs with which it was associated, was aborted by the cumulative impact of restrictions on the franchise, and by the political forces empowered by a divided and decentralized state system.

To be sure, there were reasons for believing in the possi-

[74]Wrong, 166.

bility of something like a labor party. Economic calamity had scuttled long-term Republican domination of the national government, at a time when blue collar workers constituted about half the workforce. Pressed by an escalating strike movement, Franklin Delano Roosevelt conceded his support to legislation to protect unionization efforts. And organized labor broke with its traditional policy of abstaining from national electoral politics to become a field apparatus for the Democratic party.[75] The new industrial unions rapidly allied themselves with the Democratic party, and shortly thereafter the craft unions did as well. As early as 1936, the CIO began to work for the Democratic ticket, creating a political arm that performed much like a campaign organization, spending money to stage rallies, print leaflets, and recruit voters in the industrial states where the CIO unions were strong. This was the birth of a massive and far-flung CIO campaign apparatus, supplemented in 1948 by a comparable AFL effort, that deployed "armies of trade-union precinct workers" and often took the place of the local Democratic party apparatus itself.[76] In the 1940s, the union-party formation in the United States did not look very different from Western Europe: union density levels were not much lower, and the degree of class polarization in voting was as high.[77]

These events, however, did not occur on a fresh slate. The Democrats had only become the party of Northern labor, and even there labor influence was weakened by persisting disenfranchising procedures which reduced

---

[75]A resolution adopted at the 1896 AFL convention asserted that "party politics, whether it be Democratic, Republican, Socialistic, Populistic, Prohibition, or any other shall have no place in the convention of the American Federation of Labor." Quoted in Galenson, 49.

[76]The phrase is in Davis, 90. On the impact of unions on the Democratic vote, see E. E. Schattschneider, 1960, 50, who estimated unionism added ten percentage points to the Democratic inclination of the labor vote. See also Scoble, 675, who examined this calculation under different assumptions and concluded that union influence on the way labor votes might have been larger.

[77]On class voting, see Alford.

working class voting numbers.[78] Labor influence was also countered by the renewed vigor of the urban machines, organizations made possible in the first place by decentralization, and then ironically revived by a Democratic administration which channeled funds to big city bosses in an effort to build local support. In any case, no matter the popular complexion of the party, as the strike movement subsided, the influence of business lobbyists on the Congress grew.

Even more important, the Democrats also continued to be the sectional party of the Southern Bourbons.[79] This peculiar coalition was also sustained by decentralization and disenfranchisement, as well as by the fragmentation of national government authority. Decentralization allowed the Southern oligarchy to construct a regional political system that shored up the plantation economy, and to defend that system under the banner of "states rights." The disenfranchising arrangements of the late nineteenth century (together with the regular use of state-sanctioned violence) protected the Southern system from electoral challenges from below, by the simple expedient of purging poor blacks and most poor whites from the electorate. This not only meant that an oligarchy ruled in the South, it also meant that the class tilt of the Northern wing of the party toward the working class was offset by a class tilt in the South toward the planter-merchant oligarchy. At the same time, the decentralization built into the system of national representation by the privileging of regions over population,

---

[78]In a 1959 study, Harold Sheppard and Nicholas Masters, 437–447, found that the UAW had registered 90 percent of its members, and 87 percent of them voted. However, if this was accurate, it was not typical. Sidney Lens, 298, reports that in the late 1950s, the director of the AFL-CIO's political arm estimated that overall, only 40 percent of union members were registered voters. A survey by the Amalgamated Clothing workers found even fewer registrants (cited in Davis, 98).

[79]There is a superficial parallel here to the rise to power of Scandinavian labor parties through alliances with rural parties. But, in fact, there is no parallel. The alliance with the rural South was not an alliance with family farmers, as was the case in Scandinavia, but with plantation owners.

particularly in the Senate and the electoral college, gave the oligarchical Southern section a strong grip on the national government. And a system of divided powers in the national government meant that grip could become a stranglehold on national policy, especially as powerful Southern Democrats in the Congress allied themselves with Northern Republicans beginning in the late 1930s.

As a result, the support for unionism by party leaders during the Great Depression did not last. After the war, the legislative protections of the National Labor Relations Act were whittled away and the once pro-labor National Labor Relations Board was reconstituted, largely as a result of the influence of Southerners and business-oriented Republicans in the Congress who had joined together in an alliance that was near-fatal to organized labor. Meanwhile, decentralization permitted the states to undercut the union protections won from the federal government in 1935, and a good many did just that, especially in the South. As these reversals accumulated, labor's brief political flowering faded. Most important in the longer run, the Taft Hartley Act of 1947 explicitly allowed state open shop laws which were especially prevalent in the South,[80] setting the stage for the failure of Operation Dixie, the Southern organizing drive launched by the CIO in 1946, which ran aground on intransigent Southern opposition (and union infighting).[81] This meant that as new plants dispersed to the Sunbelt in subsequent decades, the unions did not follow.[82]

---

[80]The Taft Hartley Act also granted employers "free speech" rights, introduced new curbs on strikes, and prohibited such solidarity tactics as sympathy strikes, secondary boycotts, and mass picketing. And the non-communist affidavits required of union officials under the Act spurred a long wave of union fratricide.

[81]The CIO attempted to penetrate the South early, and had scored some local organizing successes during the war. See Lichtenstein, 135–137. However, Goldfield, 1987, 185–189, thinks these efforts were fatally flawed because union leadership was conservative and racist. On the failure of Operation Dixie, see also Davis, 92–94.

[82]However, Goldfield, 1987, attributes the decline of union membership

The main American welfare state programs were inaugurated during the heady days of the New Deal. As we recounted in Chapter 2, when FDR first took office, elites everywhere, shaken by the depth of the economic crisis and by mounting protest among the unemployed, supported emergency measures, including emergency relief, and so too did Southern congressmen, whose impoverished region had been especially hard hit by the economic calamity. Even so, however, there were objections from the start by Southern elites to national relief programs that overrode local wage scales or interfered with caste arrangements. And when the Social Security Act of 1935 replaced emergency relief, Southern representatives who dominated the key committees in the Congress carried great weight.[83] Significant segments of business also organized to oppose the act because they feared income support programs would interfere with low-wage labor markets.[84] Together with Southern representatives, they used the political leverage guaranteed them by divided and decentralized government to ensure that the new national welfare state programs would conform with sectionally and sectorally diversified labor markets.[85]

The intricate provisions of the Social Security Act reflected this confluence of forces. For one thing, whole categories of low wage workers were excluded from the old age

---

more to employer opposition than to either the contraction of smokestack industries, or the shift of industry to the Sunbelt. See our discussion in Chapter 11 of this book.

[83]Both the House Ways and Means Committee and the Senate Finance Committee were chaired by Southerners. For discussions of the role of the South in the New Deal, see V. O. Key; Tindall; Piven and Cloward, 1977, Chapter 5; Alston and Ferrie; and Quadagno, 1990.

[84]On the influence of different fractions of business on the Social Security Act, see also Quadagno, 1984; Domhoff, 1990; and Jenkins and Brents.

[85]The key group in formulating the main provisions of the Social Security Act is widely agreed to have been the American Association for Labor Legislation. While the AALL is often defined as a civic reform organization, Domhoff's, 1990, 44–64, analysis makes clear that the organization drew its support from business leaders associated with the National Civic Federation.

and unemployment insurance programs. For another, eligibility was made conditional on a history of steady employment. And finally, as we have already shown, authority over the "categorical" or welfare programs (as well as over the unemployment insurance program) was largely ceded to the states and even to the counties, where local employers could ensure that conditions of eligibility and benefit levels were calibrated to their requirements.[86] These conditions were built into the foundations of the underdeveloped American welfare state.

The Welfare State Structures Welfare State Politics

The welfare state is not only the consequence of politics. It also helps to create that politics. Another strand of state-centered analysis focuses on the contribution of the welfare state itself to the politics which foster welfare state development or underdevelopment. In this argument, attention is directed away from the influence of the state on the political origins of the welfare state, and directed instead to the way welfare state agencies and programs, once they come into existence, influence popular politics. The initiating idea here is obvious: welfare state programs create constituencies that subsequently defend the programs, and promote their expansion. But this commonplace idea is only partly true. Some welfare state programs—pensions for the aged, for example—do seem to generate supportive constituencies. Others, such as the American means-tested programs, generate more opposition than support. We think the politics of the means-tested programs in the United States have even more far-reaching effects, dampening support for other welfare state programs as well. It would be useful to understand why.

---

[86]For a fuller discussion, see chapters 4 and 5 of this book. See also Piven and Cloward, 1987.

Some explanations have been advanced to explain the variable political effects of different systems of welfare state programs. First, while all welfare state programs shape constituencies, and they all influence understandings or interpretations, different programs shape different constituencies and encourage different political understandings of the meanings of the programs. Broad and inclusive programs carve out large constituencies with common stakes, while fragmented programs that reach narrowly defined groups are more likely to create divisions.[87] The incidence of the taxes that generate revenues for the programs can be similarly unifying or divisive, especially when these taxes are more visible.[88]

A number of the analysts who emphasize the role of labor parties in the politics of the welfare state also put forward a variant of just this sort of state-centered analysis. In their hands, what is important about the formative influence of the welfare state is whether over time it shores up the solidarity of the working class, and creates allies for it in electoral politics, particularly among employees of the welfare state. Thus, not only do labor parties and their union allies support the welfare state, but the welfare state in turn can strengthen the working class in electoral politics. Or, conversely, it can weaken the working class, as it appears to have done in the United States.[89]

Several features of the American welfare state deserve special scrutiny from this perspective. One is the complex system of differentiated programs which nourishes divisions among working class constituencies, not least by race. This oft-remarked upon feature of the American welfare state helped to account for the sharp conflicts evident when

---

[87]See Esping-Andersen, 1985, Chapter 5; Offe, 1991.

[88]See Wilensky, 1976.

[89]See Myles and Quadagno for this point made in a comparison of Canada and the U. S. See Piven, 1991, for a discussion of the impact of the American programs on working class allegiances to the Democratic party.

the means-tested programs were enlarged in the 1960s, largely in response to black insurgency. White working class taxpayer resentment was encouraged first because a number of programs, particularly AFDC, were identified with the minority poor, and second because the working class carried the brunt of the state and local taxes which helped fund the AFDC program.

Another feature of the American welfare state was perhaps even more important for its ultimately perverse effects on longer term political support for the welfare state, as well as the longer term prospects for something like a labor party. Simply put, there was too little of it. The Social Security Act was not the beginning of a process of welfare state growth. It was, for a long time, the high point. After World War II, Western European welfare state programs enlarged. But in the United States, the limited programs that had been inaugurated in the 1930s were allowed to languish. And new programs proved impossible to win in the Congress, owing to the vigorous resistance of Southern Democrats and business-oriented Republicans on the one hand, and the desultory support of Northern Democrats, who were also influenced by business interests, as well as by the local clientelist parties to which many congressmen remained beholden.

Meanwhile, the new industrial unions had expanded their sights not only to demand higher social security payments, but to demand national health insurance, child care facilities, government housing, and so on. Blocked by a Congress dominated by Southern Democrats and business-oriented Republicans, a still-militant and still-strong labor movement turned elsewhere for some of these protections. It used workplace power to bargain with employers for health and old age protections, and later to bargain for supplementary unemployment benefits as well.[90] The result was that,

---

[90]For an analysis, see Stevens.

over time, core working class groups looked less to government for the measures that would guarantee their security, and more to the marketplace. For example, without a national health program, most Americans relied on employers for health protections. In turn, a government that did less was less likely to generate confidence or affection or loyalty. And a party that did less was also less likely to hold the allegiance of its constituency over time.

Finally, the structure of the U. S. welfare state programs, and the poor relief practices that flourished within that structure, also had a formative influence on political culture, and specifically on popular political understandings of the causes of poverty, and the attributes of the poor. In another language, welfare state programs, like all institutional arrangements, can be understood as a text from which people derive meanings.[91] Programs which deal with beneficiaries as citizens and taxpayers shore up convictions in support of social rights. Programs which deal with recipients as supplicants or paupers weaken convictions about social rights, and even stigmatize the recipient population in the eyes of a broader citizenry.[92]

In this book we argue that the meanings communicated by poor relief practices, whether the branding of the pauper in the sixteenth century or the public excoriation of the welfare recipient in the twentieth, are of overwhelming importance, and that they can best be understood as rituals of degradation. We do not want to overstate this. We think different and even contradictory meanings can be "read" even in these means-tested welfare state programs. Programs which make subsistence more secure may be to some degree ideologically liberatory for that reason alone, nourishing ideas about social rights which contradict the stric-

---

[91]The paradigmatic exposition is Bourdieu's. See also Sewell.
[92]See Edelman (1978, 1988), and Schram, 1992.

tures of the market, and that may be one reason that more liberal relief-giving so quickly gives way to restrictive practices directed to enforcing work. As a consequence of these practices, and, just as importantly, as a consequence of the public displays of these practices, means-tested programs communicate punitive and degrading meanings which dampen political support for the programs, even among those with a clear material stake in them. Moreover, the uses of "welfare" as a symbol of income support programs generally during the 1970s and 80s suggests that the derogatory meanings associated with the means-tested programs may temper public support for other welfare state programs as well.

Protest and the Politics of Social Welfare

Fitted together, we think that the democratic class struggle, pluralist, and state-centered perspectives offer a convincing explanation of the distinctive pattern of American welfare state underdevelopment. They point to the crippling effects of disenfranchisement, of a decentered state structure, and of limited welfare state programs in inhibiting working class electoral organization and influence in the United States. Indeed, perhaps this synthesis is too compelling, for it leaves us with no way to explain why welfare state programs emerged at all in this country.

The premise common to each of these theories of welfare state politics is that political institutions shape forms of political action, or stated differently, that political structures shape political processes. Thus, developed electoral-representative institutions nourish electoral forms of action; a fragmented state structure fosters a fragmented party structure, and so on. We think this is self-evidently true. However, if disenfranchisement and weak political parties meant that electoral-representative channels were less available in the United States, particularly to the working class, agricultural laborers, and minorities,[93] other forms of collective action did remain available. The role in translating needs or systemic imperatives into politics and policy, which democratic class struggle theorists attribute to labor parties and centralized unions, and which pluralists attribute to voters and interest groups, was in the United States played by protest movements. (As we showed in Chapter 1, there is also evidence from historians such as Hobsbawm, Rude, the Hammonds, and the Tillys that protest movements played a large role in Europe, and perhaps more so before the development of electoral-representative arrangements. Steinmetz also provides evidence of the large role of protest in local government poor relief policies in imperial Germany.[94])

In the United States, protest movements were important in part because electoral-representative institutions limited the incorporation of lower-strata groups. While these movements were influenced by electoral representative processes, they did not take form mainly in electoral politics. Protest movements were undergirded by solidarities and ideas formed in the workplaces and neighborhoods where people lived their daily lives.[95] And they found expression in dramatic defiance of the authorities that gov-

---

[93]"No national parties were available to channel the demands of new groups and so elections could not play an important role in settling conflicts with established groups and institutions" (Griffin, 698).

[94]Steinmetz, 209, found that local relief spending in imperial Germany rose and fell "in tandem with extraparliamentary disorder." These findings are particularly interesting because they provide evidence of the local threat factor which may well have informed Bismarckian social policies, in contrast to treatments of these policies as the autonomous initiatives of state elites.

[95]Here we can only refer to the large literature on the dynamics of protest movements which has for the most part been developed entirely apart from the literature on the welfare state. See, for example, Hobsbawm, 1965; Smelser; Moore; Wolf; Tilly et al., 1975; Gamson, 1975; McAdam; Flacks; and Morris and Mueller. For our analysis of protest, which expands on the argument of this book, see Piven and Cloward, 1977.

erned these workplaces and neighborhoods. But if protests often welled up outside of electoral-representative spheres, their impact on electoral politics, and on welfare state policy, could be large, as we have been at pains to explain in this book.

The depression again provides a good example. When Franklin Delano Roosevelt took office, procedural disenfranchisement continued to keep voter turnout down, union membership was at a low point, and the Democratic Party remained a party of Southern politicians and big city bosses who were swept to victory by depression conditions. Consistently, the new administration offered plans oriented mainly to reviving business by bringing order to financial markets, and by adopting industrial price and production controls proposed by the U. S. Chamber of Commerce. Meanwhile, however, a series of widespread protest movements—among the unemployed, farmers, the old, and industrial workers—caused sufficient disruption and electoral dissension to prompt entirely different initiatives. The movements, galvanized in part by Roosevelt's vague campaign promises, raised contentious issues with which the Roosevelt administration had to cope, or risk escalating disruptions in the streets and factories, and spreading disaffection among its still insecure electoral constituency. Popular insurgency compelled the administration to inaugurate massive relief programs, to pass legislation lending government protection to the right of workers to organize, and to initiate social security legislation that created the framework for the American welfare state. Our term for that welfare state has been "underdeveloped." Nevertheless, it was a welfare state, eventually providing near-universal pensions for the aged, as well as benefits for the disabled and the unemployed. Compared to more developed welfare states, the programs are backward, even cruel. Compared to what they might have been in the absence of protest, the American welfare state is an achievement.

We conclude with a speculative query about the broader significance of protest politics. Our case for the persisting importance of mass insurgency in shaping relief policy is based on the American experience. We are not satisfied, however, that the role of protest in other rich industrial countries has been seriously investigated. Theory guides empirical inquiry, and accordingly most empirical research tends to search for evidence of the factors identified by preferred theories, of the role of working class electoral organization, or of voter and interest group influence, or of the formative influence of state structures or state actors. As a consequence, protest movements get less attention, and are often simply ignored. Nevertheless, there is at least preliminary cross-national evidence that working and lower class insurgency contributed to increases in aggregate welfare state expenditures in other industrial countries. According to Swank, in a study of 17 industrial countries during the postwar period, industrial strikes and working-class protests over economic conditions were correlated with general welfare state expenditure increases. And Hicks and Swank similarly conclude that the impact of lower-class protests and strikes on welfare state expansion in these same countries during the 1960–71 period was "roughly as consequential as [the impact] of governing parties and large, organized pressure groups."[96] These findings should provoke a reassessment of the role of protest movements in the evolution of welfare states in other rich countries.

Such a reassessment will not be easy for the proponents of the democratic class struggle perspective who tend to marginalize protest, treating it as an inferior form of politics which was thankfully superceded as working class organization developed. Indeed, there is a tendency to treat protest as evidence of working class weakness, as when Korpi tells us that the growing strength of the Swedish

---

[96]Hicks and Swank, 1984, 106; Swank, 1983; and Hicks and Swank, 1991.

social democratic party in the twentieth century was paralleled by a decline in the level of industrial conflicts.[97] Myles also concludes that working class political power is inversely related to strike levels and, even more simply, that the quality of citizenship entitlements is a reflection of party competition and of the size of the dependent population.[98] These conclusions suggest so much confidence in electoral organization as the instrument of working class interests as to seem to unhinge the analysis from its Marxist roots.[99]

At base, the argument for working class electoral organization is a kind of hybrid, splicing together the classical Marxist view that class interests are formed in production relations with the pluralist view that these interests are expressed in electoral politics by unions and labor parties. Perhaps so. Or perhaps sometimes, under some conditions. Or perhaps most of the time. But we need a reasoned and qualified justification for equating classes formed in production with the organizations that purport to represent them in electoral politics. Instead, the model treats as axiomatic the assumption that trade unions and social democratic parties—and only trade unions and social democratic parties—in fact represent working class interests. Thus Korpi proposes that working class power will be greatest where trade unions are centralized and collaborate closely with a socialist party.[100] But to leave it at that is a kind of nominalism: it is to assume that the politics of organizations can be understood by the names they give themselves.

There are in fact good historical reasons for questioning

[97]Korpi, 1983, 46–47. More recently, Korpi has suggested that protest in the United States is a kind of alternative to working class electoral organization. See Korpi, 1989.

[98]Myles, 1984, 89–90 and 95. See also Hibbs, 1978.

[99]Of course, this is not the complete argument. Both Myles and Esping-Andersen, for example, stress the *ultimately* contradictory consequences for capitalism of an expanding welfare state, which Esping-Andersen, 1985, says entails the "decommodification" of labor power, and which Myles, 1984, 110–111 and 114, says shifts the balance of power between capital and labor.

[100]Korpi, 1983, 39.

this sort of total confidence in electoral organization. One is simply the inevitable tendency toward oligarchy. Experience suggests that working class organizations gradually move away from their rank and file, and perhaps all the more so when they must maneuver for survival and success in an electoral environment dominated by other powerful organizations. This tendency was documented and explained by Michels in his work on the German Social Democratic Party and the effects on its leadership of the turn toward parliamentarianism,[101] although his critique has generally been acknowledged only to be then ignored.

A second reason to scrutinize rather than assume the relationship of electoral organizations to the classes and class interests they purport to represent has to do with the way the exigencies of electoral politics transform class political action. Earlier in the century, social democrats had been confident that the advance of industrial capitalism would create a working class electoral majority. They were wrong, the industrial proletariat never became a majority. As the twentieth century advanced, it became clear that social democratic parties bidding for state power through electoral processes had to seek support from other classes. Inevitably, therefore, the agenda and culture of the left parties tended to become oriented toward extra-working class voters, or toward coalition with the parties of extra-working class voters.[102] The point is not that this is reprehensible, or even avoidable. Rather it is simply that the extent to which social democratic parties (as well as centralized trade unions) do in fact represent working class interests should not be taken for granted, but should be treated as historically contingent and therefore as empirically variable.

The electoral path forces compromise for more general

---

[101]Michels, 1949.
[102]See Przeworski and Sprague, 1986.

reasons as well. On the one hand, organizations bidding for victory at the polls reach for the widest possible support, and are therefore likely to shrink from actions that may alienate potential voters from other strata, as well as those who control the resources needed to reach voters. On the other hand, working class voters themselves are susceptible to diverse appeals from party competitors. The commitment to electoralism may therefore lead class-based organizations to eschew militant conflict.

These observations about the limitations of working class electoral organization suggest a hypothesis about the relationship between electoral politics and protest. However, we think the relationship is more complicated than has hitherto been proposed. European historical trends suggest that strong electoral organizations tend to supplant protest, and perhaps even suppress protest. In other words, stronger parties mean weaker protests. But this does not mean protest is eliminated. And where parties are stronger and more centralized, and capable of effective programmatic responses, even weaker protests may play an important role in countering the tendencies toward oligarchy and class compromise inherent in organization and electoralism, and their dampening effects on welfare state programs.[103] By contrast, in the United States, where parties are weaker and more fragmented, much higher levels of protest are not only likely, but may be necessary to achieve comparable programmatic responses.

Whatever their role in the past, protest movements may well become more important in the future, as economic globalization reduces the political effectiveness of traditional working class organizations. If oligarchy and elec-

---

[103]We are indebted to Fred Block for suggesting how this hypothesis is implied in our work on the interaction of protest movements and electoral politics.

toral compromise always limited these organizations, they are likely to be much more severely limited as deindustrialization proceeds. The ranks of the old working class are shrinking, leading left parties to further dilute class appeals in order to shore up their vote totals. At the same time, the traditional left party strategy of appealing for broad voter support with promises of immediate material improvement has become ever more difficult and treacherous. In the past, this strategy always forced labor parties into accommodations with business interests who controlled investment and therefore the possibility of wage and job growth. Now, however, the terms of the accommodation are becoming increasingly unfavorable as global trends sharpen the threat of disinvestment—and heighten the power of business leaders.[104]

Protest movements have always been the resort of those who lacked institutionalized forms of political access and influence. As the new conditions of postindustrialism weaken older forms of labor organization, protest movements may become the only means to defend the welfare state, not only in the United States, but in Western Europe as well.

CHAPTER TWELVE

APPENDIX

Disruptive Protest and Relief Expansion: a Commentary on Recent Research

The publication of *Regulating the Poor*, with its emphasis on political regulation as the key dynamic in poor relief growth, provoked something akin to outrage among social

---

[104]See Przeworski, 1985.

welfare historians who were inclined to interpret relief history as shaped by the high-minded intentions of reformers allied with benign elites. At the 1980 annual meeting of the Organization of American Historians, Walter I. Trattner convened a panel of social welfare historians to evaluate *Regulating the Poor,* especially from the perspective of relief arrangements in the United States during the eighteenth and nineteenth centuries, a period which the panelists rightly claimed we had neglected. These papers, together with our rejoinder, were subsequently published in a volume edited by Trattner.[105]

What is at issue in these essays is our contention that relief rises should be understood as efforts by elites to moderate mass disorder (our claim that relief also performs the function of regulating labor is not taken up for analysis). We gave primacy to conflict and social control rather than to the consensus and social altruism which figure so largely in traditional social welfare histories.

This debate occurred at a time when the published work of a new school of general historians devoted to recovering "history from below"—especially the history of European preindustrial popular protest, whether food riots, squatting, machine-smashing, or relief riots, including mobs tearing down workhouses—had become available. We identified with this developing school, and its overall findings provide support for our analysis of the workings of poor relief in the preindustrial world. Conflict, including conflict initiated through popular collective action, was a central preoccupation in their work, as was the impact of conflict on historical change.

But the Trattner volume contains no references to Eric J. Hobsbawm, E. P. Thompson, George Rude, Charles Tilly or to other historians who saw that popular protest—

---

[105]Trattner, *Social Welfare or Social Control: Some Historical Reflections on "Regulating the Poor,"* 1983.

including "the madding crowd"—also shapes history. Instead, these social welfare historians protrayed common people merely as objects of elite benevolence. To them, relief history, and social life more generally, represented the unfolding of a consensual normative order, with philanthropists at the head of the march.

The main challenge to us was their claim that large relief rises occur without antecedent disorder, leading to the conclusion that it is intensified hardship among the poor, not intensified protest by the poor, which motivates elites to expand aid. But their case is flawed because there were no relief rises in the historical periods they examine, although they mistakenly think there were. Alexander[106] treats decisions by the overseers in colonial Philadelphia to abolish outdoor relief arrangements and to build a workhouse in 1765, and then to double its size in the 1790s, as actions which greatly expanded relief even though there was no civil turmoil. He thus ignores all of relief history which shows that relief expansion always takes place through outdoor systems (if only for practical reasons, such as cost), and that the substitution of workhouses occurs in periods of relief contraction, as the Philadelphia case in fact demonstrates. The Pumphreys[107] analyze the movement of early twentieth century reformers for a system of mothers' pensions as if it, too, led to a substantial rise in relief, when in fact very few mother-headed families were actually granted benefits. And Achenbaum's essay on the Great Depression comes to the same conclusion, although by a slightly different tack.[108] He manages to offer an explanation of the origins of the 1935 Social Security Act without even men-

---

[106]Alexander, "The Functions of Public Welfare in Late-Eighteenth Century Philadelphia: Regulating the Poor?"

[107]Pumphrey and Pumphrey, "The Widows' Pension Movement, 1900–1930: Preventive Child-Saving or Social Control?"

[108]Achenbaum, "The Formative Years of Social Security: A Test of the Piven and Cloward Thesis."

tioning marches and riots by the unemployed or spreading waves of strikes by industrial workers, arguing that this legislation resulted from the efforts of reformers alone. In an approving commentary on these papers, Leiby[109] treats them as affirming the "common sense" view that "the policy of lawmakers was that government should help people who needed and deserved help, so the number of people who got relief increased and decreased with the number of people who were needy and deserving." However, Mohl's essay contradicts all else in this volume.[110] He describes the failure of elites to extend mass relief despite the hardship during the economic downturns and depressions in the Gilded Age. He also draws attention to the failure of elites to relieve the poor despite recurrent civil disorder, and thus corrects and clarifies our view on the relationship between protest and the likelihood of winning relief concessions. We claimed that civil disorder is a prerequisite to relief rises, but Mohl points out that we left the impression that it is also a sufficient condition.[111]

The 1930s

The findings of "history from below" on the important role of protest as a determinant of relief cycles in the preindustrial world have now been broadly accepted. The question remains whether protest has been similarly crucial to welfare in the industrial world. We said it has been, at least in the United States, where poor relief arrangements still flourish. The two great periods of twentieth century relief expansion were also characterized by enormous civil dis-

---

[109]Leiby, "Social Control and Historical Explanation: Historians View the Piven and Cloward Thesis."

[110]Mohl, "The Abolition of Public Outdoor Relief, 1870–1900: A Critique of the Piven and Cloward Thesis."

[111]For our full response to this volume of essays, see Piven and Cloward, "Humanitarianism in History: A Response to the Critics."

order, first by industrial workers and the unemployed, and then by blacks; and, in both periods, relief was sharply limited when disorder subsided, as the evidence in this book shows.

Critics of our analysis of the 1930s generally accept the important role of political protest, but find other deficiencies in our argument. The main line of criticism was initiated by Domhoff. Based on his detailed studies of economic elites, he claims that we give insufficient weight to divisions among business leaders in explaining why mass protest succeeds in winning more liberal relief.[112] In the 1930s, for example, the division between "business conservatives" and "business liberals" allowed political leaders to be more responsive to protest than they might have been had they confronted a unified business opposition. Domhoff says that a fuller explanation of relief rises depends on "a better understanding of the moderates within the corporate community." Jenkins and Brent[113] incorporated Domhoff's critique in a more comprehensive analysis of the 1930s, which combines the analysis of "sustained protest" with the analysis of "hegemonic competition between capitalist blocs," the point being that protest fares better when elite divisions help create political opportunities for reform. Kerbo and Shaffer[114] go a further step by presenting evidence from the 1930s suggesting that the unemployed perceive and interpret these divisions as favorable to reform, and are therefore more likely to engage in protest.

---

[112]Domhoff, "The New Class War," 1983, 58.

[113]Jenkins and Brents, "Social Protest, Hegemonic Competition, and Social Reform: A Political Struggle Interpretation of the Origins of the American Welfare State," 1989.

[114]Kirbo and Shaffer, "Lower Class Insurgency and the Political Process: The Response of the U. S. Unemployed, 1890–1940," 1992.

The 1960s

If theories of welfare growth giving pride of place to philanthropists were losing credibility, new theories replaced them, which rooted consensus in the social system rather than in an elite stratum. *Regulating the Poor* appeared at a time when systemic and evolutionary explanations of welfare state growth were developing. At a general level, as we said earlier, these theories note that resources enlarge as a result of industrial growth, and that needs also tend to enlarge because economic growth typically leads both to populations who live longer, and to the social dislocations of urbanization. They then claim that resources get allocated to meet needs more or less automatically.

Most, but not all, of the research on the 1960s relief expansion is devoted to assessing the relative merits of systemic and conflict theories. Much of it is quantitative, reflecting advances in social science methodology. Quantitative measures of needs, resources, and protest are examined for their effects on measures of relief expansion. City, state, and national level data are variously used; both cross-sectional and time-series analyses are undertaken. And much of the debate between proponents of different perspectives is focused on methodological issues.

The substantive findings of this corpus of research, taken as a whole, provide support for the role of protest, especially for the urban riots in the 1960s. That is true of the work by Betz[115]; Jennings[116]; Isaac[117]; Isaac and Kelly[118];

---

[115]Betz, "Riots and Welfare: Are They Related?" 1974.

[116]Jennings, "Civil Turmoil and the Growth of Welfare Rolls: A Comparative State Analysis," 1979; "Urban Riots and Welfare Policy Change: A Test of the Piven-Cloward Theory," 1981; and "Racial Insurgency, the State, and Welfare Expansion: A Critical Comment and Reanalysis," 1983.

[117]Isaac, "Racial Insurgency, the State, and Welfare Expansion: A Critical Comment and Reanalysis," 1983.

[118]Isaac and Kelly, "Racial Insurgency, the State, and Welfare Expansion:

Griffin, Devine, and Wallace[119]; Hicks and Swank[120]; Schram and Turbott[121]; and Chamblin.[122] In addition, Hicks and Swank[123] as well as Sharp and Maynard-Moody[124] report that violent crime also had some impact on the relief rise in this period. In a study of Mississippi, where there were no riots, Colby[125] found a significant relationship between nonviolent protest and relief expansion in the 1960s. However, both Gronbjerg[126] and Albritton[127] found no statistically significant relationship between riots and welfare growth.

All of the studies of the 1960s relief rise also conclude that there is support for systemic interpretations, no matter whether they do or do not find support for conflict and protest. Growth in both needs and resources preceded relief growth. Again, there are difficult conceptual and methodological problems. A particular researcher may find that unemployment rates help predict the welfare rise, but not rates of female-headed households; and another researcher

---

Local and National Evidence from the Postwar United States," 1981; and "Developmental/Modernization and Political Class Struggle Theories of Welfare State Expansion: The Case of the AFDC "Explosion" in the States, 1960–70," 1982.

[119]Griffin, Devine, and Wallace, "On the Economic and Political Determinants of Welfare Spending in the Post–World War II Era," 1983.

[120]Hicks and Swank, "Civil Disorder, Relief Mobilization and AFDC Caseloads: A Reexamination of the Piven and Cloward Thesis," 1983; Swank and Hicks, "Militancy, Need, and Relief: The Piven and Cloward AFDC Caseload Thesis Revisited," 1984.

[121]Schram and Turbott, "The Welfare Explosion: Mass Society versus Social Control," 1983a; and "Civil Disorder and the Welfare Explosion: A Two-step Process," 1983b.

[122]Chamblin, "Intergroup Threat and Social Control: Welfare Expansion Among States during the 1960s and 1970s," 1992.

[123]See their 1983 article.

[124]Sharp and Maynard-Moody, "Theories of the Local Welfare Role," 1991.

[125]Colby, "A Test of the Relative Efficacy of Political Tactics," 1982.

[126]Gronbjerg, *Mass Society and the Extension of Welfare, 1960–1970,* 1977.

[127]Albritton, "Social Amelioration Through Mass Insurgency? A Reexamination of the Piven and Cloward Thesis," 1979; cf. also Piven and Cloward, "Electoral Instability, Civil Disorder, and Relief Rises: A Reply to Albritton," 1979.

may find the reverse. But none of these studies ends by dismissing either needs or resources as important explanatory variables. The great value of much of this research literature is that it moves toward explanations of poor relief expansion that are more complex. Still, many analysts continue to insist that systemic explanations are sufficient, that protest and conflict are not necessary to explain how resources get allocated to needs, and it is to them that we address our final comments.

Systemic theories may help explain relief expansion, but they can only explain contraction if there are corresponding reductions in either needs or resources, or both. Our sense of relief history is that relief was frequently contracted even though both needs and resources were enlarging. That was certainly true in the American South in the postwar period: agricultural modernization devastated the farm labor population even as industrial modernization generated vast new affluence, and yet the relief rolls in one jurisdiction after another were either slashed or kept from rising, at least until the mid-to-late 1960s when insurgency in many forms had spread throughout the nation.

The post-1960s period presents a similar puzzle for systemic analysts. Resources grew; the society became wealthier, even though the rate of growth slowed compared to earlier periods. Needs also grew; unemployment rates were higher, wage levels fell, fewer people found full-time work with adequate benefits, and substantially more people fell into poverty. But instead of liberalizing the means-tested programs, the rolls were driven down, payments were slashed, and the ritualized degradation of relief recipients was intensified. To our minds, this contradiction can only be explained by the demise of protest from below, and by the mobilizing of elites from above, in this case a politicized business community in league with Republican administrations, to force poorer people to take less even while richer people were taking more. These are circumstances which a needs/resources perspective, taken alone, cannot illuminate, and it suggest to us that what we call the "labor regulating" phase of the relief cycle deserves attention.

Kirsten A. Gronbjerg's test of T. H. Marshall's systemic theory of "mass society" illustrates this point. She reports evidence that a variety of measures of modernization showed increases between 1960 and 1970, including voter participation, median education, the professionalization of the workforce, urbanization, industrialization, and state revenue. Since modernization variables were more important by 1970 than they had been in 1960, the conclusion follows that the AFDC rise represented the incorporation by the "center" of groups at the "periphery," epitomized by a cultural shift away from definitions of welfare as a privilege to welfare as a "social right" or "entitlement." However, 1970 was not a good year to end the test of this line of argument, because it marked the beginning of the successful campaign to limit "welfare rights," not least by allowing payment levels to fall and by driving the rolls down—and this despite the fact that mass society trends continued unabated. The point, in short, is that systemic theories cannot explain the cyclical pattern of poor relief, but the rise and demise of protest can.

Finally, we offer several further comments about protest. One is that it takes many forms, including forms which are not generally defined as protest. For example, a great rise in applications for welfare can express defiance, although this is not always the case. In depressions, when the market for labor collapses and when protest sometimes erupts, elites may actively promote mass relief programs. When people then apply for aid, they are taking advantage of the fruits of protest, rather than engaging in defiant behavior itself. The period from 1960 to 1966 was different, however. Millions of poor families, separately but in concert, applied for assistance *against the resistance* of welfare and political authorities, and against the resistance of prevailing social norms prescribing self-reliance, a point we made in response to Durman's contention that it was application rises rather than riots that fueled the relief rise.[128] Then, in 1966, with the formation of the National Welfare Rights Organization, the defiance expressed by these application rises was augmented by the outbreak of more organized protest against relief authorities. In other words, mass defiance need not be organized or led, or even widely noticed, except in the form of official statistics reporting sharp rises in applications for public assistance, or sharp rises in crime reflecting defiance of civil order and property norms, or sharp rises in rent delinquencies reflecting defiance of the norms governing landlord-tenant relations. In our opinion, much defiance from below takes these forms, and it should be acknowledged.

Indeed, if there is anything distinctive about our work, it is that we assign political meaning to forms of lower-class action which are typically viewed as inchoate. Many contemporary analysts disagree, including analysts who are sympathetic to more organized forms of lower-class political action. Hobsbawm, who instructed us to appreciate "primitive rebels,"[129] nevertheless defines our support of riots and other forms of disruptive protest as "blind militancy"[130]; what the poor need instead, he says, is to find ways to organize into "bodies capable of carrying out policies" reflecting their interests.[131] Gamson and Schmeidler similarly dismiss our perspective as an "anti-organization phillipic."[132] Roach and Roach accuse us of advocating

---

[128]Durman, "Have the Poor Been Regulated? Toward a Multivariate Understanding of Welfare Growth," 1973; cf. also Piven and Cloward, "Reaffirming the Regulation of the Poor," 1974.

[129]Hobsbawm, *Primitive Rebels: Studies in Archaic Forms of Social Movement in the 19th and 20th Centuries,* 1965; and *Bandits,* 1981.

[130]Hobsbawm, "Should the Poor Organize?" 1978.

[131]*Ibid.*

[132]Gamson and Schmeidler, "Organizing the Poor: An Argument with Frances Fox Piven and Richard A. Cloward, *Poor People's Movements,* " 1984; cf. also Piven and Cloward, "Disruption and Organization: A Reply to Gamson and Schmeidler," 1984.

"turmoil in command of politics."[133] We remain unpersuaded. To our minds, many analysts have a limited conception of protest, and deny recognition to much protest by the poor.[134]

REFERENCES

Abramovitz, Mimi, *Regulating the Lives of Women: Social Welfare Policy From Colonial Times to the Present.* Boston, South End Press, 1988.

Achenbaum, W. Andrew, "The Formative Years of Social Security: A Test of the Piven and Cloward Thesis." In Walter I. Trattner, ed., *Social Welfare of Social Control: Some Historical Reflections on "Regulating the Poor."* Knoxville, University of Tennessee Press, 1983.

Acker, Joan, "From Sex Roles to Gendered Institutions, *Contemporary Sociology,* 21, 5, 1992.

Albritton, Robert B., "Social Amelioration Through Mass Insurgency? A Reexamination of the Piven and Cloward Thesis," *American Political Science Review,* 73 (December) 1979.

Alexander, John K., "The Functions of Public Welfare in Late-Eighteenth Century Philadelphia: Regulating the Poor?" In Walter I. Trattner, ed., *Social Welfare or Social Control: Some Historical Reflections on "Regulating the Poor."* Knoxville, University of Tennessee Press, 1983.

Alford, Robert, *Party and Society: The Anglo-American Democracies.* Chicago, Rand McNally, 1963.

Alston, L. J., and J. P. Ferrie, "Resisting the Welfare State: Southern Opposition to the Farm Security Administration."

---

[133]Roach and Roach, "Organizing the Poor: Road to a Dead End," 1978; cf. also Piven and Cloward, "Social Movements and Societal Conditions: A Reply to Roach and Roach," 1978. And then again, Roach and Roach, "Turmoil in Command of Politics: Organizing the Poor," 1980; and cf. also Piven and Cloward, "Doctrine in Command of Politics: A Reply to Roach and Roach," 1980.

[134]See Piven and Cloward, "Normalizing Collective Protest," 1992, for a fuller discussion of this issue.

467   *Poor Relief and Theories of the Welfare State*

In R. Higgs, ed., *The Emergence of the Modern Political Economy.*
Greenwich, Connecticut, 1985.

Barrett, Nancy, *The Welfare System as State Paternalism.* Paper
presented to Conference on Women and Structural Transformation, Institute for Research on Women, Rutgers University, 1983.

Bensel, Richard Franklin, *Sectionalism and American Political Development, 1880–1980.* Madison, University of Wisconsin
Press, 1984.

Betz, Michael, "Riots and Welfare: Are They Related?" *Social
Problems*, 21, 3, 1974.

Boris, Eileen, and Peter Bardaglio, "The Transformation of
Patriarchy: The Historic Role of the State." In Irene Dia-
mond, ed., *Families, Politics, and Public Policy.* New York,
Longman, Green, 1980.

Bourdieu, Pierre, *Outline of a Theory of Practice.* Translated by
Richard Nice. Cambridge, England, Cambridge University
Press, 1977.

Bridges, Amy, *A City in the Republic: Ante-Bellum New York and the
Origins of Machine Politics.* New York, Cambridge University
Press, 1984.

Brown, Carol, "Mothers, Fathers, and Children: From Private
to Public Patriarchy." In Irene Diamond, ed., *Families, Politics, and Public Policy.* New York, Longman, Green, 1980.

Callaghan, Polly, and Heidi Hartmann, "Contingent Work: A
Chart Book on Part-Time and Temporary Employment,"
Institute for Women's Policy Research, Economic Policy In-
stitute, Washington, D.C., 1991.

Cameron, David R., "The Expansion of the Public Economy,"
American Political Science Review, 72, December 1978.

Castles, Francis G., *The Impact of Parties: Politics and Policies in
Democratic Capitalist States.* Beverly Hills, California, Sage
Publications, 1982.

Chamblin, Mitchell B., "Intergroup Threat and Social Control: Welfare Expansion among States during the 1960s and
1970s." In Allen E. Liska, ed., *Social Threat and Social Control.*
Albany, State University of New York Press, 1992.

Cloward, Richard A., and Frances Fox Piven, "The Professional Bureaucracies: Benefit Systems as Influence Systems." In Richard A. Cloward and Frances Fox Piven, *The
Politics of Turmoil: Essays on Poverty, Race and the Urban Crisis.*
New York, Pantheon Books, 1974.

Cohen, Jean L., and Andrew Arato, *Civil Society and Political Theory.* Cambridge, MIT Press, 1992.

Colby, David C., "A Test of the Relative Efficacy of Political Tactics," *American Journal of Political Science,* 26, 4, 1982.

Collier, D., and R. Messick, "Prerequisites Versus Diffusion: Testing Alternative Explanations of Social Security Adoption," *American Political Science Review,* 69, 1975.

Cutright, Phillip, "Political Structure, Economic Development, and National Social Security Programs," *American Journal of Sociology,* 70, 1965.

Cutright, Phillip, "Income Distribution: A Cross-National Analysis," *Social Forces,* 46, 1967.

Dahl, Robert, *Dilemmas of Pluralist Democracy.* New Haven, Yale University Press, 1982.

Davis, Mike, *Prisoners of the American Dream.* London, Verso, 1986.

Dawson, Richard E., and James A. Robinson, "The Politics of Welfare." In Herbert Jacob and Kenneth N. Vines, eds., *Politics in the American States.* Boston, Little Brown and Co., 1965.

Derthick, Martha, *Policymaking for Social Security.* Washington D.C., Brookings Institution, 1979.

Derthick, Martha, "Up-to-Date in Kansas City: Reflections on American Federalism, The 1992 Gaus Lecture," *PS: Political Science and Politics,* 25, 4, December 1992.

Diamond, Irene, ed., *Families, Politics, and Public Policy.* New York, Longman, Green, 1983.

Domhoff, G. William, "The New Class War," *Social Policy,* Winter 1983.

Domhoff, G. William, *The Power Elite and The State: How Policy is Made in America.* New York, Aldine de Gruyter, 1990.

Downs, Anthony, *An Economic Theory of Democracy.* New York, Harper and Row, 1957.

Durman, Eugene, "Have the Poor Been Regulated? Toward a Multivariate Understanding of Welfare Growth," *Social Service Review,* 47, September 1973.

Dye, Thomas R., *Politics, Economics and the Public: Policy Outcomes in the American States.* Chicago, Rand McNally, 1966.

Dye, Thomas R., "Politics Versus Economics: The Development of Literature on Policy Determination," *Policy Studies Journal,* 1979.

Edelman, Murray, *Political Language.* New York, Academic Press, 1978.

Edelman, Murray, *Constructing the Political Spectacle.* Chicago, University of Chicago Press, 1988.

Eisenstadt, S. N., and Luis Roniger, "The Study of Patron-Client Relations and Recent Development in Sociological Theory." In S. N. Eisenstadt and Rene Lemarchand, eds., *Political Clientelism, Patronage and Development.* Beverly Hills, California, Sage Publications, 1981.

Eisenstein, Zillah, *The Radical Future of Liberal Feminism.* New York, Longman, Green, 1981.

Eisenstein, Zillah, "The State, the Patriarchal Family, a. d Working Mothers." In Irene Diamond, ed., *Families, Politics, and Public Policy.* New York, Longman, Green, 1983.

Esping-Andersen, Gosta, *Politics Against Markets: The Social Democratic Road to Power.* Princeton, Princeton University Press, 1988.

Esping-Andersen, Gosta, *The Three Worlds of Welfare Capitalism.* Princeton, Princeton University Press, 1990.

Esping-Andersen, Gosta, "Postindustrial Cleavage Structures: A Comparison of Evolving Patterns of Social Stratification in Germany, Sweden and the United States." In Frances Fox Piven, ed., *Labor Parties in Postindustrial Societies.* Oxford, Oxford University Press, 1991.

Flacks, Richard, *Making History: The Radical Tradition in American Life.* New York, Columbia University Press, 1988.

Flora, Peter, and Arnold J. Heidenheimer, "The Historical Core and Changing Boundaries of the Welfare State." In Peter Flora and Arnold J. Heidenheimer, eds., *The Development of Welfare States in Europe and America.* New Brunswick, New Jersey, Transaction Books, 1984.

Flora, Peter, and Jens Albert, "Modernization, Democratization and the Development of Welfare States in Western Europe." In Peter Flora and Arnold J. Heidenheimer, eds., *The Development of Welfare States in Europe and America.* New Brunswick, New Jersey, Transaction Books, 1984.

Fraser, Nancy, "Women, Welfare and the Politics of Need Interpretation," *Thesis Eleven,* 17, 1987.

Fraser, Nancy, *Unruly Practices: Power Discourse and Gender in Contemporary Social Theory.* Minneapolis, University of Minnesota Press, 1989.

Friedland, Roger, and Jimy Sanders, "The Public Economy and Economic Growth in Western Market Economies," *American Sociological Review,* 50, 1985.

Gamson, William A., *The Strategy of Social Protest.* Homewood, Illinois, Dorsey, 1975.

Gamson, William A., and Emile Schmeidler, "Organizing the Poor: An Argument with Frances Fox Piven and Richard A. Cloward, *Poor People's Movements,*" *Theory and Society,* 13, 1984.

Galenson, W., "The Historical Role of American Trade Unionism." In S. M. Lipset, ed., *Unions in Transition.* San Francisco, Institute for Contemporary Studies, 1986.

Gary, Lawrence E., "Policy Decisions in the Aid to Families With Dependent Children Program: A Comparative State Analysis," *The Journal of Politics,* 35, 1973.

Giddens, Anthony, "Classical Social Theory and the Origins of Modern Social Theory," *American Journal of Sociology,* 81, January 1976.

Goldfield, Michael, "Labor in American Politics—Its Current Weakness," *The Journal of Politics,* 48, 1986.

Goldfield, Michael, *The Decline of Organized Labor in the United States.* Chicago, University of Chicago Press, 1987.

Goldfield, Michael, "Class, Race, and Politics in the United States," *Research in Political Economy,* 12, Greenwich, Connecticut, JAI Press, 1990.

Goldfield, Michael, "Worker Insurgency, Radical Organization, and New Deal Labor Legislation," *American Political Science Review,* 83, 1991.

Gordon, Linda, "What Does Welfare Regulate?" *Social Research,* 75, 4, 1988.

Gough, Ian, *The Political Economy of the Welfare State.* London, Macmillan Press, Ltd., 1979.

Griffin, Stephen M., "Bringing the State into Constitutional Theory: Public Authority and the Constitution," *Law and Social Inquiry,* 16, 4, 1991.

Griffin, Larry J., Joel A. Devine, and Michael Wallace, "On the Economic and Political Determinants of Welfare Spending in the Post–World War II Era," *Politics and Society,* 12, 3, 1983.

Gronbjerg, Kirsten A., *Mass Society and the Extension of Welfare, 1960–1970.* Chicago, University of Chicago Press, 1977.

Haber, Samuel, *Efficiency and Uplift: Scientific Management in the Progressive Era, 1890–1920.* Chicago, University of Chicago Press, 1964.

Habermas, Jurgen, *The Theory of Communicative Action. Volume Two, Lifeworld and System: A Critique of Functionalist Reason.*

Translated by Thomas McCarthy. Boston, Beacon Press, 1987.

Hays, Samuel P., *Conservatism and the Gospel of Efficiency.* Cambridge, Harvard University Press, 1958.

Heidenheimer, Arnold J., "Secularization Patterns and the Westward Spread of the Welfare State, 1883–1975." In R. F. Tomasson, ed., *The Welfare State, 1883–1983,* Comparative Social Research Annual, 6, Greenwich, Connecticut, JAI Press, 1983.

Hibbs, Douglas A., "Political Parties and Macroeconomic Policy," *American Political Science Review,* 71, December 1977.

Hibbs, Douglas A., "On the Political Economy of Long-Run Trends in Strike Activity," *British Journal of Political Science,* 8, 2, 1978.

Hibbs, Douglas A., *The Political Economy of Industrial Democracies.* Cambridge, Harvard University Press, 1987.

Hicks, Alexander M., "Ascent and Crisis of Welfare Effort." Paper presented at the Workshop on Comparative Studies of Welfare State Development of the International Sociological Association, August 29–September 1, 1991, Vuoranta, Finland, unpublished.

Hicks, Alexander, and Duane H. Swank, "The Domestic and International Political Economy of Welfare Expansion: The Case of 17 OECD Nations, 1960–1971. Paper presented at the Annual Meeting of the American Political Science Association, St. Louis, Missouri, 1982.

Hicks, Alexander, and Duane H. Swank, "Civil Disorder, Relief Mobilization and AFDC Caseloads: A Reexamination of the Piven and Cloward Thesis," *American Journal of Political Science,* 27, November 1983.

Hicks, Alexander, and Duane H. Swank, "On the Political Economy of Welfare Expansion: A Comparative Analysis of 18 Advanced Capitalist Democracies, 1960–71," *Comparative Political Studies,* 17, 1, April 1984.

Hicks, Alexander, and Duane H. Swank, "Politics, Institutions, and Welfare Spending in Industrialized Democracies," *American Political Science Review,* 86, 3, September 1992.

Hobsbawm, E. J., *Primitive Rebels.* New York, W. W. Norton, 1965.

Hobsbawm, E. J., "Should the Poor Organize?" *The New York Review of Books,* XXV, 4, March 28, 1978.

Hofstadter, Richard A., *The Idea of a Party System.* Berkeley, University of California Press, 1969.

Holmstrom, N., " 'Women's Work,' The Family, and Capitalism," *Science and Society,* 45, 1981.

Huntington, Samuel, *Political Order in Changing Societies.* New Haven, Yale University Press, 1968.

Isaac, Larry, and William R. Kelly, "Racial Insurgency, the State, and Welfare Expansion: Local and National Evidence from the Postwar United States," *American Journal of Sociology,* 86, 6, 1981.

Isaac, Larry, and William R. Kelly, "Developmental/Modernization and Political Class Struggle Theories of Welfare State Expansion: The Case of the AFDC "Explosion" in the States, 1960–70," *Journal of Political and Military Sociology,* 10, 2, Fall 1982.

Isaac, Larry, and William R. Kelly, "Racial Insurgency, the State, and Welfare Expansion: A Critical Comment and Reanalysis," *American Journal of Sociology,* 88, May 1983.

Janowitz, Morris, *Social Control of the Welfare State.* Chicago, University of Chicago Press, 1976.

Jenkins, J. Craig, and Barbara Brents, "Social Protest, Hegemonic Competition, and Social Reform: A Political Struggle Interpretation of the Origins of the American Welfare State," *American Sociological Review,* 54, 6, December 1989.

Jennings, Edward T., "Civil Turmoil and the Growth of Welfare Rolls: A Comparative State Analysis," *Policy Studies Journal,* 7, Summer 1979.

Jennings, Edward T., "Urban Riots and Welfare Policy Change: A Test of the Piven-Cloward Theory." In Helen M. Ingram and Dean E. Manns, eds., *Why Policies Succeed or Fail.* Beverly Hills, California, Sage Publications, 1981.

Jennings, Edward T., "Racial Insurgency, the State, and Welfare Expansion: A Critical Comment and Reanalysis," *American Journal of Sociology,* 88, 6, 1983.

Katznelson, Ira, "Rethinking the Silences of Social and Economic Policy," *Political Science Quarterly,* 101, 1986.

Keller, Morton, *Affairs of State: Public Life in the Nineteenth Century.* Cambridge, Harvard University Press, 1977.

Kerr, Clark, J.T. Dunlop, Frederick Harbison, and Charles Myers, *Industrialism and Industrial Man.* New York, Oxford University Press, 1964.

Key, V. O., *Southern Politics in the State and Nation.* New York, Alfred A. Knopf, 1949.

Kirbo, Harold R., and Richard A. Shaffer, "Lower Class Insurgency and the Political Process: The Response of the U.S. Unemployed, 1890–1940," *Social Problems*, 39, 2, 1992.

Korpi, Walter, and Goste Esping-Andersen, "Social Policy as Class Politics in Post-War Capitalism: Scandinavia, Austria and Germany." In John Goldthorpe, ed., *Order and Conflict in Contemporary Capitalism*. New York, Oxford University Press, 1984.

Korpi, Walter, *The Democratic Class Struggle*. London, Routledge & Kegan Paul, 1983.

Korpi, Walter, "Power, Politics, and State Autonomy in the Development of Social Citizenship," *American Sociological Review*, 54, 3, 1989.

Korpi, Walter, "Institutions and the Cost of Power." Paper delivered at the Workshop on Comparative Studies of Welfare State Development organized by the Research Committee on Poverty, Social Welfare and Social Policy in Helsinki, August 1991.

Kousser, J. Morgan, *The Shaping of Southern Politics: Suffrage Restrictions and the Establishment of the One-Party South*. New Haven, Yale University Press, 1974.

Kristensen, Ole, "On the Futility of the 'Demand Approach' to Public-sector Growth," *European Journal of Political Research*, 12, 1984.

Kudrle, Robert T., and Theodore R. Marmor, "The Development of Welfare States in North America." In Peter Flora and Arnold J. Heidenheimer, eds., *The Development of Welfare States in Europe and America*. New Brunswick, New Jersey, Transaction Books, 1981.

Leiby, James, "Social Control and Historical Explanation: Historians View the Piven and Cloward Thesis." In Walter I. Trattner, ed., *Social Welfare or Social Control: Some Historical Reflections on "Regulating the Poor."* Knoxville, University of Tennessee Press, 1983.

Lenski, Gerhard, *Power and Privilege*. Toronto, McGraw-Hill, 1966.

Lichtenstein, Nelson, "From Corporatism to Collective Bargaining: Organized Labor and the Eclipse of Social Democracy in the Postwar Era." In Steven Fraser and Gary Gerstle, eds., *The Rise and Fall of the New Deal Era.* Princeton, Princeton University Press, 1989.

Lipset, S. M., and Stein Rokkan, "Cleavage Structures, Party Systems, and Voter Alignments: An Introduction." In S. M.

Lipset and Stein Rokkan, eds., *Party Systems and Voter Alignments: Cross-National Perspectives.* New York, Free Press, 1967.

Lockard, Duane, *New England State Politics.* Princeton, Princeton University Press, 1959.

Lukes, Steven, *Essays in Social Theory.* New York, Columbia University Press, 1977.

Marshal, T. H., *Class, Citizenship and Social Development.* Chicago, University of Chicago Press, 1964.

Marx, Karl, *Capital,* Volume I. Moscow, Progress Publishers, no date.

McAdam, Doug, *Political Process and the Development of Black Insurgency, 1930–1970.* Chicago, University of Chicago Press, 1982.

McCormick, Richard P., "The Party Period and Public Policy: An Exploratory Hypothesis," *Journal of American History,* September, 66, 2, 1979.

McIntosh, Mary, "The State and the Repression of Women." In A. Kuhn and A. Wolpe, eds., *Feminism and Materialism.* London, Routledge and Kegan Paul, 1978.

Michels, Robert, *Political Parties.* Glencoe, Illinois, The Free Press, 1949.

Mohl, Raymond A., "The Abolition of Public Outdoor Relief, 1870–1900: A Critique of the Piven and Cloward Thesis." In Walter I. Trattner, ed., *Social Welfare or Social Control: Some Historical Reflections on "Regulating the Poor."* Knoxville, University of Tennessee Press, 1983.

Moore, Barrington, *Social Origins of Dictatorship and Democracy.* Boston, Beacon Press, 1966.

Morris, Aldon D., and Carol McClurg Mueller, *Frontiers in Social Movement Theory.* New Haven, Yale University Press, 1992.

Myles, John, *Old Age in the Welfare State.* Toronto, Little Brown, 1984.

Myles, John, "Social Structures and Welfare Policies: Perspectives for Canada and the United States." Departmental Working Paper 91–8, Carleton University, Ottawa, 1991.

Myles, John, and Jill Quadagno, "Explaining the Difference: The Politics of Old Age Security in Canada and the United States." Unpublished and undated paper.

Niskanen, William A., "Bureaucrats and Politicians," *Journal of Law and Economics,* 18, 1971.

Noble, Charles, "Institutional Impediments to Social Policy in the U.S." Paper presented at the 1990 Meetings of the

American Political Science Association. San Francisco, August 30–September 2.

O'Connor, James, *The Fiscal Crisis of the State.* New York, St. Martin's Press, 1973.

Oestreicher, Richard, "Urban Working-Class Political Behavior and Theories of American Electoral Politics, 1870–1940," *The Journal of American History,* 74, 4, 1988.

Offe, Claus, "Advanced Capitalism and the Welfare State," *Politics and Society,* 2, 4, 1972.

Offe, Claus, "Smooth Consolidation in the West German Welfare State: Structural Change, Fiscal Policies, and Populist Politics." In Frances Fox Piven, ed., *Labor Parties in Postindustrial Societies.* New York, Oxford University Press, 1991.

Orloff, Ann Shola, "The Politics of Pensions in Britain, the United States and Canada, 1880s–1930s: The Role of State Formation and State Building in Policy Developments." Paper presented at the Workshop on Comparative Studies of Welfare State Development of the International Sociological Association, August 29–September 1, 1991, Vuoranta, Helsinki, Finland.

Orloff, Ann Shola, and Theda Skocpol, "Explaining the Politics of Public Social Spending," *American Sociological Review,* 49, 6, 1984.

Pampel, Fred C., and John Williamson, "Welfare Spending in Advanced Industrial Democracies, 1950–1980," *American Journal of Sociology,* 93, 6, 1988.

Pampel, Fred C., and John Williamson, "Age Structure, Politics, and Cross-National Patterns of Public Pension Expenditures," *American Sociological Review,* 1985, 50, 787–98.

Piven, Frances Fox, "Structural Constraints and Party Development: The Case of the American Democratic Party." In Frances Fox Piven, ed., *Labor Parties in Postindustrial Societies.* New York, Oxford University Press, 1991.

Piven, Frances Fox, and Richard A. Cloward, "Reaffirming the Regulation of the Poor: A Reply to Durman," *Social Service Review,* 48 (June) 1974.

Piven, Frances Fox, and Richard A. Cloward, *Poor Peoples' Movements: Why They Succeed, How They Fail.* New York, Pantheon Books, 1977.

Piven, Frances Fox, and Richard A. Cloward, "Social Movements and Societal Conditions: A Reply to Roach and Roach," *Social Problems,* 26, 2, 1978.

Piven, Frances Fox, and Richard A. Cloward, "Electoral Instability, Civil Disorder, and Relief Rises: A Reply to Albritton," *American Political Science Review*, 73, 1979.

Piven, Frances Fox, and Richard A. Cloward, "Doctrine in Command of Politics: A Reply to Roach and Roach," *Sociological Quarterly*, 21, 1980.

Piven, Frances Fox, and Richard A. Cloward, "Humanitarianism in History: A Response to the Critics." In Walter I. Trattner, ed., *Social Welfare or Social Control: Some Historical Reflections on "Regulating the Poor."* Knoxville, University of Tennessee Press, 1983.

Piven, Frances Fox, and Richard A. Cloward, "Disruption and Organization: A Reply to Gamson and Schmeidler," *Theory and Society*, 13, 1984.

Piven, Frances Fox, and Richard A. Cloward, *The New Class War: Reagan's Attack on the Welfare State and its Consequences.* Revised and expanded edition. New York, Pantheon Books, 1985.

Piven, Frances Fox, and Richard A. Cloward, "The Historical Sources of the Contemporary Relief Debate." In Fred Block, Richard A. Cloward, Barbara Ehrenreich, and Frances Fox Piven, *The Mean Season: The Attack on the Welfare State.* New York, Pantheon Books, 1987.

Piven, Frances Fox, and Richard A. Cloward, "Welfare Doesn't Shore Up Traditional Family Roles: A Reply to Linda Gordon," *Social Research*, 55, 4, 1988.

Piven, Frances Fox, and Richard A. Cloward, "Normalizing Collective Protest." In Aldon Morris and Carol McClurg Mueller, eds., *Frontiers in Social Movement Theory.* New Haven, Yale University Press, 1992.

Piven, Frances Fox, and Richard A. Cloward, "Movements and Dissensus Politics," forthcoming.

Polan, D., "Toward a Theory of Law and Patriarchy." In David Kairys, ed., *The Politics of Law.* New York, Pantheon, 1982.

Polanyi, Karl, 1957, *The Great Transformation.* Boston, Beacon Press.

Powell, G. Bingham, "Voter Turnout in Comparative Perspective," *American Political Science Review*, 80, 1, 1986.

Przeworski, Adam, *Capitalism and Social Democracy.* New York, Cambridge University Press, 1985.

Przeworski, Adam, and John Sprague, *Paper Stones: A History of Electoral Socialism.* Chicago, University of Chicago Press, 1986.

Pumphrey, Muriel, and Ralph E. Pumphrey, "The Widows' Pension Movement, 1900–1930: Preventive Child-Saving or

Social Control?" In Walter I. Trattner, ed., *Social Welfare or Social Control: Some Historical Reflections on "Regulating the Poor."* Knoxville, University of Tennessee Press, 1983.

Quadagno, Jill, "Welfare Capitalism and the Social Security Act of 1935," *American Sociological Review*, 49, 1984.

Quadagno, Jill, "Race, Class, and Gender in the U.S. Welfare State," *American Sociological Review*, 55, 1, 1990.

Quadagno, Jill, "Theories of the Welfare State," *Annual Review of Sociology*, 13, 1987.

Rainwater, Lee, Martin Rein, and Joseph Schwarts, *Income Packaging in the Welfare State: A Comparative Study of Family Income.* Oxford, England, Clarendon Press, 1986.

Roach, Jack L., and Janet K. Roach, "Organizing the Poor: Road to a Dead End," *Social Problems*, 26, 2, 1978.

Roach, Jack L., and Janet K. Roach, "Turmoil in Command of Politics: Organizing the Poor," *Sociological Quarterly*, 21, 1980.

Robinson, D., *Slavery in the Structure of American Politics, 1765–1820.* New York, Norton, 1979.

Rokkan, Stein, "Geography, Religion and Social Class: Cross-cutting Cleavages in Norwegian Politics." In S. M. Lipset and Stein Rokkan, eds., *Party Systems and Voter Alignments.* New York, Free Press, 1967.

Rusk, Jerrold G., and John J. Stucker, "The Effect of the Southern System of Election Laws on Voter Participation: A Reply to V. O. Key." In Joel H. Silbey, Allan G. Bogue, and William H. Flanigan, eds., *The History of American Electoral Behavior.* Princeton, Princeton University Press, 1978.

Schattschneider, E. E., *Party Government.* New York, Rinehart, 1942.

Schattschneider, E. E., *The Semisovereign People.* New York, Holt, Rinehart & Winston, 1960.

Schram, Sanford F., "Post-Positivistic Policy Analysis and the Family Support Act of 1988: Symbols at the Expense of Substance," *Polity*, Summer 1992, 24, 4, 633–655.

Schram, Sanford F., and J. Patrick Turbott, "The Welfare Explosion: Mass Society versus Social Control," *Social Service Review*, 57, 1983a.

Schram, Sanford F., and J. Patrick Turbott, "Civil Disorder and the Welfare Explosion: A Two-step Process," *American Sociological Review*, 48, 1983b.

Schumpeter, Joseph, *Capitalism, Socialism and Democracy.* New York, Harper Brothers, 1950.

Scoble, Harry, "Organized Labor in the Electoral Process: Some Questions," *Western Political Science Quarterly*, 16, 1963.

Sewell, William, "A Theory of Structure: Duality, Agency, and Transformation," *American Journal of Sociology*, 98, 1, July 1992.

Shalev, Michael, "The Social Democratic Model and Beyond: Two Generations of Comparative Research on the Welfare State," *Comparative Social Research*, 6, 1983.

Shalev, Michael, "The Political Economy of Employment-Based Social Protection: An Approach and an Illustration." Paper prepared for the ISA Workshop on Comparative Research in Social Policy, Labor Markets, Inequality, and Distributive Conflict, Stockholm, August 25–28, 1988.

Sharp, Elaine B., and Steven Maynard-Moody, "Theories of the Local Welfare Role," *American Journal of Political Science*, 35, 4, 1991.

Shaver, Sheila, "Gender, Class and the Welfare State: The Case of Income Security." Sociology Program, Graduate Center, City University of New York, 1987, unpublished.

Smith, Joan, "Transforming Households: Working-Class Women and Economic Crisis," *Social Problems*, 34, 1987.

Shefter, Martin, "Party, Bureaucracy, and Political Change in the United States." In Louis Maisel and Joseph Cooper, eds., *Political Parties: Development and Decay*. Sage Electoral Studies Yearbook, 4, Beverly Hills, California, 1978a.

Shefter, Martin, "The Electoral Foundations of the Political Machine: New York City, 1884–1897." In Joel H. Sibley et al., eds., *The History of American Electoral Behavior*. Princeton, Princeton University Press, 1978b.

Sheppard, Harold, and Nicholas Masters, "The Political Attitudes and Preferences of Union Members: The Case of the Detroit Auto Workers," *American Political Science Review*, 53, 1959.

Skocpol, Theda, and Edwin Amenta, "States and Social Policies," *Annual Review of Sociology*, 12, 1986.

Smeeding, Timothy, Michael O'Higgins, and Lee Rainwater, *Poverty, Inequality and Income Distribution in Comparative Perspective*. The Luxembourg Income Study, London, Harvester Wheatsheaf, 1990.

Smelser, Neil, *Theory of Collective Behavior*. New York, The Free Press, 1962.

Steinmetz, George, "The Local Welfare State: Social Domination in Urban Imperial Germany," *American Sociological Review*, 55, 6, 1990.

Stephens, John, *The Transition from Capitalism to Socialism.* London, Macmillan, 1979.

Stevens, Beth, "Labor Unions, Employee Benefits, and the Privatizations of the American Welfare State," *Journal of Policy History*, 2, 3, 1990.

Swank, Duane H., "Between Incrementalism and Revolution: Group Protest and the Welfare State," *American Behavior Scientist*, 26, 3, 1983.

Swank, Duane H., and Alexander Hicks, "Militancy, Need, and Relief: The Piven and Cloward AFDC Caseload Thesis Revisited." In Richard Ratcliff, ed., *Research in Social Movements, Conflict and Change.* Greenwich, Connecticut, JAI Press, 1984.

Tarrow, Sidney, *Democracy and Disorder.* New York, Oxford University Press, 1989.

Therborn, Goran, "Karl Marx Returning: The Welfare State and Neo-Marxist, Corporatist and Statist Theories," *International Political Science Review*, 7, 2, 1987.

Thompson, E. P., *The Making of the English Working Class.* New York, Vintage Books, 1963.

Tilly, Charles, *From Mobilization to Revolution.* Reading, Massachusetts, Addison Wesley, 1978.

Tilly, Charles, Louise Tilly, and Richard Tilly, *The Rebellious Century, 1830–1930.* Cambridge, Harvard University Press, 1975.

Tindall, George B., *The Disruption of the Solid South.* Athens, Georgia, University of Georgia Press, 1965.

Trattner, Walter I., ed., *Social Welfare or Social Control: Some Historical Reflections on "Regulating the Poor."* Knoxville, University of Tennessee Press, 1983.

Tufte, Edward R., *Political Control of the Economy.* Princeton, Princeton University Press, 1978.

Ursel, Jane, "The State and the Maintenance of Patriarchy." In James Dickinson and Bob Russell, eds., *Family, Economy and State.* New York, St. Martin's Press, 1988.

van Arnheim, J., Corinia M., and Geurt J. Schotsman, "Do Parties Affect the Distribution of Incomes? The Case of the Advanced Capitalist Democracies." In Francis G. Castles, ed., *The Impact of Parties: Politics and Policies in Democratic Capitalist States.* Beverly Hills, California, Sage Publications, 1982.

Weibe, Robert H., *The Search for Order*. New York, Hill & Wang, 1967.

Weinstein, James, *The Corporate Ideal in the Liberal State, 1900–1918*. Boston, Beacon Press, 1968.

Weir, Margaret, Ann Shola Orloff, and Theda Skocpol, eds., *The Politics of Social Policy in the United States*. Princeton, Princeton University Press, 1988.

Wilensky, Harold L., *The Welfare State and Equality*. Berkeley, University of California Press, 1975.

Wilensky, Harold L., *The "New Corporatism," Centralization, and the Welfare State*. London and Beverly Hills, Sage Publications, 1976.

Wilensky, Harold L., and Charles N. Lebeaux, *Industrial Society and Social Welfare*. Glencoe, Illinois, The Free Press, 1965.

Wilson, Elizabeth, *Women and the Welfare State*. London, Tavistock, 1977.

Wolfe, Eric, *Peasant Wars of the Twentieth Century*. New York, Harper and Row, 1973.

Wrong, Dennis, *Power: Its Forms, Bases and Uses*. New York, Harper & Row, 1979.

APPENDIX

*Statistical Source
Tables*

AFDC Caseloads by Region and State for Selected Years Since 1940 (in thousands) [a]

	December 1940		December 1945			December 1950			
	# FAMILIES	% TOTAL	# FAMILIES	% TOTAL	% CHANGE 1940–1945	# FAMILIES	% TOTAL	% CHANGE 1945–1950	% CHANGE 194?–195?
NATIONAL	360	100	274	100	−24	635	99	132	7
Northeast	102	28	68	25	−33	136	21	100	9
Connecticut	1		2		100	5		150	40
Maine	2		1		−50	4		300	10
Massachusetts	12		7		−42	13		86	
New Hampshire	1		1		—	2		100	10
New Jersey	11		3		−73	5		67	−5
New York	24		25		4	56		124	1
Pennsylvania	49		26		−47	46		77	−
Rhode Island	1		1		—	4		300	3
Vermont	1		1		—	1		—	
North Central	110	31	82	30	−25	135	21	65	
Illinois	7		20		186	23		15	2
Indiana	17		6		−65	11		83	−
Iowa	3		3		—	5		67	
Kansas	6		3		−50	5		67	−
Michigan	20		14		−30	26		86	
Minnesota	9		5		−44	8		60	−
Missouri	13		12		−8	25		108	
Nebraska	6		2		−67	4		100	−
North Dakota	2		1		−50	2		100	
Ohio	11		8		−27	15		88	
South Dakota	2		1		−50	2		100	
Wisconsin	13		6		−54	9		50	−
West	43	12	24	9	−44	95	15	296	
Arizona	3		1		−67	4		300	

Source: HEW

[a] Includes AFDC-UP; coterminous United States; columns may not add to totals because of rounding errors. December of each year except February 1969.

	December 1960			December 1964			February 1969			% 1960–69
# FAM-ILIES	% TO-TAL	% CHANGE 1950–1960	# FAM-ILIES	% TO-TAL	% CHANGE 1960–1964	# FAM-ILIES	% TO-TAL	% CHANGE 1964–1969	% CHANGE 1960–1969	INCREASE OCCURRING AFTER 1964
---	---	---	---	---	---	---	---	---	---	---
45	100	17	975	100	31	1,545	100	58	107	71
72	23	26	267	27	55	481	31	80	180	69
8		60	15		88	20		33	150	42
6		50	5		−17	7		40	17	100
15		15	25		67	48		92	220	70
1		−50	1		—	2		100	100	100
16		220	26		63	50		92	213	71
69		23	119		72	256		115	271	73
52		13	69		33	86		25	65	50
5		25	6		20	9		50	80	75
1		—	1		—	3		200	200	100
72	23	27	227	23	32	306	20	35	78	59
37		61	55		48	74		35	100	51
11		—	12		9	14		17	27	67
9		80	11		22	15		36	67	67
6		20	9		50	11		22	83	40
27		4	39		44	51		31	89	50
10		25	14		40	18		29	80	50
26		4	26		—	30		15	15	100
3		−25	4		33	7		75	133	75
2		—	2		—	3		50	50	100
28		87	42		50	61		45	118	58
3		50	3		—	4		33	33	100
10		11	11		10	21		91	110	91
1	18	38	191	20	46	342	22	79	161	72
8		100	9		13	10		11	25	50

	December 1940		December 1945			December 1950			
	# FAM- ILIES	% TO- TAL	# FAM- ILIES	% TO- TAL	% CHANGE 1940– 1945	# FAM- ILIES	% TO- TAL	% CHANGE 1945– 1950	% CHANGE 194_– 195_
California	16		7		—56	56		700	25
Colorado	6		3		—50	5		67	—1
Idaho	3		1		—67	3		200	-
Montana	2		1		—50	2		100	-
Nevada	—		—		—	—		—	-
New Mexico	2		3		50	5		67	1
Oregon	2		1		—50	4		300	1
Utah	4		2		—50	3		50	—2
Washington	5		4		—20	11		175	1
Wyoming	1		—		—100	1		—	-
South	103	29	100	36	—3	269	42	169	1
Other South	75	21	74	27	—1	188	30	154	1
Arkansas	6		4		—33	19		375	2
Delaware	1		—		—100	1		—	-
Dist. of Columbia	1		1		—	2		100	1
Florida	4		6		50	28		367	6
Kentucky	—		5		—	24		380	-
Maryland	7		3		—57	6		100	-
North Carolina	10		6		—40	16		167	
Oklahoma	19		16		—16	21		31	
Tennessee	14		11		—21	25		127	
Texas	—		10		—	19		90	
Virginia	4		4		—	8		100	1
West Virginia	9		7		—22	18		157	1
Deep South	28	8	26	9	—7	81	12	212	18
Alabama	6		6		—	19		217	2
Georgia	5		4		—20	17		325	2
Louisiana	15		9		—40	28		211	
Mississippi	—		3		—	11		267	
South Carolina	3		4		33	7		75	

| December 1960 | | | December 1964 | | | February 1969 | | | | % 1960–69 |
# FAM-ILIES	% TO-TAL	% CHANGE 1950–1960	# FAM-ILIES	% TO-TAL	% CHANGE 1960–1964	# FAM-ILIES	% TO-TAL	% CHANGE 1964–1969	% CHANGE 1960–1969	INCREASE OCCURRING AFTER 1964
79		41	127		61	252		98	219	72
8		60	11		38	15		36	88	57
2		−33	3		50	3		—	50	—
2		—	2		—	3		50	50	100
1		—	1		—	2		100	100	100
8		60	7		−13	11		57	38	100
6		50	8		33	13		63	117	71
4		33	5		25	8		60	100	75
12		9	17		42	22		29	83	50
1		—	1		—	1		—	—	—
70	36	—	290	30	7	416	27	43	54	86
83	25	−3	201	21	10	278	18	38	52	81
7		−63	7		—	10		43	43	100
2		100	3		50	5		67	150	67
5		150	4		−20	7		75	40	100
23		−18	28		22	45		61	96	77
1		−13	21		—	30		43	43	100
9		50	19		111	30		58	233	52
7		69	27		—	28		4	4	100
8		−14	18		—	23		28	28	100
2		−12	19		−14	28		47	27	100
9		—	20		5	37		85	95	94
0		25	11		10	16		45	60	83
0		11	25		25	20		−20	—	—
7	12	7	88	9	1	137	9	56	57	98
1		11	19		−10	25		32	19	100
6		−6	18		13	38		111	138	91
1		−25	24		14	39		63	86	83
0		82	21		5	26		24	30	83
9		29	7		−22	10		43	11	100

AFDC Caseloads in Urban Counties for Selected Years Since 1950 (in hundreds)[a]

URBAN COUNTIES BY REGION AND STATE	1950 CASE-LOAD	1960 CASE-LOAD	% CHANGE 1950-60	1964 CASE-LOAD	% CHANGE 1960-64	1969 CASE-LOAD	% CHANGE 1964-69	% CHANGE 1960-69	% OF 1960-69 INCREASE OCCURRING AFTER 1964
National Summary (All Counties)	6352	7445	17%	9750	31%	15453	58%	107%	71%
121 Urban Counties [b]	2510	3391	35	4999	47	8978	80	165	71
5 Largest Urban Counties [c]	988	1244	26	1925	55	3938	105	217	75
116 Other Urban Counties	1522	2147	41	3074	43	5040	64	135	68
78 Northern Urban Counties [d]	1955	2765	41	4223	53	7594	80	175	70
43 Southern Urban Counties	555	626	13	776	24	1384	78	121	80
All Non-Urban Counties	3842	4054	6	4751	17	6475	36	60	71
Northern Non-Urban Counties	1702	1984	17	2631	33	3701	41	87	62
Southern Non-Urban Counties	2140	2071	−3	2120	2	2774	31	34	93
Northeast (All Urban Counties)	930	1180	27	1926	63	3669	91	211	70
Connecticut	47	68	45	132	94	171	30	151	38
Fairfield (Bridgeport)	12	17	42	34	100	44	29	159	37
Hartford	16	25	56	55	120	68	24	172	30
New Haven	19	26	37	43	65	59	37	127	48
Massachusetts	100	111	11	192	73	365	90	229	68
Bristol (New Bedford)	11	14	27	23	64	42	83	200	68

	7	10	43%	18	80%	35	94%	250%	68%
Hampden (Springfield)									
Middlesex (Cambridge)	26	21	−19	36	71	67	86	219	67
Suffolk (Boston)	46	52	13	92	77	179	95	244	69
Worcester	10	14	40	23	64	42	83	200	68
New Jersey	34	116	241	190	64	349	84	201	68
Camden	5	18	260	24	33	36	50	100	67
Essex (Newark)	15	50	233	99	98	175	77	250	61
Hudson (Jersey City)	5	17	240	24	41	54	125	218	81
Mercer (Trenton)	3	11	267	15	36	25	67	217	71
Passaic (Patterson)	3	11	267	18	64	39	117	255	75
Union (Elizabeth)	3	9	200	10	11	20	100	122	91
New York	488	588	20	1005	71	2224	121	278	75
Albany	5	4	−20	7	75	15	114	275	73
Erie (Buffalo)	27	43	59	75	74	92	23	114	35
Monroe (Rochester)	12	15	25	28	87	43	54	187	54
New York City	413	481	16	810	68	1922	137	300	77
Niagara (Niagara Falls)	5	5	—	15	200	18	20	260	23
Oneida (Utica)	8	10	25	17	70	23	35	130	46
Onondaga (Syracuse)	7	15	114	28	87	50	79	233	63
Westchester (Yonkers)	11	15	36	25	67	61	144	307	78
Pennsylvania	232	258	11	358	39	486	36	88	56
Allegheny (Pittsburgh)	79	94	19	140	49	147	5	56	13

SOURCE TABLE 2 (Cont.)

URBAN COUNTIES BY REGION AND STATE	1950 CASE-LOAD	1960 CASE-LOAD	% CHANGE 1950–60	1964 CASE-LOAD	% CHANGE 1960–64	1969 CASE-LOAD	% CHANGE 1964–69	% CHANGE 1960–69	% OF 1960–69 INCREASE OCCURRING AFTER 1964
Erie	5	11	120%	12	9%	17	42%	55%	83%
Lackawanna (Scranton)	14	14	—	14	—	11	–21	–21	—
Lehigh (Allentown)	2	2	—	4	100	5	25	150	33
Philadelphia	132	137	4	188	37	306	63	123	70
Rhode Island	29	39	34	49	26	74	51	90	71
Providence	29	39	34	49	26	74	51	90	71
North Central (All Urban Counties)	543	900	66	1289	43	1863	45	107	60
Illinois	141	261	85	359	38	549	53	110	66
Cook (Chicago)	188	252	83	345	37	527	53	109	66
Peoria	2	4	100	6	50	12	100	200	75
Winnebago (Rockford)	1	5	400	8	60	10	25	100	40
Indiana	45	65	44	67	3	84	25	29	89
Allen (Fort Wayne)	3	7	133	7	—	9	29	29	100
Lake (Gary)	15	23	53	27	17	43	59	87	80
Marion (Indianapolis)	18	22	22	20	–9	19	–5	–14	—
St Joseph (South Bend)	5	8	60	9	13	9	—	13	—

Polk (Des Moines)	6	16	167	17	6	22	29	38	83
Kansas	15	25	67	38	52	59	55	136	62
Sedgwick (Wichita)	8	16	100	23	44	31	35	94	53
Shawnee (Topeka)	2	4	100	6	50	8	33	100	50
Wyandotte (Kansas City)	5	5	—	9	80	20	122	300	73
Michigan	113	156	38	235	51	297	26	90	44
Ingham (Lansing)	5	7	40	9	29	12	33	71	60
Genesee (Flint)	9	7	-22	14	100	30	114	329	70
Kent (Grand Rapids)	6	9	50	16	78	19	19	111	30
Wayne (Detroit)	93	133	43	196	47	236	20	77	39
Minnesota	30	50	67	81	62	115	42	130	52
Hennepin (Minneapolis)	16	30	88	50	67	70	40	133	50
Ramsey (St. Paul)	7	12	71	21	75	33	57	175	57
St. Louis (Duluth)	7	8	14	10	25	12	20	50	50
Missouri	89	112	26	124	11	152	23	36	70
Jackson (Kansas City)	24	30	25	33	10	40	21	33	70
St. Louis	65	82	26	91	11	112	23	37	70
Nebraska	13	11	15	18	64	38	111	245	74
Douglas (Omaha)	11	9	-18	15	67	32	113	256	74
Lancaster (Lincoln)	2	2	—	3	50	6	100	200	75

SOURCE TABLE 2 (Cont.)

URBAN COUNTIES BY REGION AND STATE	1950 CASE-LOAD	1960 CASE-LOAD	% CHANGE 1950-60	1964 CASE-LOAD	% CHANGE 1960-64	1969 CASE-LOAD	% CHANGE 1964-69	% CHANGE 1960-69	% OF 1960-69 INCREASE OCCURRING AFTER 1964
Ohio	69	164	138%	298	82%	443	49%	170%	52%
Cuyahoga (Cleveland)	23	51	122	100	96	153	53	200	52
Franklin (Columbus)	6	28	367	51	82	83	63	196	58
Hamilton (Cincinnati)	23	36	57	58	61	69	19	92	33
Lucas (Toledo)	5	14	180	28	100	43	54	207	52
Mahoning (Youngstown)	2	2	—	8	300	18	125	800	63
Montgomery (Dayton)	4	15	275	20	33	34	70	127	74
Stark (Canton)	2	7	250	9	29	11	22	57	50
Summit (Akron)	4	11	175	24	118	32	33	191	38
Wisconsin	22	40	82	52	30	104	100	160	81
Dane (Madison)	6	6	—	7	16	13	86	117	86
Milwaukee	16	34	113	45	32	91	102	168	81
West (All Urban Counties)	482	685	42	1008	47	2062	105	201	77
Arizona	24	46	92	63	37	69	10	50	26
Maricopa (Phoenix)	18	37	106	50	35	49	−2	32	—
Pima (Tucson)	6	9	50	13	44	20	54	122	64
California	359	499	39	742	49	1691	128	239	80

		36%	35	49%	92	67%	142%	69%
Los Angeles	212	241	14	386	60	947	145	293	79
Orange (Anaheim)	5	13	160	20	54	59	195	354	85
Sacramento	14	32	129	53	66	102	92	219	70
San Diego	28	40	43	46	15	107	133	168	91
San Francisco	27	43	59	56	30	114	104	165	82
Santa Clara (San Jose)	16	33	106	52	58	112	115	239	76
Colorado	20	29	45	44	52	66	50	128	59
Denver	20	29	45	44	52	66	50	128	59
New Mexico	—	16	—	21	31	38	81	138	77
Bernalillo (Albuquerque)	—	16	—	21	31	38	81	138	77
Oregon	17	25	47	31	24	47	52	88	73
Multnomah (Portland)	17	25	47	31	24	47	52	88	73
Washington	51	54	6	83	54	110	33	104	48
King (Seattle)	29	25	-14	46	84	57	24	128	84
Pierce (Tacoma)	12	13	8	16	23	26	63	100	77
Spokane	10	16	60	21	31	27	29	69	55
Utah	11	16	45	24	50	41	71	156	68
Salt Lake (Salt Lake City)	11	16	46	24	50	41	71	156	68
South (All Urban Counties)	555	626	13	776	24	1384	78	121	80
Deep South	193	146	-24	174	19	337	94	131	85
Alabama	48	41	-15	44	7	70	59	71	90
Jefferson (Birmingham)	32	24	-25	23	-4	34	48	42	100
Mobile	7	13	86	17	31	31	82	138	78
Montgomery	9	4	-56	4	—	5	25	25	100

SOURCE TABLE 2 (Cont.)

URBAN COUNTIES BY REGION AND STATE	1950 CASE-LOAD	1960 CASE-LOAD	% CHANGE 1950-60	1964 CASE-LOAD	% CHANGE 1960-64	1969 CASE-LOAD	% CHANGE 1964-69	% CHANGE 1960-69	% OF 1960-69 INCREASE OCCURRING AFTER 1964
Georgia	46	31	-33%	38	23%	106	179%	242%	91%
Chatham (Savannah)	10	6	-40	9	50	22	144	267	81
Fulton (Atlanta)	30	21	-30	25	19	71	184	238	92
Muscogee (Columbus)	6	4	-33	4	—	13	225	225	100
Louisiana	94	57	-39	73	28	136	86	139	80
Caddo (Shreveport)	18	13	-28	18	38	22	22	69	44
East Baton Rouge (Baton Rouge)	10	10	—	9	-10	17	89	70	100
Orleans (New Orleans)	66	34	-48	46	35	97	111	185	81
Mississippi	5	17	240	19	12	25	32	47	75
Hinds (Jackson)	5	17	240	19	12	25	32	47	75
Other South	362	480	33	602	25	1047	74	118	78
Arkansas	15	8	-47	8	—	13	63	63	100
Pulaski (Little Rock)	15	8	-47	8	—	13	63	63	100
Washington, D.C.	22	50	127	42	-16	70	67	40	100
Florida	71	78	10	100	28	181	81	132	79
Dade (Miami)	16	25	56	37	48	66	78	164	71
Duval (Jacksonville)	29	27	-7	29	7	49	69	81	91
Hillsborough (Tampa)	19	16	-16	21	31	43	105	169	81

Jefferson (Louisville)	17	27	59	32	19	59	84	119	84
Maryland	43	53	23	121	128	202	67	281	54
Baltimore	43	53	23	121	128	202	67	281	54
North Carolina	18	38	111	43	13	45	5	18	29
Forsyth (Winston-Salem)	6	14	133	19	36	18	−5	29	—
Guilford (Greensboro)	6	12	100	13	8	12	−8	—	—
Mecklenburg (Charlotte)	6	12	100	11	−8	15	36	25	100
Oklahoma	23	46	100	55	20	79	44	72	73
Oklahoma (Oklahoma City)	10	25	150	30	20	48	60	92	78
Tulsa	13	21	62	25	19	31	24	48	60
Tennessee	53	68	28	70	3	130	86	91	97
Davidson (Nashville)	10	9	−10	9	—	18	100	100	100
Hamilton (Chattanooga)	11	13	18	14	8	19	36	46	83
Knox (Knoxville)	16	14	−13	13	−7	21	62	50	100
Shelby (Memphis)	16	32	100	34	6	72	112	125	95
Texas	72	80	11	92	15	195	112	144	90
Bexar (San Antonio)	17	19	12	26	37	46	77	142	74
Dallas	12	13	8	16	23	47	194	262	91
El Paso	4	6	50	6	—	9	50	50	100
Harris (Houston)	19	13	−32	14	8	39	179	200	96
Jefferson (Beaumont)	2	3	50	4	33	7	75	133	75
Lubbock	—	1	—	1	—	4	300	300	100
Nueces (Corpus Christi)	4	7	75	6	14	10	67	43	100
Potter (Amarillo)	1	1	—	1	—	1	—	—	—
Tarrant (Fort Worth)	8	11	38	11	—	15	36	36	100

SOURCE TABLE 2 (Cont.)

URBAN COUNTIES BY REGION AND STATE	1950 CASE-LOAD	1960 CASE-LOAD	% CHANGE 1950-60	1964 CASE-LOAD	% CHANGE 1960-64	1969 CASE-LOAD	% CHANGE 1964-69	% CHANGE 1960-69	% OF 1960-69 INCREASE OCCURRING AFTER 1964
Travis (Austin)	4	5	25%	5	—%	14	180%	180%	100%
Wichita (Wichita Falls)	1	1	—	2	100	3	50	200	50
Virginia	28	32	14	39	22	73	87	128	83
Arlington	1	1	—	1	—	1	—	—	—
Newport News	2	3	50	5	67	8	60	167	60
Norfolk	12	11	-8	11	—	25	127	127	100
Portsmouth	2	4	100	5	25	9	80	125	80
Richmond	11	13	18	17	31	30	76	131	76

Source: HEW

a Includes AFDC-UP; includes cases receiving vendor payments for medical care only in 1969. December of each year except February 1969. Figures may not total properly because of rounding errors.

b Any county containing a main city of at least 100,000 persons. In 1960, there were 121 counties which contained 130 main cities in the coterminous United States. Six counties—Alameda, Los Angeles, and Orange in California, New Haven in Connecticut, Lake in Indiana, and Wayne in Michigan—contained two or more main cities for a total of 15 cities. The result is 121 urban counties with one or more main cities of at least 100,000 persons.

Eleven cities fell in more than one county. New York City, which falls in five counties, has been treated as a single county. Since at least 70% of the population of each of the remaining ten cities fell within a single county, that county was treated as urbanized. Hence Atlanta was designated as falling in Fulton County; Shreveport in Caddo County; Kansas City in Jackson County; Youngstown in Mahoning County; Oklahoma City in Oklahoma County; Chicago in Cook County; Tulsa in Tulsa County; Portland in Multnomah County; Amarillo in Potter County; and Wichita Falls in Wichita County.

c Counties containing a main city of at least 1,000,000 persons: Los Angeles, Wayne (Detroit), Cook (Chicago), Philadelphia, and New

Characteristics of AFDC-UP Increases

	%	Number
AFDC-UP Caseloads		
1964	—	66,841
1969	—	78,863
As a % of Combined AFDC		
and AFDC-UP Increase		
1960–64	29%	66,841/230,499
1964–69	2%	12,022/570,271
1960–69	10%	78,863/800,770
% AFDC-UP 1960–69 Increase		
Occurring Before 1965	85%	66,841/ 78,863

Source: HEW; December of each year except February 1969

Percentage of Black Families on AFDC Rolls [a]

	1948	1953	1961	1967[c]	% CHANGE 1948–53	% CHANGE 1953–61	% CHANGE 1961–67
NORTHEAST							
Connecticut	17%	23%	42%	46%	35%	83%	10%
Maine	0	2[b]	1	0	—	−50	−100
Massachusetts	8	13	NA	20	63	NA	NA
N. Hampshire	1	1[b]	1	2	—	—	100
New Jersey	35	46	64	66	31	39	31
New York	42	48	43	48	14	−10	12
Pennsylvania	43	41	40	48	−5	−2	20
Rhode Island	14	14	18	20	—	29	11
Vermont	0	0	1	0	—	—	−100
NORTH CENTRAL							
Illinois	50	66	73	73	32	11	—
Indiana	23	39	48	51	70	23	6
Iowa	4	6	14	11	50	133	21
Kansas	22	23	23	36	5	43	9
Michigan	30	44	55	54	47	25	−2
Minnesota	1	3	7	8	200	133	14
Missouri	27	38	48	55	41	26	15
Nebraska	13	20	21	28	54	5	33
North Dakota	0	0	0	0	—	—	—
Ohio	27	33	50	55	22	52	10
South Dakota	0	0	0	1	—	—	—
Wisconsin	3	7	21	27	133	200	29
WEST							
Arizona	11	10	16	18	−9	60	13
California	16	27	34	32	7	26	−6
Colorado	5	9[b]	12	3	8	44	−75
Idaho	0	7[b]	2	0	—	−71	−100
Montana	0	0	1	1	—	—	—

Nevada	NA	NA	36	46	NA	NA	28
New Mexico	1	1	6	6	—	500	—
Oregon	6	9	NA	9	50	NA	NA
Utah	1	5 [b]	3	2	400	—40	—33
Washington	5	8	8	10	60	—	25
Wyoming	1	4 [b]	6	8	300	50	33

SOUTH

Other South

Arkansas	25	35	40	61	40	14	53
Delaware	47	62	73	71	32	18	—3
D. of C.	83	90	93	97	8	3	4
Florida	50	66	66	76	32	—	15
Kentucky	14	21	21	27	50	—	29
Maryland	62	69	66	74	11	4	12
N. Carolina	36	44	54	69	22	23	28
Oklahoma	25	38	38	38	52	—	—
Tennessee	16	28	41	53	75	46	27
Texas	43	36	38	41	—16	6	8
Virginia	46	52	59	67	13	13	14
West Virginia	6	8	10	9	33	25	—10

Deep South

Alabama	37	55	62	70	49	13	13
Georgia	32	43	48	70	34	12	46
Louisiana	53	67	68	77	26	1	13
Mississippi	25	62	76	86	148	23	13
S. Carolina	55	61	64	75	11	5	17

Source: HEW
[a] AFDC-UP excluded except where indicated.
[b] Total nonwhite population.
[c] AFDC-UP included.
NA Not Available.

Number of AFDC Applications Received and Approved,
1960–68 (in thousands) [a]

	1960	1961	1962	1963	1964	1965	1966	1967	1968
National									
Approvals	323	451	440	449	520	531	577	679	762
Received	588	751	746	788	853	858	902	998	1088
Northeast									
Approvals	100	155	155	168	167	165	176	221	260
Received	159	231	239	254	249	246	252	294	329
North Central									
Approvals	61	88	89	81	101	95	93	97	113
Received	107	142	137	135	155	146	145	144	162
West									
Approvals	64	74	76	86	136	152	170	205	234
Received	113	133	134	156	206	223	261	306	349
South									
Approvals	101	127	119	117	122	123	134	152	161
Received	210	245	237	244	243	242	244	254	248
Deep South									
Approvals	36	38	33	33	35	35	39	45	59
Received	80	82	77	79	77	77	79	84	89
Other South									
Approvals	65	91	84	84	86	87	96	105	103
Received	130	163	159	164	166	165	165	170	159

[a] Coterminous United States; 1968 figures were estimated, and may differ slightly from the official figures which were published subsequently by HEW; AFDC-UP included; column totals may not equal the national totals due to rounding.

INDEX

"Committee to Save Unemployed Fathers" (East Kentucky), 322

Communist Party (communism), 63–64, 67–68, 81, 91, 102, 104; Unemployed Councils, 105, 107–8

community-action agencies, 288–90; preparation of welfare manuals by, 301; and neighborhood service center programs, 303–4; *see also* advocacy services; neighborhood legal services

Community Action Program (CAP), 256, 258, 269, 271 *n.*, 274, 289

Community Advancement, Inc., 328

Community Chests, 57–58

Community Council of Greater New York, 150

Community Mental Health Centers Act (1967), 257

community social fabric: women and stability of, 393–94

Comprehensive Education and Training Act, 360

Conference Board (business forum), 359

Conference for Progressive Labor Action, 108

Conference of Mayors, United States, 271 *n.*

conformity, as force to regulate behavior, 228

Congress of Industrial Organizations (CIO), 441, 443

Congress for Progressive Labor Action, 105

Congress of Racial Equality (CORE), 260 *n.*, 273 *n.*, 321–22; "Gandhi Award," 281

Connecticut: welfare increase in, 332

construction industry, racial discrimination in, 224

Continental Congress of Workers and Farmers, 107

Corn Laws, 31 *n.*

Costigan, Edward, 52, 54, 73

cotton industry, mechanization of, 201–3, 210

Coughlin, Father Charles E., 88, 101–4

crime, 228; and weakening of family controls, 226; in the ghettoes, 227, 231

Cromwell, Oliver, 16

cultural theories of social life, 415–17

culture of poverty, 392

Daley, Richard J., 271

Davis, John W., 70, 87

Day, Edwin, 322

day-care centers, 170–71

Dearborn (Michigan): demonstration against Ford River Rouge Plant, 65

decentralism: political activity and governmental, 435–39; Southern plantation political system and, 442–43; trade unions affected by, 443

Deficit Reduction Act of 1984, 386

degradation of welfare recipients, 395–97

Deindustrialization of America, The (Bluestone and Harrison), 347

Delaware: welfare increase in, 133, 332 *n.*

democracy: welfare state and, 430–32

democratic class struggle: political and electoral activity and, 424–27

Democratic Party, 68, 262, 276, 280; congressional election (1930), 54; ERA (1932), 56; election of 1932, 69–70, 91–92, 107, 111; congressional election of 1934, 87; election of 1936, 98–100, 103–4, 111; urban blacks in, 250–51; fragmentation of, 252–54; election of 1960, 255; enfranchising of blacks, 279–80;